1976

THE EXILE OF TERROR

Jorge Majfud

HUMANUS
SAN DIEGO-ACAPULCO

1976. The Exile of Terror
1st edition, September 2024.
© Jorge Majfud 2024
© Humanus Editores 2024
ISBN: 978-1-956760-17-0
Humanus.info
editor@humanus.com / cuauhtemoceditorial@gmail.com

All rights reserved for any commercialization of the full text. Any part of this book up to five consecutive pages may be reproduced or used by any graphic, electronic, or mechanical means, including photocopying or information and retrieval systems, with the sole condition of not altering the original text.

"Back then, in 1976, everything seemed reasonable, even murder."
Mariana Callejas

"In this war, there are no civilians. Everyone is a combatant."
Luis Posada Carriles

"This is a global war. There are no civilians or innocents. Everyone is a combatant and should be treated as such."
Orlando Bosch

"There is no better way to get rid of an undesirable than with a drop of Staphylococcus aureus."
Eugenio Berríos

"I regret nothing. If I had to kill 273 instead of 73, I would do it again. Let them suffer as we have suffered."
Ricardo Morales

"The only thing they haven't accused us of is killing Jesus"
Ignacio Novo Sampol

"The leaders of the main Cuban exile organizations that the Agency was trying to organize were essentially selfish and egomaniacal; they were more concerned with what their positions in Cuba would be once Castro was overthrown than with working for the common cause."
Internal CIA Investigation in the Bay of Pigs

"If they're really so anti-communist and truly have guts, they should be in Cuba fighting like men. Cubans live here for the money, but they act like patriots. If they truly hate Castro so much, what the hell are they doing here? They're all like dogs barking from the other side of the fence."
Mariana Callejas

"If Posada Carriles were a member of the National Union of Cuban Writers and Artists instead of a terrorist, he wouldn't be able to dream of entering the United States. The Department of Homeland Security denies visas to Cuban poets and artists but grants free entry to the country to terrorists."
José Pertierra

"No one here in Miami is interested in freedom of expression. Only in Havana."

Bernardo Benes

"Modern wars are, above all, psychological wars; the goal is to twist public opinion… Never leave traces of our actions; if this is not possible, always and under any circumstance deny any involvement in the events. Always. Even when the opposite is the most obvious…. If the interests of others align with ours, then they are allies; if they have no interest, they are instruments; if they oppose our interests, they are enemies."

Antonio Veciana

"I hate the United States. They have betrayed us. Every day that passes I want to grab a rifle and shoot at this country."

José Alfredo Pérez San Román, commander of the CIA's failed invasion of Cuba.

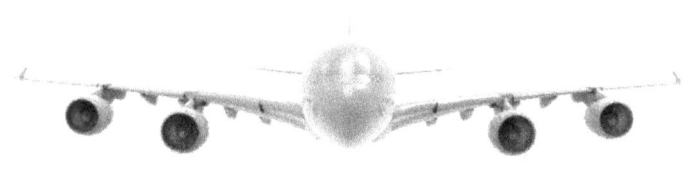

WARNING

Any resemblance to reality is not mere coincidence. The events narrated have been strictly documented. The only fictional characters in this story are Ernest and Hunter.

CHAPTERS

JANUARY
Happy Birthday, America 9
Little Havana 11
First clipping...14
At the Copa, Copacabana 17
Cuba über alles 22
Non-fiction novel 23
Quetropillán, Chile 25
Fidel and Malcolm X 29
Dictators and dictators 38
The Apprentices 40
Bay of Pigs..44
Kill Fidel. Or Kennedy..49
Pinochet carried his luggage 57
The pediatrician Orlando Bosch 58
Michael and Mariana before Townley and Callejas 60
The CIA, DINA, and the Townleys..69
The gringo from electronics 72
First attempt to kill Pascal Allende 73
Roland Otero in Santo Domingo 80
New betrayals, new failure 82
Augusto Lutz 86

FEBRUARY
My Hero, Al Capone 91
Those who didn't rise from bombers...94
That long road trip in a caravan..96
Vice in Miami: the Largest CIA Base 110
Miami. The capital of terrorism 115
Copacabana. Lola, death, and rum in Havana 121
Well, then let the dogs loose 123
Cuban coffee. A very dynamic culture. 127
Union City, the Miami of the cold...131
Biological Weapons 137
Bombs and Votes 142
Bob Marley: Another island of drug-addicted blacks.................143

Santiago is not Havana, and Bosch is not El Che 145
El Mono Morales and Orlando Bosch 153
Bosch Arrested in Costa Rica 154
Dictators for freedom 161
Orlando and Isabel separate for a while..........................163
I couldn't forget Dawson Island 165

MARCH
From the Southern Cone to the Northern Patio 171
At IPS 176
Raymond Molina in Buenos Aires 181
The can of tuna 187
Townley's first victim 189
Coup in Argentina 192

APRIL
Let them sink a ship, or a plane 197
The best way to eliminate an undesirable 201
Vendettas in Miami 205
The Church Commission and the Parallel State 212
Townley demonstrates the virtues of sarin gas..............214
The literary gatherings of Mariana 214
An example of fascist democracy..................................215
The CIA, El Mercurio, Pinochet and the final solution 217

MAY
The Internal Struggles of Santiago 223
Ritoque 224
Gathering with Stefano delle Chiaie...............................226
More literature: Borges, Sábato, Videla 227
Rolando Otero, the missing link....................................229
It's not just ideas; it's something deeper.......................233
Threats..235

JUNE
Ideological Patriotism 239
Let him leave and never return 240
Welcome, Mister Kissinger..243
The condor spreads its wings 248
Make it look like the reds from Argentina did it 250
Chaos has no name 253
The organized chaos with a single name 258
The wandering Caribbean 265

"Cubans don't have balls" 267

JULIO
We are all one under God...271
Praying costs nothing...275
Among all the forms that deserve silence 276
The Queen represents freedom..278
Cubana 615..281
The best way to get rid of an undesirable 284
Bombs and marches for freedom 288

AUGUST
Letelier and Kubitschek must be neutralized 293
To kill and whom to kill, that is the question...................................294
Bombs and Articles 296
Kill the future president..297
Two fake passports, another missing link 299
The Captain and the Dancer..301

SEPTEMBER
The sensual art of killing a man..307
Stateless by Decree...310
Enemy of freedom and of wars 313
The cross and the brothel...314
A Good-for-Nothing to the Rescue of Civilization............................316
Nothing like a good bomb 319
Acronyms for freedom 321
What matters is the psychological effect 323
A savior's call from an enemy..324
The Strategic Ambiguity of Carlos Andrés Pérez 327
Bosch in Caracas 332
Letelier. First Attempt 333
Final interview 336
This time it can't fail...337
In the midst of the fire, you will be with me......................................338
The mysterious labyrinth of infamy...341
The Patriotic Businessman...343
The Embassy of Chile informs the public 344
September, Love 345
A More Ambitious Gamble 346
It was the DINA..349
Collective fantasy, pure and harsh reality 352

Borges and Pinochet...354
It hadn't been the perfect crime 355
It was the Communists 359
Media protection by intelligence begins.............................362
The CIA of George H. Bush 364

OCTOBER
The First Pieces of the Puzzle 373
The happiest day 374
They think the Revolution gave them superpowers 375
Posada Carriles sells out Bosch 376
Walking on Clouds..378
Falling from the Sky 380
They are all fighters...383
As always, the rest died slowly 384
The same patio, the same chairs 385
It went over the cliff with all the dogs inside 386
There were no other suspects. There never were........390
Prison and a New Escape...392
Luckily Pinochet wasn't a Marxist......................................397
If I've seen you, I don't remember....................................398
Orlando has the details...400
With Allende, thousands of dissidents would have disappeared......403
To understand the drug trade, you have to be part of it 404
In a global war, there are no innocents 405
Three inappropriate journalists 408
El Mono's skills...412
Why do they always blame us?..414
The Stone in the Hornet's Nest 415

NOVEMBER
It was unintentionally intentional 421
I didn't go either...422
Investigate, from here on down. 423
Kill it once more..425

DECEMBER
Pragmatists, kill that one too...431
The fight with the drug trade 432
Letelier's Briefcase...434

YEARS LATER

Otero, the link found 439
The blond Chilean 441
They have abandoned you 443
Father, ask God to heal my son 448
I am a Christian, not a murderer 450
The fall of Michael Townley 451
Without money, there is no justice 453
The Cold War Within 459
Long live freedom of expression in Cuba, not in Miami 461
We don't mix business with politics 465
The Failed Trade of Goodwill 468
Everyone wanted El Mono, dead 470
In Miami, the definition of terrorism is flexible 471
Let Bush call his father 473
Of course, Pinochet gave the order 475
The two shadows of the car following us 478
A New Era: Going After the Laws 480
The law is equal for all; not all are equal under the law 482
If we do it, it's not terrorism 485
From Terrorism to Lobbying 486
The Free World seeks a winnable war 488
Butterflies learn to fly 490
Freedom Lovers, Yours 494
CIA orders, sir 497
Heroes, but not quite 499
Terrorists yes, poets no 504
PEOPLE AND CHARACTERS 505
SOURCES 530

JANUARY

Happy Birthday, America

ON THE NIGHT OF MONDAY, JANUARY 19, sitting on a bench in Congress, expressionless and always in profile no matter where you look at him, Henry Kissinger watches the president. Gerald Ford delivers his last State of the Union address, though he doesn't know it yet:
"*This year we celebrate the two hundred years of our country...*"
The president's voice fills the interior of a Chevrolet that slowly drives away toward its garage in Bethesda.[1] The snowflakes enlarge in the car's light and crash against the windshield.
"*In the long, upward march of man*" said the president, "*from savagery and slavery along the nearly two thousand years of the Christian calendar and nearly six thousand years according to the Jewish calculation, there have been many deep and terrifying valleys, but also many bright and admirable peaks.*"
Seventeen hundred kilometers to the south, on a bar TV in a nearly empty Little Havana in Miami, two men in white guayaberas watch the president's yellowed face and then glance at each other without a word. Outside, a man urinates behind a bush and looks at them thoughtfully.
"*We must introduce a new balance between spending on social programs and spending on defense. A balance that ensures we fully meet our obligation to the needy and, at the same time, allows us to strengthen our security in a world that remains hostile to freedom...*"
The men in guayaberas smoke and drink rum half-heartedly, almost out of obligation, as if existence was unbearable without the slow suicide of each day. The man on the other side of the sign *raB otijoM* seems to announce the culmination of his urinary urgency with a subtle tremble, just as a young woman enters, demanding something from the bar owner, and a brief argument in Spanish begins, making it even harder to understand the president's words.

The young woman had told him twice she wanted old clothes from beef, and he'd been given pork.

"*Our country has played a unique role in the world since the day of its independence, two hundred years ago. Since the end of World War II, we have successfully assumed the great responsibility of ensuring a stable world order, full of hope for the progress of Humanity…*"

—Want me to change the channel?—the bartender shouts from behind the counter.

—*We've tried to be the world's police and understanding parents here at home.*

—No, leave it like this—says one—. We're not going to understand much more anyway.

—For the shit that's out there…

"*The truth is we are the greatest democracy in the world. We remain the symbol of man's aspiration to freedom and well-being. We are the embodiment of hope for progress… We continue to work to improve the efficiency of our military forces. The budget I will present this year represents the needs of the United States to face the world in which we live. While conflicts persist, our intelligence capabilities must be the best.*"

—Channel 23 plays the same thing but translated—insists the bartender.

—Worse. Leave it like this, we're leaving anyway.

"*The key elements for peace among the nations of the Middle East already exist. Our traditional friendships in Latin America, Africa, and Asia continue. We have taken on the leadership role by initiating serious and hopeful dialogue between the industrial world and the developing world.*"

—He's not a bad guy—said the mustached one— but that Congress filled up with communists, dammit.

—Not all of them—said the other, pointing at the screen, which at that moment focused on the Secretary of State, in profile, arms crossed, and lips tight.

—Well, that reminds me I have to get up early tomorrow. Let me grab a ten.

He stood up, jingled some coins in one hand, as if trying to keep them from escaping the table, and headed for the door.

"*...the words I remember best are Dwight Eisenhower's. 'America is not good because it is great. America is great because it is good.'*"

The unanimous applause of Congress echoed in the bar. The two men stopped silently before leaving. The gardener was already gone.

"*President Eisenhower was raised in a poor but religious home*" continued the president, "*in the heart of America. His simple words echoed the eloquent testimony of President Lincoln when he said, "being right gives us strength." In turn, Lincoln invoked the humble image of George Washington, kneeling and praying at Valley Forge... Let us engrave it now in each of our hearts as we begin our Bicentennial.*"

—Well, see you later, pescao—said one—. Hasta mañana.

The television announced for Monday, February 1st at 9:00 PM, the first episode of the series *Rich Man, Poor Man*. The conflicted poor brother, Tom Jordache, and the rich brother, Peter Haskell, owner of Tricorp, lead very different lives, but united by blood ties. On ABC.

When the customers at table 8 got up, the bartender took the opportunity to put on S.W.A.T. just as, in Maryland, the Chevrolet almost had an accident. On a right turn, black ice caused it to skid to the left and nearly collide head-on with a truck coming the opposite way.

When Orlando got home, Isabel asked him how his day had been.

—Everything's fine, as usual—replied Orlando, hiding an envelope he had just taken from the mailbox.

LITTLE Havana

LAST FRIDAY I RECEIVED ANOTHER LETTER, unsigned and signed *Zero*. It had been redirected to me by the Social Sciences secretary to the motel where I've been staying since July. Few know what a threat signed by *Zero* means, because the executions signed by that group almost disappeared several years ago, which proves that the same people (who are now into politics and business, mostly legal) knew about my latest investigation.

It was written in Spanish. The fact that it was sent to my university office indicated that they hadn't escalated the intimidation or that they didn't even know my home address. It's true that I'm not the owner of the apartment where I live in Jacksonville, which makes it harder to locate me. To find out where I work, just Google me. The note said they'd seen me near the Versailles restaurant.

I had breakfast there only once, black coffee with churros. Very well made, like my grandmother's. The waitresses, besides, are very friendly and almost all of them speak Spanish. Calle Ocho, Little Havana is like Havana, but with lots of new cars and plenty, plenty of asphalt, enough so that a Cuban can't hear another's shouts walking on the opposite sidewalk and feel betrayed by it.

—Miami is Cuba with food—Jesus had told me, with the typical hand gestures some Cubans use—. In Cuba, there's Count Fidel.

—Count?

—Fidel is a count. He hides the rice, the sugar, the meat, the chicken...

Cuban women don't raise their arms as much. Instead, they place the back of their hands on their hips, after a full-body sway, which indicates it's time to agree with them.

—Do people in Havana pee in the streets?—I asked, provoking him.

—No—he said, laughing fully—. It's just that in Cuba, people don't drink as much as here. Over there, we're all skinny. There's not so much food and even less beer.

—That's why they live longer than here.

I read the note again. It was true, I had breakfast at Versailles, but being seen on Calle Ocho was more of a safe bet, like saying they saw me walking on Fifth Avenue after flying to New York. From there, I had gone to meet Jesus. Jesus is a retired mechanic and had known Jorge Mas Canosa and his brother.

Zero, or whoever was hiding behind it, knew that I was reconstructing the murder of Orlando Letelier and Ronni Moffitt in Washington. The case was solved by the FBI some time ago. Although of significant importance, it was still just another terrorist attack like many others from that era. What mattered now, I thought, was understanding the context. I wasn't interested in stretching any mystery about who the killer was, those clichés so often repeated in commercial Anglo-Saxon literature and Hollywood films. For me, the mystery wasn't in the excitement of cowboy vs. Indian stories, but in understanding how the cowboys had become the undisputed heroes and had come to dominate the political center of the empire of the time.

I knew I wasn't going to uncover any new suspects, anyone who had slipped past the FBI, but someone was clearly bothered by any review of the facts. Facts, whether simple or sinister, that hid a powerful network with roots in the Havana mafia of the 1940s.

It was even less my intention to bring anyone to justice. All the accused and prosecuted were and are free. Some were protected by the FBI itself as witnesses against their comrades. Others were acquitted by flawed trials or by judges under threat. Some were simply pardoned by presidents, both ours and theirs, like the Bushes here or the Moscosos there.

Something I discovered over time was that, like hundreds of criminals living today in Florida, New Jersey, or New York, they are unrecognizable from the photos of their glory days—from the guards of various Latin American presidents to the colonels and generals of the dictatorships in the South. Like any man who matures before entering the thinness of old age, their faces are wider, their facial muscles no longer hold the frequent beauty of youth, their impeccable business suits or cheerful guayaberas in front of a glass of rum and behind an unlit cigar, their friendly smiles of generous friends and wise grandfathers don't betray their dark pasts. Much less the unshakable conviction that each of the thousand bombs, each of the deaths of innocents that lengthened lists in various countries, was justified by The Struggle for freedom, not by their personal interests.

Any one of them could be sitting in front of me right now, watching me over their Cuban coffee, their Salvadoran papusa, without me having the slightest chance of identifying them, no matter how many times their names and stories appear in this report.

First Clipping

The attack on Letelier in Washington was better investigated by the journalists of the time than by academics. Things have changed. The need for survival and professional advancement at any cost has tamed them to perfection: "sit Sultan, stay Simba, down Lion, up Captain, jump Conan."

On occasion, some journalists did a better job than the specialized police themselves. It can't be said that they solved more cases than the CIA, because the CIA was part of the very crimes it claimed to investigate and knew where the salt and spices were. In most cases, it was the conductor of the orchestra. In all cases, it abandoned the orchestra when its musicians started to falter or, simply, because letting them act without involvement had been part of the operations manual.

In the library at the University of Miami, I found some original documents from that time. One of them was The Incident, dated March 1, 1977. It was signed by journalists Taylor Branch and John Rothchild. Just as the FBI dealt with the CIA's arrogance, the most troublesome journalists had to deal with the FBI and local police.

—I also became a man of three phones—Rothchild had said.

—What's that?—asked Branch.

—You have one of their numbers—Rothchild explained—. You call them, and they say "phone number X." You go to the payphone marked with number X and, before calling them, you look for another phone Z and take down the number. Then you call them again from phone X. When they ask you for the number of another phone nearby, you give them the number Z. You hang up and then go to phone Z, and they call you there.

—Seems a bit complicated.

—That's how it works—said Rothchild—. The last time, the feds informed me that there are four *nests of assassins* working hard: one is the Cuban exiles; another, Venezuelan intelligence, the DISIP; another, Chilean Intelligence, the DINA; and another, the CIA. For the FBI, all four are terrorists, except some are legal. Untouchable. Not a few acknowledge themselves as terrorists, albeit for a good cause, like the fight against terrorism.

I photocopied this and other articles from the time and reread them at a bar on Calle Ocho. From experience, I knew that two readings of the same text in different contexts often turn out slightly different. The dialogue between Branch and Rothchild was just a small piece of the puzzle. In a corner of page 52, the Miami News of March 16, 1977, echoed this publication about Luis Posada Carriles, Orlando Bosch, and El Mono Ricardo Morales in Venezuela.

It took me three years to begin to understand the chaos of the Cuban groups in this country. They were united only by their obsession with killing Fidel Castro at any cost, an ideological passion that functioned like a single mask for a thousand faces and, through money by any means, a lust for power that frustrated the Revolution in 1959. The chaos was abundant in data, interviews, and documents. The most important ones remained classified and had probably already been destroyed. Despite everything, at least for me, things began to clarify. The story had four chapters:

1. *(1946-1959) The mafia of the Havana casinos during Batista's time.*

2. *(1959-1968) The powerful and founding Cuban exile in Florida in the 1960s, their training at the CIA schools, and their notorious failures to regain power in Cuba.*

3. *(1968-1980) Their period of unleashed terrorism, without CIA oversight, with bombs and settling of scores.*

4. *(1980-present) Their conversion to politics and lobbying in the U.S. Congress.*

I transcribe here, verbatim, the note I wrote that night in a bar. I don't remember which one, nor does it add anything to know it. I always keep my notes when I've had a couple of drinks. For caution's sake. Creativity and sensibility don't usually go hand in hand, but they collaborate.

I tore the page from my notebook, folded it in four, and put it in a pocket of my guayabera to consider it the next day, with a cup of Cuban coffee. I drank the rest of the beer and finished reading the lengthy article "The Incident." What was becoming clear to me about my characters under the magnifying glass was that some had manic episodes, suffered from or enjoyed megalomania, or something like a Napoleon Complex.

There were many obvious examples. One was Ricardo Morales Navarrete, known in the Cuban exile community as El Mono. I think this one, though not as important as others, was one of the most mysterious due to his ability to be in different scenarios, in different countries, to work for different organizations (like Cuba's G-2, the CIA, the FBI, Venezuela's DISIP, and even Chile's DINA) and betray almost all of them equally.

After belonging to the secret services of revolutionary Cuba, Morales Navarrete went into exile in Miami and there he rose to the highest echelons of power within secret intelligence, including that of Venezuela. Venezuelan intelligence and its secret police were filled with Cubans from Miami due to what was called the "disposal problem," an excess of CIA-trained Cuban agents who had proliferated on U.S. soil, operating on their own in numerous bombings and terrorist attacks. The U.S. government maintained an ambiguous position, investigating on one hand while avoiding condemning those responsible for blood crimes on the other. Even John Kennedy was the first to realize that they had "created a monster" beyond control. The first to realize it and the first to suffer the fire of its foul breath.

Like Bosch and Luis Posada Carriles, Morales became a CIA agent and a protected informant for the FBI. He had no qualms about eliminating some of his fellow Agency comrades who were trouble, more for their ineptitude than their lack of loyalty to the cause, those useless Cubans whom Orlando Bosch had called "the CIA's Crazies," and there were far more than just three. According to El Mono (according to Bosch, according to everyone), no one was innocent in a global war. Any person, child, man, or woman walking down the street was a combatant, even if they didn't know it. Therefore, if it was necessary to eliminate them, it was more of an obligation than an opportunity. If it was with a bomb, even better, because bombings always have a much greater psychological effect on the enemy, that is to say, on Fidel Castro, his global government, and the American communists.

By then, after three years of investigation, only one thing was clear to me: every time I thought I had the entire puzzle put together, I found that there were several pieces that didn't fit. So I kept at it, for two more years.

AT THE COPA, COPACABANA

IN FEBRUARY 1946, THE YOUNG FRANK SINATRA arrived in Havana with two million dollars in a suitcase. Two Chicago mobsters, the brothers Rocco and Charlie Fischetti, followed him even when he went to the bathroom. The brothers were cousins of Al Capone and had a well-earned reputation in the business of brothels, gambling, and organized crime.² Sinatra entertained with his songs the attendees of the mafia summit in the region.

Havana, like Tijuana and other cities along the southern border of the United States, had prospered in the alcohol and prostitution business thanks to the 18th Amendment of the U.S. Constitution. This constitutional reform, better known as *Prohibition*, was approved in 1919 with 76 percent of the Senate vote and had banned the greatest addiction of the Great Nation since its founding: alcohol.

Since the early 19th century, liquor and cheap whiskey from the saloons of Georgia and Pennsylvania had fueled wars of expansion over Indian and Mexican territories. A side effect, and later historical obsession, was sex with the disposable women of the conquered inferior races. In a letter to the Secretary of State, dated 1846, General Winfield Scott, tasked with wresting away more than half of Mexico's territory in a war invented by his despised president, James Polk, and by Southern politicians to expand slavery, wrote: "our militias and our volunteers have committed atrocities, horrors in Mexico. Robbery, murder, and the rape of mothers and daughters in front of their bound husbands have been common occurrences throughout this region along the Rio Grande."

A tradition that, naturally, continued with the expansion of the same power, often legitimized with money. The statistics of the following century would confirm that one of the greatest sexual fantasies of Anglo-Saxon men, after the trauma of Vietnam, is not blondes like Marilyn Monroe but Asian women—defenseless, fragile women in need of being saved and protected. In other words, nothing like the women who defeated the great empire.

On December 22, 1946, just under a year before Frank Sinatra's arrival in Havana with his suitcases full of dollars, the hemisphere's largest mafia conference of the last generation had taken place in the city. It had been organized by Charles "Lucky" Luciano, the weathered Italian mobster, considered the father of organized crime in the United States in the 20th century and an expert in gambling and prostitution. Luciano was one of the main allies of the other American mafia with operations in Cuba, whose boss was Meyer Lansky, the godfather of the Jewish mafia network known as the Kosher Mafia. Lansky owned numerous casinos and betting houses in the United States and Cuba, such as the one located in his luxurious Hotel Riviera in Havana. Under the gold-decorated ceilings, legal gambling, legalized gambling, and illegal gambling flourished. Along with roulette and the bolita game, prostitution and drug trafficking also thrived. In 1952, Fulgencio Batista appointed him Director of Gambling in Cuba.

One could speculate (I noted, but this should not be taken as fact but as a mere theory) that since the late 19th century, the most persecuted and harassed immigrants, such as the Irish, Italians, and Jews, produced (like the Central American gangs today) a phenomenon of mafias and criminal defense groups that later became legal lobbies of harassment and extortion. The historical logic of these groups indicates that, ironically emerging from social and political marginalization, they often reach economic power and, later, political power in their countries, continuing a much older historical pattern: from persecuted to persecutors.

But let's return to the simple and hard facts. During the days leading up to Christmas in '46, the biggest mafia bosses in the United States gathered at Cuba's luxurious Hotel Nacional. Following the coup by Senator and General Fulgencio Batista in 1952, the dream of turning Havana into the Las Vegas of the Caribbean began to materialize without bureaucratic delays. Foreign investments and the laws protecting them proliferated. When in 1957 Senator John Kennedy made an official trip to Cuba, Santo Trafficante provided him with three young prostitutes at a brothel where they spied on him through a mirrored wall.[3] Six years later, the same mafias of Santo Trafficante Jr., Frank Costello, Albert Anastasia, Vito Genovese, and one of Fulgencio Batista's protégés, Meyer Lansky, were implicated in several investigations and named by multiple witnesses as accomplices in the assassination of President Kennedy.

Few residents of the island, such as Ernest Hemingway, opposed this organized crime convention.

—After the Cuban Revolution—admitted a retired FBI agent—the Havana mafia was relocated to the United States with the arrival of the first exiles.

People like Rolando Masferrer, José Miguel Battle, Orlando Piedra, and the former Havana police chief, Colonel Esteban Ventura, set up their businesses here, in Miami, just as they had in Cuba. They thrived on illegal gambling like la bolita, long before the lottery was legalized.[4] As often happens within the mafia, many of these anti-Castro figures were killed by other anti-Castro individuals. Rolando Masferrer, to give just one example, was eliminated in Miami in 1975 with a bomb. A settling of scores. Not without irony, the senator from Batista's bloody dictatorship, the influential director of Cuba's Libertad newspaper and later a protagonist in terrorist explosions (like the one that ended a hundred lives in Havana's port or the assassination of President John Kennedy) had summed up the philosophy of his struggle in an exceptionally clear way: "the only language communists understand is that of dynamite."[5] Of course, from his ideological paranoia and according to FBI agents, even Orlando Bosch and Guillermo Novo appeared as dangerous communists.[6] According to Miami police reports, one night Masferrer stopped Ignacio Novo at the entrance of his newspaper, Libertad, disarmed him, and left him in the middle of the street in his underwear. Something neither Ignacio nor his older brother, Guillermo, would forget.

By 1990, Miami was still known in FBI offices as the capital of mafia and terrorism in the United States, due to its epidemic of bombings in the homes and businesses of those Cuban exiles who favored opening relations with the island.[7] Every so often, media like Radio Mambí organized telethons to raise funds for *La lucha* or for *La guerra*.[8] In 1993 alone, they managed to raise half a million dollars in just a few days, threatening to blow up any business that refused to cooperate, as some unhinged individuals like the lawyer

Alberto Millán reported. No one could account for where that slush fund ended up.

—*Vice in Miami*—Hunter reminded me— that series with Don Johnson and Philip Thomas, the one who played Ricardo Rico, came after Dallas and Dynasty, if I recall correctly.

—True—I replied—. We had to salute the new opulence of the Confederate South.

—Only now, instead of cotton plantations, there were oil companies and a lot of tourism dazzled by the eternal happiness of Miami and Disney World.

—Nothing has changed as much as it seems. In fact, some things remain constant...

—Like, for example?—Hunter asked.

—Like how the super-rich still don't know how to be happy.

—Do you think they're less happy than us?

—I think so—I said, hesitating—. At least their billions of dollars don't achieve a minimum and reasonable proportion of happiness. How is it possible to be happy and live obsessed with maintaining financial empires, controlling even the breath of their senators? How can they be so happy from trial to trial, which often end in suicide? How can billionaires be happy when they're always busy defending their own paradise and others' hell? Because, in all that madness, there can be no winners without losers. About something, even something very small, they are mistaken. They keep uncorking champagne, but the poor still have wine.

—What do you have against millionaires? Why the hate?

—The first is true. I don't like them.

—But why? It's typical class hatred.

—You don't like communists, right?

—That's right—Hunter said, holding his belly—. I dislike them a lot, like chicharrón.

—Why?

—Damn, don't quiz me, professor.

—Why do you hate communists?

—Because they're against freedom, because they steal the work of decent people, because they manipulate the press, because they're experts in propaganda, because they're sick with ideology...

—Well, I don't like millionaires for those same reasons. But me, who's not even a communist, I don't stop them from taking their private planes and landing in whatever country they fancy.

Her name is Lola, she was a showgirl
But that was thirty years ago
When they used to have a show
Now it's a disco, but not for Lola
Still in the dress she used to wear
Faded feathers in her hair

CUBA ÜBER ALLES

I WROTE IN MY NOTEBOOK *Conversation with Allende*, an interview I thought I should watch before fully diving into 1976. It had been recorded in Chile by the journalist and professor Saul Landau. I had already gathered some relevant information about Landau. I was quite familiar with the Cuban exile community in Union City.

—They are all creatures of U.S. foreign policy—said Landau—. These lunatics, some with portraits of Hitler, also had the führer's motto hanging in their offices, only with a slight variation: "Cuba über alles."

—Cuba Above All. Cuba First.

I saw it firsthand. In the bars of Miami it became a cocktail and a tradition that spanned generations. "Cuba über alles, our beer-fueled take on a Cuba libre", the signs and chalkboards announced. An exotic mix of beer, rum, and lots of freedom.

Cuba above all. Even if it burns. After the explosion in Havana's port, which took 101 lives and left hundreds more disabled, the sabotage continued systematically. Just the first week of 1965, a wave of fires broke out in different regions of the island.

—If we had the resources—said Orlando Bosch to the journalists in Miami on January 17, 1965— Cuba would burn from one end to the other.

The next day, the *Press of Atlantic City* in New Jersey reported on its 17th page about several fires in Cuban sugar mills. From Miami, the MIRR confirmed that they had bombed several facilities, managing to set extensive areas of plantations on fire.

—For three days—reported the organization led by Orlando Bosch— our planes dropped napalm bombs and five thousand phosphorus bombs on Cuba. We lost a ship loaded with weapons and propaganda, but none of ours were captured, as the government claims.[9]

Three decades later, Luis Posada Carriles would sum up one of his frustrations, which were never few, in a conversation with the Cuban journalist Ann Louise Bardach: Cuba was a very different country from the one he left in 1959. He no longer cared who took power on the island. It would never be the country he knew in his youth.

—When I left Cuba—said Posada Carriles, without citing sources— twenty percent were Black. Now Black people make up seventy percent.[10]

Non-Fiction Novel

BACK AT THE LIBRARY, I PICKED UP a book about the attack that brought down the Cubana plane shortly after Letelier's death. I opened it to the page where I left off and closed it again. I noted my own difficulties:

Why do non-fiction novels take up an entire page describing details that are impossible to verify and, worse yet, completely irrelevant? In a plane that is crashing, they reproduce dialogues, tics: "she wiped the sweat with the back of her hand, clicked her tongue, and saw her companion crossing herself while thinking that morning she had bid her father farewell with a hug that had lasted an eternity..." Now, *if you are mentioning a dinner among four people, like Orlando Letelier's* last supper, an event documented in several records, and you write: "on the television the kids were watching Rich Man, Poor Man", well, that is also a detail very difficult to verify. Maybe the television was off, but you check the TV schedule in that city and, in addition to verifying that at that time channel X was airing that series and you know that it was a very popular show at the time, it is entirely valid to set the scene with a real, probable, and illustrative detail of the sensitivities of the moment.

I still had not figured out how I was going to write *1976*. All the options were negative. Like when one needs to choose the name for their unborn child and all the names remind them of people whom, for some good or bad reason, they prefer to avoid.

—A minor detail—I thought or wanted to think.

I had the unpleasant feeling that that genre, so sacred to me, the novel, was a zombie or had died. Though not its forms... Had it been killed by the McDonaldization of the market? A growing lack of ability and taste among new generations to distinguish between fiction and reality had severely wounded both. Maybe it was just humanity returning to times when myths and religions occupied the place that sciences and critical thinking had taken for a few centuries—though more than religious narrative, now it was about a pornographic faith in self-deception. After all, in a world where one can no longer look a woman in the eyes without being accused of harassment, fantasy is the most real thing we have left.

—I wouldn't worry about the form—Hunter had told me—. It's the subject. I already told you to write a detective story, without so many real references. But no, you are determined to get into trouble. At your age, you should already be thinking about...

—About what?

—The same thing as me—Hunter lamented—. About something more publishable, something pleasant to read. If you come to me with another one of your heavy tomes that, worse, must be read twice to understand, we are not going to publish it. I am sorry to tell you, but we already talked about this with my partners. On the other hand, no matter how many documents you cite from here and there, no more than a dozen readers are going to believe you. They will kill the messenger first.

—What could I care if they don't believe me?—I said—. I am neither a pastor of some sect nor are they the judges of some final judgment.

—Well, I am more pragmatic—said Hunter—. Since I am not a capitalist because I live off my work, as you have said yourself, I am not going to kill myself over any idealism. Apart from publishing unmarketable authors like you, I must save money for my retirement. My idea is to get the hell out of here, to go live in Italy or Mexico. I will leave later, not now, for obvious reasons. There is no money in Mexico and no life in the United States.

QUETROPILLÁN, CHILE

ONE HOT JANUARY AFTERNOON, THE DOORBELL RANG at the Townley household. It was Mamo. Mariana answered the door, who would remember this moment in her memoirs, nine years later. The documents of the time will not contradict her, quite the opposite.

They greeted each other with a kiss and a hug. Behind them appeared Michael. They embraced with less restraint and Mamo asked:

—Well, Don Miguel, what do you think of your new residence?

—I have no words to thank you in any language, Colonel—said Michael, in nearly perfect Spanish, though unable to hide his gringo accent—. As my wife says, there is no more beautiful view in all of Latin America than what we have here.

—Some people are saying that Chile is a country or a landscape.
—Heretics.

Michael Townley was surprised that Colonel Manuel Contreras had deigned to visit them. More likely was a visit from Colonel Espinosa, the second-in-command of DINA. His deep inferiority complex made him the perfect servant. Oedipus complex, some biographers would say. The perfect psychopath, the CIA recruitment office would have concluded.

Besides his many merits (like his dual nationality, his perfect command of English and Spanish, and certain self-taught knowledge of electronics), Michael didn't know how to say no to any order that came from above.

—Having two passports isn't a merit. I'm not so sure about your bilingualism either.

—Call it whatever you want.

Although Callejas, ten years older, like any mother, had a great influence over him, she was still his wife. Often, like any son, Michael lied to her when he knew she would question some higher order. He wasn't a womanizer, like Colonel Espinosa, like Orlando Letelier, and like so many other Latin men. He was only obsessed with power, with keeping the chaos of life under control, like the British imperial lawn that later became a cultural brand of the United States: keeping nature under artificial, geometric control, even if it meant enslaving its own lawnmowers and polluting nature itself in a completely surreal enterprise.

—I'm sure this place will be filled with pleasure and work—said Colonel Contreras, looking at Mariana.

—The two are the same thing—Michael clarified.

The colonel slumped into the armchair by the window and said:
—*La dolce vita* ... Did you see it?
—No.
—Yes, of course.
—I always remember the beginning. I don't remember anything else, but Mr. Jesus Christ flying all over Rome tied to a helicopter

always seemed like the pinnacle to me... When the shadow passes over the wall of a building, it seems to rise to the heavens. A whole message.

—As if he were leaving us...

—Very good interpretation. I hadn't thought of that. We're alone, then. We'll be alone until he returns.

In the hall on the third floor, Mariana had planned the new center for the literary gatherings of Chile, the new literature of the new Latin America. Her fondness for organizing salons where she was the gravitational center had begun years earlier. In the modest apartment in Santiago, upon her return from Miami (while Townley was culminating his passionate courtship with another woman in San Francisco), Callejas had maintained the tradition of late-night gatherings with the younger members of Patria y Libertad, where they analyzed the disintegration of the country at the hands of the Allende regime.[11] "Allende fueled class hatred," confirmed Callejas in his 1995 memoirs. "The hatred between the dispossessed and the rich hung in the air like a stench...I noticed the corruption of the government. It was impossible to blame Yankee imperialism."[12]

According to Callejas, these were gatherings similar to the ones held during Allende's time, in the heroic little apartment in Santiago, with the members of Patria y Libertad. The theme of freedom and the role of the state were always present in some form. The freedom of art, the freedom of man, the freedom of society, if such a thing as society even existed...

—The first thing a human being has at birth is freedom—recited Hunter—. Then the state takes it away...

—Yes, I'm familiar with the idea—I reproached him—. It's very nice, but no less a fiction than *One Hundred Years of Solitude*. The first thing a human being has at birth is a list of urgent needs. Any mother knows that. Freedom? Zero. Not even the freedom to choose between the left or right breast. Freedom is something that is conquered, and only in small doses, after years of struggle. The same goes for societies. Freedom is a construction and involves the progressive reduction of basic needs, the conquest of justice, and the dignity of each individual—three things that only make sense in society and long after being born.

—Well, as you wish—said Hunter—. It doesn't matter now. I've already told you that if you want a publishable book, you must start by stripping it of your own ideas, especially any political ones. People like concrete details. Plots...

—A murder, not many. Lots of blood and lots of sex, but with some logic so that the reader feels like the detective. Some rape without too much description, to avoid offending sensibilities. Short sentences, something that can be read at the beach...

—Let's return to Chile of Townley and Callejas.

That's where the cacerolazos were organized, a stroke of genius invented in Chile by CIA agent David Atlee Phillips more than two decades ago. The marches weren't made up of starving poor people, who resisted destroying their few pots by banging them with a ladle, but by members of the upper class, mostly housewives. One of the recurring topics in these gatherings was the rumor that the socialist doctor and president wore expensive suits and (like Virgilio Paz in Miami, said Callejas) drank Chivas Regal while his people went hungry.

—I know what I'm talking about—said Callejas—. I live nine blocks from the president's residence.[13]

Days before, Colonel Contreras had informed Michael about the start of a secret plan to develop chemical weapons. They also needed to make progress in better using electronic resources. He had suggested several locations, but Michael and Mariana decided to set up the lab in the wealthy northeast suburbs of Santiago, at 4925 Orange Avenue, right where the new government was developing an area exclusively for officers, military officials, and important visitors. Not famous visitors. Important visitors, like Orlando Bosch and other valuable fighters for the Free World.

FIDEL AND MALCOLM X

—Well, you have to understand the times—said Hunter—. We're talking about the Cold War. The United States couldn't allow a Soviet stronghold in its hemisphere.

—Its hemisphere?—I asked.

—Well, I understand that this Monroe Doctrine thing isn't very likable, but...

—Superman fighting for justice against the villains who want to take over the world. Don't the villains realize that the world already has an owner? Or they don't respect private property. Still, at the time, Cuba wasn't even a Soviet stronghold. Just a dangerous and arrogant attempt to be independent. How could those blacks and those white islanders think of doing without us? Didn't they learn anything from Guatemala? That was the problem. They learned too much from Guatemala.

—Timidity was never a very effective strategy.

Exactly. But, beyond the nationalizations and the aspirations for autonomy of the New Cuba, the Revolution wasn't thinking of cutting ties with its largest trading partner. In fact, when Fidel Castro visited the United States on April 7, 1959, he hired an American public relations agency, Bernard Relin & Associates Inc. According to Time magazine on July 8 of that year, the firm charged the Cuban government $72,000, a paltry sum considering Fulgencio Batista's personal dealings with U.S. companies, which amounted to nearly $46 million.[14] Aside from some interesting details revealed by the Bernard Relin firm, Castro did not take their recommendations very seriously, such as shaving his beard and swapping his olive-green uniform for a businessman's suit.[15] Instead, he gave his own instructions to the delegation: he forbade them from talking about money. Not even by accident.

—We are not beggars,—he said.[16]

Secretary of State Christian Herter met with the young revolutionary in Washington. Herter reported to Eisenhower: "It's a shame you did not meet with Fidel *Castro*. He is more than an interesting character... In many ways, he's like a child."[17]

At a lunch, he was introduced to William Wieland.

—Who is this gentleman?

—Mister Wieland,—said Wieland's assistant,—is the director of the Office of Mexican and Caribbean Affairs and currently the official in charge of the State Department for Cuban Affairs.

—Well, well,—said Castro,—I thought I was the one in charge of Cuban affairs.[18]

After a long conversation at a New York hotel, CIA agent Gerry Droller (then Frank Bender) concluded:

—Castro is not only not a communist, but he's a committed anticommunist.

Vice President Richard Nixon reached the same conclusion when he met with the Cuban for two and a half hours in his Capitol office twelve days later.

None of these assessments stopped the invasion plan for the island, which had already been on CIA desks weeks before the new revolutionary leader's first visit. The original sin wasn't about being or not being, but about challenging Washington, the sugar companies, and the casino mobs for control of the Pearl of the Caribbean. And, worse than that, setting a terrible precedent. Once again, as in 1898, the problem was the independence advocates, the unacceptable bad example of a Republic of free Blacks, no longer cutting off their masters' heads, as in Haiti, but nationalizing land and businesses, as President Árbenz attempted in Guatemala.

Months before leaving office, Eisenhower decided to postpone the invasion and leave it to the new administration, John Kennedy. By late 1960, Havana had already discovered the CIA training camps in Guatemala. The CIA had to spread the rumor in the press that it was a group of communist guerrillas, and to maintain the element of surprise, switched the landing from Trinidad to the Bay of Pigs, an area closer to Havana but less populated.

In the midst of the Cold War, allowing a friendly dictator to fall without Washington's approval and, worse, daring to talk about national sovereignty in the face of the companies leading the freedom of the Developed World could set a terrible precedent in the banana republics of the South. For the CIA and the White House, the quickest and cheapest solution was the same one that solved the problem in Guatemala: media warfare, invasion, and regime change in the name of the fight against communism. Easy as pie.

—Cochinos?—protested David Atlee Phillips, the CIA agent who mastered Spanish thanks to his sabotage work in Chile since the end of World War II— How do you think Cubans will support an invasion with that name?

Perhaps for the same reason, Ernesto Che Guevara preferred to call Playa Girón the most significant defeat of U.S. imperialism in the century up to that point. Of course, it wasn't just a matter of names. At the time, polls showed that the Revolution had the support of ninety percent of the population. The discovery of clandestine cemeteries across the island, filled with Batista's disappeared, only deepened the rejection of U.S. support and the Cuban mafia, now exiled in Miami.

—It's very hard to find a Cuban without a family member killed by Batista's regime—said Ruby Hart Phillips, the New York Times journalist based in Cuba.[19]

On August 17, 1961, a few months after the Bay of Pigs fiasco and seven thousand kilometers to the south, Che gave a speech in the auditorium of the University of the Republic of Uruguay. That afternoon, beside him, intently listening was the senator and former presidential candidate of Chile, Salvador Allende. As the crowd exited, someone shot and killed the history professor Arbelio Ramírez. Apparently, the bullet was meant for Che. It was the first unsolved assassination of the Cold War in that country, typical of cases orchestrated by secret agencies operating at the highest level. In his speech, Che had noted that Uruguay didn't need any revolution, as its democratic system was functioning. He didn't know that, at the time, the powerful Howard Hunt was stationed in Montevideo, the same man who had successfully promoted his candidate for the presidency of that country, Benito Nardone. The same man who had hijacked the media to destroy democracy in Guatemala, had used them again to place his candidate in the presidency, this time without much scandal. The democracy continued to function very well, for some, for the same old players. But, as tradition dictated, inconvenient influences had to be removed, if possible without attacking freedom of expression. Cuba's example of independence, Che's anti-imperialist speech, fell into that category of undesirables.

Surely not by coincidence, the Cuban CIA agent Orlando Bosch was among the crowd that afternoon in Montevideo when Professor Arbelio Ramírez was killed. Surely he hadn't gone to listen to Che's lecture.

The plans to assassinate Castro and reinstall a less arrogant dictator in Havana had begun the very night Batista fled to the Dominican Republic in a plane loaded with suitcases of cash. Washington, the CIA, and the casino mafia didn't hesitate for a moment. Fidel Castro knew it, but he needed the U.S. market and believed a new agreement with the northern giant was possible. So, on September 18, 1960, he landed again in Long Island, this time to participate in the annual United Nations Assembly, four days later.

The delegation's arrival was greeted by the American left and met with threats from La Rosa Blanca, a pro-Batista group that later, due to the discrediting of El General Mulato, would operate alongside other Miami groups as anti-Castro exiles.

This time, the Cuban plane carrying Fidel Castro to New York was forced to return to Cuba, while the delegation was escorted to the Shelburne Hotel, located on Lexington Avenue and 37th Street. The hotel demanded an exorbitant deposit of twenty thousand dollars. The State Department decreed that the delegation could not leave Manhattan, but no other hotel in the area dared to take them in. Castro quipped that if New York could not provide lodging for a diplomatic delegation from another country, then the UN should be moved to another city, like Havana.

It was a rainy day, and the Cuban delegation stacked their suitcases at the main entrance without a confirmed hotel. Minutes later, a Black man entered the lobby of the Shelburne and asked to speak with the Cuban prime minister. When the bearded man appeared, the stranger said:

—Mr. Malcolm X has reserved a hotel for your delegation.
—Wonderful, my friend. Where is it?
—It's the Hotel Theresa. It's an hour from here, in Harlem.

Castro didn't know it, but the Hotel Theresa, far cheaper than the Shelburne, had welcomed Black celebrities who were not accepted in downtown Manhattan, like Duke Ellington, Louis Armstrong, and Nat King Cole.

—We'll go there at once—said Castro.

The Harlem newspaper, the New York Citizen-Call, noting that Cuba's official delegation included both white and Black members, published:

"*On Monday night, two thousand Black New Yorkers waited in the rain for the Cuban prime minister, Fidel Castro, to arrive at the famous and historic Hotel Theresa in Harlem... For the oppressed residents of the Harlem ghetto, Castro is that bearded revolutionary who expelled the corrupt from his nation and dared to tell white America: go to hell.*"[20]

A smaller group of Batista supporters also gathered to protest against the revolution.

The *New York Times* on September 21 headlined: "*Castro Seeks Support of the Negroes.*" In his column, journalist Wyne Phillips highlighted Dr. Castro's strategy: pretending there is no racial segregation in Cuba, when a year earlier he forcibly removed a Cuban leader, Fulgencio Batista, who was half Black. Despite everything, Phillips himself admits that numerous testimonies from Black

Americans visiting Havana acknowledged feeling like people, like any white person walking the streets.

With the ink still fresh from the newspapers the day after their expulsion from the Shelburne Hotel and their improvised entry into the Harlem hotel, Manhattan's most luxurious hotels offered free lodging to the Cuban delegation. But Castro decided to turn the initial humiliation into another moral blow to the arrogance of the giant. He rejected the offers, and the delegation stayed in Harlem.

The history of the Hotel Theresa became a headache for Washington and an offense to a country suffering from a strong segregationist backlash, where the more moderate racists supported the solution of the interpretive law of the constitution, known as Separate but Equal—equal, but separate. To make matters worse, the Cuban delegation received a visit right there from the President of Egypt, Gamal Abdel Nasser, Soviet Premier Nikita Khrushchev, the Prime Minister of India, Minister Jawaharlal Nehru, and renowned intellectuals such as Langston Hughes, Allen Ginsberg, and Columbia University professor Wright Mills, author of *The Power Elite*, a book where he exposed the existing conflict of interests between military corporate power and politicians. Several researchers will recognize this book as the unacknowledged inspiration for President Eisenhower's famous farewell speech on the dangers of the Military-Industrial Complex, for which he would be accused of being a communist.

Malcolm X visited Castro in his room. Upon leaving, questioned by journalists about his sympathies for Castro and Che Guevara, he declared:

—Please don't tell us who our friends should be and who our enemies should be.[21]

Sidney Gottlieb, the chemical genius in charge of the CIA's MK-Ultra Project, proposed humiliating the dangerous leader in front of the whole world. For the CBS interview, which was intended to reach the largest possible audience worldwide, he proposed contaminating Castro's shoes with thallium. This would cause excessive salivation while he spoke. At the same time, he would be exposed to LSD to make him appear drunk. It wasn't a new idea of propaganda sabotage (Howard Hunt had used similar tactics in Mexico, against the painter Diego Rivera), but this time it didn't work on the interviewee.

President Eisenhower and Vice President Nixon did not hide their frustration. The FBI took note. One of their agents managed to enter the Hotel Theresa and spy on a meeting between Castro and Malcolm X. The CIA, lacking jurisdiction in the territory, employed the mercenary firm founded by one of its former agents, Robert Maheu, to plan the first of the six hundred attempts to assassinate Castro. The private agency Maheu was the same one that, serving the dictator Rafael Trujillo, had made the professor Jesús Galíndez disappear in New York, four years earlier. The same firm that served as the basis for one of the most popular TV series in history: Mission: Impossible. The same series cherished by several Batista supporters of the failed Bay of Pigs invasion, such as Orlando Bosch.

At the Plaza Hotel, Bob Maheu met with the CIA agent Jim O'Connell and with John Roselli, one of the leaders of the Italian-American mafia, which owned the cabarets, brothels, and casinos in Cuba, protected by Batista and nostalgically remembered by generations of nostalgic Cubans in the United States as the golden era when all the Cuban people lived by dancing salsa, drinking rum, and making lots of money from legal corruption.

These mafias had been displaced by the Revolution of 1959, so the CIA understood they shared a common objective. To assassinate the bad dictator, who had been in power for only a few months, Mr. Roselli connected Maheu with other mobsters in Tampa, Florida. Two of them were Sam Giancana and Santo Trafficante Jr., both donors to Kennedy's presidential campaign and later collaborators in the conspiracy to assassinate him. Although, for some very good reason, the documents that would definitively prove this information have not been declassified by Washington, the clues and testimonies that point to the involvement of the CIA and the Cuban mafia have accumulated over the years like manure in a chicken coop.

Giancana was assassinated in Chicago in 1975, just before he was to testify before the Church Commission of the U.S. Senate, which was investigating the CIA's systematic assassination plans. In a predictable manner, the CIA director, William Colby, assured: "we had nothing to do with that."[22]

Fidel Castro would have been an easy target in a black hotel that couldn't even control the hot water in the bathrooms. But Maheu and the CIA knew that the assassination of a foreign leader on US soil would only worsen Washington's reputation, so they decided to take the big moment to Havana. Upon his return, Castro gave a predictable speech from the balcony of Government House, which was interrupted by a bomb. A few minutes later, a second one exploded, and a few hours later, a third. It would have been a piece of cake to claim that the assassination was the work of the heroic Cuban dissidents and that "we had nothing to do with it." That was one of 638 failed attempts to assassinate the only dictator that Washington, the CIA, and the mainstream media could see in the Caribbean, Latin America, and the rest of the world.

Other poisoning attempts followed, carried out by various Cuban mercenaries, such as Juan Orta and other infiltrators for hefty sums in dollars, but none achieved their goal. Plans involving gases during interviews or weapons hidden in press microphones also failed, like the one organized from Bolivia, with the support of the Cuban Antonio Veciana, when Castro visited Chile in 1971.

In his speech at the UN on Thursday the 22nd, Castro responded to the accusations from the dominant press that the Cubans had chosen a brothel to stay in:

—For some gentlemen, a humble hotel in the Harlem neighborhood, the neighborhood of Black Americans, has to be a brothel.[23]

Years later, in response to a journalist's provocation, Malcolm X replied:

—The only white man I've ever liked was Fidel Castro.

The CIA failed to assassinate the bearded man of the Caribbean, but the FBI managed to have Malcolm X assassinated in 1965, as always, as if it were someone else's doing, lone wolves. The same strategy of indirect solutions had been practiced with Martin Luther King Jr.. The FBI pursued him for years to document his weakness for women. They knew he suffered from depression and, as a young man, had attempted suicide. The idea was to expose some possible infidelity, destroy his marriage, and push him to suicide. When this didn't work, they facilitated an assassination at the hands of some mentally ill lone individual, which occurred in 1968, at the Lorraine Motel, when the Black leader was preparing to support a healthcare workers' strike in Tennessee. In the collective memory, only these two assassinations will remain, attributed to lone wolves, not the FBI's plan refined and executed over two decades, later known as COINTELPRO (Counter Intelligence Program), through which the FBI infiltrated Black and Latino communities; it infiltrated unions, feminist groups, and anti-imperial war groups to monitor and discredit them with provocateurs; to demoralize them and dismantle their resistance organizations. An FBI memorandum dated March 3, 1968, reported that "Martin Luther King, Jr. was targeted because (among other things) he might abandon his supposed obedience to white liberal doctrines (of nonviolence) and embrace Black nationalism." Eight years later, in April 1976, a Senate investigation led by Senator Frank Church concluded that this psychological warfare led to moral harassment through false reports and rumors planted in the media. "Many of the techniques used would be intolerable in a democratic society, even if all the targets had been involved in violent activities, but COINTELPRO went much further. The main unstated premise of the programs was that a law enforcement agency has the duty to do whatever is necessary to combat perceived threats to the existing social and political order."[24]

In 1967, the CIA had better luck with its plan to assassinate Che Guevara in Bolivia. Che, accused for decades by the media center of Miami of being a cruel killer, had returned to his habit of leading his battles from the front, a habit to which the heroes of the Batista exile, like Orlando Bosch and Luis Posada Carriles, were not very inclined. Nor was it a characteristic of the many mercenaries who, according to the FBI, turned Miami into "the capital of terrorism in the United States."[25] Also Mono Morales Navarrete, José Dionisio Suárez, Virgilio Paz, and the Novo Sampol brothers were more fond of dynamite and the CIA's plastic explosives C4, always from a distance, than of smuggled cigars.

Weeks after the Hotel Theresa scandal, on October 12, 1960, the young Senator John F. Kennedy set up his vendor's stand in front of the hotel and gave a speech against racial discrimination and the socialist ideas of the Cuban Revolution. There's nothing better than hijacking the struggle of the underclass and then limiting it to a specific area, the national one, just as firefighters burn a forest boundary to stop a larger fire. A couple of years earlier, in Congress, Senator Kennedy had recommended continuing funding Latin American armies to maintain Washington's political influence in those countries.

—Latin American armies are useless in any war—the young senator had said in 1958— but in their countries, they are the most important institutions. The money we send them as aid is money down the drain, in a military sense, but it's money very well invested in a political sense.

Dictators and Dictators

—It sounds like another one of those conspiracy theories—said Hunter, scratching his Hemingway beard— like everything surrounding Kennedy.

—It's in the Congressional transcripts—I reminded him.

—Ah, I forgot you burn hours of your life at the stake of primary sources. But what do you mean by… what do you call it…?

Batisteros. What's up with those damn batisteros?—asked Hunter, without losing the habit of inserting one of those curse words he had picked up in some Latin American country.

—I think it's explained pretty well in the book you're not going to publish.

—I haven't told you yet that we're not going to publish it. You haven't even sent us the first manuscript. I'm trying to see things from our readers' perspective. For example, when you say Batista, that Pinochet were dictators, wasn't Fidel also a dictator? Why don't you present the story from a more neutral point of view?

—Neutrality doesn't exist, not even in relativistic physics or quantum physics. But look, I have no problem saying it: Fidel Castro was also a dictator. At least according to the definition from the liberal democracies of the civilized First World, which have, throughout modern history, been the most brutal and genocidal imperial regimes.

—So, there's no difference between one dictator and another.

—Of course there is, like the difference between Earth and Mars. The Batistas and the Pinochets preceded the Castros by generations. Haven't I said before that Washington and U.S. corporations have been the most important promoters of communism in Latin America? The real problem for Washington has always been democracy, true democracy, where ordinary people without capital dared to say no and their decision actually mattered.

—Yes, I think I've heard you say that before. I thought it was one of those provocations you're known for.

—Call it what you want, but let's focus on what's important. Some, the Batistas, the Somozas, the Trujillos, the Pinochets, the Videla, the Sese Secos were dictators installed by the international dictatorship, the dominant imperialism of the time, and the others were dictators who resisted it. Were they the only solution? History shows and proves that democracies in the Periphery were always either hijacked or destroyed whenever they bothered the will of the

Center. One thing was Mohammad Gaddaf and another the Saudi monarchy. Do you understand the difference?

—I'll make the effort.

THe APPrenTices

Luis Posada Carriles and Orlando Bosch knew each other from their student days. They got to know each other even more when, through CIA agents David Atlee Phillips and Howard Hunt, they were recruited in Havana to overthrow the new revolutionary government. The strategies were multiple, from planting bombs in clothing stores to a massive paramilitary invasion. The founder of Alpha 66, Antonio Veciana, started in the same way.

—Maurice Bishop, that is, David Atlee Phillips—Veciana acknowledged—, knew I was responsible for the fire in one of Havana's most famous stores. A young mother of two burned to death. He also knew I was responsible for spreading the rumor that led to the exodus of thousands of Cuban children to the United States. The genius plan was called Operation Pedro Pan. It was made possible with the help of the Catholic Church in Florida. The transferred children, by air, were classified as orphans. Bishop knew it was I who almost managed to collapse Cuba's economy by distributing thousands of pamphlets and running a rumor campaign that sowed panic. We had invented that the new government was going to kidnap the younger children to be sent to Russia.

Before the revolution, Veciana had been a bank employee of the richest man in Cuba, the Sugar King, Julio Lobo. The new president of the National Bank of Cuba, Ernesto Guevara, offered him the job of recruiting accountants and administrators for the new financial system of Cuba, but Veciana opted for a much more attractive offer from the CIA.

—Che was fanatical about telling the truth at any cost—said Veciana in his memoirs, written with the help of Carlos Harrison in 2017, Trained to Kill: The Inside Story of CIA *Plots against Castro, Kennedy*, and *Che*—. He never pursued me, maybe because we were both asthmatic.

—You're kidding me, asshole—said Hunter— Sorry. Go on, go on...

Like other mercenaries, Veciana admitted to having bombed economic centers in Cuba. Bombs in tobacco factories, mattress factories, bars, hotels, and even the oil refinery were part of his résumé while he was on the island. Twenty years later, the CIA and other exiles would introduce pests into the plantations, with the same goal.

When Veciana went into exile, he continued doing what he had learned with the CIA. But the CIA was never satisfied with his work, from missing Fidel Castro with a bazooka that almost killed astronaut Yuri Gagarin to his costly failures in Chile and Bolivia to assassinate Castro with journalists and fake microphones.

Veciana wasn't the only one tasked with taking advantage of Castro's visit to Chile in 1971. After being treated with indifference by the CIA, Michael Townley got in closer contact with the Cubans at the AAMCO mechanics, where he worked. In Miami, and with the mediation of El Mono Morales, they prepared a shipment of weapons for Patria y Libertad. The plan was to assassinate two of Castro's aides in Santiago. Once again, the plan failed.[26]

The most important operation (to kill Fidel Castro) was in the hands of the CIA, but it was canceled at the last moment when the hired Cubans deserted.

—Cubans have no balls—shouted agent David Atlee Phillips—; they're all cowards. Eliminate Medina and Rodríguez.

—I can't do that—replied Veciana.

—How much does it cost to kill a man in Bolivia?—insisted Phillips— A hundred, two hundred dollars? Invite them to a meeting and pay someone to do the job. They're a risk. We can't let the State

Department be exposed. Imagine if any of them implicate you, now that you're a member of the diplomatic corps of the United States in Bolivia?

—But that was the risk we were taking—said Veciana, on the verge of losing his mansion in La Paz and his wife's happiness giving orders to her domestic workers—. If the plan had been successful and Fidel Castro were now dead, my men could have been arrested...

—Arrested?—Phillips replied—. You think they would have survived this mission?"

—I can't do it—, Veciana answered.

—Go back to Bolivia—, Phillips ordered and hung up.[27]

The same procedure had been applied to the assassin of President Kennedy, when Lee Oswald was killed shortly after being captured and before being questioned by the FBI about his contacts with the CIA and the Cuban exiles in Miami.[28] Veciana himself would later acknowledge having seen Oswald in Dallas, weeks before the president's assassination, talking with his boss, Maurice Bishop, that is, David Atlee Phillips.

Although the Revolution had appointed the liberal Christian Manuel Urrutia Lleó as president of Cuba, Washington could not tolerate any gesture of independence from any of the Southern republics. It never had and didn't know how to. Before, because they were Black people who didn't know how to govern themselves. Now, because they were communists. Always, because we had important business there, and allowing a bad example could set off a catastrophic domino effect. Especially when the bad example had been achieved against one of their allied dictators and against the casino and brothel business of the mafias from Chicago, New York, and Miami, led by celebrities like Santo Trafficante, Meyer Lansky, Bugsy Siegel, Frank Ragano, Angelo Bruno, and Carlos Marcello. Moreover, when six years earlier the same CIA had resolved the issue of another too-independent president in Guatemala at a very low cost, with an intense media war and an invasion more suited to Hollywood than the Pentagon.

On February 12, 1959, during the National Security Council meeting, Allen Dulles, the director of the CIA and personal enemy of the future president, made it more than clear:

—The new leaders of Cuba must be treated like children: it's better to try to guide them where we want, rather than directly contradict them; if contradicted, they are capable of any disaster.

Although, at that time, Fidel Castro had not declared himself a communist, he had demonstrated aspirations of independence, especially during his visit to the White House, four months after the triumph of the Revolution. Castro's proposal was to confirm trade relations between the two countries but based on the never-achieved sovereignty of the island. Although Vice President Nixon confirmed that he saw nothing communist in the young, bearded man, he found him a bit naive. Mainly because, both Nixon and President Eisenhower, already had in motion the CIA's plan to neutralize the Revolution with another invasion, similar to the one achieved in Guatemala in 1954 and in Iran a year earlier.

President Eisenhower did not receive Fidel Castro at the White House. He went to play golf in Georgia. When the invasion of his Invincible Fleet fails at the Bay of Pigs, Fidel Castro and Ernesto Che Guevara will go play golf, not because they were fans of the sport, but because of their sarcastic sense of humor.29

—I understand that far—said Hunter—. But it's always bothered me a bit that they blame everything on us Yankees. Haven't they ever done things wrong over there?

—Yes, many times—I said—. In fact, I believe we have been the main culprits... Or rather, not *us*, without discrimination, but, to start with, our beautiful oligarchy and its two long arms: its armed arm, the armies; and its feathered arm, the media. In the name of freedom and national defense, oppression and selling out. But let's continue, if you want, with this idea of the victimization of the victim; with the notion of 'they always blame everything on us so they don't have to take responsibility for their own problems.'

—Socially resentful—said Hunter—. It's an accusation I've heard a lot down south...

—True. Especially during the military dictatorships and now from their heirs. But I never understood why *socially resentful* was used as an insult. A socially resentful person is someone who has gone through negative social experiences and has developed class consciousness. The complete opposite of a lackey or who Malcolm X called the house Negro.

Bay of Pigs

This time, the military invasion, preceded by a media war campaign, just like the previous ones, didn't work. The explanation was given by one of the main figures involved in the latest operations, CIA agent Howard Hunt:

"Castro and Guevara learned from history. We didn't."[30]

Faced with the refusal to establish commercial relations with Fidel Castro, Eisenhower's personal enemy, former president Harry Truman, said:

"That son of a bitch Eisenhower is stupid enough to do something like that. When Castro decided to go in the other direction in search of support, Eisenhower was still waiting for a damn report to decide what to think."

The first Cuban exiles were not poor, though the poor were the most abundant in the Cuba that didn't appear in magazines. Many were businessmen protected by Fulgencio Batista or were his worthy heirs. Others were former officials of the regime or aspirants to the freedom of Havana's nightlife, such as the manager of the Banco Financiero de La Habana, Roberto Vale, and one of his employees, José Boada, who emptied the bank's vault in the early hours of Saturday, March 11, 1961. Both fled to Miami, where they received automatic asylum. The money would have been donated to the Batista supporters in Havana, as Vale declared to the Miami Herald on Sunday, March 26.

—I did it for the Cuban cause—said Roberto Vale—. I have no doubt that Castro will fall very soon. None.[31]

Of course, it wasn't money that the CIA lacked, but volunteers willing to submit to a military regime. On their side were the salary offers, the glory, and the high positions of the freedom fighters in the new government of Cuba. The first group the agency recruited to train in Guatemala was the Batista supporters. They weren't major Batista supporters, but rather frustrated aspirants due to the Revolution.

One of the recruits, Raúl Martínez Urioste, was only twenty years old when he was sent to the training camp in Guatemala. When the long-awaited invasion day arrived, Martínez lined up to board one of the modern combat planes. They had the CIA and the most powerful nation in the world behind them. What could go wrong? The euphoria was contagious, and the breeze that caressed their faces was the wind of war, the sweet breath of history.

As he climbed the stairs of the plane, Martínez noticed a detail that paralyzed him for a second. The number painted on the ribs of the majestic mechanical bird was 846. Raised in the banned lottery game La bolita, Martínez read the meaning of the three numbers like a fortune teller reads cards: *"death-plane-soldier."*

The operation on April 17, 1961, involved the invasion of 1,400 paramilitaries by sea and air from Guatemala and Nicaragua, hours after a bombing operation from modern B-26 planes targeting the island's military facilities, which left seven dead and dozens seriously injured. The CIA equipped the ships with food for several weeks and several boxes with counterfeit bills of 20 Cuban pesos. The U.S. Navy supported with a massive aircraft carrier, the antisubmarine destroyer USS Essex, which had successfully participated in the destruction of Korea and in assisting the French Empire against the independence fighters in Vietnam, then Indochina, a few years earlier.

The Cuban patriots chosen by the agency were never known for their combat skills, so the original explanation for the failure shifted to President Kennedy, for his lack of support with airstrikes, first, and later against the CIA itself, for having used them as an experiment.

Thousands of Cubans died in the operation. Ten members of Battalion 2506 were tried for torture and murder during Batista's regime and executed. Six died from wounds received in combat. The remaining 1113 were sentenced to thirty years in prison for treason. 60 were released a year later for health reasons and sent to Miami and on December 21, 1962, Fidel Castro exchanged them for medicine and food.

Eight days later, eleven months before his assassination, at the American football final in Miami on December 29, President Kennedy gave a laudatory speech in honor of Brigade 2506. Several released members presented him with the Brigade 2506 flag. One of them, one of the three leaders of the failed invasion, Pepe San Román, listened to Kennedy's flattering speech. Years later he confessed:

—I hate the United States. They have betrayed us. Every day that passes I want to grab a rifle and shoot at this country.[32]

A Batista military man, José Alfredo Pérez San Román had studied at Fort Belvoir in Virginia and later at Fort Benning, Georgia. Just three days after the Bay of Pigs invasion began, Pérez San Román was captured in a swamp by Cuban volunteers from the island.

At the Orange Bowl in Miami, the president's wife, Jacqueline Kennedy, dazzled with a speech in Spanish before 75 thousand people, adorned with members of Brigade 2506.

—It is an honor foorr me—said Jackie, with rolled Rs as if they were German, interrupted by every phrase she remembered— to be here today among a grrroup of the bravest men in the world... I feel prrroud that my son has known your officers. He is too young to underrrstand what has happened here, but I will make it my duty to

El exilio del terror 47

tell him the story of your courrrage as he grrrows up. It is my wish and my hooope that someday he may become a man at least half as brave as the members of Brigade 2506.

—I couldn't stop looking at the First Lady—said Raúl Martínez—. She was speaking in a very sexy Spanish.[33]

A year later, her husband was assassinated. For the decades to come, countless testimonies, both from insiders and outsiders, implicated members of the Cuban exile community in their collusion with the CIA to kill him. For decades, the failures of the members of Battalion 2506 multiplied, to the point where the concept of success shifted to the goal of detonating a few hundred bombs, most of them in Florida, New Jersey, and New York, targeting their own comrades. Later, in the 1980s, the same groups transitioned into politics, where they found more success. Their corporate organization and lobbying power in Washington were modeled after the American Israel Public Affairs Committee, better known, as is customary in the Anglo-Saxon world, by its acronym AIPAC.

Before the invasion, the CIA managed to place a group of militiamen on the island, a kind of improved version of the Granma landing. Since they couldn't rely on local support, they dropped bags of rice and beans from planes. Due to poor aim, the bags often landed far from the camp, and the militiamen on the ground had to walk long distances to retrieve the supplies. Thanks to experience, the pilots improved their aim, but they soon began receiving messages with a new round of complaints:

—Sons of bitches, what are you trying to do? Kill us all with bags of rice?

At that time, Fidel Castro began accusing Washington of repeated sabotage and a maneuver in progress, mentioning operational bases in Florida and Guatemala. The United States ambassador to the UN, Adlai Ewing Stevenson, informed of the details of the plan to invade Cuba, categorically denied it:

—The accusations of a plot orchestrated in Washington are completely false—he said—. The United States is committed to a policy of non-aggression.

As the best defense is a counterattack, he immediately accused the Soviet ambassador of meddling in the affairs of the American hemisphere. The training camps in Guatemala had been reported in the press as maneuvers by communists aiming to overthrow sovereign governments in the region.

Agent David Phillips would recall in 1977 that while listening to their ambassador at the UN, they were doubled over with laughter:

—Adlai Stevenson was a great actor; no one could beat him at lying.

In March 1960, a French ship with Belgian weaponry exploded in the port of Havana, killing dozens of people. A second explosion killed even more, especially those who came to the rescue, a tactic known in the manuals of organized crime of secret agencies. Fidel Castro closed his funeral speech for the victims with a phrase that would remain as the motto: "Homeland or death. We shall prevail."

Shortly after, a Miami television channel reported attacks by rebel Cubans on the island against Castro's regime.

—They are rebellious Cubans—, the journalist says—but the Cuban government, as always, blames the United States for everything.

On the same front page where the *Miami Herald* on March 26, 1961, had published the confession of the robbery of the Financial Bank of Havana, an article titled:

"*It's Wrong. Then Blame the Yankees*"

The article, signed by William L. Ryan of the Associated Press, continued with an alliteration, a literary device favored in political speeches:

Are nearly half of Latin Americans illiterate?
Blame the Yankees!
Is Latin America populated by a swarm of poor amidst immense riches?

Blame the Yankees!
Does Latin America need more roads, more railways, and more industries, but its agriculture remains stuck in the feudal era?
Blame the Yankees!
That's the habit of left-wing politicians and even some right-wing politicians. The anti-Yankee mentality blames others for their own shortcomings.

This narrative capsule—I noted—, which can be summarized with any of the verses, was reproduced in different contexts as if it were a copy, following a known pattern of the CIA when planting their articles in major media outlets in different countries. After some time, the seeds germinated, and it was no longer necessary to tend to the forest.

On the same front page, further down, another piece titled *"The Great Political Factor"* continued the same complaint of the victor:

"Sometimes this is due to their denial of feelings of inferiority and envy... Even businessmen in Argentina do not believe in Washington's Food for Peace plan, claiming that it's about dumping excess production from Northern markets onto the South."[34]

KILL FIDEL. OR KENNEDY

A YEAR AND A HALF BEFORE THE ASSASSINATION OF LETELIER, on Tuesday, March 4, 1975, Howard Hunt and his daughter Lisa were questioned in Washington by the Senate committee investigating the assassination of John Kennedy. Lisa confirmed that her father was at home on November 22, 1963. In fact, her father asked everyone to witness a historic, unprecedented event on television.[35]

All that history will continue to be labeled as a grand conspiracy theory or simply a conspiracy, especially since the CIA has either destroyed or not declassified the most important documents that could help clarify it. What is beyond doubt is that Hunt was one of the main agents in the conspiracies in Guatemala, Mexico, and Uruguay, among other stations, and was later implicated in the Watergate scandal, which ended with the resignation of President Richard Nixon in 1974.

According to Hunt, the mistake in Cuba lay in the unforgivable decision of President Kennedy not to bomb Havana before the invasion. The Cuban exiles clung to this argument like a fossil to its stone. The same lament was used to justify the defeat in Vietnam, but this time the blame fell on the intellectuals... Many years later, from his yacht docked at his residence on 82nd Street in Miami, Hunt began writing his memoirs. Hunt mentioned a report that he himself (then Edward J. Hamilton) wrote from Havana, which not only explains the failure of the invasion but also the mysterious claim of Che Guevara, who had assured that Cuba would not be another Guatemala: "any possible support from Cubans for the invasion must be flatly dismissed; Castro must be assassinated before the invasion, and it must be done by Cuban patriots."

Castro's secretary, Juan Orta, hired to poison his drink with pills a week before the invasion, also lost courage. The pills had been manufactured by the CIA's Technical Services Division and sent to the island through the Batista mafia bosses, Santo Trafficante and John Rosselli. Orta took refuge in the Venezuelan embassy on April 11, 1961, where he remained for over three years before landing in Miami. At least the mercenaries tasked with poisoning Patrice Lumumba's toothpaste in the Congo didn't get the chance to prove their bravery. Other mercenaries, part-time CIA collaborators, were responsible for handing Lumumba over to the rebels of the chosen future dictator, Mobutu Sese Seko.

In December 1964, two other participants in the assassination of Orlando Letelier, the brothers Guillermo and Ignacio Novo, had planned a bazooka attack on Che Guevara, who was set to speak at the annual UN conference.

This time, the shot was to be fired from the opposite shore of the East River. The use of the bazooka and its poor outcome sparked memories of other failed plots to assassinate Fidel Castro, such as when the famous Russian astronaut Yuri Gagarin visited him in Havana. On September 15, 1960, at 11:00 PM, Antonio Veciana Blanch had returned to Apartment 8-A on the eighth floor of Avenida de las Misiones 29, carrying an anti-tank bazooka wrapped like a gift. The apartment was a CIA office in Havana, but Veciana believed he was the first to rent it, under his mother-in-law's name. The long-planned shot missed its target.

Four years later, in December 1964, the Novo brothers bought a bazooka for $35 at a store on Eighth Avenue. They had to modify it to increase its power. When they believed Che was heading to the UN building, they fired the powerful projectile from the East River promenade in Long Island. The projectile fell into the river, about two hundred meters from the UN building, causing a five-meter geyser of water.

—We will not submit to any inspection by the United States— said Guevara in his speech before the Assembly—but instead to multilateral agreements with equal obligations for all parties. U.S. aircraft, with complete impunity, navigate our airspace... Low-altitude flights, pirate attacks, as well as sabotage by spies...

The same story of Juan Orta repeated itself several times. When Fidel Castro visited Chile in 1971, for the press conference on July 9 in Santiago, the CIA initiated a new plan to eliminate him without leaving a trace, that is, attributing the act to someone else or, at the very least, as outlined in their operations manual, leaving the door of denial always open. A strategy that the Mossad would copy in various operations, such as (according to some testimonies) the attacks in London and Buenos Aires in the nineties.[36]

In Chile, the Cubans hired by agent Antonio Veciana, accredited as journalists from *Venevisión*, were supposed to use their microphones as guns. They also backed out a day earlier. Agent David Atlee Phillips had planned everything so that the assassination would appear as the work of Cuban exiles. From Caracas, Luis Posada Carriles had a better story, meticulously prepared: like a fly in a wound, it would implicate Cuban assassins in a Soviet plan. The logic of the plan was unclear, which, in terms of psychological warfare, was an irrelevant detail and even necessary to keep the global population speculating and arguing over the resolution of the mystery. In the end, the entire discussion would always be resolved by accusing the dissidents of being conspiracy theory enthusiasts.

By 1971, Veciana had been stationed by the CIA in La Paz, Bolivia, posed as an elite banker, though all he knew about banks was what he had learned as a teller at the Bank of Cuba. Phillips stole the idea from Posada Carriles. As Veciana would later admit in his 2017 memoir, Trained to Kill, the idea was to blame the Russians for the assassination, causing Cuba to enter into conflict with its main economic partner, which would plunge the island into misery and total crisis. If it wasn't through bombs, it had to be through diplomacy.

The idea wasn't very brilliant. More optimistic than a newlywed, it never even came to fruition. A hiccup occurred. At the last moment, the Cubans Marcos Rodríguez and Diego Medina, the fake journalists, offered various excuses to cancel the operation. A chronic peritonitis in one and the possibility of being recognized by a cousin in Castro's secret service in the other.

Furious, David Atlee Phillips (who, as the manual suggests, always organized and never participated) yelled at Veciana over the phone:

—Cubans have no guts. They're all cowards.

He ordered Rodríguez and Medina to be eliminated.

—How much does it cost to kill a man in Bolivia?—asked Phillips— A hundred, two hundred dollars? You're not short on money. Invite them to a meeting and pay someone to eliminate them. Under no circumstances can we afford to let them stay alive. They're a risk. We cannot allow the State Department to be exposed in any way. Imagine if either of these men implicates you, now that you're a member of the U.S. diplomatic corps in Bolivia?

—But that was the risk we were taking—Veciana responded—even if the plan had succeeded and right now Fidel Castro were dead. My men could have been arrested...

Phillips, furious, replied:

—Arrested? Under no circumstances were they going to survive. I didn't tell you before, but that had already been decided.

—I can't do it—said Veciana.

Veciana must have known it very well. The same procedure had been applied to the assassin of President Kennedy, Lee Oswald, when he was silenced shortly after being captured, on November 24, 1961, by Jack Ruby. Veciana himself confirmed it with his own eyes when he saw Lee Oswald and his boss David Phillips together in Dallas weeks before Kennedy's assassination. He must have known it, but working in intelligence never meant its members had passed any IQ test.

Another 632 attempts by the CIA to assassinate Castro failed. The first ones were institutionalized under the name Operation 40, in which Orlando Bosch, Luis Posada Carriles, and their CIA bosses, Howard Hunt and Frank Sturgis—both implicated in the Watergate scandal, participated.

Also involved in some of these failed attempts was Marita Lorenz, the daughter of a German father and an American mother. Lorenz was Fidel Castro's lover and a CIA agent. Like the others, she failed to attempt to poison him in 1960 with a capsule in an ice cream.

—Operation 40—declared Marita Lorenz—, was a group trained to assassinate members of the military or any political party in foreign countries. We were to infiltrate and often received orders to eliminate certain individuals, even some of our own members suspected of being foreign agents.

In November 1977, Lorenz would acknowledge that she was part of Operation 40, organized by the CIA and including Orlando

Bosch, Frank Sturgis, and the assassin of President Kennedy, Lee Harvey Oswald. Despite the CIA's unlimited resources, Operation 40 failed in its attempt to invade Cuba and failed in its multiple attempts to kill Fidel Castro, but they had better luck with their own president, whom they not only blamed for the Bay of Pigs fiasco but also feared would fulfill his promise to dissolve the CIA. According to Lorenz, Lee Oswald trained with the Cubans in Florida. When she was called before the Congressional investigation committee, she stated that the Cuban CIA agent under Howard Hunt's orders and part of the Operation 40 group, Frank Sturgis, was the second sniper who shot at the president. Frank Sturgis was the stage name of Frank Angelo Fiorini. Before becoming a CIA agent, he was known in the mafia network of Havana's Copacabana Club.

The committee investigating Kennedy's assassination dismissed Marita Lorenz's testimony for lacking evidence to support her sworn statements, even though her testimony did not contradict but rather confirmed many others.

—We left in two cars loaded with rifles, from Miami to Dallas— insisted Marita Lorenz in an interview with the New York Daily News—. It took us two days, driving nonstop. We went with Lee Oswald, Frank Sturgis, Orlando Bosch, Pedro Díaz Lanz, and two Cuban brothers I had never seen before...

The brothers were Guillermo and Ignacio Novo Sampol, both with a certain reputation within the Miami Free Cuba circles. A reputation adorned with violent failures but one that would grow exponentially when they became involved in the assassination of Chilean Orlando Letelier, in Washington.

In Dallas, they checked into a motel so they could come and go without passing through any reception area. Is there a more quintessential symbol of American freedom than gas stations and motels? Like supermarkets, drive-through banks, coffee shops, and restaurants, and all those places where the unpleasant experience of having to interact with others has been resolved.

—Remove that paragraph—said Hunter—. It's too, how should I put it... too biased. Besides, readers aren't interested in the author's opinion. Keep only the first sentence.

In Dallas, they checked into a motel so they could come and go without passing through reception. They unloaded some weapons and went over the map again. Shortly after, while the sun was still setting, the powerful CIA agent Howard Hunt arrived and stayed with the group for 45 minutes. Before leaving, he left a package with a stack of dollars.

—Jack Ruby showed up right after—said Marita Lorenz—. The last time I saw Frank Sturgis was at Orlando Bosch's house, in Miami.

Lorentz stopped giving her testimony due to anonymous threats against her and her daughter. Jack Ruby, the assassin of Lee Oswald, had died in 1967 at Parkland Hospital, the same hospital where Lee Oswald and John Kennedy had died. Ruby, alias of Jacob Rubenstein, was a powerful casino owner, manager of illegal gambling in Texas, and had extensive connections with the Tropicana Club in Havana and, later, with the Cuban exiles. He boasted of always being accompanied by a Colt Cobra .38 revolver. The Warren Commission chose to believe that Ruby had killed Oswald out of patriotic sentiment and dismissed multiple testimonies that could implicate him in a plot against the president.

Perhaps not by coincidence, the CIA invested millions of dollars in propaganda against all those who questioned the conclusions of the Warren Commission. In a cable dated April 1, 1967, it ordered all its stations to "use propaganda resources to respond and refute the attacks of the critics" who were skeptical of the Commission's conclusions as "conspiracy theorists."[37, 38]

Later, Marita Lorenz learned that Sturgis was behind some of the threats against her. Her daughter, then 15 years old, defended herself by saying she was the daughter of the former dictator of Venezuela, Marcos Pérez Jiménez, decorated by Washington in 1954 with the Legion of Merit medal, for his services to freedom.

Millions of adults will follow this same precarious line of reasoning.

—The communists are pressuring her to testify against me—Sturgis said to the *The Boston Globe*, on November 9, 1977, after being arrested by New York police and released without charges two days later—What they want is to discredit Cubans, accusing them of being conspirators... I'm protecting the United States against those who want to destroy this country. I'm fighting for the flag.[39]

That same year, Rolando Otero, another Cuban agent of the CIA, by then in prison for one of several bombings attributed to him, confirmed the agency's vast plan to get rid of the young and inexperienced president. In a report dated March 20, 1977, the FBI recorded his testimony stating that the CIA had sent Lee Oswald to Moscow and, before bringing him back, had the assassination plan ready, including the version that it had been done by the Cuban mafia, with no involvement from the Agency.

The Warren Commission also questioned the Cuban Silvia Odio, who testified that weeks before the president's assassination, Lee Oswald and three other members of JURE had shown up at her apartment to ask for a donation to support the fight against Castro.

—The assassination of Kennedy was discussed in my house, in Dallas. Oswald was there. It doesn't matter what the hell the Warren Commission says—Silvia Odio said years later to the Tampa Bay Times of Florida.[40] Odio accused the members of the Warren Commission of discrediting her testimony because it implicated the Cuban exiles as participants in the assassination.

Lee Oswald had also visited the store of the Cuban businessman Carlos Bringuier, but Bringuier considered Oswald a communist agent. In fact, the two got into a fistfight when Bringuier saw Oswald on a street corner handing out pamphlets in favor of Fidel Castro, a scene that was at least ridiculous, and various researchers would attribute it to the CIA, as another way of distracting from the facts about the enemy.

—On November 22, 1963—Otero declared— there were between 30 and 35 CIA agents in Dallas... After that, at least three assassinations of Cubans in Miami served to silence those agents who were directly involved in the plan.

—Can you provide names?

—Of course—said Otero, according to a secret CIA document dated August 1, 1966—: Howard Hunt, Bernardo Torres, Norman Díaz, Orlando Urra, Niledo Acevedo... Recently, Díaz narrowly escaped being assassinated for the same reason.[41]

Pinochet carried his luggage

ON THE WAY TO THE IPS OFFICES, Orlando Letelier drove by in his Chevrolet Malibu past his former residence on Massachusetts Avenue 2305. It was still the residence of the Chilean ambassador, but now it was Pinochet's ambassador. He would pass by there every morning, but this time he couldn't help but stop for a moment to look at the garden, the moderate Baroque facade, the Art Nouveau entrance, and the tall windows through which he once glimpsed something that he mistook for a new horizon.

—Pinochet carried Orlando's luggage—his wife, Isabel, once recalled—. I never liked that general. The first time he saw me, he said, "The minister's wife is as beautiful as the previous ones." I detested him. He wouldn't stop flirting with me, but he would shut up when Orlando appeared. With him, he was servile, to the point of being pathetic. His eldest son, Francisco, didn't like him either. Despite being only fourteen, the boy felt uncomfortable with that soldier being in his father's study every day, silently browsing through books, staring at the Andes through the window as if he owned the place.

Poor Augusto had been a mediocre student all his life. But he had climbed the ranks by mastering the art of boot-licking, as one of his fellow soldiers once said. Neither Allende nor Letelier managed to see it in time. General Pinochet presented himself as a politically neutral radical, bound by military discipline. In fact, he was considered the most loyal officer to Allende's government. Maybe that was true for a while. He didn't have clear political ideas. Fascism isn't an ideology; it's a mental condition that rarely gets cured. His wife, Lucía Hiriart, knew more about history and politics than he did, and she was no less authoritarian. Quite the opposite. She once admitted:

—If I were the head of government, I would undoubtedly be much tougher than my husband. I would already have all of Chile under a state of siege.

By chance or design, General Pinochet had gained the trust of everyone in the new government. Except Isabel. When the coup attempt of June 1973 failed, General Pinochet sided with the constitutional order, and President Allende promoted him to Commander in Chief. Only he knew what strings he was pulling within the military. Only he knew he had the full support of Washington and the CIA to launch his own adventure three months later.

On September 10, 1973, hours before the coup and when Allende already sensed the outcome, General Augusto Pinochet said to Letelier:

—No one admires Dr. Allende more than I do.

—Pinochet is a genius of betrayal—Letelier would say on February 18, 1975.

The Pediatrician Orlando Bosch

UNLIKE POSADA CARRILES (who also harbored an uncontrollable hatred for the Cuban Revolution and, especially, for anyone who might question him) Orlando Bosch had an inflated ego. According to the NSA agent, Perry Fellwock, alias Winslow Peck, "Pediatrician

Bosch had the habit of assassinating anyone who disagreed with him." When he wasn't thinking about an attack that the entire world would recognize as a masterpiece, he was painting tropical landscapes that never reached the mastery of Van Gogh, though they did fetch high prices in Miami galleries. Only in Miami and in a couple of bars in Union City.

At the University of Havana, Bosch had been, for a brief period, the leader of the medical students' union. His rivalry with the leader of the law faculty was uneven. Fidel Castro had the same energy and the same determination to succeed, but he stood out for his dialectical skills and his ability to sway a student assembly. Bosch didn't even know how to speak. He was clumsy with words and even clumsier with ideas. This inability to express himself verbally was evident in the paintings bought by the donors of the cause and, above all, in covert actions, which increasingly became more violent. According to his explosives comrades, Bosch never missed an opportunity to take credit for any attack. When he hadn't been directly involved, he preferred to leave the matter in a haze of ambiguity and mystery.

After graduating as a pediatrician in Cuba, he had left a child with walking difficulties permanently disabled. He never demonstrated any aptitude for science, either. After the Revolution and some time in Miami, he returned to Cuba as a Red Cross volunteer, but the indifference of his former university rival turned him into what he would forever remain. For him, Fidel and all the revolutionaries were arrogant, conceited. He heard them on the radio. He saw them on television. They appeared every day in the printed press. A triumphalist fever prevented them from thinking clearly, Bosch thought. They believed themselves more than they were for having defeated Batista's powerful army in the Sierra Maestra, on the dusty roads of Santa Clara, and on the pristine streets of Havana. But freedom was something else. It had to be something else.

Having ended his brief career as a pediatrician and ignored by the new revolution in Cuba, Bosch took refuge for the second time in Miami. From the beginning, he associated with groups that, between rum and cigars, would plan bombs with some publicity effect every night. On December 12, 1966, The Palm Beach Post reported again that "the leader of the militant groups of Cuban exiles has been charged in federal court for his threats against Cuban exiles, in order to raise funds for his organization. Dr. Orlando Bosch, aged 40, who has had frequent conflicts with U.S. authorities, and Marcelino García, aged 58, have been charged with conspiracy and extortion for twenty thousand dollars. Several letters with bomb threats will be presented by the prosecution."

Michael and Mariana Before Townley and Callejas

Bearing an unquestionable record, Michael Townley, one of the assassins of Letelier and other troublesome activists, was born in Iowa. The young man with a horseshoe mustache and excellent command of Spanish had served as a channel to finance the candidacy of President Jorge Alessandri against Salvador Allende in 1958. The CIA's money had been enough for victory in the elections, although (or precisely because of that) the margin had been minimal. The same story repeated itself in the elections against the same Allende in 1964, but this time the candidate chosen by the CIA had been Eduardo Frei.

In 1970, Washington's money and that of the transnational corporations were not enough (finally, Allende had won the elections), so it was necessary to resort to a Plan B, a Plan C, and another Plan D… B: prevent the election winner from being sworn in as president. C: in the worst-case scenario of his reaching La Moneda, destabilize him with another "War of the Worlds," Orson Wells-style, creating social unrest and international opinion that would justify anything to come. D: as a final solution, resort once again to a patriotic army to remove the elected from a place he did not deserve. The same CIA analysts concluded that with Plans B and C, it would be enough for the left to lose the 1976 elections. The problem wasn't so much Allende and the left, but democracy, or some form of democracy in a peripheral country that would continue the nationalizing obstacles initiated by the previous president, Eduardo Frei. Those democracies that every so often were used by their people to say no.

For each of those plans detailed in Washington by President Richard Nixon, Secretary of State Henry Kissinger and CIA Director Richard Helms, some volunteers were necessary. Money was not what was lacking. Michael Townley was one of them. He had the almost perfect psychological profile. He hadn't been the son that the successful businessman, Vernon Townley, would have wanted.

He wasn't a bad kid; he was just good for nothing or didn't do anything right. In 1961, Michael returned to Chile and settled in Valparaíso. At 19 years old, on July 22, he married a 29-year-old woman with a dominant, almost maternal personality, who was then a Chilean Intelligence infiltrator in the Socialist Party and who, whenever she could, boasted of having carried arms in Israel.

None of his parents attended the wedding. Callejas' mother ended up accepting the couple and her three children in her home but didn't speak to Michael until Christmas, when everything is forgiven. He wasn't allowed upstairs until his father-in-law died. Since the Callejas were broke and couldn't pay for funeral services, Michael built his father-in-law's coffin with his own hands and smuggled the body in a truck to the north of Chile, where he was buried. Upon his return, he went door to door selling the Collins Concise Encyclopedia, a collection of eight heavy red-bound volumes, to the wealthiest families in Santiago who knew or wanted to know how to read English. A few months later, one of them, the future president of Chile Eduardo Frei, agreed to place an order for the encyclopedia, which he later refused to pay for when Michael delivered it to his home. This bad experience left a lasting impression on him about the irresponsibility of Chilean democrats.

From Venezuela, his father got him a job at the Ford subsidiary in Lima, but it lasted only four months. He returned to Santiago, claiming that Peruvians were lazy. He didn't do too badly when he got a job at an investment company called Investors Overseas Service, whose function was to help wealthy families in Chile to invest their capital abroad under false names, since the law prohibited Chileans from this type of operation.[42] IOS, had been founded by Bernard Cornfeld with the goal of making a lot of money in a short time thanks to the illegal manipulation of investment funds worldwide. Although in 1973 Cornfeld would be arrested and convicted of fraud in Switzerland, he would only spend a few months in prison, after which he would dedicate himself to investing his fortune in luxuries until his death in 1995.

In 1967, Mariana and Michael moved to Miami. They were welcomed and housed by Michael's grandparents who lived in Pompano Beach. Michael dedicated himself to selling Ford trucks but, for some reason, was fired after a few weeks. Mariana enrolled in a literature course at the University of Miami, where she wrote a story titled "Pigs in the Greenhouse" about an invasion of pigs that destroyed years of work by a diligent farmer. A sort of George Orwell's Animal Farm, but upside down.

At the time, Callejas was outraged by President Eduardo Frei's agrarian reform and by the leftward shift of Chile's conservative Christian Democratic Party. In the 1964 elections, to prevent a victory by the socialist Salvador Allende, the CIA had supported Eduardo Frei with millions of dollars and with planted articles in the media. Once in power, the same administration of Lyndon Johnson recommended that he carry out a timid reform, to calm the growing discontent of landless peasants, something that was beginning to resemble a pressure cooker about to explode. Frei's reform only forced the sale of land by the largest landowners in the country, something that affected almost no one but resembled the modest agrarian reform of Jacobo Árbenz in Guatemala just over a decade earlier, which ended with a coup d'état promoted by the largest American banana company and organized by the CIA. The Chilean oligarchy, in control of most of their country's economy, saw it as a betrayal and as an unacceptable bad example for decent people. According to Callejas, because of these irresponsible policies, the pigs (the poor, the workers) were going to destroy everything the rich had built with their own effort. All her acquaintances applauded her latest story as a masterpiece, worthy of Borges' genius.

Apparently, no one bought utility vehicles in an area dedicated to tourism and entertainment. He managed to stay for some time in the ARAMCO mechanical workshops in Little Havana and a couple of years later managed to buy some shares in another branch of the chain of workshops in Hialeah, the popular Cuban district of Miami where no one speaks English.

One night, after several bars on Calle Ocho, Callejas encouraged him to work for the CIA. Working as a mechanic for minimum wage did not align with the expectations of the son of a Ford Company manager or a successful secret employee of IOS. Least of all, his wife.

But Callejas was another bundle of contradictions. While attending university in Miami, she had participated in street protests against the Vietnam War. When Vietnam Moratorium Day came, she told Michael that he should join the protest and not go to work if the workshop decided to open.

—If they don't open tomorrow—said Townley—they'll end up closing permanently. Almost all our clients are Cuban, and they are for the war.

—Well, I have no respect for those people—said Callejas—. If they're really so anti-communist and truly have balls, they should be in Cuba fighting like men. If a communist like Castro had taken power in Chile, I'd be there fighting right now. The Cubans are here for the money, but they act like patriots.

—Well…

—Nothing—Mariana concluded—. If these Cubans really hate Castro so much, what the hell are they doing here? They're all like dogs barking from the other side of the fence.⁴³

But business is business. To get into the CIA a mere phone call wasn't enough. First, he had to get noticed. Preferably through the agency's own contacts. For this reason, Michael reached out to what remained of the Chicago Junta, a group of Cuban exiles that included Frank Sturgis, Orlando Bosch, Aldo Vera Serafín, and Antonio Veciana until its dissolution, 24 hours before the assassination of President John Kennedy. The Cuban CIA agent Antonio Veciana would later insist that his boss, David Atlee Phillips, had met with Lee Harvey Oswald, the president's assassin, a few weeks earlier in Dallas. Phillips would deny this. He would also deny using the pseudonym Maurice Bishop. At a cocktail party in Washington, he would feign not recognizing Veciana, despite the many years they had worked together in Cuba, Bolivia, Chile, and the United States. None of this was meant to embarrass agents like Phillips—quite the opposite: in every lie, in every act of deception, he gave a masterclass in professionalism with the James Bond style that many admired and emulated.

The appeal of fictional characters like James Bond wasn't just a decorative detail. Prominent Cubans in Miami, like Orlando Bosch and El Mono Morales Navarrete, were avid fans of TV series like Mission: Impossible. By 1967, the series, in color, opened with the iconic musical theme by Argentine composer Lalo Schifrin, and its central image was a ticking bomb, from the match igniting the fuse to the grand mercenary exploits of Hollywood heroes. The series that inspired the new terrorists had, in turn, been inspired by reality. When in 1956 the Dominican dictator Rafael Trujillo ordered the kidnapping of Professor Jesús Galíndez from Columbia University in New York, he hired a private firm from Washington called Robert A. Maheu & Associates. The firm, led by John Frank, had been founded by a former CIA and FBI agent to operate within U.S. territory where the CIA had no jurisdiction. Maheu admitted that the

TV series Mission: Impossible was based on the actions of his team, and both Bosch and Posada Carriles, when they weren't planning some bombing, worked for their own private detective agencies, with far less success than Mission: Impossible or The Magnificent Seven but with no shortage of real casualties.

By 1970, Townley too was eager to become a secret hero, a true Martin Landau or a Peter Graves; a new Hernán Cortés or a Don Quixote intoxicated by chivalric romances. The CIA not only recognized the benefits of TV series but later didn't hesitate to invest heavily in promoting films like Top Gun or Zero Dark Thirty, which naturally became box office hits and led to a notable increase in the number of young volunteers, both for secret agents and the Marine Corps.

Unable to contain his anxiety, on November 25th Michael looked through a phone book and called a CIA office in Miami. He gave the best references about himself. He spoke Spanish fluently and knew Chile as well as agent Davis Atlee Phillips. He had a Chilean and an American passport. He could travel across the American continent like a condor or a chalchalero. He hated the current Chilean government like any good anti-communist, but he was determined to take action.

—I'll leave you my address and phone number in Pompano Beach.

Townley was no stranger to the CIA. For their recruitment office, the candidate had advantages and disadvantages. He hadn't finished high school (one of their requirements at the time), he had no idea what Marxism was, but he hated Marxists, and he demonstrated he had the required profile: an obsession, a deep psychological conflict that, in his specific case, would reveal itself as an inferiority complex, driving him to venerate authority and submit to it automatically. A wife ten years older could suggest an Oedipus complex or a tendency towards submission. A conflictual relationship with his father that hadn't translated into youthful rebellion, but rather into a search for paternal recognition through disproportionate acts.

Later, once Allende's government was overthrown, Townley repeated the same request in Chile to the CIA's phone number. But the CIA preferred to use him without registering him as their own agent, like Luis Posada Carriles, Antonio Veciana, or Manuel Noriega. So when Pinochet's new secret agency, the DINA, added him to their roster of permanent agents, he felt important for the first time in his life. He no longer needed a mistress in the United States nor the money that Calleja's ex-husband continued to send them.

To earn the trust of his superiors, who, like Espinosa and Contreras were only colonels, he didn't refuse any orders to assassinate dissidents in Chile, Argentina, Italy, and the United States. In a phone conversation with his mother-in-law, he informed her that the Chilean army had promised him the rank of Major.

—Don't pay attention to him, mom—Mariana corrected him then—. It's a ridiculous idea. How are they going to give the rank of Major to someone who isn't even a military officer?

Mariana didn't have many scruples when it came to advancing her literary career, but she didn't beat around the bush when it came to deflating her young husband's pretensions.

—When they need you—Mariana once told him— you're an officer. When you need them, you're just a civilian...

Colonel Contreras, aware of how difficult Mariana could be, managed to calm her down for a while with a diamond ring.[44]

Aside from the expectations of her father, the successful Ford manager, her husband's first big desire, Michael Townley, was to be part of the CIA's payroll. Michael called them from Miami even before Allende's victory in Chile. He boasted about his knowledge of South America and his almost perfect command of Spanish. The CIA never contacted him to congratulate him, but they made an exception to their requirement that candidates must have a university degree or at least some experience related to any intellectual capacity. They didn't include him on their list of permanent agents, but used him as a fuse collaborator through third parties.

After ten years, the Townley Callejas couldn't achieve a stable income, but their travels and their lifestyle didn't belong to that of a working-class family. For almost a decade, the new couple survived on the money sent monthly from the United States by her ex-husband, Allan Earnest, the father of her two eldest children. Allen had once shared with Mariana the fantasy of socialist Zionism in the kibbutzim of Israel, but later his pacifism clashed with the government's policies. He refused to enlist in the army and had to leave the Holy Land.[45]

Months after his collaboration with Patria y Libertad, the murder of the night watchman in Concepción, and days after the coup d'état, the DINA became Michael's great opportunity. One of his first major missions was to harass General Carlos Prats, who was then the commander-in-chief of the Chilean army during the government of Salvador Allende. The logistics weren't too complicated. On June 27, 1973, when Prats passed through the exclusive and nearby neighborhood of Las Condes, a small group began to insult him. Soon after, a red Renault began to follow him until the general fired a shot at the car's fender. Naturally, due to the incident, he was forced to resign. He went into exile in Argentina and was executed in Buenos Aires in 1974 (in September, as is often the case) with a bomb crafted by Townley himself.

Callejas had returned a year earlier from "a forced exile" of four months in Miami, as he would write in his 1994 memoirs. He had returned immediately and urgently, as soon as he learned of the coup on September 11, 1973. Michael took a few weeks. Upon his return, he made contact with Colonel Pedro Espinosa, introducing himself under the alias Andrés Wilson.

Colonel Espinosa smiled. He knew very well what his real name was. He had been following him since his days with Patria y Libertad, at 214 Rafael Cañas Street. He knew about his calls from the phone number 23 27 05 at the headquarters of the patriotic group, his clandestine mobile radio transmissions through the neighborhoods, and even the fiasco in Concepción, when they decided to fight for freedom of expression on Channel 5 and ended up killing the night watchman.

Mariana Callejas flew from Miami and in Chile adopted the name María Luisa Pizarro. When the captain announced the approach to Santiago's airport, a passenger shouted:

—*Viva Chile, carajo!*

The other passengers echoed loudly:

—*Viva Chile, carajo!*

A second later, the passengers were singing the national anthem with their right hands over their hearts.

Marina was euphoric. She stood up from her seat, clapping. Two hands weren't enough to express so much happiness. Someone invited the passengers to toast, and the flight attendants began serving champagne.

—My father used to tell me—Callejas would write in his memoirs—: There is no army in the world braver, nobler, or better prepared than Chile's. I know this because I served in the military. It's a source of pride, Our Army.

When Mariana looked back, she saw a woman dressed in black, sitting in the last seat of the plane, crying and holding her two children.

Townley returned to Chile a few months after Callejas. Jokingly, his kids called him Uncle Kenny because they had seen his passport was in the name of Kenneth Enyart.

—You should be more careful with those things—Mariana scolded him.

—He's a friend—said Michael.

The friend, Kenneth Enyart, was actually a client at the mechanic shop in Miami where Townley worked as an automatic transmission specialist. One day Enyart left his car for repairs and forgot to remove the documents from the glove compartment. Michael took them, went to the nearest post office, and processed his new passport. He processed it at the post office. He received it by mail.

—Poor Kenneth will never in his fucking life travel abroad—said Michael— and I needed to come to Chile without a record, start from scratch.

Twenty years later, in a secret interview in Miami with journalist Marcelo Araya for Chilean television, Townley won't mention Enyart but will regret having abused a friend's trust.

One of the few things he'll regret.

THE CIA, DINA, AND THE TOWNLEYS

COLONEL MANUEL CONTRERAS, Colonel Pedro Espinosa, DINA, and General Augusto Pinochet himself were part of the old CIA triangulation tactic. These triangulations follow the same logic as Tor, the most secure internet browser, invented by U.S. intelligence services before it got out of control: when a user visits a page, they send and receive information through three other computers around the world, chosen at random, making it harder to trace.

This formula, powerful for its simplicity and effectiveness, had been taught and practiced by the agency since its founding in 1947, but it wasn't new. It was already present in the principles of propagandist Edward Bernays since the early 20th century and could be summarized as:

Never do or say anything directly;

Organize everything so that what you want done is done by someone else, convinced they're acting of their own free will.

If something goes wrong, neither the mastermind nor their client can be implicated.

Even if the evidence against us is undeniable, never accept it; keep denying it at any cost.

The same principles worked, like a fractal, at different levels. This was the case for the Chilean dictatorship, its intelligence service, its collaborators, and its mercenaries. To the CIA, Townley was, in the eyes of DINA, a highly valuable asset. He was American, held a legal U.S. passport, and aside from speaking English and Spanish perfectly, he knew both cultures like the back of his hand and was a fanatical anti-communist. He had married the Chilean Mariana Callejas, another great potential asset due to her family background and psychological profile. The CIA didn't let in any collaborator without first tracking and studying them for a reasonable time and then subjecting them to various truth tests, some of which involved an electronic belt around the chest and multiple questions ranging from homosexual concerns to capitalist loyalty.

Still young, Callejas had a long personal record. Years before, she had converted to socialist Zionism and had lived, worked, and formed close bonds in Israel. Later, she grew tired of socialism, though not Zionism, and returned to Chile. In Miami, she had participated in some anti-Vietnam War protests, but that was because she was studying at a university, the University of Miami.

The ultimate test came in 1970 when Salvador Allende won the elections. Consistent with her criticism of the Cubans in Miami, whom she accused of lacking the guts to go fight Castro on the Island itself, Mariana returned to Chile to fight against the elected dictator. Michael resisted for a while, until he gave in to his wife's conviction. She, being ten years older, seemed to have a clearer perspective than her husband, who at the time was enjoying doubt and a youth he had never experienced with a lover in San Francisco.

In Chile, both joined the far-right group called, as it could not be otherwise, Patria y Libertad. A couple of years later, Michael managed to collaborate with this group by bringing in a hundred assault rifles from Argentina. He also organized multiple protests based on false stories. Among the group's other achievements was the supposed disappearance of its number two, Roberto Thieme, in a plane crash that never happened. Thieme's funeral, held in January 1973, was as fake as the stories that adorned the event.

They were not as successful with Callejas herself, when they showed up at her apartment urgently to confiscate the radios used to broadcast propaganda against Allende.

—Allende's police has discovered them—Roberto Thieme himself had said, before the disappearance operation—. They could be here any moment. We must take them somewhere else.

—I don't think they've discovered anything—Callejas told them—. If they've really discovered something, it's because you informed the police.[46]

Thieme and the members of Patria y Libertad disappeared into the night, but Allende's police never showed up.

Despite this minor and insignificant incident, *Patria y Libertad* and Colonel Pedro Espinosa facilitated Townley's entry into the DINA. Allende had defined this group as "another fascist group funded by the CIA." Over the years, the CIA would at least confirm the latter part of the accusation. Additionally, Mr. Henry Kissinger contributed $38,000 of the time plus $5,000 monthly to support this group. One of the leaders of Patria y Libertad would confess to at least five hundred terrorist attacks and confirm the conviction of the time and of many in the future: "the military are the true guardians of the country's constitution." Townley and Callejas agreed. Moreover, Townley had said, repeating an old idea of President Richard Nixon: "in Latin America, the masses are not ready for democracy."[47]

Michael and Mariana's first adventure against the regime involved the manufacture of Molotov cocktails. The innovation they were most proud of was the inclusion of sawdust, which made the flames last longer. The sense of impunity might have been due to some psychological trait they both shared, but also to the idea that if something went wrong, they would have the support of the most powerful secret agency in the world. Of course, they first had to make them aware of all the work they were doing, and for that, they also needed their own operational triangulations.

At first, Townley thought that Patria y Libertad could be that lower vertex.

—Actually, it's not that hard to kill the president—Townley said one night during a meeting with Pablo Rodríguez and other members of Patria y Libertad at their small house in Santiago.

—Does it seem that way to you?

—I have no doubts.

—And how would it be?

—On any corner—explained Townley— there's a... how do you say it? A... sewer lid.

—*Manhole cover*— Mariana helped him.

—Yes, a manhole cover. One night you go in, place fifty or sixty kilos of dynamite, and when the chosen one passes... boom!

Townley drew a big heart in the air with his hands, while drawing out the word booooom. The attendees looked at each other. After a moment of skepticism, Rodríguez asked:

—Dynamite? And where would we get the dynamite?

—You're sitting on it— said Townley.

Mariana looked at him like a mother looks at a child who has said a bad word at a family gathering.

The Gringo from Electronics

—THE GRINGO IS WORTH HIS WEIGHT—said Colonel Pedro Espinosa—. He's an expert in electronics, he's a U.S. citizen, and he'll be able to enter and leave the country whenever required. He speaks both languages perfectly. You could say he was born and raised both there and here at the same time.

—Do you know if he's a CIA agent?

—We don't know yet, but I'd bet anything that he is.

—We can offer him four hundred dollars a month.
—Too little.
—We also shouldn't sugarcoat it...
—Let's offer him six hundred... Something between six hundred and eight hundred dollars, no more. Not too much or too little, so that the woman also needs to get involved at some point. It's not good for a woman to be as independent as Mrs. Callejas.
—She's much older than him, and it wouldn't be strange if they end up divorced because of some affair of the gringo's. You know what a scorned woman is like.
—Tell me about it, Colonel!
—We'll tell him to get a stage name. Writers love that. Especially if they're women.

Michael Townley received a monthly salary of fourteen thousand pesos, and his wife two thousand, although she would insist in her memoirs that she was never assigned a specific mission.

First Attempt to Kill Pascal Allende

In its cover on January 25, the *Miami Herald* reported on the good health of President Gerald Ford (in the photo he is seen smiling and ready for the electoral battle against Jimmy Carter), on Henry Kissinger's trip to Madrid to sign a new "Defense Pact" prior to Spain's accession to NATO, and on an interview with its editor in the Dominican Republic of Joaquín Balaguer.

The article was titled "*Is the Dominican Republic* a haven for terrorists?." The journalist and editor of the paper, Don Bohning, had met at a restaurant in Santo Domingo with two Cubans from the CIA, Frank Castro and Rolando Otero. Younger, Otero was an aspiring member of the paramilitary group led by Frank Castro, thanks to his recent involvement in the bombs successfully detonated in Miami, for which he was wanted by the State Police and the FBI. Months earlier, he had participated in a wave of attacks against the main institutions of Florida's legal system. At least nine bombs had exploded in the buildings of the Miami police, the FBI, the State Attorney's Office, and at Miami International Airport, forcing him to flee to South America.

El Mono Morales located him at Caracas airport at 9:30 p.m., as if by coincidence. He allowed him to pass through immigration without the usual protocol checks, put him in a DISIP car, and took him to one of the exclusive apartments at the Arauco Hilton Hotel.

El Mono Morales, an FBI informant, warned him:

—The FBI is hot on your heels—he said—. You can't stay here long.

The next day Morales returned with his superior and chief of the DISIP, the Cuban CIA agent Orlando García. García had worked for Venezuela's secret services for over a decade. More recently, he had been promoted to head of the international division. Despite the ideological distrust that had led veteran Luis Posada Carriles to resign, García had managed to adapt the DISIP and its core, composed of Cubans from Miami, to the new political reality, becoming a very close associate of the new president, Carlos Andrés Pérez.

—You can't stay here for long—said Morales—. The Yankees are putting a lot of pressure on us because of the recent attacks in December. Tell me how it all happened.

García remained silent throughout the entire interview, which made Otero nervous. For a Cuban and considering that, without knowing it, both had been comrades during the good old days of the CIA, his silence couldn't mean anything good. In any case, García Vásquez was known for his secrecy. In restaurants, he always sat in a corner. He never turned his back on anyone and preferred to monitor the other tables while he ate, talked, or digested.

—Where can I go?—asked Otero, with few options.

—Santiago—said Morales—. Chile's new secret police has already contacted one of ours for a mission in Rome, and the plan seems to have worked quite well. The communist senator didn't die, but he and his wife were left like vegetables.

—I like the idea—, said Otero.

In the afternoon, El Mono Morales called the FBI and informed them that Otero had confessed to being the perpetrator of the bombings from last December at the post office, the district attorney's office, and the federal building in Miami.

—Where is he right now?—In Caracas—, said Morales—, at the Arauco Hilton.

The FBI agents hung up and discussed the next steps. They acknowledged that Morales had a special talent. Over the years, he had worked for the CIA, the FBI, the DEA, the paramilitary organizations of the Cuban exile, and, most likely, for the G-2, Cuba's secret police in the early 1960s, like many other exiles from Miami. Like a black widow, he had spun a web that kept him untouchable at the center of his own network of betrayals and conspiracies.

The FBI could accuse him of various crimes, but, aside from being an immunized witness in several cases, he was the best informant the feds had ever had, which was also why they couldn't detain Otero in Caracas. Only that fact could end Morales's life or his valuable collaboration.

Almost at the same time, Morales handed Otero an Iberia ticket to Santiago, and some money; not too much, so that his desperation would lead him to seek a permanent and strategic connection with the DINA. By the end of 1975, the government of General Pinochet had already received and granted secret refugee status to several Cubans from Florida and New Jersey, from the most well-known Orlando Bosch to Guillermo Novo Sampol, who was beginning to challenge Bosch's leadership of the Cuban paramilitary organizations in the United States. Novo had entered the country on December 4, 1974, and left two weeks later, bound for Colombia. Only this record, later in the hands of the FBI, proved yet another violation of the parole imposed by U.S. courts, which prohibited him from leaving the country. As in Bosch's case, Novo was also not detained.[48]

Shortly after arriving in Santiago, Otero headed to the Diego Portales Building in the city center, where Pinochet maintained his offices while repairs on La Moneda continued. There, they ordered him to return to the hotel and wait. Otero wandered the streets of Santiago, awaiting a response.

A few days later, a man named Major Torres, Michael Townley, posing as Captain Andrés Wilson, along with Mariana Callejas, who was not formally introduced and simply took notes, visited him. For an hour, they interrogated him about his activities in Miami, his knowledge of explosives, and his past experience as the youngest member of the 2506 Brigade that had invaded Cuba in 1961, when he had just turned 16 years old.[49]

A week later, he received a visit from another agent of the DINA, a red-haired man who introduced himself as Marcelo Estrobel. He told Otero that he preferred to talk somewhere else. A hotel is never a reliable place. They went out to the street, and the agent pointed to a restaurant, where they settled in a corner. Without introductions, he offered Otero his first mission, a job suited to his profile and experience: to travel to Costa Rica and assassinate Salvador Allende's nephew, Andrés Pascal Allende, and his girlfriend, the dancer Mary-Anne Beausire.

—Two communist terrorists—said the red-haired man, handing him a Manila envelope with photos of both—. Pascal Allende is a member of the MIR, an armed resistance group since September 11, 1973. We've already liquidated all of them. Almost all of them. Pascal Allende escaped and fled to Costa Rica. A few months ago, the Costa Rican government granted him asylum and refuses to extradite him so we can complete the cleanup operation.

—My God—said Otero—. She is a beautiful woman.

According to the FBI, at first, Otero agreed to kill Pascal Allende, but he resisted killing the dancer.

—We don't kill women—said Otero.

—Take it or leave it—said the red-haired man—. You have two weeks to prove you're committed to the cause.

—That's too short of a time—complained Otero, while looking back at the dancer's photo.

—We could agree not to kill her—said the redhead—. Of course, if they plant a bomb in her car and the beauty dies by accident, we'll give you an extra bonus for the job.

Otero remained silent, looking at the two photos. Beneath them, another paper contained relevant data, such as the two biographies and the addresses where the targets were usually found in Costa Rica. The envelope and the black-and-white photos reminded him of Mission Impossible, the favorite TV series of Orlando Bosch and other comrades from the failed Brigade 2506.

—If you really want to establish an anticommunist base here—said the redhead— you must first prove you can successfully execute this mission. We'll provide assistance for the trip, but you must complete the rest of the mission on your own. Once you pass this first test, our government will provide you with weapons and money for our shared struggle against communism.

Otero didn't respond.

—That's all I can say—concluded the redhead—. Take it or leave it.

Otero accepted.

—But if you sell us out to the FBI—said the redhead— as Cubans tend to do, we'll have to kill you.

—There's no need to worry about that—said Otero—. To me, the FBI is just like Fidel Castro.[50]

In Santiago, Otero took the scheduled flight to Costa Rica, but during the layover in Lima, he hesitated again. Now he had a mission of a different magnitude and feared falling into the hands of the FBI or the local police. He had to do something unexpected, he thought, something even he wouldn't have planned. Flying directly to Costa Rica on the orders of a stranger wasn't a very good idea. He could ask Mono Morales or Orlando García for advice, but he couldn't do it over the phone, so he decided to return to Caracas, even though he had been warned not to go back for a while.

While standing in the immigration line at Caracas International Airport, Orlando García approached him and pulled him aside.

—What the hell are you doing here?—said García.

—I have important information—said Otero— but I can only give it to you in person.

—You're an idiot. Kissinger arrives in three days, and this place is crawling with Yankee agents.

—What about Mono?

—In Miami—said García—. I'll take you to his apartment until you get out of here.

After a meeting with FBI agents in Miami, Mono flew to Caracas on February 15 and found Otero in his apartment. Only Otero's manila envelope, with the photos and details of the two sentenced by DINA, managed to calm him down. If there was one thing Mono valued, it was sensitive information.

Shortly after, Frank Castro urgently flew from the Dominican Republic to join Mono and Otero in a long conversation at Mono's apartment. Castro secured ten thousand dollars from the Cuban Liberation Front for the double assassination in Costa Rica, which, moreover, would be handled by two off-the-radar members of the FBI, currently residing in Somoza's Nicaragua. Otero, who according to the new plan had to return to Santiago and wait for the success of the operation, couldn't be happier.

Frank Castro's FLC competed with other exile groups (like the one led by Orlando Bosch) for a full partnership with DINA in Chile and, for him, this opportunity presented by Otero was more than timely. Frank Castro did not trust The Mono Morales, but he needed him. El Mono, for his part, knew that the DINA had also offered Orlando Bosch, then a protected resident of Pinochet in Lo Curro, Santiago, the mission to assassinate Pascal Allende and his girlfriend in Costa Rica. He probably also knew (this will never be known without some degree of doubt) that Bosch planned to complement his mission with a more significant attack, a bomb against Henry Kissinger in San José. It wouldn't have the same effect as the assassination of Kennedy (whom many still associate with the dark man beside the umbrella man in Dallas) but something is something.

Why an anti-communist ally like Kissinger? So that Washington would stop persecuting the Cubans who "*have suffered too much.*" If we suffer, others must suffer twice, ten times more, if necessary. Two months later, a secret FBI report will conclude that, in Kissinger's case, the terrorists' intention was not to kill him. The welcoming bomb had a publicity objective.[51]

Rolando Otero returned to Santiago, but the operation was another failure. After several days trying to contact the DINA, someone knocked on the door of room 711 at the Hotel Emperador and, when Otero answered, a man without identifying himself said:

—Estrobel is going to kill you.

Orlando Bosch had been arrested in Costa Rica and his name, Rolando Otero, had been leaked to the press.

—Can't you ever do anything right? If you still want to stay alive, take a flight to Costa Rica and eliminate Pascal Allende once and for all. Redeem yourself, you and your team of good-for-nothings.

—Tell your boss that if anything happens to me—said a nervous and cornered Otero— planes in Chile are going to start exploding mid-flight...

The shadow smiled, but said nothing.

The next morning, Otero moved to a modest boarding house on the outskirts of Santiago, called Providencia. The FBI agent based in Buenos Aires, Robert Scherrer, one of the first to detect the Condor Plan originating in Pinochet's government and with the CIA's approval, recorded Otero's move thanks to his informants, but he didn't want to arrest him. Apart from the international complications with the new Chilean government, that would have hindered the investigation of operations still unjudged in the United States.

Frank Castro was also not arrested for the failed attempt on Pascal Allende's life, which fueled several suspicions of a new betrayal among the Cuban exiles. Everyone seemed convinced that someone had leaked the information about the attempts on Pascal Allende and Henry Kissinger's lives.

—It must have been El Mono—concluded Frank Castro.

In Santiago, the DINA debated whether to attribute the high-profile and compromising failure to a new betrayal or the well-known inefficiency of the CIA's Cubans.

—They're great at crying, setting bombs everywhere, and drinking rum—said Captain Miller—, but don't ask them for anything more. Cubans can't even light a cigarette without the CIA's help, and even then, the cigarette doesn't light or explodes in their face. They're not *Mission Impossible*, they're The Three Stooges.

Roland Otero in Santo Domingo

In Santiago, Michael Townley and other agents of the DINA located the new hotel where Ronaldo Otero was staying and searched his room. They grabbed him by the arm and threw him into a car that began speeding through different routes on the outskirts of Santiago. At a deserted bend in the road, Townley parked. He took out a recorder and started asking questions.

Interrogated about the failed operation in Costa Rica, Otero confessed to his meeting with DISIP officers in Caracas.

—Who, specifically?

—Ricardo Morales, Orlando García, and Frank Castro...

Townley turned off the recorder and said:

—We entrusted you with a secret operation... and the first thing you do is run and tell Mono Morales, a known informant?[52]

Townley was right. What Otero did was naive, clumsy, stupid, but it wasn't Townley, speaking with such authority, reprimanding a trembling fool, unable to think straight for a moment. The real Townley was a boy with a horseshoe mustache, plagued by an inferiority complex that he would one day admit, when he'd get out of

El exilio del terror

prison and disappear in Florida under the protection of the very same FBI that captured him. He had learned in Pinochet's Chile a character that fascinated him, someone he had wanted to be his whole life since his childhood in Iowa, since he became the useless son of a successful Ford manager in Chile, since he worked as a modest mechanic with Cuban exiles in Miami, in the late 1960s.

He returned to the hotel without saying more. He stopped and said, again with authority and repeating a verbal capsule, typical of the secret services of the time, as ambiguous as it was effective:

—Get out. You'll receive new orders soon.

Otero waited for days. The new orders never came. He became a vagabond in Santiago until he was detained by military intelligence agents. They interrogated him for his own lies in his desperate attempt to survive in a sports club, such as the claim that he was on a mission for the CIA.

—I work for the DINA—he lied again, or rather exaggerated—. You can call Mr. Estrobel to… I'm also an agent of the Venezuelan DISIP.

The information reached Lieutenant Contreras. For a would-be spy, the little Cuban talked too much. He didn't even know how to lie. Shortly after, Otero was put on a plane to Miami. From there, by the grace of the Lord, he managed to fly to the Dominican Republic. In Santo Domingo, he was arrested by the local police at the request of the FBI. Soon after, Frank Castro visited him in jail and assured him he wouldn't be there long. Besides being a CIA collaborator, Castro was the son-in-law of Admiral César de Windt, an important Dominican military officer in Joaquín Balaguer's government. When he spoke, he would often caress his Rolex, a special edition designed as a CIA badge, much like the throat-slitting knives so cherished by the Nicaraguan Contras.

A few days later, Otero was having lunch on the sidewalk of a restaurant in Santo Domingo with Franz Castro and the editor of the *Miami Herald*, Don Bohning. They ordered Cuba Libres, according to an FBI report.

—The U.S. government trained us to kill for Cuba's freedom—Otero told Bohning—. Now they betray us and want to put us in jail.

Another Cuban fugitive from American justice and refugee on the island was Umberto López. Bohning wondered about several coincidences, such as how all the individuals accused of terrorism in the U.S. had passed through Caracas, like Orlando Bosch, a pediatrician on the FBI's most-wanted list, who remained free and conspired from one country to another. "The Cuban exiles in the Dominican Republic—wrote Bohning— are also involved in car sales. Some import and export. The most important administrators of Gulf operations are almost all Cubans." Not a few were friends of President Balaguer. Or relatives, like Frank Castro.

—Umberto López is also one of us—Castro said—. I have no reason to deny it. More than a friend, he's like a brother. We met in the CIA training camps.[53]

In the Dominican Republic, Rolando Otero took up skydiving at the military airport in San Isidro. Later, he returned to Chile on a new mission, where he was finally arrested by FBI agent Robert Scherrer. He arrived in Miami on Thursday, May 20, at 6:30 p.m., handcuffed. Scherrer arrived with a bandaged hand. Otero had bitten him so hard during the trip that it cost him a tooth.

New Betrayals, New Failure

BETRAYALS AND VENDETTAS WERE PART of the tradition of the feared Cuban paramilitary and parapolitical exile groups. In many cases, they were motivated by differences in interpretation over who was more anti-Castro. In others, they were simple vendettas and internal power struggles in Miami and Union City. When not for personal gain. Not infrequently, it involved leaking information to the FBI or court testimonies, as was the case with "El Mono" Ricardo

Morales, who testified against Orlando Bosch in the attack on the Polish ship stranded in a Miami port, which nearly cost him his life when his car exploded as he started it.

At a private meeting in Santiago, FBI agent Robert Scherrer reported that the head of DINA, Colonel Manuel Contreras, assured him he had no doubt that El Mono Morales had leaked the information about the plan to assassinate Pascal Allende. According to Contreras,

—El Mono is a damn communist—said Colonel Contreras, as he smiled kindly at Scherrer, whom he also considered an enemy within his greatest ally, the United States—. In my mind, I have no doubt that it was him who sold the information.[54]

Although El Mono Morales had spent his entire career selling information about his own comrades whenever he needed to gain some personal benefit, the "I have no doubts" from the head of the bloodiest and most ruthless police force in the hemisphere not only meant that he had no evidence, but that it could well be false intelligence, an authorized speculation meant to complicate and distract from the investigation that directly implicated him.

Later documents would indicate that the traitor was Luis Posada Carriles, who at the time was desperately and persistently trying to reintegrate into the CIA's payroll. A few years earlier, when the CIA had removed him for his habit of operating without informing his superiors, he hadn't been too concerned. He had a well-established career in Venezuela's secret police and held a high-ranking position that made him nearly untouchable. He was a feared repressor of dissidents and an expert in torturing his interrogated subjects. With the arrival of Carlos Andrés Pérez, he began to grow wary. The new president was the vice president of the Socialist International and, although it wasn't difficult to infiltrate or even bribe him, Posada Carriles knew that trust was not a family asset. He never stopped being a sporadic collaborator with the CIA, but by 1976 he needed the salary security of the agency and, above all, a more committed protection. For this, he went to great lengths to earn the trust of his new directors. His main weapon to convince them was selling goodwill by providing information about his colleagues and friends, such as Orlando Bosch.

The first in this new series of betrayals involved the plan of Chile's secret police to assassinate Andrés Pascal Allende, nephew of the deposed president Allende, and his companion Mary-Anne Beausire. Posada Carriles passed the information to one of his potential enemies, President Andrés Pérez, knowing that he would communicate it to the president of Costa Rica, Daniel Oduber. Both Pérez and Oduber were enemies due to their leftist ideas and their diplomatic relations with Cuba, but for Posada Carriles, any information had value if it generated a return. The death of Pascal Allende was a Chilean matter; it didn't mean as much to him as the potential favors generated by the leak. In his case, it would return as trust from the governments of Venezuela and Costa Rica and from the CIA, as proof of the quality of his collaboration.

One of the Chilean plans to assassinate Pascal Allende was under Otero's responsibility. The other was under his friend Orlando Bosch. More secretly, Michael Townley had been working on a new explosive with Petn (a chemical stronger than nitroglycerin) that could be hidden in a cigarette and had enough power to obliterate the face of the enemy of freedom, exiled in Mexico.[55] Bosch was arrested. The second leak was even more serious for U.S. intelligence. In Costa Rica, Bosch was accused of planning an attack against Secretary of State Henry Kissinger.

Despite the high quality of the information provided by Posada Carriles, the CIA remained reluctant to officially reinstate him. They kept him as an informant. Unhappy with this, Posada Carriles persisted and requested the Agency's intervention to obtain special entry visas to the United States. As a gesture of goodwill, on June 22, he informed them of a plan by Cuban exiles to blow up a Cubana flight mid-air from Panama. The attack will fail due to a detonator malfunction. Another detonator error will cause the Cubana flight on July 9 to explode before the plane takes off in Jamaica.

This endless series of failures, where most of the dead were other Cuban exiles from Miami and Union City, was capitalized as experience by Posada Carriles, Orlando Bosch and other less prominent leaders, though no less active, such as El Mono Ricardo Morales Navarrete, Frank Castro, Guillermo Novo, Dionisio Suárez, Virgilio Paz and Orlando García Vásquez. The greatest achievements of their careers, in terms of media impact rather than political objectives, will be the assassination of Orlando Letelier and his assistant Ronni Moffitt in Washington and the explosion of Cubana Flight 455 two weeks later, which killed 73 people shortly after takeoff from Bermuda.[56, 57]

In September of this year, Bosch and Posada Carriles will celebrate together (with plenty of rum, cigars, and bucolic paintings of their own making, in an apartment in Caracas) the two greatest achievements of their careers. Two events with which they will play with mystery, as they could neither claim nor reject the credit. Often, they did both, depending on the political climate. Both will be elevated to the status of heroes in Miami, with museums, monuments, marches, fundraisers, presidential pardons, commemorative days in their honor, and politicians who would continue their fight in the lobbies and the U.S. Congress. In 1983, the Miami City Council established a holiday as "Doctor Orlando Bosch Day," and in 2010, despite protests from teachers, he was awarded an honorary plaque at the Bacardi House of the Institute for Cuban and Cuban-American Studies (ICCAS) at the University of Miami.

In June 1976, Otero will be tried in Jacksonville for the explosion of nine bombs. Despite the evidence, he will be acquitted. When a year later his case is reopened and he is convicted, he will become the link connecting the assassination of Letelier to the DINA, through the Cuban paramilitaries. He will do so out of spite for the Chileans who, in his view, did not treat him as a veteran anti-communist fighter deserved. The FBI detectives will exploit this sentiment of the convicted man to solve their most difficult case yet. Otero's confession will reveal the true identity of Michael Townley.

With that domino piece fallen, Virgilio Paz, Dionisio Suárez, and Alvin Ross Díaz will fall as well. But not many more. Some, like El Mono Morales, will be executed by their own comrades. Not by U.S. justice.

AUGUSTO LUTZ

COLONEL CONTRERAS SHARED WITH TOWNLEY a certain inability to imagine the pain of others. At military school, he would often humiliate and torture his cadets by shoving their heads into toilets, to teach them not to make mistakes. He had the ideal profile of the Latin American dictator that CIA agents sought around the world. He had returned from Fort Benning in 1969 convinced that the world was in an all-out war against communism, that the ends justified the means—no matter what they were—and that reality was what one believed it to be, regardless of what the evidence might suggest.

Like other officers trained at the School of the Americas, Contreras had returned to Chile with a strong sense of superiority. When Pinochet declared himself the leader of Chile in 1973, he founded the Dirección de Inteligencia de Chile, DINA. When it began to act without limits against its enemies, such as the members of the MIR who had taken up arms after the coup, and against any man or woman suspected of thinking differently, some army officers protested.

One night, General Augusto Lutz called Contreras to demand information about the disappeared husband of his daughter's teacher. Contreras refused.

—I demand that you provide me with the information—insisted Lutz—. You are a lieutenant colonel in the army, and I am a general.

—The only orders I follow—interrupted the colonel— are those of my commander, General Pinochet.

Contreras had met Pinochet in 1960, when he was a lieutenant and had decided to take courses at the School of War. At the time, Captain Pinochet taught Strategy.

Lutz was transferred to Punta Arenas, at the far south of the country, very close to the Dawson concentration camp, where key figures of the previous government were languishing.

—If I ever get sick—he told his wife— do not take me to the military hospital.

Lutz had collaborated in the military coup and in the disappearance of the young journalist from New York, Charles Horman, among other crimes against dissidents, and he knew his fellow soldiers quite well.

Shortly after, following an officers' party, he fell ill and was admitted to the military hospital in Punta Arenas, where he was hospitalized for three weeks. He was then transferred to the military hospital in Santiago.

Before he died, he passed a note to his daughter that said, "*Get me out of here*," but the nurses said all the patients said the same thing. The news of his death was announced on radio and television a day before he died. He was 51 years old.

Deaths of figures inconvenient to the dictatorship in hospitals were numerous. One of the techniques to achieve this without leaving traces was developed by the chemists of the DINA, among them engineer Eugenio Berríos and his American friend, Michael Townley, in Lo Curro. The experiments continued with prisoners in the regiments.

FEBRUARY

My Hero, Al Capone

According to the Department of Justice of the United States, between 1961 and 1968 alone, Orlando Bosch was involved in thirty terrorist operations. None were a landing on the island against the dictatorship. None were hand-to-hand combat that could risk his physical integrity. In no case did he attempt (much less succeed) to convince the majority of Cubans to join a successful counterrevolution that would force Castro to flee to some resort in Russia. All were actions from a distance, against someone else with possible dealings with the dictatorship. Always in hiding. Always denying every action. Never condemning any.

—Do you think all that was a new phenomenon, emerging after the Revolution?—asked Hunter.

—I don't think so—I said—. The culture and organizations of the mafia established in Batista's Cuba were already old traditions. In history, nothing is created or destroyed; everything is transformed.

José Miguel Battle, Santo Trafficante, Meyer Lansky... All it took was a little shake to send them to other places, to other countries, where they continued doing the only thing they knew how to do, albeit adapted to the new context. With some exiled fortunes and the support of a top-secret agency, the miracle was guaranteed. The mafia of gambling, alcohol, and brothels had created, for decades, a culture of power in Havana. The high-society parties hosted by American giants like the Caribbean Octopus, that is, the United Fruit Company (the same company that destroyed democracies in the Backyard and supported its tropical dictators), lavish parties and receptions to please the dictator's wife, María Fernández de Batista, represented the Golden Age of Cuba, longed for by generations.

Even by its butlers. The golden age of the mafia and easy money that never reached the rest of illiterate and starving Cuba, the one that didn't appear in newspapers or on television. The one that doesn't and never will appear in the memories of the nostalgic Batista supporters in the U.S. Congress. Even the so-called Palestinians of Havana, named not because they were Palestinians but because they were peasants from the Province of Oriente, who didn't even have a piece of land to die on.

Santo Trafficante and Meyer Lansky were already powerful mobsters in the forties and fifties. Rolando Masferrer was a powerful businessman and senator before the Revolution. Others were no more than errand boys but with the same aspirations of becoming millionaires. This was the case of José Miguel Battle. He had been a police officer under Fulgencio Batista, promoted to Batista's secret police, the SIM, which was dedicated to hunting down and assassinating dissidents. At the same time, he was an employee and frontman for Meyer Lansky's bribes. The Revolution not only ruined the business of casinos, prostitution, and drug trafficking, but also the dreams of its more modest employees, like Battle, of becoming rich and respected overnight. Like Martín Fox, a modest entrepreneur in the La bolita gambling business in Matanzas who, within a few years, ended up becoming the owner of the famous Tropicana nightclub in Havana.

In Miami, he was quickly recruited by the CIA and promoted to Second Lieutenant in the U.S. Army. Months later, he was tasked with leading one of the groups that invaded the Bay of Pigs by air. After the failure and becoming a prisoner of war in Cuba for over a year (along with a thousand other comrades, all heroes and political prisoners of the communist regime, for the Miami exile), he was released. In Union City, the modest police officer, now a soldier and CIA agent, founded the mafia group The Corporation. In 1977, Battle was sentenced to thirty years for his illegal gambling, drug trafficking, and murder businesses in the U.S., businesses that provided him with $45 million a year. He pleaded guilty to murder and was

El exilio del terror

pardoned two years later. In Miami, The Godfather became the richest man in Florida and one of the top political campaign donors. In 2004, he was charged again with murder and drug trafficking, a business that left the family over 1.5 trillion dollars.

—The Revolution was his downfall and his fortune.

—When Castro and Che expelled Batista, the casino mafia didn't believe their business would be shut down. They were moving too much money and were used to commanding or killing for any government to dare do so much. They were wrong. The first thing the Revolution did was expropriate their hotels and close casinos and brothels.

—Aside from the economic loss—said Hunter— it must have been an affront to the mafia's honor.

—The revolutionaries released pigs in the casinos, in case it wasn't clear enough.[58]

—As if the pigs and the insults to honor weren't enough, two years later came the Bay of Pigs fiasco.

—That's right, and not just for the Batista supporters. *"Like many others involved,"* the powerful CIA agent, Howard Hunt, would acknowledge half a century after the fiasco, "I could never get over the trauma of the Bay of Pigs". David Atlee Phillips, another powerful CIA agent in Havana, got drunk on half a liter of whiskey the night the failure was confirmed. Later he admitted: "It wasn't just that Castro and Che had won. What deeply affected me was not having done a good job."

—A true professional—said Hunter.

—Mercenary, in other words—I noted—. Another example of the Protestant divorce between faith and morality: the right faith saves; bad deeds don't condemn. Hence that terrifying fear of losing faith and that pale hatred of critics or spokesmen of other beliefs.

—Well, let's not meddle in God's business—cut Hunter, calling the waiter.

Those Who Didn't Rise from Bombers

ON FEBRUARY 4, 1976, THE DEA IN VENEZUELA received a request (number 02406) from headquarters in the United States to allow the Cuban Manuel de Armas to travel to Caracas to purchase a kilo of Colombian heroin. De Armas was a collaborator and informant for the CIA, defined in the files of his own employers as "a mobster, a killer, a ruthless and pathological liar."[59]

The request was approved, and De Armas arrived in the country on February 11. The following day, he reported being taken to the Cuban Embassy for questioning. There, he was allegedly offered the chance to collaborate with the island's government. Immediately, the CIA requested that he return to Miami, but later concluded that the information was highly improbable, yet another product of his imagination. On February 20, an FBI agent wrote a report acknowledging that "for two months, the FBI has avoided any contact with Manuel de Armas due to his unstable psychological condition."[60]

Possibly due to the Agency's notorious indifference to his recent actions, Manuel de Armas held a press conference in Miami, where he acknowledged his ties to U.S. secret agencies, which had trained him in the prestigious CIA schools.

The press conference was documented in the FBI and CIA reports, but it was never published in the commercial press. De Armas went to Mexico and on April 22, he reappeared in a New York Times article as the protagonist of two assassination attempts on Fidel Castro, one in 1971 in Chile (years later acknowledged and detailed by CIA agent David Atlee Phillips and Cuban agent Antonio Veciana) and another in Havana, thwarted by Cuba's secret service, when they arrested Cuban exiles in the Bahamas.[61] For years, though vastly poorer, Havana's secret service proved to be more effective than that of the United States in preventing the assassination of leaders and presidents, or attacks against the population, such as the one on the Twin Towers.

Manuel de Armas will be one of the hundreds, if not thousands, of cases that will end up forgotten. In the Miami offices, the CIA reported in 1976 that, months earlier (on October 17, 1975, and again on January 7 of that year), de Armas had offered himself as a double agent, in addition to working for the Drug Enforcement Administration, DEA. The same CIA document defined de Armas and other candidates as "unstable, so any contact must be carried out with extreme caution," with a particular interest in making money from the U.S. government.[62] With the same psychological profile, others would go down in history for their terrorist actions. The House Select Committee on Assassinations described him as "a possible source of information on Masferrer's connection to the assassination of President Kennedy."

Unlike De Armas, Rolando Masferrer was able to build a name for himself. He was a prominent politician in the Batista regime and one of the most mentioned names in the investigations into the assassination of President Kennedy. But, without a doubt, one of the most recognized names in this story of rum, cigars, and bombs is Luis Posada Carriles. With the same psychological profile as Manuel de Armas detailed by the FBI, his actions stood out for the consistency of his philosophy, his practice of terror, and his ambiguous game between claiming credit in the press for a terrorist attack and denying it in the courts of any country.

As in all cases, without exception, the relationship between the CIA and its Cuban recruits was tainted by conflict and betrayal. Two days after Manuel de Armas arrived in Caracas on one of his last important missions, on February 13, the CIA decided to cut ties with Luis Posada Carriles, due to some tax payment issues with which it did not want to be associated.

"Posada didn't smell too good," according to the CIA's man for Latin America, Jack Devine, who was responsible for the coup against Salvador Allende and the terrorist campaigns of the Contras in Nicaragua.

After an interesting list of failures, Devine had been very clear with Posada Carriles:

—From now on, that matter of assassinating Fidel Castro is in your hands, okay?

On June 23, 1976, the CIA reported that Manuel de Armas had fled to Cuba. On April 21, de Armas had held another press conference, this time in Havana, where he admitted to being a member of the Miami paramilitary group Abdala and a CIA agent. He denounced an ongoing plan to get Cuba and Venezuela to break off diplomatic relations.[63] Although he mentioned several names, including that of "El Mono" Ricardo Morales, he could not specify what this plan entailed.

That Long road trip in a caravan

A YEAR EARLIER, COLONEL MANUEL CONTRERAS had handed twenty-five thousand dollars to Townley to assassinate Allende's former Minister of Economy, Pedro Vuskovic, and other members of the Popular Unity. The Chilean exiles were planning another dangerous meeting in Mexico City. Shortly after, DINA sent Mariana Callejas to Mexico, via Miami, to assassinate Allende's widow, among other exiles. By then, Townley was Andrés Wilson and Callejas was sometimes María Luisa Pizarro and other times Ana Pizarro.

Both plans failed for a hard-to-believe reason, both for Townley and for his Cuban collaborator who traveled with them to Mexico, always distrustful of the gringo and the Chilean woman. The socialist meeting in the Mexican capital had ended by the time they arrived. It could have been due to a clever calculation by the enemies of freedom or an error by its defenders. The event meant a deep disappointment that undermined the morale of the new association while reinforcing the confidence that would lead them to collaborate once more to assassinate Orlando Letelier and Ronni Moffitt in September.

The first contact with the Cuban freedom fighters had begun years earlier in Miami, where Townley had contacts from his days as a mechanic at Aamco in Little Havana, when he had offered his services to the CIA several times. Now, a closer encounter with the leaders of the Cuban exile had started off on the wrong foot, as everything did.

Guillermo Novo didn't trust the blond man with the English accent. He could be a CIA spy, although the Agency wouldn't be so foolish as to use someone who spoke Spanish as a second language to communicate with The Community, especially after the famous operations of David Atlee Philips who, since the 1950s, also spoke Chilean as a second language. Not to mention the availability of Cubans willing to collaborate on every corner of Calle Ocho or in any nightclub in Miami Beach. It's true that recruiting proven and reliable collaborators takes years, but it wasn't organization or patience that the Agency lacked most.

—The Chilean government hasn't treated my people as we expected—Novo said.

—The thing is, until now, we haven't always been able to trust—Townley said—. We know you've been compromised by the CIA and by the Cuban government. I know that you, Dionisio Suárez, and Orlando Bosch were in Chile in December. I know because I was there, with all of them. I didn't know who Novo and Dionisio were, but I recognized Bosch, obviously. El Mono Morales leaked information about all of you, and Bosch ended up in jail. I myself informed my superiors that Bosch's Acción Cubana branch was infiltrated by the CIA, and I advised them not to trust the other Cubans. So now I can only offer my apologies.[64]

—I'm not surprised about Bosch—said the FBI, in Novo's words, who at the time was vying for leadership with Bosch over the Cuban exile paramilitary groups—. He talks too much. He's a politician, and we need soldiers. What is this mission about?

Novo, Suarez, Ana Pizarro (Mariana Callejas), and El Gringo Andrés Wilson (Michael Townley) agreed to meet at a motel, to discuss the matter more privately, at 1:00 PM the following day. This encounter was documented by the FBI and later in Callejas's memoirs.

The Cubans arrived shortly after twelve, while Townley was in the bathroom. They entered brandishing .45 caliber pistols and accused them of being CIA agents. Both Townley and the Cubans had been CIA collaborators, but different events had kept them sidelined from their paychecks.

—You are from the CIA—said Novo—. You want us to believe you are from DINA, but you are from the CIA...

Townley did not know them personally, nor did they know him beforehand, even though they all worked in car repair and sales at the same shops in Florida and New Jersey.

—I told you we couldn't trust these fools—said Callejas.

—You have no idea how much we Cubans have suffered by trusting the CIA—Novo told her.

More subdued, as was his nature, Townley tried to convince the Cubans they were mistaken. It wasn't just about saving the mission but saving their own lives. Guillermo Novo wouldn't have hesitated to eliminate any potential threat by unloading his Beretta 92 in a motel. His bodyguard was known in Elizabeth, New Jersey, as José "Blood Pool" Suárez.

Suárez had been a colonel in Fidel Castro's army. Witnesses in Miami had recognized him as one of the executioners in the trials against those accused of murders and violations during Batista's regime. He himself admitted to participating in executions during the previous regime of Fulgencio Batista and shortly after the triumph of the Revolution, as was the case of Lieutenant Colonel Armando Suarez Suquet in March 1959, when the lieutenant was admitted to the military hospital of Camagüey and was accused of ordering a recent massacre.

El exilio del terror 99

—Don't play dumb, I told you—Suárez acknowledged in a conversation recorded on July 18, 2016, in Miami—. Act like a man... He was tried by a court and executed by a firing squad, as he should have been. He received no different treatment than what was applied to other convicts at that time... It's possible I was part of the firing squad, but I'm not sure if I was there... I'm almost certain I was part of the court that condemned him... In the end, not all the convicts were executed because an order came to suspend the trials. The order was given by Fidel Castro from the plane bringing him back from the United Nations.[65]

Later, like Orlando Bosch, José Suárez felt sidelined by the Revolution and defected to Miami. He was recruited by the CIA for the Bay of Pigs invasion in 1961. After the failure and the release of the thousand captured in Cuba, he became one of the leaders of the Cuban Nationalist Movement, receiving several decorations from his own group. Guillermo Novo was more well-known. In December 1964, he had planned a bazooka attack from across the East River against the UN, just as Che Guevara was giving his speech. But the missile fell into the middle of the river. The same story as the bazooka attack the CIA tasked Antonio Veciana with to kill Yuri Gagarin in Havana. The Novo brothers were detained for a few months by the New York police. In 1967, they bombed a Cuban ship again in Montreal, Canada. They were arrested in June 1967 by the New Jersey Police Department for illegal possession of explosives and fined $250 with two years of probation. In 1973, they were arrested again and detained for six months for the attack in Montreal. Between 1974 and 1976, there were two hundred bombings in Miami, from the airport to the FBI offices. Five Cuban exiles were killed. There were also executions using less spectacular methods, such as a simple Baretta pistol.

—We are from DINA—said Callejas— and we have an important job to do. If you want to kill us like the communists do, just do it already.

Novo and Suárez began unpacking Callejas' suitcases.

—If you have doubts, why don't you call Chile?—insisted Townley.

—They're clowns—said Callejas. Apart from not being impressed by Novo and Suárez, she never wanted to work with them.

Callejas held a deep disdain for the Cuban exiles since her time at the University of Miami. First, because during the anti-Vietnam War protests, they threw eggs and tomatoes, and later, once the ideological barrier was overcome, because in every dinner she shared with any of them, their antisemitism always came up, and she had to remind them of her past in the kibbutzim of Israel. Those failed experiments, like all socialist experiments, they said. Perhaps because Karl Marx was Jewish, the anticommunists mixed their hatred of communism with a Jewish plan to dominate the world.

—They looked down on us because of the way we dressed—Callejas had recalled, from her experience in Miami—. The Cubans dressed very elegantly, and their women were covered in jewels, but we wore jeans.

After what Callejas defined in the moment as a clown act, Paz and Suárez agreed to collaborate with the DINA envoys.

—If you stay in this room—said Novo— you'll soon have a response from us.

When they left, Michael silently looked at Mariana.

—Well—said Mariana—. I still think Mr. Novo is a gentleman, but it would be better to leave here.

—Let's wait—said Townley—. We can't add to the disappointments.

Hours later, someone knocked on the door and handed Townley a package and left without saying a word. The package contained two and a half blocks of C4 plastic explosive, two pistols, rolls of detonator wire, and several blasting caps.[66]

The next day, Townley and Callejas flew to Miami to rent the motorhome. They picked up Virgilio Paz at the airport, where they found him smoking a thick cigar. Paz, introduced as Javier, was not a recent acquaintance of Callejas. Years earlier, in Miami, she had thrown him out of her house. She was tired of his antisemitism, Callejas had said, of the thick smoke of his cigars, of his habit of picking his nose and spitting constantly.

Townley did not rent the motorhome. He preferred to buy it for six thousand dollars with an option to return it. On February 12, he also bought a rifle with a telescopic sight, the favorite of snipers, and a beep Fanon Courier, a medical intercom that he modified himself to turn it into a remote detonator for explosives. Half an hour further north, at Audio Intelligence Devices Inc. in Fort Lauderdale, he purchased electronic equipment worth $13,000. For less, he could have bought a house in Florida. The equipment was sent to his DINA laboratory in Santiago, via Buenos Aires. Months later, in September, Townley would visit the corner of Consultants International, a similar but higher-end establishment in Washington DC, days before the successful operation to eliminate Orlando Letelier.

By February 18, 1975, the caravan was on its way to the southern border, traveling at 120 kilometers per hour as anxiety subsided. In Mexico, the III Convention of dissidents and former members of Allende's government discussed the crimes against humanity committed by Pinochet and the options available from various countries. Allende's widow, Hortensia Bussi, took the floor. Then the former Chilean president Clodomiro Almeyda. Then the secretary of the Socialist Party, Carlos Altamirano.

—They all deserve to die—Mariana told Virgilio, according to prosecutor Propper's reconstruction—. Those are the wealthy leftists who caused all the problems in Chile XE "leftists who caused all the problems in Chile" and then left, letting the poor suffer the consequences of their criminal policies.

Townley, Callejas, and Paz sped through their three-day journey to the Federal District, armed and loaded with explosives, confident that Mexican customs would never suspect a family of American tourists. On the other side, in the lawless country, in the wild South, they would occasionally stop to rest and test some explosives in a semi-desert reminiscent of classic Hollywood.

Townley had to drive the whole time, while Callejas kept Virgilio Paz company in the back seats, where he amused himself by making small sculptures with the C4's modeling clay. Paz didn't stop talking to Mariana about his experiences in Cuba until he managed to captivate her for a moment, as always happens at some point in a long, endless conversation between two people. Callejas, still identified as Ana Pizarro, didn't reveal her real name, but Virgilio Paz did.

—I'm not called Javier.

—I don't care.

—My real name is Virgilio Paz

—Why are you telling me this?

—I like people to know who I am, and I take this mission very personally.

—That doesn't sound good for a combatant.

—My father is buried in Mexico City. Fidel expelled him from General Batista's army, and he had to leave for Spain. With the weather there, two years later he caught pneumonia. He ended up dying in Mexico, just before reaching Miami. I'll never forgive the dictator for that. I also won't forgive the Mexican doctors or the U.S. bureaucrats who delayed his visa paperwork. I was ten years old, and I've never been able to forget that injustice. That's why I haven't stopped killing every time there's been a need to fight against communism. I could build you a bomb right now with a stick of dynamite and a twenty-dollar watch…[67]

—You must've bought a lot of watches…

—No self-respecting Cuban goes without at least two watches. One for work and another for going out. I don't mind spending two hundred dollars on a Saturday night.

—I can imagine. I've noticed you wear brand-name clothes.

—Pierre Cardin, kid.

—The cigars you smoke aren't from Connecticut.

—No. They're Cohiba Behike.

—Cohiba Behike 56? With a box of those, you could have paid for the Caravan's rental.

—Cohiba Behike 55. I don't always have enough for the 56. You know it's illegal to import Cuban cigars, but those who know can find them in Miami. What can't you find in Miami? I know they bother you a bit, girl. I've seen it when I light one up. I do it on purpose, because when a woman gets annoyed, she becomes even more beautiful. As if she's getting ready for a party.

—A bit macho, but still a gentleman.

—A gentleman on every occasion. Do you remember the passport I got you last year?—asked Paz.

—I processed it myself—replied Callejas.

—Of course. You processed it with the driver's license and a birth certificate I bought from a Puerto Rican prostitute in a New York bar. Years ago. It cost me 150 dollars.

—It cost you? DINA paid for it.

—Yes, but I provided the experience. With the certificate and a utility bill, you got the driver's license, and with the driver's license and the prostitute's certificate, they gave you the passport at the post office. Do you remember the name?

—No. I've been many women. Even a Marxist prostitute.

—With that name, you traveled to Frankfurt.

—Luxembourg—she corrected—. There, they suspected the passport and deported me and Michael.

—To Germany—he said—. In Frankfurt, we saw each other again. I took you to several apartments…

—You boasted about knowing the Chilean exiles, and we pretended to be exiles from fascism too.

—You have a good memory.

—You showed me Fidelma Allende's apartment.

—No, that was Pedro Rojas.

—What was his real name?

—I forgot—he lied.

—It was Guillermo Riveros—she said— a member of the Christian Democracy of Chile. It had to be a Chilean because you guys can't pass for Chileans. It doesn't work, apart from being dumb and motherfuckers. We can't pull off Cuban either, not just the idiot or dick this and dick that and all that act. Guillermo knew many Chilean socialists in Germany. That afternoon, since Fidelma Allende wasn't in her apartment, we went down one floor and got ourselves invited by a Chilean lawyer couple. They had music by the Parra family, the same songs I had sung in Miami to celebrate when I heard about the coup against Allende. I cried with their stories.

—Stories of undesirables. Each time there are fewer left. We are eliminating them one by one.

—In the end, it was never clear to me why we also had to kill Frei Montalva's minister and his wife.

Virgilio Paz must have looked at her carefully before answering:

—It was clear—he said—.DINA also knew it. Bernardo Leighton was bringing the Christian Democratic Party closer to the Communist Party of Italy.

Mariana Callejas was having dinner with her in-laws in Miami when she heard the news of the attack on the Leightons in Rome. None of them made any comment. They said something about the salt because those who don't know are blind and deaf, but not mute. Only she paid attention to the details of the shooting that left the couple like two vegetables for the rest of their lives. It would have been better if the undesirables had died on the spot, she thought. But not even that could those freedom fighters do right.

Townley took note of the great paramilitary efficiency of the European right in organizing action groups, which would have a significant impact in the not-so-distant future. He reported it to his superior, Colonel Contreras. The French of the Organisation de l'Armée Secrète, led by Raoul Salan, had participated in various massacres in Algeria, and for Townley, it was the fulfilled dream of a boy. He had seen the film *The Day of the Jackal* countless times, inspired by the same events starred by his new friends. The same year of Patrice Lumumba's assassination, the CIA had also participated in an attempted coup d'état against the French president to prevent Algeria's independence. The agency's director, Allen Dulles, considered that an independent Algeria would be an open door for communists in Africa. Not coincidentally, and according to the U.S. Energy Information Administration, Algeria was "the main natural gas producer in Africa, the second-largest supplier of natural gas to Europe outside the region, and one of the top three oil producers in Africa."[68]

Two years later, frustrated by the loss of their largest African colony, the Organisation armée secrète attempted to assassinate de Gaulle. Albert *Bert* Spaggiari (alias Daniel) was one of its members based in Algeria. To finance this organization, in July 1976, he participated in the multi-million-dollar robbery of the Société Générale bank in Nice, for which he was convicted but never arrested. Aside from the jewels and money stolen, worth ten million dollars at the time, the goal was to steal compromising documents that, it was believed, would provoke a national scandal in favor of the French right in that year's elections. By then, Spaggiari was already working for the DINA, and they hoped the robbery of the century would provide more sensitive information about Chilean exiles in Europe, in their successful enterprise of eliminating dissidents under Operation Condor.[69]

—These European groups—reported Townley to Colonel Contreras—, have the military efficiency of the Organisation de l'Armée Secrète and the trust based on the honor of the Italian mafia.

Colonel Contreras took this report seriously. Under the guise of accompanying General Pinochet to Francisco Franco's funeral, he met with the Italians in Madrid.

If necessary—, Contreras informed them, after congratulating them on the operation in Rome—, you can count on our protection in Chile... We can still work together on a couple of pending issues with Peru and Argentina.

—It will be a pleasure to work with Michael again—said the envoy of the Alfa group.

After the attack on Bernardo Leighton and his wife in Italy, Townley flew to New York with the passport stolen from his friend Kenneth Enyart and thanked Guillermo Novo for the great work done by Virgilio Paz in Europe. The two decided to transfer the credit for the high-profile attack to Zero. Although this Miami group had played a minor, almost irrelevant role in recent years, it had achieved some notoriety by executing other Cuban exiles in Florida. By then, the lists of names signed by Zero, as if they were the Z of Zorro, were feared as a death sentence.

The information about the attack in Italy, attributed to Zero, was planted in the Spanish-language newspapers in Miami and, from there, spread to the rest of the country's media.

Years later, Callejas would write in her memoirs: "How could we believe such stories…? The military is bound to obedience, by training, by oath, who knows. But what induced us, rational and thinking beings, to obey absurd orders, to believe in children's tales?"

That is, to kill on command, as if it were something normal, like delivering a pizza. One of Callejas's favorite maxims, not for its beauty but for its effectiveness, went:

—First in the head. Second in the head. Third in the head. Fourth in the heart.[70]

During a break, with the motorhome parked by the side of the road on the way to Mexico, Townley taught Paz how to remove the speakers from the Fanon Courier beeper receiver and replace it with a device capable of producing the small spark needed to detonate the plastic explosive. One evening in the desert, the two men conducted a test. Mariana watched them from where she sat beside the motorhome, several hundred meters away, until they returned and Michael turned the ignition knob. In a fraction of a second, a bright flash contrasted with the dark silhouette of the ground under the twilight, and a moment later, the brief sound of the explosion

El exilio del terror   107

reached them. The two men celebrated like NASA engineers after successfully verifying an operation. Townley then placed the rest of the C4 in the Camper's refrigerator and they continued their journey.

The mission in Mexico ended in another failure, except for the new contacts and the extension of credit between DINA and the Cubans. The convention of foxes had not been the first in that endless city. It was the third session of the International Commission of Inquiry into the Crimes of the Military Junta in Chile, and among its participants was the general secretary of the Socialist Party of Chile, Carlos Altamirano, who months earlier had narrowly escaped an assassination attempt by the Santiago-Miami in Paris, when the French police, alerted by intelligence about the operation, whisked him away from Orly Airport in a black limousine, straight to a relative's house.[71] For some reason, the powerful intelligence services of Europe and the United States often aborted some assassinations but never, or rarely, led to the arrest of the perpetrators. When the FBI (after the death of Edgard Hoover in 1972, which cooled the ideological paranoia of the Bureau, begun in 1919) starts to professionally investigate the assassination of Letelier, the CIA will be one of the biggest obstacles to unraveling the tangled conspiracy. Its director, George H. Bush, will personally warn the investigators in charge of the case not to touch a certain category of Cubans who were above a line drawn by himself. More than agents or ex-CIA agents, the untouchables were successful businessmen, mostly based in Miami.

To justify the trip and the expenses charged to DINA, Paz and Townley decided they had to return with something in hand. They headed to Casa de Chile, a residence housing Chilean dissidents. The idea was to gather intelligence data or explore the possibility of something more media-savvy.

—Are you crazy?—Mariana told Michael—. Someone there is going to recognize us.

—Relax, girl—Paz said—. Let me go in and pretend to be a Cuban communist.

Paz returned with a gold mine. On a piece of paper, he had written the details of where the Allendistas in Mexico usually met to eat, which hotels they stayed at. Even which dentist they usually went to.

—Nothing easier than planting a bomb there—Paz said.

—What for?—Townley questioned..

—The Casa de Chile is a symbol—said Paz, according to one of the FBI reports—. A symbol of Marxism. For Cubans, symbols are important. More than important. They are everything.

—Well, I follow orders—said Townley—. We are not going to place a bomb in a location if there isn't one of the marked individuals to be eliminated.

—Why not?—complained Paz—. This mission is to prove that we are here for important things. We came here for that, and I'm not leaving Mexico empty-handed.

After a discussion that threatened the very partnership between Chileans and Cubans, Townley proposed to Paz to place the bomb he so wanted in the Cuban embassy. Paz agreed. The only problem was that the embassy turned out to be an impregnable residence, surrounded by exaggerated, paranoid walls.[72]

At the edge of frustration, Michael remembered something about the dentist of the Chilean exiles. They went there. Mariana and Paz entered the dentist's office pretending there was an emergency. Paz complained about a severe toothache in a way that allowed him to distract the secretary's attention, which enabled Calleja to steal several client files. Among them, as expected, were several Chilean exiles, with their phone numbers and addresses in Mexico City. Another piece of gold for Colonel Espinosa in Chile, after receiving news of the mission's failure.

The three mercenaries continued searching for their targets all over Mexico City, but they didn't even manage to find a trace of something resembling an international communist conspiracy meeting or the home of any of them. Simply eliminating one person from the list was enough to change the word *failure* to *success*.

Despite everything, when (weeks after Callejas, who was supposed to take care of his children) Townley returned to Santiago on May 17, 1975, and without delay, reported the details of the operation, even Colonel Contreras encouraged him to keep working. Failures were gained experience. The idea of establishing a clandestine laboratory in the Lo Curro mansion was going to facilitate future plans. With sarin gas and other biological materials, Townley could count on a new weapon, easier to transport and more discreet than car explosives, as its victims would die of an unexpected heart attack. If any dangerous radical suspected, it was always possible to cast doubt on everything. Proving any death would take them decades, if not centuries.

There were only one or two points of disagreement: the spectacular nature of the bombings wasn't a weakness of the strategy but part of its strength. The Cuban exiles knew this very well: every time they claimed responsibility for an attack widely covered in the press, donations and sympathies from potential supporters increased. The fear among the undesirables did too. The more fear, the fewer books, fewer articles, and fewer speeches up North. Nothing happens without collateral effects. Unplanned deaths had occurred after the use of sarin gas on various dissidents: some doctors and people close to the victim ended up dying for the same mysterious reasons.

At that time, Townley hadn't yet turned thirty, but everyone thought he was much older. Tall and thin, he had blue eyes and, quite often, a horseshoe or padlock-shaped mustache that defined him. His father didn't believe in him. The CIA didn't either.

The impressive facilities at Quetropillán in Santiago, the almost unlimited power over other people's lives, the messianic feeling of saving the world were irresistible to Townley and Callejas, who had arrived at the right place, at the right time, with the right paranoia.

Vice in Miami: The Largest CIA Base

In 1981, FBI AGENT ROBERT SCHERRER wrote that his colleague Carter Cornick was working in Miami, "since that's where the bomb experts live, along with drug traffickers and former Latin American dictators; the legendary Cuban mobster and former senator, Rolando 'El Tigre' Masferrer was executed there in 1975... Orlando Bosch is still raising funds in Miami."[73] Both agents had been assigned to the car bomb case that killed Orlando Letelier and Ronni Moffitt and, like other federal agents, they knew Miami as "the capital of terrorism in the United States." The record of executions and car bombs in public and private buildings left no room for doubt.

This consensus among FBI detectives had an explanation in history, I thought, I noted, I crossed out, I rewrote. The wave of terrorist attacks in Florida, New Jersey, and New York was the natural result of a historical development that had begun with the mafia organizations that dominated the Cuban economy even before Fulgencio Batista's government. Later, it was a side effect of the CIA's plans starting with the coup d'état in Guatemala in 1954 and, especially, after the Cuban Revolution of 1959.

In 1961, south of the University of Miami campus, the CIA established its largest operational station in the world, which it named JMWAVE, with a budget of 50 million dollars (equivalent to 500 million, half a century later), which resulted in a miraculous boom for small businesses in the area, while demonstrating the virtues of capitalism, the free market, and freedom from the tyranny of governments. There, 300 American employees and 6,000 Cuban exiles, recruited as collaborators, began working. All, according to records, eventually ended up on the CIA payroll. The project was shut down in 1968 due to persistent failures, including the most significant one, which was the assassination of Fidel Castro and the frequent sabotage and bombings of the island, which, far from diminishing the power of the new regime, ended up strengthening it.[74]

Among the direct collaborators were figures who would later wield significant power in politics and business, such as the gastronomic and media entrepreneur Jorge Mas Canosa. During the 1961 invasion of Cuba, Mas Canosa led the Niño Díaz group. He was also a broadcaster for Radio Swan and Radio Américas, the pirate radio station that the CIA set up on the CIA-owned island off the coast of Honduras, to prepare for the invasion of Cuba with its psychological warfare manual. The radio station was a replica of Radio Liberación, the shortwave station created in 1954 to destabilize the democracy of Guatemala, led by Jacobo Árbenz, which at the time was an absolute success. In Guatemala at the time was a young doctor named Ernesto Guevara, who would take his experience to Cuba and become part of the resistance to the CIA's plan to turn Cuba "into another Guatemala."

In April 1965, this CIA station in Miami incorporated Luis Posada Carriles. In June 1967, Posada was sent to Caracas to pursue a career in Venezuela's secret police (where he distinguished himself for his violent interrogation techniques) and pave the way for a dozen other Cubans from Miami, who would not work as second-tier agents or sergeants, but in high-ranking positions within the Disip as soon as they arrived at Maiquetía Airport. One of them would be the Cuban Ricardo Morales Navarrete, who was recruited that same year into the CIA station in Miami.

Known as El Mono, Morales had been a secret agent of the G-2 in Cuba until 1960 and a member of "Commandos L" of Miami in 1963. He was recruited a year later by the CIA "for paramilitary activities" in Florida. El Mono would become a central figure in the Cuban exile. He was a CIA agent during the massacres in Congo and Angola (for 350 dollars a month); one of the chiefs of Venezuela's secret police in the 1970s; and a protected informant for the FBI (at 700 dollars a month) against his own comrades, despite having admitted to a murder in Florida in 1972.[75] Ultimately, he would dedicate himself to drug trafficking until his execution in a Miami bar in 1982.

Due to the infamous failure of the Bay of Pigs, the future businessman and powerful financier of various paramilitary operations from Miami, Jorge Mas Canosa, was awarded the rank of ensign as soon as he enlisted in the United States Army to end his time as a paramilitary. At Fort Benning, he was in charge of training Cubans in propaganda and clandestine operations.[76]

Fort Benning, in Georgia, was named in honor of Henry Lewis Benning, a general of the pro-slavery Confederate forces, exactly a century earlier and, at the time, the headquarters of the School of the Americas—the "School of Assassins," according to Robert Richter's translation. There, Mas Canosa met and became an unconditional friend of Félix Rodríguez, Luis Posada Carriles, and Oliver North. He would meet Oliver North again at the White House during Ronald Reagan's presidency. Despite insisting that he was not the Jorge Mas Canosa mentioned by Lieutenant North during the Iran-Contra scandal, later investigations revealed that the donations to North to fund the Contras came from the only Mas Canosa known in Miami—and who used the same phone numbers under investigation. Colonel Oliver North would build a career training the Contras in Honduras and Nicaragua. He would be convicted of lying to the U.S. Congress about the Iran-Contras case and, shortly after, pardoned by the White House. He would also be recognized for other unpunished massacres, such as those in Afghanistan, decades later.

With some inaccuracy, Rodríguez took credit for the execution of prisoner Ernesto "Che" Guevara in Bolivia under the influence of the Standard Oil Company and Nazis sent by the CIA, such as war criminal Klaus Barbie.

Posada Carriles failed in all his attempts to kill Fidel Castro, but Mas Canosa would help him several times to stay in various countries and escape from uncomfortable situations, such as the Caracas, after being convicted of blowing up the Cubana plane with 73 passengers.

The smartest of all seems to have been Mas Canosa. By the late 1960s, he was already managing million-dollar businesses in Miami and, in his spare time, financing paramilitary groups like Comandos L. If Orlando Bosch had failed in his attempt to become the Che Guevara of capitalism (the reference was explicit in a letter he sent from Chile), Mas Canosa had failed in his obsession to replicate the success of the Granma, when in 1956 a few surviving rebels landed in Cuba and, in three years, managed to overthrow the dictatorship of Fulgencio Batista, a dictatorship even better armed than Castro's and with the unconditional support of the U.S. government and the powerful mafia of the casinos and brothels of Havana. His attempts to land in Cuba on sophisticated yachts to overthrow Fidel Castro failed time and again. For some reason, nothing worked, not even close. For some reason, not even God trusted us, even though we trusted God so much. Nothing would ever work, a frustration that only increased the level of inbred violence.

By the 1970s, as was the case with other exiles and the CIA on a larger scale, Mas Canosa became involved with various drug traffickers, such as Rafael de Arce and Antonio Canaves.[77]

—These people visited Jorge once or twice a week—declared under oath and before a judge his brother, Ricardo Mas Canosa— until they got into trouble with the law, due to their dealings with the drug traffickers. I remember them well, because they would show up at the offices in their luxurious Cadillacs, smoking huge cigars. As soon as they entered Jorge's office, they would close the door and leave me outside.[78]

A series of declassified FBI documents (with the approval of the CIA, which by then no longer considered these collaborators important) record multiple illegal activities by Mas Canosa and Posada Carriles, from international drug trafficking to the creation of paramilitary training camps in Florida; the continued arms trafficking from Venezuela; the placement of bombs in Mexico and Central

America, and (according to another secret CIA report from July 26, 1965) the attempted overthrow of another president of Guatemala, this time Colonel Alfredo Peralta Azurdia, at the request of another Miami Beach resident, the millionaire businessman Roberto Alejos Arzú.[79]

According to a classified document eleven years later, dated November 26, 1976, Posada Carriles, *"expert in demolitions"*, also worked with Alejos Arzú on his coup plan in Guatemala.[80] The plan, loaded with weapons and bombs against Peralta Azurdia, another dictator protecting banana corporations and with some bedroom friends, was thwarted by Washington in Mexico. Years later, the colonel and dictator Peralta Azurdia, in whose government the Death Squads reigned, as well as his personal enemies, also retired in Miami.

The role of Posada Carriles in Venezuela was very similar to that of Dan Mitrione in other countries on the continent, such as Uruguay. In June 1967, the CIA ended its working relationship with Posada Carriles, citing tax issues, independent activities, not reported to Headquarters. By August, he was already working for Digepol, in Caracas.[81] While he was head of Venezuela's secret police, he was known as Commissioner Basilio. He not only oversaw the torture and disappearance of Venezuelan dissidents subjected to special interrogation techniques, but also facilitated drug trafficking from Colombia to Miami, as recorded in FBI memos from March 1973. A month later, the CIA confirmed Posada Carriles' connection to drug trafficking, being reported in the company of "powerful drug lords." Federal investigators chose not to formalize charges, to keep him as a source of information. In May 1973, he was found "guilty only of having the wrong friends." Not just friends. By March 1976, the DEA was still after his wife, Nieves Elina González, suspected of participating in drug trafficking from Colombia to Miami via Venezuela.

Three months later, Posada Carriles requested a special visa from the CIA to spend his vacation in the United States.[82]

MIAMI. THE CAPITAL OF TERRORISM

IN THE 1950S, THE CIA HAD LAUNCHED WITH SEVERAL SUCCESSES, SUCH AS THE OVERTHROW OF MOHAMMED MOSSADEGH in Iran, coups d'état like in Guatemala, and, a few years later, repeating the same recipe in Brazil, Indonesia, Bolivia, and Chile, apart from the assassination of leaders like Patrice Lumumba in Congo and, more than likely, with the assassination of John Kennedy.

But the resounding failures based on absent intelligence began with the Bay of Pigs fiasco in the sixties and continued with Vietnam in the seventies, with their inability to foresee the suicide of the Soviet Union in the eighties, with terrorist attacks like the one on the Twin Towers in the new century, and with the alleged "intelligence failures" that led to the invasion of Iraq and the destabilization of the Middle East.

To assassinate Fidel Castro and carry out another regime change in a foreign country, the CIA turned to their Cuban exile employees and Italian mafia mercenaries who, before Castro, ruled the island in the alcohol, casino, and prostitution businesses. Among their most important figures were Santo Trafficante, Salvatore Sam Giancana, and John Roselli (Filippo Sacco). The latter two were assassinated in 1975 and 1976 before testifying before the Church Commission of the Senate, which was investigating the CIA's covert assassinations in foreign countries—including the assassination of President Kennedy.

With a few exceptions (like the successful introduction of lab-engineered biological pest agents into Cuba in the early eighties), the CIA failures almost all their previous objectives began to deteriorate their relationship with their Cuban employees. The Cubans took no blame for the failures. On the contrary, starting in 1968, they began to blame the CIA and Washington for everything, to the point of becoming, for decades, allied enemies.

The seventies would translate the new currents of social liberation from the previous years, such as the civil rights movement, independence movements in Africa, and resistance against the wars in Cambodia, Laos, and Vietnam. These popular movements would culminate in the most progressive congress in the history of the United States.

Another event that worsened the discontent among Cuban exiles was when on March 4, 1975, Senator Ted Kennedy proposed lifting the blockade against Cuba. According to polls at the time, the majority of the U.S. population was against the blockade, and an increasing number of countries dared to reestablish diplomatic relations with Havana.

Bombs began to explode. Several flights from Miami were evacuated to detonate bombs planted by the Fighters for Freedom. On December 4, 1975, the New York Times reported that a student narrowly escaped another bomb placed at the door of his apartment at the University of Miami, for having spoken in favor of dialogue with the island.[83]

Luis Posada Carriles, Orlando Bosch, Orlando García, and El Mono Ricardo Morales Navarrete, among many others, exploded with indignation over the new proposals for dialogue and negotiation. Hundreds of bombs in the United States and in the backyard exploded as well. Miami mobilized against the proposal of the dialoguers that materialized in the Committee of the 75, once Jimmy Carter took office in the White House.

Big and small businesses suffered attacks. As soon as Mackey International Airlines announced plans to resume flights to Cuba, their offices were destroyed by a bomb. The cruise line Carras had to cancel its bookings due to multiple bomb threats. Humble stores in Miami, such as El Español, owned by Cuban Alberto Rodríguez, suffered bomb explosions to prevent them from helping neighborhood Cubans arrange temporary family visits to the island.[84] Bombs and execution threats were also used against businesses that did not donate as expected, in the best style of the Judeo-Italian mafia of Havana, until the damned Revolution ended the lucrative business.

This tradition, which extended to kidnapping to collect unpaid debts, continued into the nineties, albeit in different scenarios and for other interests. CIA agent Roberto Parsons spent some time trafficking people from Cuba. By then, the agency had distanced itself from the house painter due to his well-known illegal businesses in gambling, drug trafficking, and contract killings, which did not recognize the hierarchical order or respond to the agency's plans, but to his own personal interests. Frequently disappearing, the FBI once reported that the main suspect in his death and disappearance was El Mono Morales Navarrete. However, Parsons would die in prison in 1994, twelve years after the murder of El Mono in Miami and for a cause more biological than political, without being tried for any of his murders.

In this same year of 1976, Valentín Hernández and Jesús Lazo executed another Cuban exile, Luciano Nieves, for joining the proposal of the then recently elected president Jimmy Carter. Nieves was shot in a parking lot of the Miami hospital where he had gone to visit his eleven-year-old son. Shortly after, Hernández and Lazo also murdered Juan José Peruyero, former president of the Bay of Pigs Association of Florida.

According to an FBI report dated November 5, 1976, the group of Cubans self-titled "Youth of the Star" were responsible for several attacks in Miami, including the bombing of the Dominican Republic consulate, on Monday, October 6, 1975; the bombing of the Broward County courthouse on Friday of the same week; the bombing at the offices of the Dominican airline on the 20th of the same month; the bombing at Bahamasair of the Bahamas, on November 27. By then, some of its members, such as Gaspar Jiménez and Ruiz Hernández, were already imprisoned in Mexico for attempting to harm the Cuban consul. But these were just precursors to the new tradition; new not because of the bombs or the deaths, but because of the independence of the Cubans once contracted by the CIA a few years earlier.

The pediatrician Orlando Bosch, by then a rising star among Cuban exiles and a CIA agent, claimed responsibility for the deaths of some "stupid servants of the CIA." According to the FBI, between 1973 and 1976 alone, Bosch was responsible for more than a hundred attacks in Florida and likely dozens of deaths. One of his associates, Héctor Cornillot Llano (brother-in-law of El Mono Morales Navarrete and partner of Omar Soto Pujol), in July 1968 managed to plant five bombs within a span of two hours.[85] The targets were any company that maintained or was suspected of having any commercial relationship with Cuba. Those executed in cold blood were mostly members of their own organizations, not entirely orthodox or radical, judged by the executor's criteria. Exiled figures of weight, anti-communists by conviction and convenience, such as Héctor Díaz Limonta, Arturo Rodríguez Vives, Ramón Donestévez, José Elías de la Torriente, and Rolando Masferrer were executed with remote-detonated bombs. Héctor Cornillot was convicted in the 1990s and pardoned in 2001 by President George W. Bush, at the request of Florida's powerful congressmen.

If the CIA considered their Cuban collaborators as pathological egocentrics, "selfish, egomaniacal, and macho" trapped in "petty infantile rivalries, with a penchant for impulsiveness", the pathological egocentrics considered the CIA as an ineffective and treacherous institution.

—I felt betrayed by President Kennedy and by the CIA—said Orlando Bosch to journalist Blake Fleetwood—. First, they made us dream, then they abandoned us.

—We can remove them from our payrolls—acknowledged a CIA agent— but we cannot take away what we have taught them.

Following the impulsive divorce with several collaborators in the late 1960s, U.S. police records reported two hundred bombs planted and detonated by various exile groups in just a few years. The victims were not communists, but old comrades. Bosch, and some of his rum-drinking friends, managed to eliminate six out of nine comrades.

One of the survivors (at the time, since he would be executed on Christmas 1982 in an exclusive Miami Beach restaurant) was El Mono Morales Navarrete, also Cuban, also a CIA agent and explosives expert. In fact, El Mono would survive two assassination attempts by the comrade Bosch. On one occasion, miraculously, when his car, which he had just gotten into, was completely destroyed by a bomb on a Miami street corner. When the journalists arrived, almost at the same time as the police, El Mono mocked the incident. From the first minute, he knew who had done it.[86] Someone who, two years later, in 1976, had to reluctantly accept his help to escape to Venezuela of Andrés Pérez: Orlando Bosch.

The attacks planned in Miami (and in the second pole of Cuban terrorism, Union City, in New Jersey) targeted both U.S. territory and foreign lands. A source from the Department of Justice cited by the New York Times on July 16, 1978, stated:

—Terrorism is primarily exported from South Florida.

The FBI would confirm it in another way:

—Miami is the capital of terrorism in the United States.

In 1976, prosecutor Jerry Sanford apologized to agent Robert Propper for carrying a weapon.

—You're the first prosecutor I've seen armed—said Propper.

—That's because I'm the only attorney in the Prosecutor's Office working on Cuban terrorism—explained Sanford—. Just in the last two and a half years, a dozen prominent Cuban leaders have been assassinated. The drug-related killings amount to two or three deaths a day. Not infrequently, they're riddled with machine guns. Some Cuban activists have taken over the cocaine trade, and others have rebelled against the CIA and against any other Cuban exiles they consider to be too moderate in their anti-communism. The chaos is such that it's almost impossible to distinguish a politically motivated murder from a mere drug-related score-settling. It's very difficult to solve each of these cases...

—Why?

—The terrorists have strong support from the community—explained Sanford—in addition to a great deal of money that comes from the drug trade and their connections with big business. Mountains of dollars go to their legal defenses or to corrupt the police, and probably some judges too. It's no different from Al Capone's mafia in Chicago. Do you understand now why I carry a gun?

Sanford forgot to mention politicians ranging from district representatives to governors and presidents, like those from the Bush family, some of whom would later receive presidential pardons. All in the name of freedom.

The feds had not only identified the wave of terrorist attacks by Cuban exiles but also their sources of funding, which ranged from donations from big businesses to drug trafficking, especially during the rise of the Somocista counterrevolutionaries in Nicaragua, regrouped under the name Contras, and the renewed support of the CIA and the White House. Investigator T.D. Alleman reported that in 1981, federal police estimated that 70 percent of all the cocaine entering the United States came through Miami.

—Miami's morgue—reported Alleman—is so full of drug-related corpses that the city has to store bodies in refrigerated trucks.[87]

In the 1960s, armed groups had sprouted like mushrooms in that tropical corner of the United States: some of the most well-known were the Cuban Nationalist Movement, the Secret Cuban Government, the Cuban National Liberation Front, Cuban Power, El Alacrán, Cuban Scorpion, Youth of the Star, Cuban Action, Omega 7, and the Pedro Luis Boitel Command. During the 1960s, these organizations carried out 731 attacks on the island and 156 in the United States, in addition to death threats, beatings, vandalism, extortion, and targeted assassinations.

Some exiles, like the former senator of Fulgencio Batista and director of the newspaper Libertad in Santiago, Cuba, Rolando Masferrer Rojas, also disappointed with the inefficiency of the CIA in their costly attempt to overthrow Fidel Castro, began stockpiling weapons in Haiti, to create a base for the invasion of Cuba. As a businessman, he managed to convince several organizations, including CBS, to invest in this new venture to overthrow another Caribbean dictator in the name of freedom.[88] This time, a dictator they hadn't installed themselves.

Copacabana. Lola, Death, and Rum in Havana

THE POWERFUL BUSINESSMAN, Rolando Masferrer, was executed in Miami in 1975 with sticks of dynamite, likely placed by an expert, Guillermo Novo. He had a romantic past that was enough to capture the media's attention. A fervent anti-communist, in his youth, he had been a socialist. In the 1930s, he had fought in Spain in defense of the Second Republic, alongside the American communists of the Lincoln Brigade, but something broke or simply matured upon his return to Cuba. By the late 1940s, he had shifted from revolutionary socialism to become part of the Havana mafia. There, he was the leader of the mafia group Los Tigres, which, in Miami, would later make him known and recognized as El Tigre.

Like other figures of the exile, such as Orlando Bosch, Masferrer participated in arms trafficking and sabotage flights targeting sugar plantations and energy centers in Cuba, organized by the CIA. One of the most successful operations took place on March 4, 1960, when Masferrer and other exiles managed to blow up the French vessel La Coubre in the port of Havana. The attack claimed 101 lives and left several hundred seriously injured. The explosion and sinking were reminiscent of the explosion that sank the Maine in the same place in 1898, but without the same consequences. La Coubre was carrying weapons and ammunition for the defense of an imminent invasion of the island. The international press attributed the explosion to an accident, despite witnesses at the time insisting on identifying Rolando Masferrer as the man who handed over two thousand dollars to sailor Alain Mouriat in the port of Belgium. By pure coincidence, the attack followed the classic pattern of planned attacks to this day: an explosion followed by a second, more deadly explosion fifteen minutes later, when more people gather at the scene of the disaster to help the victims or out of sheer curiosity.

Purely by coincidence, a few months earlier, the CIA had received information from Masferrer about this arms shipment to Cuba with the purpose of resisting their invasion plan at the Bay of Pigs, which was then underway.[89] Shortly before, the CIA agent and vice president of Johnson and Johnson, Colonel Joseph Caldwell (J.C.) King, had met with Masferrer in Miami. When the Cuban Revolution had not yet reached its first year, according to a classified document on December 11, 1959, Colonel J.C. King, then head of the CIA's Western Hemisphere Division and CEO of the pharmaceutical company created by the CIA, Amazon Natural Drug Company (a participant in the MK-Ultra project to control minds through the use of drugs), reported the need to assassinate Fidel Castro.

—No other revolutionary leader is as attractive and hypnotic to the masses. *He must be eliminated.*[90]

The day after the attack on La Coubre, Fidel Castro denounced the U.S. government as the main instigator of the tragedy, closing his speech with the slogan "Patria o Muerte," which would become the motto of the island's revolutionaries. Also, the image captured by photographer Alberto Korda of El Che Guevara attending the victims' funeral would multiply across generations in various corners of the world, to the displeasure of many others. As is often the case with the CIA's masterpieces, no one was ever convicted for this terrorist attack.

The attempts to assassinate Fidel Castro became a historical obsession and a multi-million-dollar business. They were initiated by the mafias of Johnny Roselli and Santo Trafficante, then continued by the CIA and by the ex-members of the battalion that failed at the Bay of Pigs. Years later, J.C. King would provide Miami groups with

$50,000 of the time and technical support, as needed, to whoever managed to kill the monster of the Caribbean.[91]

To silence critics of the previous dictatorship, the dictatorship of freedom of Fulgencio Batista, Masferrer founded Los Tigres, a paramilitary group that was never defined as such. When the members of the Club Copacabana of Havana lost their privileges in 1959, he fled to Miami on his yacht Ola Kun I with over ten million dollars, according to Cuban authorities. Although this figure has been disputed, since customs in Miami reported no money entering the country, what is clear is that Masferrer took with him enough to avoid starting from scratch in the Land of Freedom and unbreakable connections with other disinherited individuals, like the Havana mafia boss Santo Trafficante Jr., and an infinite hatred for the Revolution of the mob that hates freedom. In Florida, he raised funds for the Cuban Cause by extorting resentful Cubans.

Despite everything, he was not the most radical member of the Cuban exile in Miami, and it cost him his life. As noted earlier, in 1975, he was assassinated by his own anti-Castro comrades with a car bomb, in retaliation for his own attempt to blow up a package of dynamite at the yacht factory of Ramón Donestévez. Donestévez, editor of a Miami Spanish-language newspaper like Masferrer, would also be executed by the same mafia a few months later, in April 1976, not with dynamite but with a shot behind his right ear, as a promotional symbol for one of the many extortion and execution groups in Miami.[92]

WELL, THEN LET THE DOGS LOOSE

WHILE IT IS TRUE THAT THE CIA HAD a policy of letting their mad dogs out of the house to bite at will, a kind of strategic laissez-faire, it did not tolerate them planning attacks without reporting them to Headquarters in Virginia. This will be one of the biggest issues for

Luis Posada Carriles. For the mad dogs that ran out desperately looking for something to bite, it was a matter of reputation. Groups like Omega 7 didn't stop killing members of the Hispanic community in the style of Al Capone or the Cuban mafia from the Batista era; they also terrorized several states and countries with bombings against embassies, consulates, and any kind of private company suspected of doing business with Cuba.

Not just businesses. A simple word too much or too little in a newspaper could amount to a death sentence. The unexpected divorce with the CIA in the early 1970s did not change their love for dynamite, C4, or summary executions, but it did change several strategies—and drastically. It was at that precise moment that, for many members of the Cuban exile, there was no other option but to resort to donations from big businesses, extortion of small shops, drug trafficking, and the anti-communist dictatorships of the south, like Pinochet's in Chile.

The CIA's and the Cuban exile's history with drug trafficking has multiple precedents. Although the files with their records grew thicker in the offices of the state police, the FBI, and the CIA itself, their collaborators were never, or almost never, linked to the agency and never, or almost never, ended up in jail. Orlando García Vásquez, another of those implicated in the murder of Orlando Letelier, was a known figure in these secret reports. Among the few published photos of him, one stands out where he is seen wearing dark glasses next to Venezuelan President Andrés Pérez, with a delegation, descending an escalator, a symbol of the oil-rich country's prosperity during the 1970s.[93] At the time, García was a security agent and friend of the group of Cubans in Miami who, since the 1960s, had led the DISIP, Venezuela's secret police, whose third leader had been, thanks to the CIA, Luis Posada Carriles. García also improved his income through the illegal sale of weapons to the Venezuelan army, thanks to the friendship of one of his lovers with the president of the Margold Corporation, whose president was a lover of

President Pérez. In 1991, he was accused of being a shareholder of the same company that benefited from the arms sale.

—Orlando didn't sell us a single knife, not even a blade—defended Andrés Pérez to the press.

Indeed, it wasn't knives or blades but grenades. A few days later, Orlando García resigned as President Pérez's security guard and disappeared from the map.

An update from the Agency's files, dated February 25, 1976, described García as *"a political mafioso, a murderer, a fraudster, a pathological liar, and ruthless... García has always been on the side of the powerful and has earned the trust of many presidents in the Caribbean."*[94] Long before the luxuries and power he enjoyed for a good time in Caracas, García had been a member of the Revolutionary Insurrectional Union and had participated in student protests with Fidel Castro at the University of Havana. In 1952, he fled to Miami over a murder he was allegedly involved in but for which he was never prosecuted. This was quite common during the heroic sixties for the Cuban upper class, long before Fidel Castro opened the island's prisons in 1980, allowing thousands of common criminals and poorer individuals to be received in Miami as refugees, indistinguishable from genuine dissidents.

In Havana, García met the exiled future president of Venezuela, Rómulo Betancourt. Shortly after the triumph of the Cuban Revolution, like Orlando Bosch and many others, García Vásquez did not feel adequately appreciated. He left for Costa Rica, where he managed to become a guard for President José Figueres, who introduced him to another exiled Venezuelan leftist, future minister under Betancourt and future president, Carlos Andrés Pérez. García and Pérez became close friends until both fell from grace in the early nineties.

This brief experience of self-imposed exile in Miami and Costa Rica enabled Orlando García to establish the contacts and trust that would land him in the secret police of Caracas, once Betancourt was elected president in 1958.[95] At the time, as a result of the fall of another Washington-backed dictatorship, that of Marcos Pérez Jiménez, the region was experiencing a surge of moderate leftism. This new wave was not looked down upon by the CIA; it was a way to curb a wave of nationalist revolutions against the major corporations of the North, and being democratic, they were easy to influence and sabotage when the time came, as indeed happened in all cases. The new moderate left democracies like Figueres' Costa Rica or Betancourt's Venezuela came into conflict with some of their mad dogs, such as the dictator Rafael Trujillo in the Dominican Republic, who felt threatened, wary of their new neighbors, and jealous of Washington's unconditional love.

worked later became an office of various services of the Venezuelan secret police, eventually leading to the creation of the intelligence service DISIP, whose head was the Cuban Rafael Rivas Vásquez and one of its most feared policemen was also the Cuban Luis Posada Carriles. DISIP was founded in 1968 by President Rafael Caldera, and two years later, one of its greatest pretexts emerged, the leftist armed group Bandera Roja. Although composed of guerrillas convinced of their Marxist ideas, Bandera Roja would accumulate a history full of suspicions. It would oppose the government of Hugo Chávez and, later, support the CIA-backed candidate, the self-proclaimed president of Venezuela, Juan Guaidó.

Shortly after its foundation, El Mono Ricardo Morales would join DISIP and, in a meteoric and inexplicable rise for the rest of the Venezuelan aspirants, would reach high positions, very close to the president. The Cuban exile and Chile's DINA would come to know El Mono as a mysterious character, admired, feared, and hated by both friends and foes. He was an agent of Cuba's intelligence service, the DGI, a CIA bomber in Congo, a mercenary, a traitor, and later an informant for the CIA and FBI, someone harder to capture than Al Capone.

Years later, a CIA memorandum recorded that on September 6, 1973, the DEA had requested information about one of its collaborators, Orlando García Vásquez, and four other Cubans, due to their involvement in drug trafficking from Venezuela. García was confirmed to be a close friend of the region's major drug lords. The connection between the DEA, Washington's anti-drug trafficking department, and drug trafficking itself is historical for many reasons. It's not just about the money but also their justifications. In 2024, it would be revealed that the DEA had attempted to frame the government of Hugo Chávez and later Nicolás Maduro in Venezuela to make them appear as collaborators of the drug trafficking mafia.[96]

At the time, another Orlando, Bosch, was reaching out to contact the intelligence services of Chile first, and then Venezuela. Bosch would end up working for both organizations, the DINA and the Disip, thanks to favors from other Cuban exiles, some of whom, like El Mono Ricardo Morales and his closest friend, Luis Posada Carriles, would use and betray him as the moment required.

Cuban Coffee. A Very Dynamic Culture.

DURING THE 1970S, TERRORIST ATTACKS for freedom, most planned in Florida and New Jersey, continued with even greater virulence. The same groups of Cuban exiles based in Miami carried out 16 attacks in Cuba and 279 in the United States. Between 1974 and 1976 alone, Washington acknowledged 113 attacks in the country and 202 in 23 other countries. In Miami, in just two years, they managed to detonate 200 bombs, some of them at the Office of the Prosecutor, the FBI offices, and the Police Department. Five Cuban exiles were killed by their own comrades. One of the well-known exile leaders and FBI informants, El Mono Ricardo Morales, did not show up on the day of the trial against one of the suspects.

In the 1980s and 1990s, the bombings did not stop with the entry into politics of the major businessmen who supported them, like Jorge Mas Canosa. In 1989 alone, 18 bombings were recorded.

Almost all of them went unpunished. Almost all of their perpetrators were forgotten by the press, except for a few, like Luis Posada Carriles, Orlando Bosch, and El Mono Morales.

According to the U.S. Attorney General, Dick Thornburgh, Bosch was *"a terrorist who never repented."* For Deputy Attorney General Joe Whitley, he was always *"a threat to National Security."* None of which prevented him and other terrorists like Posada Carriles from retiring and living protected in Miami. By then, a hundred murderers and genocidaires from those horrible southern countries were living freely in Florida as if they were respectable businessmen in suits and ties. Generals Carlos Eugenio Vides Casanova and José Guillermo García, responsible for rapes and massacres under the proxy dictatorship in El Salvador, will be just three of the most well-known cases in the Sunshine State—Florida.

—The Miami community," summarized an FBI agent, "doesn't want to cooperate with the police to solve these attacks." With their proudly complicit silence, they feel they are supporting the cause of the Cuban exile every time they violate the laws of the United States.

—We are not obligated to obey the laws of any country that steals our right to fight for freedom—explained Ignacio Novo.[97]

—One of the reasons why Miami became a banana republic—said Alberto Millán— is because people like Janet Reno made sure to create the conditions under which prosecutors never investigate anything. When they find a mountain of evidence, they simply decide not to charge anyone.[98]

The Operation Court Broom investigation will conclude, in April 1996, that the judges of Florida, particularly those in the southern part of the peninsula, were especially vulnerable to corruption due to the fact that they were elected by vote. Fearful of a deeper investigation, some judges resigned, and others pleaded guilty to accepting bribes and extortion.

By 1974, these organized groups in Miami were responsible for 45 percent of all terrorist attacks on the planet. According to federal police, just between 1973 and 1976, there were more than a hundred politically motivated attacks in Miami, all carried out by Cuban exile groups.⁹⁹

—The good thing about car bombs—admitted Guillermo Novo himself— is that you don't need to be on location to carry it out. You plan everything, and the clock takes care of the rest.

By the 90s, the Cuban political lobby had largely replaced their paramilitary organizations in Florida and New Jersey. The mafia and illegal paramilitarism did not disappear, but the votes of their representatives and senators in Congress proved to be more effective than a hundred bombs on the Atlantic Coast or throughout the Caribbean. None of these powerful lobbies in Washington succeeded in overthrowing the communist regime of Fidel Castro, but at least they ensured the impoverishment of Cubans on the island, serving as a cautionary example of the failure of socialism, essential to discredit any internal critic or dissident.

At the Versailles restaurant of Felipe Valls, located on Calle Ocho in Miami, everyone gathered, from terrorists like Orlando Bosch and Posada Carriles to presidents like Ronald Reagan, Bush Sr., Bush Jr., Bush's brother, Bill Clinton, Donald Trump and his daughter Ivanka; renowned artists like Beyoncé and rappers Jay-Z and Pitbull, and world-famous athletes like Lionel Messi and Luis Suárez, all courted by the home club of Mas Canosa, Inter Miami.

In 2021, NBC quoted one of the founder's granddaughters, Nicole Valls:

—Anyone running a political campaign always comes to Versailles and takes the same photo at the little window, sipping their Cuban coffee.

According to NBC, *"for any politician on the campaign trail, making a stop at Versailles is essential. The tradition began with Democrat Bob Graham in 1977. As a gubernatorial candidate, he took on different jobs for a day. One was as a waiter's assistant, serving food at Versailles. Graham won. Versailles is a restaurant that has shaped the growth and history of the vibrant Cuban-American community in Miami."*¹⁰⁰

Vibrant, without a doubt. Aside from Bosch and Posada Carriles, one of the house's friends was the powerful businessman Jorge Mas Canosa, whose money backed various freedom fighters.

—Mas Canosa—said Gaeton Fonzi, investigator for the House Select Committee on Assassinations— is a creation of the CIA. He became a master in the manipulation of psychological warfare.[101]

A powerful businessman due to his unsuspected connections, he was the czar of Latino media in Florida, founder of the Cuban American National Foundation lobby and the construction company MasTec. Thanks to a fortune estimated in billions of dollars, the Mas family would buy the pink Inter Miami team in 2021 and, in 2023, the best player in the world, Lionel Messi.

Later, Fonzi would summarize his experience in the 1990s:

—There are two Cubas. One is the real Cuba and the other is the Cuba that Mas Canosa invented in the minds of the exiles, convincing them that there is a volatile dissident community in Cuba ready to overthrow the government. A myth that he has upheld for many years.[102]

Although in Miami a fairly uniform ideology and narrative consolidated, the beneficiaries were and will continue to be a few. According to some moderate Cuban exiles, the only beneficiary of President Bill Clinton's new policy was Mas Canosa. His economic and political empire grew like a supernova. The faith and hopes of the rest, who survived on an unstable salary, never disappeared. With a few exceptions, U.S. politicians and diplomats also shared the same Miami exile narrative, but they were somewhat more realistic.

—The only way someone like Mas Canosa could come to power in Cuba—said the former chief of the U.S. Interests Section in Havana, Wayne Smith— is a total collapse of the country, a civil war leading to intervention...

Plans, attempts, and resources were not lacking. Prayers either, but frustration led more than one to suspect that even God was a communist.

Jorge Mas Canosa managed to get Luis Posada Carriles to escape from the Caracas prison where he was held for participating in the terrorist attack that brought down Cubana Flight 455 with 73 people on board, most of them young athletes.

UNION CITY, THE MIAMI OF THE COLD

THE SECOND CAPITAL OF THE CUBAN paramilitary exile is in Union City, New Jersey, a few minutes from Manhattan. The main avenue of the Little Havana of the Hudson is Bergenline. If someone doesn't know Spanish, they get lost walking there, or don't know which local business they're entering. In 1960, almost no Cubans lived there, but fifteen years later they were the majority of the population.

Half a block from Bergenline Avenue, Omega-7 and the Cuban Nationalist Movement had their headquarters. It was a two-story building, with the windows painted black, either to disguise or to impress. The dominant slogan that pedestrians could read on one of the boarded-up windows was "Cuba Above All," which many recalled the Nazi anthem and Hitler's most recognized phrase, Deutschland über alles, "Germany Above All," "Germany First." Not in a few Miami pubs, the idea will be even more explicit "Cuba über alles."[103]

—The Nazis hijacked that phrase from the German anthem—said Hunter— until it became politically incorrect.

—Correct. In the 19th century, the anthem aimed to consolidate the National State over regional warlords. That was the great existential conflict of the time. Something very similar to the past feudal system, where feudal lords dominated their regions, and neither the king nor the State had any influence. "Germany above all" meant "the country above the regions, above the states." The Nazis turned it into "the country above other countries." A case where language

and its interpretations define reality, much like in the Bible or the Quran. The same thing happened here in the United States, with the Pledge of Allegiance. What does it say? I don't remember it by heart.
"I pledge allegiance to the flag of..."

"I pledge allegiance to the flag of the United States of America and to the Republic for which it stands, one Nation under God, indivisible, with liberty and justice for all."

—In the late 19th century, the socialist Francis Bellamy wrote those lines to overcome the divisive scars of the Civil War. Later, the anti-communist paranoia of Senator McCarthy added in 1954 the phrase "One nation under God" and the older, even lamer idea of a country chosen by the Creator of the Universe, with a divine right to rain bombs at will on any undemocratic country, that is, inconvenient, too independent.

—Lame idea—clarified Hunter— but embraced by millions, in the blink of an eye, by aspirants to paradise.

—Yes, that thing you apparently earn if you pray the right way. That place, according to the McCarthyites and the Jimmy Swaggarts, full of deranged criminals. Just thinking about it gives me a Hatuey panic.

—Imagine you die—said Hunter— you arrive in Heaven and are greeted by the prosperity preacher, Kenneth Copeland... But let's move on to that page.

Omega-7 and the MLC collected their own taxes from businesses in the district, a practice well-known not only to Al Capone's mafia, but also to the feared Italian and Jewish mafias in Batista's, whose most famous names were Santo Trafficante and Meyer Lansky. Businesses that refused to pay would end up with shattered storefronts as a warning. Thanks to this logistics, methods, and media preaching, the annual collection amounted to $100,000, but it only covered some operational costs. The rest came from some CIA salaries, donations from large companies, drug trafficking through Venezuela, and even the local mayors' offices, according to FBI reports.

At the time, Julia Valdivia was the assistant to the mayor of Union City, but everyone knew her as The Lady Mayor because of her mysterious influence over the mayor. According to NSA agent Winslow Peck, one of the smaller groups based in Miami, Cuban Action, had more capitalist methods. In Little Havana, they used to sell bonds and stocks. Each bond cost between ten and a thousand dollars, which could be sold at a much higher price once Fidel Castro was assassinated. With these funds, Cuban Action had managed to detonate several bombs at different Cuban embassies and consulates. The biggest problem, noted Winslow Peck by the end of 1976, was the assassinations and score-settling among the gusanos for reasons ranging from financial disagreements to differences in interpretation on how to kill Fidel Castro. From Miami to New York, the anti-Castro groups were numerous, some of which identified themselves as Young Star, F14, Zero, The Condor, Secret Government of Cuba, Jure, Gin, April 17, Brigade 2506 and Omega 7, almost all composed of veterans from the failed Bay of Pigs invasion or directly organized by the CIA, such as the Mambises Command. In the words of agent Perry Fellwock, "all the worm-terrorist groups were infiltrated or used by the CIA for their Operation Mongoose, one of the largest terrorist campaigns against Cuba organized by Washington after the defeat in the Bay of Pigs." The CIA extended this operation to the University of Miami, creating the Zenith Technical Enterprises department, with an annual budget of 50 million dollars at the time. The operations of this base, composed of six thousand Cuban exiles, despite the license to bomb indiscriminately any suspect vill-age, also failed in Congo and Angola. By 1964, the CIA was paying El Mono Morales 270 dollars a month while he resided in Miami and 370 dollars when he was in Congo, collaborating with the repression of Mobutu Sese Seko, until in 1965 he became a dictator and ally of the Free World.[104]

But a time came of accumulated failures and too much independence on the part of these groups, mercenaries for freedom. According to the CIA, the Cuban exiles failed because they lacked guts.

According to the Cubans of Miami, the failure was due to a commitment that wasn't total, like that of a good marriage.

By the end of the 60s, the Cubans started to act like the English pirates and the American filibusters, like William Walker, who operated outside the law but in favor of the English Crown and the democratic government of Washington. They weren't recognized or condemned. They were left to act according to the convenience of the moment, and without anyone taking responsibility.

When the income from the CIA through various channels started drying up due to tactical disagreements, the Freedom Fighters turned to the Moon Sect. Since then, the South Korean Reverend Sun Myung Moon of the Unification Church, known for his Divine Principle that he applied to large donations for far-right politicians worldwide. According to Moon, this mission was given to him by Jesus one day in 1936 when he appeared to him on a mountain in Korea and asked him to continue the work that God's Son couldn't finish due to his crucifixion. None of the Cubans in the MLC or Omega-7 believed a single word of this story, but the donations were a testament to their faith in the Cuban cause.

At the same time, Virgilio Paz and José Suárez supplemented the income through deal-ings with Colombian drug cartels.

—Virgilio Paz likes Chivas Regal and fine clothes— declared Cuban Silvia Odio be-fore the Warren Commission, who also accused Cuban exiles of participating in a meeting at her Dallas home with Lee Oswald, the assassin of President Kenn-edy.

Others, like Felipe Rivero, were respon-sible for opening doors with his preferred regime and his most dedicated ally, Augusto Pinoc-het's regime in Chile. One of his greatest achievements was establishing the connection between the Miami groups and the DINA in Santiago through Townley, as was the case with Virgilio Paz and Dionisio Suárez (alias "Pool of Blood"), who were responsible for detonating the bomb that killed Orlando Letelier and Ronni Moffitt in Washington.

On weekends, they would have meetings and take photos dressed as combatants or award themselves medals and military promotions. The brothers Ignacio and Guillermo Novo Sampol, José Cueto, El Mono José Luis Gómez, José Papiro González, Bilito Sampol, Felipe Martínez, Jorge Domínguez, Jorge Romeu, and José Ramon Egues were often present. On some occasions, intergroup summits were organized with the flags of Cuba and the United States, with a sign that read: "Welcome Home, Cuban Freedom Fighters" ("Bienvenidos a casa, cubanos luchadores por la libertad").

Some members, like the Novo brothers, had emigrated in 1952 during Batista's dictatorship, but they were considered Castro exiles. Unlike other exiled militants, the Novos never worked for the CIA or participated in the failed Bay of Pigs invasion.[105] In 1976, the older brother, Guillermo, quietly began to challenge Orlando Bosch for leadership in terrorist activities.

Lourdes Casal, a young Cuban woman who worked for the CIA and later became a professor at Rutgers University, then a classmate of one of the MNC members, said:

—They're strange people. They award themselves medals and military distinctions every time someone hits another person over the head with a stick in a bar.[106]

Between 1975 and 1983 alone, the group Omega 7 set off a series of bombs from New York to Miami. In February 1975, they managed to detonate a bomb at the Venezuelan consulate in New York. According to the FBI, one of their key members and a former member of Brigade 2506 who participated in the Bay of Pigs fiasco, was Eduardo Arocena. On the night of October 27, 1978, another bomb exploded at the Cuban Embassy at the United Nations, a déjà vu of another bomb that had gone off in the same place two years earlier. Not far from there, another bomb exploded at Avery Fisher Hall, where a Cuban ballet troupe was performing. The attacks were claimed by Omega 7.

For a time, Puerto Rican nationalists also resorted to bombing innocent people as a way to promote their political cause, but the scale never reached the national and international extent of Cuban terrorism in the United States.

—The best communist is a dead communist—Arocena told the press.

A common saying that, in the case of Cuban exile paramilitarism, didn't even reflect reality. Very few of those assassinated by these groups were communists. Almost all were anti-communists, too moderate, or members of other groups with the same goal, recalling the tradition of the Mafia and drug cartels.

This was the case, for example, of Eulalio José Negrín, a Cuban exile who agreed to reestablish diplomatic relations with the island so that Cuban exiles could visit their families. After his office was destroyed by a bomb, he was shot on 10th Street in Union City, New Jersey, by Omega 7, in front of his 12-year-old son, Richard.

Arocena and Omega 7 were responsible for other bombings and assassinations, including multiple bombs at businesses owned by Cubans considered neutral or without a clear political stance, as well as diplomatic buildings. On September 11, 1980, they assassinated the Cuban consular attaché in New York, Félix García Rodríguez, with a shot to the back of the head while he was walking down the street at six in the evening. The killer, Pedro Remón, disappeared from the scene before anyone could react in horror. On September 11 of the following year, 1981, Arocena planted bombs in the Mexican consulates in Manhattan and Miami.

Two decades later, Arocena would be arrested in Panama, along with other Cuban terrorists with notorious histories, such as Guillermo Novo Sampol, Gaspar Jiménez, and Luis Posada Carriles. In this case, they were linked to another international terrorist attack. Naturally, they were all pardoned by the country's president, Mireya Moscoso, in 2004.

Months before eliminating Negrín, Omega 7 had killed Carlos Munos in Puerto Rico, another member of the Committee of 75, established by the government of Jimmy Carter to negotiate the release of prisoners in Cuba and the opening of travel. The president of this committee, Bernardo Benes Baikowitz, had to wear a bulletproof vest for a long time, as he was branded a traitor by the terrorist group Alpha 66, founded by CIA agent Antonio Veciana, despite having secured the release of thousands of prisoners in Cuba.

"We will continue with these executions," an anonymous caller told the FBI offices, "until we have eliminated all the traitors living in this country."

Years later, Arocena was arrested by the police before he could assassinate the Cuban ambassador Raúl Roa Kouri on March 25, 1980. He was accused of detonating thirty bombs, carrying out several executions, and being one of the main leaders of the terrorist group Omega 7, under the alias Omar. In his defense, Arocena denied all the information gathered by the police and the FBI. He denied knowing what Omega 7 was and denied his involvement in any violent acts against innocents—a strategy from the CIA's yellow manuals, although by then they were more enemies than bosses or allies.

The Miami press labeled him a "Cuban patriot." Several politicians interceded for him when he was tried and convicted, such as the mayor of Miami, Xavier Suárez:

—For me, Arocena is not a terrorist. He is a *freedom fighter*.

Biological Weapons

ON FEBRUARY 19, HENRY KISSINGER traveled to Brazil to sign a cooperation agreement with another friendly dictator, General Ernesto Geisel. In Brasília, he had to endure an entire soccer match, of which he did not even understand the offside rule. At the same time in Colombia, the government declared a state of emergency due to student protests against the imminent visit of the Secretary of State.

The *New York Times* on Sunday the 22nd, on its front page, reported: *"The agreement provides a strong boost to Brazil's aspirations* to be recognized as an emerging world power."[107]

The same article reproduced the statements of the Secretary of State:

—We have expressed several times—Kissinger had said—our opinions on the issue of human rights. The United States supports respect for the democratic governments of each country... I would like to make it clear that I do not want to turn our policy for the hemisphere into an obsession with a small Caribbean country... Our conversations in Brazil have focused exclusively on market issues.

It wasn't the first nor the last time that Mr. Kissinger lied to the press shamelessly. It wasn't the first nor the last time that the press collaborated in the attempt. One of his masterpieces was appearing on television on September 12, 1973, claiming and confirming that his government had nothing to do with the coup d'état in Chile. Despite having been a survivor of Nazi barbarism, he was, above all, a fervent enemy of the Soviets, the only enemies of Nazism when all of the West loved Hitler's ideas.

In 1976, despite the scandals that forced Nixon to resign and the discoveries of the Church Commission about the systematic manipulation of the press and the multiple plans of covert assassinations, the CIA and its unrecognized branches remained in charge. The Brazilian dictatorship, with ten more years of experience than the Chilean one, had already worked on biological weapons at the Butantan laboratory of the University of São Paulo. From this laboratory, Michael Townley received information on the production and effects of nerve toxins that were used to eliminate dissenters without leaving traces. The Pinochet government received shipments of botulinum neurotoxin, a toxin derived from the clostridium botulinum bacteria, with an effect much more potent than cyanide. The dissidents on whom this new discovery was tested suffered poisoning and muscular paralysis. The painful death usually occurred due to paralysis of the lungs, rather than the suffocation from poisoning. The effectiveness of this new marvel was received with enthusiasm.

At that time, from the Southern Cone to Europe, the deaths of prisoners and dissidents by poisoning of wines, pastries, and medications in hospitals became common. Sarin gas was also used. This gas had been discovered by the Nazi government of Germany and one of its greatest virtues was the absence of traces after its application. After World War II, not only a thousand Nazi engineers were hired by NASA, but many more were channeled by the CIA to support friendly dictatorships around the world, as was the well-known case of Klaus Barbie in Bolivia. All were hired for their knowledge and their fanatical anti-communism. Not for their superior race. The same CIA invested decades and mountains of dollars developing their own experiments with drugs and poisons. One of their experiments consisted of inoculating syphilis and gonorrhea to a thousand poor people in Guatemala. One of their projects was MK-Ultra, to find the truth drug, which started the first focus of LSD and other drug addiction in the United States. All for a good cause.

After several of these state-planned assassination projects were exposed by the Church Commission of the U.S. Senate in 1975, the agency continued its tradition of deciding who deserves to live and who does not, as if nothing had happened. By the end of the decade, biological weapons had multiplied their offerings. One of their targets was, as it could not be otherwise, the cursed and indomitable island of the Caribbean. Orlando Bosch and other recognized historical heroes of Miami participated in the napalm and phosphorus bombings of the mills and sugar fields of Cuba, which ruined several harvests. However, this brutal sabotage also did not yield the expected results, so they resorted to other, more devastating means.

In 1980, the Cuban Eduardo Arocena was accused, among other things, of introducing into Cuba the epidemic of hemorrhagic dengue, which severely sickened more than 300 thousand people. In 1984, before a federal jury in the United States, Arocena admitted to participating in this massive biological attack, planned and executed by his Miami.

—We brought to Cuba some germs to use them against the Soviets and the Cuban economy—said Arocena—. It was not my intention to harm any innocent Cuban...[108]

Shortly before, the State Department had dismissed this accusation as absurd, although it was nothing new—neither the sabotage nor the denial of any responsibility for the sabotage. The CIA, an agency which almost never informs other branches of the state about its activities and only respects laws when they do not stand in its way, had done it long before. None of its agents has ever been brought before a court for their crimes. Nor will they be, for generations to come. Their crimes, when partially known, are only revealed decades later, when all those involved are dead and there is no longer any need to redact their names when some unpatriotic individual requests official declassification under the Freedom of Information Act.

According to the *Washington Post* in 1979, the use of biological weapons developed by the CIA to subdue other troublesome countries, such as Vietnam, was focused on the destruction of Cuban agriculture with agents such as the thrips palmi, the deadly Newcastle virus against chickens, first, and African swine fever later, in 1971, which cost half a million dead pigs on the island.[109]

By pure coincidence (or not?), the catastrophe in Cuba coincided with African swine fever on the nearest island. There is no study that links these two events, so we could classify this observation as mere speculation. However, around the same time, the Dominican Republic suffered a devastating plague that wiped out its pigs. To prevent the plague from spreading to the US, Washington came up with a brilliant idea: kill and bury one million black pigs in Haiti. The big business of preventive extermination of Haiti's black pigs and their replacement with the delicate white pigs from Iowa generated substantial income for some northern companies, but caused another economic crisis in Hispaniola.[110] Haiti's poorest peasants received no compensation for killing their black pigs. The OAS and Washington invested the promised 23 million dollars, but only seven million reached the affected individuals, who never knew that, in reality, they had lost 600 million dollars thanks to the great idea of the country that knows how things are done. According to the University of Minnesota, if the disease had reached the American market, the country could have lost up to five billion dollars. The country or the corporations. Either way, Haiti's black pigs were replaced with white pigs from Iowa. For centuries, black pigs had adapted to the island's conditions, while the replacement plan by Washington's experts required that the new Iowa pigs be cared for better than the farmers could care for their own children. The Iowa's pigs, whiter and fatter than the traditional black pigs, could only drink filtered water. The gossips of that country claimed that they needed air conditioning to survive the island's heat.

In Cuba, the catastrophe occurred two years after Nixon announced that the United States would abandon the development and use of biological weapons. In all cases, the CIA's biological attacks against Cuba were carried out by Cubans, sometimes stationed in Panama and introduced to Cuba from the Guantanamo base.[111] When the CIA was questioned by Congress, it blamed the outbreak first on Europe and later on Africa. The contradictory versions provided by the CIA to the congressional committee were refuted by scientists of the time, since, among other reasons, the viruses in question were not consistent with the very high mortality rate caused.

Finally, an intelligence agent (responsible for delivering the virus to the Cubans) leaked the information to journalists Drew Fetherston and John Cummings of The Washington Post. The information confirmed that these pathogens had been introduced to Cuba by Cuban exiles from Miami.

Due to the blockade, the White House denied Cuba a supply of the larvicide temephos, which would have reduced the catastrophe of the dengue sabotage. As a usual detail that almost no one cares about, it is necessary to recall that, thanks to this brilliant idea, 158 people died, mostly children, and hundreds of thousands more were severely affected by the epidemic. Two decades later, on May 7, 2002, U.S. Deputy Secretary of State under George W. Bush, John Bolton, would accuse Cuba of developing biological weapons.

The leader of Omega 7, Eduardo Arocena (known as Omar), would be one of the few involved in multiple terrorist acts to end up in a U.S. prison. The FBI accused him of at least two murders and the detonation of thirty bombs along the East Coast. Miami journalists, like Ángel Cuadra of Diario de las Américas, would describe him as "a man convicted for reasons related to the long-standing struggle of the anti-Castro Cubans for the freedom of Cuba, their homeland. Arocena is perhaps the longest-held political prisoner in the world."[112] That is, a political prisoner. After a long signature campaign in his favor, he would be released in 2021. In Miami, he would be welcomed as a hero.

BOMBS AND VOTES

THE 2506 BRIGADE AND OTHER GROUPS managed to ensure that cinemas and theaters did not show films or stage plays that, in one way or another, might discuss Cuba without condemning its regime.

I picked up the black notebook (the same one I'm using now to write these words) and jotted down, as a reminder for the next day:

Could anyone imagine that this culture (deeply rooted since its birth, since its founding as a community) might one day stop planning terrorist attacks and dedicate itself to music and rice with beans? To find an answer, it is necessary to study history from the beginning. Especially the sources of funding.

I looked outside. Then at the ceiling. There was a camera there too. Perhaps it was one of those fake cameras that are always present in supermarkets. Maybe it was just a surveillance camera for theft or one of those minor incidents that YouTubers love so much. Maybe it was all that, and the NSA had access to that camera as well. How could I know? Well, part of the secret lies in eternal doubt.

I closed the yellow-paged notebook and tried to take refuge in my thoughts, which probably were still part of my private property. After a moment, I attempted to close the notebook, and, as if unintentionally, I read a much older note, probably written last month:

In the 19th century, the poor drank cheap whiskey in pubs and sang songs against the dirty Mexicans. Many of them ended up enlisting in the war against the immoral neighbor to the south, a war invented and sold by President James Polk as a provocation that, in reality, had been a timid response by the Mexicans to his persistent provocation to go to war and take California. More than a century later, Henry Kissinger observed that Richard Nixon made military decisions late at night when he was drunk. Ronald Reagan would fall asleep while his advisors briefed him on international politics and, when he woke up, he would only reach for the jar of colorful jellybeans always waiting for him on his Oval Office desk. Another president may be abstinent, but the story will be the same.

BOB MARLEY: ANOTHER ISLAND OF DRUG-ADDICTED BLACKS

As the brand-new director of the CIA, and under the orders of Henry Kissinger, George H. Bush directed much of his beginner's enthusiasm toward the campaign to destabilize Jamaica's prime minister, Michael Manley, by far the most popular leader on the island.

From day one, Manley had presented himself as a socialist. He had won the 1972 elections by a wide margin. After four years in government, and taking advantage of his undeniable popularity, he ran for reelection. Almost at the same time, accused of being a populist, the mood on the island shifted as quickly as the weather in the

Caribbean. Violence swept the country like a hurricane, and no one knew why.

Neither the CIA nor Kissinger forgave Manley for his alignment with the Cuban government, supporting the independence of Angola and condemning South Africa's Apartheid regime. The CIA's destabilization operation involved an injection of ten million dollars and the illegal shipment of voluminous arsenals of weapons.

The prime minister survived three assassination attempts planned by the CIA and, to make matters worse, he won the elections that year, in December 1976, but the violence would not end until his rival, the American Edward Seaga, defeated by a historic margin of votes, finally won the 1980 elections.

Despite the sudden and widespread violence on the island, half the population sang *War*, Bob Marley's latest song, based on a pacifist speech given by Ethiopia's leader, Haile Selassie I, at the UN in 1963.

Until there are no
first and second-class citizens of any nation
Until the color of a man's skin
has no more significance than the color of his eyes
There will be wars.

Although Bob Marley had been careful not to take a political stance in his country, he was accused of being a supporter of the socialist minister. On the night of December 3, he survived an assassination attempt at his home on 56 Hope Road, carried out by seven armed men. His wife Rita, still inside their blue Land Rover, was shot in the head. Marley was hit once in the chest and once in the hand. His musicians were also shot, but everyone survived. Bandaged and without their usual strength, Rita, Marley, and his musicians performed at the Smile concert that same Sunday. The concert had been scheduled months earlier, as a call for peace and a response to the rising tide of national violence.

To the dismay of George H. Bush, eighty thousand people filled the National Heroes Park stadium. Not even the CIA's hefty budgets could compete with the chords of reggae. They had to focus on more important islands, on more serious countries. All long before investing fortunes in promoting rappers who would sing about money and the women who kneel for it.

Santiago is not Havana, and Bosch is not El Che

IN FEBRUARY 1976, ORLANDO BOSCH landed in Costa Rica with a fake passport, issued in Santiago on September 25, 1975, under the name Héctor Emilio Ramón Davanzo Cintolesi. His wife was listed as Elinor Matzner.[113] According to the stamps on this passport, Bosch had entered Panama on December 28, 1975, then landed in El Salvador on a flight from Chile, on January 7, 1976. On January 30, he entered Nicaragua from where he traveled to Costa Rica a week later. His plan to assassinate Pascal Allende and the U.S. Secretary of State also failed. His friend Luis Posada Carriles sold the information to the CIA from Caracas, so Bosch ended up being arrested before he could assassinate at least one of his targets. He was detained at the house rented by Orlando Flores, the Miami connection.

Bosch had been sent by the generals of the Chilean navy, who competed in repressive efficiency with the colonels of the DINA. The jealousy of the former over the breakdown of military hierarchy and the resentment of the latter had turned the assassination of one of the men most hated by Pinochet into a race where all protocols of international espionage were broken.

Michael Townley and Major Torres had interrogated Rolando Otero on the outskirts of Santiago and the Cuban had left a very bad impression on them. He was unstable, a charlatan, impulsive, and not at all trustworthy. Despite Townley's negative report (which recommended ignoring Otero), the DINA sent him on the mission to assassinate Pascal Allende in Costa Rica, almost at the same time the navy sent another Cuban from Miami, Orlando Bosch. In the efficiency for killing, true agents are tested. One had to experiment to know in whom to continue investing time and money.

Both Bosch and Otero proved that a failed mission could be much worse than no attempt at all. It also seemed to demonstrate, once again, that any mission entrusted to any paramilitary group of the Cuban exile was a guaranteed failure—apart from new unforeseen enemies, nourished by the same frustration as always, unjustly defined by the powerful CIA agent David Atlee Philips, after yet another failure to assassinate Fidel Castro in Chile: "it's that the Cubans have no balls."[114]

On April 29, 1975, the newspaper *Pueblo* of Costa Rica reported the presence of Orlando Bosch in the country, as well as in the Dominican Republic and Venezuela. On August 2, 1976, a bomb destroyed his offices. This incident was never investigated, as Costa Rica's National Security Office operated with several Cuban exiles and protected the Movimiento Costa Rica Libre, which used to publish its columns in El Nacional.[115]

Now accompanied by his new wife and newborn daughter, Orlando Bosch and Adriana Delgado had met in Santiago, in the house of the military complex where Augusto Pinochet had been protecting the pediatrician since December 4, 1974. Bosch had arrived in Chile on Tuesday, the 3rd (with a fake passport under the name Pedro Antonio Peña, number 85668) to avoid extradition to the United States, due to the explosion of two bombs he acknowledged as his own work in November of that year. He had arrived in Venezuela from the Dutch colony of Curaçao, accompanied by his comrades and enemies, the Cubans Guillermo Novo and Dionisio Suarez. The three had been invited by the deputy director of operations of DISIP, the also Cuban Rafael Rivas.[116] Another Cuban, Virgilio Paz, was also a special guest of Colonel Contreras to continue collaborating on international operations and to reside in Santiago, with all expenses paid whenever needed. One of the biggest conflicts among the new guests was the dismissive or, at the very least, noncommittal treatment given to Rolando Otero, an incident that became public in the Cuban community in Miami as an offense to be repaid, by any means. The other issue, no less important, was the perpetual state of siege imposed by Pinochet's regime, making any form of nightlife impossible.117 Without rum-filled cantinas, without hot prostitutes, and with too much cold, there was no way counterrevolution could thrive. Obviously, Santiago was not Batista's Havana. Much less the Miami of Mas Canosa.

According to the NSA agent, Perry Fellwock, shortly after Bosch was arrested in Caracas for the two bombs, but the FBI did not proceed with his extradition request due to pressure from the State Department. The Cuban lobby in Venezuela and Rivas's express dealings had secured his release and sent him to Chile.

—How did you end up in chilly Chile, Doctor?—his San Juan contact asked him at the hotel bar.

—It's a very long story— Bosch replied, looking at the bartender through the bottom of his glass. His glasses were almost as thick as the glass holding the rum, and his sight somewhat better than a mole's. Without rum, the mysterious Cuban mixed fiction and memories. Luckily, the police and intelligence services of several countries, especially the CIA and the FBI, kept much clearer records.

In Chile, Bosch was a protégé of Pinochet and the DINA, but neither was generous with money. It wasn't due to any scarcity in the fight against communism, nor was it a cultural trait of the Southern country. It was pure strategy, the result of cold academic studies. Nothing is as productive as need, and Bosch never had enough money. In the same way that El Mono Morales and others supplemented their income with drug trafficking, Bosch was known in the Miami exile community for his requests for donations in exchange for promises of heroic and historic victories.

In a letter addressed to Dionisio Suárez in February, Bosch complained of being depressed and ill, unable to speak too long on the phone without being recorded.

"After all these years of struggle, I think we have much to learn from the communists... You must maintain a certain silence to create a mystery about where I am and what I might be doing. Remember Che. His two years of absence were more important than his own death... Perhaps you think I spend too much money here, but that's not the case. The problem is that, since you left, everything has become three times more expensive. Rent now costs 294,000 escudos. The electricity bill is never less than 35,000 escudos. Gas has also gone up... I have to pay 29,000 escudos for hot water and the girl who washes and cooks for me, because I no longer have the strength. That's why I'm asking you to send me one or two thousand dollars or as much as you can in the next 72 hours. You know I don't ask for money for myself. I'm happy fighting alone against thousands of communists and assassins across the continent... Keep in mind that my rent here is due on the 7th of each month."[118]

According to the FBI agent in possession of these letters, Dionisio Suárez was a faithful servant of Bosch, but he was tired, fed up, with the boss's constant requests for money and decided to act as if he hadn't received the letter. His new boss, Guillermo Novo, was also tired of Bosch's begging. What leader, other than an evangelical pastor, lives off the begging of their followers? Everyone knew that the pediatrician lived off his fame and prestige and never stopped spending his money on cigars and rum, especially Cuban rum when he could find it, or Scotch whisky when he couldn't. Most likely, all those letters had been written under the euphoric influence of liquor and would have been sent by the girl who did everything for him, even cleaning his toilet when he left it in conditions unbecoming of an international leader.

He probably didn't even remember a word of what he had written a few hours earlier, but this last part will forever remain in the twilight of speculation.

—As if we didn't have enough problems here—said Novo.

Bosch's star seemed to be fading in Miami and in Union City. Guillermo Novo (one of the few who couldn't boast of having participated in the Bay of Pigs invasion) was there to replace him. The doctor had his moment of fame in the 60s when the Miami Herald and other local media reported on his flights with CIA napalm bombs over the "shithole island", his explosives on foreign ships in Miami on his own, and his mysterious disappearances as a fugitive from American justice.

Weeks later, in April, frustrated and probably under the same effects of alcohol, Bosch would send a new letter to Miami in the form of a combative missive, announcing a new congress in Santiago, Chile, ahead of a sublime moment in the "fight for freedom against communism." For such a relevant and significant moment in the hemisphere's history, "and under careful consideration of the needs of the case, the Treasury of Cuba demands the urgent transfer of 25,000 dollars for the war." 119

Bosch was the same age as Fidel Castro. Both were doctors, one in medicine and the other in law. Both had been leaders in their student organizations at the University of Havana during the time of Fulgencio Batista. Back then, the medical students knew the leader of their faculty, Orlando Bosch, as "The Pyro" because of his temperament and penchant for pyromania.

He competed in leadership with Fidel Castro. Fidel was arrogant. Taller, more attractive. He had a special talent for speaking at meetings and assemblies. He loved crowds as much as he now loves microphones and television cameras, interviews with famous journalists, speeches that were broadcast as far as Europe and reproduced in magazines across South America…

Bosch had lived in Miami for a time until the triumph of the Revolution in 1959. That same year, he returned to Cuba, confident that someone, somewhere, would recognize his leadership from the heroic university days. He worked in Santa Clara as a practicing pediatrician, but it didn't take long for him to clash with the indifference of the Castros.

—He left my daughter disabled—complained a patient's father.

There he realized that the Revolution had pushed him aside.

—In a year, I'll go back to Miami—he said—. I miss the real Cuba. Here, in Cuba, everything is and isn't...

He returned to Miami with his wife Myriam and their four children. After sixty days, when their tourist visas expired, they stayed as illegal immigrants. Naturally, it wasn't a problem.

—I'll be brief and clear— Bosch remembered Fidel, saying on September 26, 1960, before the United Nations Assembly, where he spoke for four hours. Four hours. Back then, Bosch couldn't even stand the first forty minutes. He didn't remember what Fidel had said. He only recalled getting up from his armchair in his Miami home and turning off the TV with a kick, something improbable but which had crystallized in his memory that way.

After leaving Cuba for the last time in 1960, Bosch started working at Abbey Hospital in Coral Gables. For Miami, as for almost everything, he harbored a deep love-hate. For years, he was addicted to the TV series SWAT and, above all, Mission Impossible, his favorite. Later, at the beginning of the seventies, when he had to flee the United States, Toma became more popular among his comrades. Back then, the shows flooding the American continent were the Cop Shows about police officers and private detectives. The main character was a real detective, Dave Toma, and the series an early version of Miami Vice. Dave Toma roamed the streets of Union City dispensing justice with his Baretta pistol. Two years later, the series was renamed Baretta, and its character became Tony Baretta, with an opening theme song that seemed born in Rio de Janeiro and matured in Chicago. Baretta wasn't just one of the most popular pistols of the time, with an Italian design, but its protagonist, Tony Baretta, catered to the public's taste for attributing all the mafia and plots to

Italians. The central idea that attracted viewers was: sometimes (often) it's necessary to break the law and the most cherished moral principles to catch the bad guys.

More or less from then on, Bosch began sleeping two hours a day. He was determined to overthrow Fidel from Cuba's government and knew that the longer he delayed, the harder it would be to achieve that goal, which became the only thing he thought about day and night. He was fired soon after, not for lacking papers but for storing explosives in the hospital basement.

He founded several armed groups, among them the Movement for Revolutionary Insurrection and Recuperation, with which he organized several attacks against sugar mills in Cuba and against Cuban ships in the ports of other countries. Several times, the FBI raided his home and other locations of his organization. Several times they confiscated dozens of bombs destined to be sent abroad. The Florida police arrested him in 1964 while he was towing a torpedo through downtown Miami in broad daylight. On another occasion, during a routine stop, they found several kilos of dynamite in his blue Cadillac, enough to blow up all four corners of any red light intersection.

By then, Bosch had already been arrested six times for conspiracy and for a dozen bombs. A classified FBI report dated March 23, 1968, mentions that Bosch had called the wife of a CIA informant, radio host Oscar Angulo Reyes, at 3:05 a.m. on January 20.

—I need to talk to Oscar—he said.

—He's not home—said his wife, who immediately recognized Bosch's voice.

—Then, tell him we planted a bomb on the plane going to Mérida—he said, and hung up without waiting for a response.

His actions, rarely punished, and his sporadic collaborations with the CIA, gave him a sense of impunity. Until finally, in 1968, he was sentenced to ten years in prison for attempting to blow up a stranded Polish ship in the port of Miami.[120] During the trial, the decisive testimony against him came from Ricardo Morales Navarrete, El Mono.

El Mono Morales was a purebred mercenary. Informant, hitman, police officer, anti-Castro terrorist, and drug trafficker, he had been an agent of Castro's secret police, then a CIA agent, bomber in Africa, paid informant for the FBI, and high-ranking official of the DISIP, Venezuela's secret police and partner of Chile's DINA. Eight years later, the DISIP, through El Mono, would hire Bosch for other special operations in the Caribbean, some on behalf of Cuban paramilitaries, like the bomb that claimed 73 lives on Cubana de Aviación flight 455, in the Bahamas. In his later years of early retirement in Miami, he turned to drug trafficking. By 1977, the Miami police department had already documented his involvement alongside other anti-Castro militants, such as Frank Sosa and Orlando Batista. Batista had been a military officer under the Batista regime, a DEA agent, and owner of the private security firm Interamerican Detective Bureau, responsible for the death of a young man at a quinceañera party in 1975. He had been recorded by Miami police as the perpetrator of at least one kidnapping.

El Mono, Batista, and Castro, among others, often met at the house on 1724 SW, 16th Street in Miami, just a few blocks from Calle Ocho, to organize "the sale of large quantities of drugs," according to the local police report.121 After building a solid reputation as untouchable in the United States and several Caribbean countries, and shortly after participating in several Miami television programs as a hero and witness to various terrorist attacks, such as the bombing of Cubana flight 455 who cost the lives of 73 people, El Mono Morales was assassinated in an exclusive bar in Miami Beach in 1982, shortly before Christmas. The crime was never solved. No one was brought to court, as tradition dictates.

EL MONO MORALES AND ORLANDO BOSCH

IN 1968, EL MONO HAD SUPPLIED ORLANDO BOSCH with dynamite and C4 plastic explosive to blow up several ships, one of them the Osaka Maru of Japan, stranded in the port of Tampa. At the time, almost all of them were experts in preparing bombs with plastique because the CIA had trained dozens of Cubans in the use of their preferred explosive. For the Osaka Maru, Bosch used four and a half kilograms and, according to Bosch himself, the deliveries of the explosives had been carried out with the knowledge of the FBI, although this detail has not been confirmed to this day.

According to El Mono, in his testimony before the judge on June 12, 1968, and just a few meters from the accused Orlando Bosch, the only thing Bosch regretted was that the bomb on the Japanese cargo ship had exploded prematurely, a problem that would recur multiple times years later but was solved in other cases, thanks to experience. Bosch wished to see, or at least imagine, the Japanese screaming as they sank into the open sea. An obsession rooted in World War II and, in particular, in General Curtis LeMay, who had dropped 1,500 tons of explosives from 300 B-29 bombers over Tokyo, killing tens of thousands in a single night. Years later, LeMay stated that he had no qualms about killing Japanese and recommended doing to Havana what they had done to Hiroshima and Nagasaki.

Bosch had informed El Mono of all the details of the plan. El Mono acknowledged that none of the bombed ships had any commercial relationship with Cuba or its government.

—Did Mr. Bosch tell you all that, Mr. Morales?
—Yes—replied El Mono, in the trial.
—Where did he tell you?
—At a restaurant in Miami.

El Mono knew that none of the bombed ships had any commercial relationship with Cuba or its government.

When Bosch was sent to prison for the first time, his wife Myriam took the opportunity to divorce him, claiming that her husband no longer thought of anything but Fidel. Fidel was in his soup and in his bed. He was sentenced to ten years in prison but released after four years, on the condition that he cease his political activities.

—*The struggle* cost me those five years in prison, my family, and my four children," Bosch would tell reporter Fleetwood years later, sitting at a visitor's table in the Caracas prison, convicted for the terrorist attack that claimed the lives of 73 people on a Cubana de Aviación flight. They are very proud of their father, but they couldn't have me when they needed me most because I was in prison. If I had just dedicated myself to medicine in Miami, I would have made many millions of dollars... I have paid a very high price for fighting for my country, but that is a higher obligation than that of a father to his children.

Fleetwood returned to Washington with six hours of recordings from the Caracas prison and an interview that not even the FBI had managed to obtain.

BOSCH ARRESTED IN COSTA RICA

—Mr. Bosch, do you accept your conditional freedom in exchange for never again participating in violent actions with political motivations?
—Yes, I do, Sir.

Governor Claude R. Kirk Jr., known as the first Republican governor of Florida, had been a key figure in the pardon granted to Bosch in 1972. But Bosch was not comfortable with non-violent activism, and even though leaving the country also meant breaking his commitment and U.S. law, in April 1974 he decided to move away from Miami, his main base of operations, and took refuge in

Venezuela, where the new president, Carlos Andrés Pérez, had taken office just a month earlier.

—Why are you smiling?—Adriana asked him two years later, rocking their daughter in her arms.

The new Bosch family had just arrived in Costa Rica from Santiago, Chile. It was February 1976.

—I'm not smiling—said Orlando—. I'm just shaving.

If Bosch said he was just shaving, that was a reason to think he was not shaving or, at least, that he was *not only* shaving. When he claimed credit for an action, few believed him; when he denied it, even fewer.

Bosch would declare many times that he had abandoned his illegal activities, especially regarding bombs, but the FBI didn't believe him either. Shortly after being released on parole, a wave of vendettas against some Cuban exiles began. In the early 70s, the Cuban National Liberation Front, formed by veterans of the Bay of Pigs and led by CIA agent Frank Castro, circulated death lists in Miami, each with 15 or 20 names. All were accused of being traitors, if not communists.

Investigating the chaos proved particularly difficult for the police, who were accustomed to dealing with a different type of maniac. The head of the Strategic Investigation Section, Thomas Lyons, at one point discovered a peculiarity about those under investigation.

—When you have an entire population talking day and night about the same thing—acknowledged the homicide expert, Lieutenant Gary Minium—thinking and talking about guns, bombs, conspiracies, attacks, and never managing to achieve their goal, eventually something has to develop. We're not trained to handle this. It's something new for us. It's a mentality that's quite difficult to understand.[122]

—Many people include themselves in their own death lists—said Lieutenant Lyons—just to gain notoriety. So it's even harder for us to identify the genuinely condemned.

In 1974, the anti-Castro activist José de la Torriente was murdered in Coral Gables.

—I swear it wasn't me—Bosch told a reporter days later—but I'm very glad José is dead.

The police were unable to locate Bosch, who secretly gave an interview to the *Miami* News, where he stated that the execution of Torriente was "a good lesson for the Cuban exile community, so that no one else presents false theories to deceive and rob the people."

—If you're innocent, why did you disappear the day Torriente was killed?

—I thought the people of action should leave the United States to operate from different bases in Central and South America.

—Have you re-entered the United States?—asked the reporter.

Bosch laughed:

—If I have to go back in, I will.

In just over a year, four of the ten people on an FLNC list were murdered in Miami. One, who survived the explosion in his car, was left without legs.

The murders continued. Executed by snipers or dynamite explosions, other exiles like Ramón Donestévez and Rolando Masferrer were killed one by one. Others, like Higinio Díaz, survived several shootings. Another bomb, attributed to Bosch as revenge, almost killed El Mono Navarrete. The bomb destroyed his car on a corner in Miami, but miraculously, El Mono neither died nor was maimed from the experience. Had he armored his car against something that was his specialty? If there was ever any clue about this, time buried it in its deepest and darkest pits.

Shortly after the investigation into Torriente's murder began, Bosch fled the country to Venezuela. In June 1974, he arrived in Caracas with a fake passport under the name Pedro Penya, invited by Luis Posada Carriles, at the time an important and feared agent of the Venezuelan secret police.

Later, the rest of the country's intelligence officers learned that Bosch had arrived not because of Posada Carriles, but when someone threw a dynamite cartridge over a wall, right into a courtyard where there was a meeting of diplomats from Cuba and Venezuela. He also placed explosives in a cultural center and the Embassy of Panama in October, during the commemoration of Cuba's Independence.

—Shortly after, we placed a bomb in the embassy of Panama in Caracas—Bosch told Fleetwood—. We chose October 10 because that's the date when Cuba's liberation was announced in 1898, and we did it because the dictator Torrijos announced he would go to Cuba. He went and kissed Castro... About two weeks later, a Cuban communist official was invited to speak at the Friends of Venezuela club. Before the yuma could speak, the bomb we had placed in the middle of the audience exploded. We had to do it. We didn't want to hurt anyone, but we couldn't let that man speak.

A few days later, the Venezuelan intelligence services met with Bosch and agreed to let him go if he led them to the rest of the explosives. They weren't far. They were right there, in his apartment.

—I had to promise the authorities that I wouldn't carry out any more actions against Castro's friends in Venezuela—said Bosch, with a smile— and they promised me, in the name of President Andrés Pérez, that no high-ranking official of the Cuban regime would be allowed entry into Venezuela.

More than that. They gave him a fake passport under the name Pedro Pena and he left for Santiago de Chile, where he arrived on December 10, 1974. On December 12, businessman Jorge Mas Canosa and Ramiro de la Fe contacted General Pinochet from Miami to request that he kindly receive and protect the leader of the Cuban Government in Exile. Bosch was housed in a government apartment. Shortly after, General Augusto Pinochet reported to Washington that Orlando Bosch was living in a military complex, "peaceful as an artist," even though the FBI had already classified him as a "dangerous terrorist."

It was there that he met Adriana. Much younger than him, in love or without Myriam's questioning. He married her a few months later, in February 1975. In August, he traveled to Buenos Aires to kill the Cuban ambassador Emilio Aragonés. The attack took place on the 13th, and a week later, the organization Latin American Anti-Communist Revolutionary Council (CRAL) claimed responsibility for the attack. In their libertarian statement, they warned that *"the bursts of machine gun fire and shrapnel will make the Castroists understand that there are no borders that can stop the actions of men who love liberty. Since Cuba is the only country in America ruled by a declared communist regime and since it is the country that has suffered the most under this inhumane system, we had to agree that Cuban Action and its leader Orlando Bosch, should lead this first action in the new and promising stage that is beginning."*[123]

—I crossed several times from Chile to Argentina—Bosch boasted to Fleetwood—. We tried to execute some Cuban diplomats in mid-1975 and detonated a bomb at the Mexican embassy in Buenos Aires. There we made very good contacts with members of the Triple A. Thanks to them, we were able to successfully execute the assassination of two other Cuban diplomats.

The young Cuban diplomats disappeared on August 9 of that year and were never seen again because, it was later discovered, they were thrown into the foundations of a building under construction in Buenos Aires.

Months later, the newlywed couple traveled to Nicaragua where they met with a group of close friends of the dictator Anastasio Somoza. From there, they flew to Costa Rica with the assignment from the Chilean government to assassinate the nephew of the dead president. Andrés Pascal Allende was in Mexico at the time. Other undesirables were on the list to be eliminated: the former Minister of Economy, Pedro Vuskovic, and the former ambassador Hugo Vigorena, among others.

But something went wrong. Two days later, when they were about to leave their hotel in San José to celebrate their first wedding anniversary, Orlando Bosch was arrested for traveling with a fake passport under the name of Héctor D'Avanzo Cintolessi. Six months later, the press in the United States would report that Bosch had been arrested on Wednesday the 18th in Costa Rica for planning the assassination of Secretary of State Henry Kissinger, whose visit to San José was scheduled for five days later, on Monday, February 23, and that the U.S. government had kept the matter secret. The Leaf-Chronicle on August 23, on page 6, would explain that the attack was motivated by the displeasure of the Cuban community in Miami over a potential improvement in diplomatic relations between Cuba and the United States.

A few days earlier, the CIA, concerned about the growing independence of Cuban actions, had decided to terminate its contract with Posada Carriles. Desperate over the loss of his salary, logistical support, and the impenetrable legal protection of the Agency, Posada Carriles contacted his superior and offered valuable information in exchange for being reinstated on the payroll. He tried to prove he was still a valuable asset and handed over information about Orlando Bosch and his next strike in Costa Rica, coinciding with the visit of Secretary of State Henry Kissinger to San Juan.

Posada Carriles was not readmitted into the super agency's ranks, but his friend of rum, paint, and explosives had to suffer the consequences. Orlando Bosch was detained in the rented house in San José by the Cuban Orlando Flores Mendoza, just as he was meeting with his daughter Teresa and her husband Rubén. The family shared the same passion. The Argentine Rubén Blinder was a member of the far-right terrorist organization, the Triple A, and six months later he would participate in the disappearance of two Cuban diplomats in Buenos Aires. Shortly after, another of Bosch's daughters, Miriam, would be prosecuted in Argentina alongside her husband, Carlos Rogers, for cocaine trafficking from Bolivia.

The Bosch family and the advisor and ambassador of Isabel Perón in Spain, José López Rega, funded part of their paramilitary organizations with cocaine trafficking across the borders of Bolivia and Paraguay, both countries secured by two dictatorships friendly to Washington, those of generals Hugo Banzer and Alfredo

Stroessner, always supported by CIA agents, such as the notorious Nazi criminal Klaus Barbie.

A few years earlier, a strategic partner of Bosch was the French CIA agent (and classified as a fascist by the agency itself) Christian David. The Frenchman managed to infiltrate the Tupamaros, the urban guerrilla group of Uruguay, sending several of its members to torture and then to the prisons of Punta Carretas and Libertad. According to the U.S. Drug Enforcement Administration, David, known as "El guapo Serge" (holder of false documentation issued in Uruguay and an Argentine passport under the name Carlos Eduardo Devreux-Bergere), was, at the time, responsible for ten percent of the world's cocaine trafficking.[124, 125]

Urgently, the intelligence services were able to verify much of Posada Carriles' information about Bosch's intentions in Costa Rica Another Cuban FBI informant, Carlos Rivero Collado, provided more details about the assassination plans against Kissinger. The idea was to send a clear signal against any negotiations with the Cuban government. Costa Rica's Minister of Foreign Affairs, Gonzalo Facio, reported that, once arrested, Bosch had confessed to investigative officers that one of his plans was to assassinate the U.S. Secretary of State. He was detained and had to remain in a cell for the duration of Kissinger's visit to Costa Rica, but later Washington dropped the charges against him.

—My only crime—lamented Bosch— was entering the country with a fake passport.

Later, Bosch corrected himself, claiming that the assassination plan only included the nephew of former President Allende, not Henry Kissinger. Washington declined to proceed with his extradition, but Costa Rica didn't want him there either and, ultimately, decided to deport him to the Dominican Republic.

—What a mafia—said Hunter.
—But all for freedom.

Dictators for Freedom

A YEAR LATER, COSTA RICA'S Minister of Foreign Affairs, González Facio, was informed by a "prominent member of the Cuban exile community in Miami" that Somoza had hired a commando led by Raymond Molina to destabilize the Costa Rican government with a media campaign, terrorist acts, and the assassinations of Venezuelan and Costa Rican diplomats. Molina was part of the failed CIA invasion of Cuba in 1961, and in March he traveled to Buenos Aires to finalize the details of the global media reaction to the planned coup d'état by General Rafael Videla against Isabel Perón.[126]

The businessman Raymond Molina also had his long track record in the fight for freedom. Before the House Committee on Foreign Affairs in Washington investigating human rights violations in Central America, Molina would acknowledge having conducted several business dealings with the government of Somoza in Nicaragua. Of course, in this case, it was a dictatorship that defended freedom. The freedom of enterprise.

In the official transcript of the April 5, 1977 session, one can read (translated here from the original English):

Raymond Molina *(vice president of Petersen Enterprise): I think I can contribute something to the area of human rights and to the analysis this committee is conducting that could put into perspective the reality of Nicaragua...* My participation has been as part of an American private enterprise focused on the development of human resources... The education system they have at the moment is only producing more intellectuals and more frustrated individuals... Here I have been listening to testimonies from several qualified and highly motivated individuals, but I think none of them are truly in touch with the realistic context of what is being carried out in Nicaragua... I believe there is biased information here, and this committee should very closely examine the information provided by individuals and organizations.

Clarence Long *(representative from Maryland)*: *Are you saying, Mr. Molina, that in Nicaragua there have been no human rights violations?*

Molina: *I'm not saying that, sir. I'm very concerned about human rights. In fact, I have been a militant in defense of human rights to the extent that I participated in the Bay of Pigs Invasion to fight against human rights violations in Cuba. I never heard during the course of these hearings here any reference to human rights violations in Cuba.*

Long: *Today we are talking about Nicaragua and the Philippines.*

Edward I. Koch *(Representative of New York)*: *I will be happy to send you my statements denouncing Castro and Cuba on human rights so you don't leave here thinking we are being selective… The reason we are discussing Nicaragua is that the United States is sending weapons to Nicaragua. We have not sent weapons to Cuba…*

Molina: *What I want to say, Mr. Koch and Mr. Long, is that I don't speak because I read it somewhere. I travel, I live there. I don't get information through third parties. I don't gather information from the New York Times. I have lived very intensely in that country and I know what it's about. True, there have been human rights violations, but we have evidence that it wasn't the government who started all this. The human rights violations were started by the Sandinista Front… No mention has been made of the human rights of businessmen who are being threatened, who are now afraid to live in Nicaragua, nor of the members of the armed forces, nor of other people, the ordinary people who cannot walk safely on the streets because they are afraid of being hit by a bullet from the Sandinistas*

Long: *Mr. Molina, do you have any contract with the Government of Nicaragua?*

Molina: *Not at this time.*

Long: *Did you have one?*

Molina: *Yes. I had a contract with the Government. As I say, my area was human rights.*

Long: *How much was the contract for?*
Molina: *Two and a half million dollars. Let me add that the Government of Nicaragua has allocated 28 percent of its budget to education and only about six percent of its budget to the National Guard.*

Another transcript, from the session of June 22 of that same year, captured this testimony from businessman Raymond Molina, who justified his support for the Somoza regime by stating that the rebels had been funded by Cuba. On that occasion, Representative Edward Koch had requested information from the US government about the allegations of Cuba's role in the Nicaraguan guerrilla. According to the House transcript, "the memorandum provided by the State Department indicates that neither the internal threat nor the Cuban support for that threat are as massive as some witnesses would have led the United States to believe… the most important element of Cuban support now is ideological and psychological, such as radio broadcasts."[127]

Orlando and Isabel separate for a while

Orlando left the house in Bethesda and moved to a small apartment in Dupont Circle, a few blocks from downtown DC.
—How's your new apartment going?—asked the friend from IPS he had met at the café on Connecticut Avenue.
—Bad. Even my food gets burned. When it's not raw.
—You survived a concentration camp and can't even make scrambled eggs.
—I've gone crazy—said Orlando—. I've lost my mind. I don't know how I could have fallen for that girl when I still love Isabel. We've been through the worst of the storm together. Isabel is the most wonderful person in the world…

—What you're feeling is the whim of a man who knows he stopped being young a long time ago. The girl grabbed you by the balls just when you were destroyed and had just landed free in Caracas, like a man reborn.

—Poor Isabel...

—The problem with men is that we have two heads, and they never agree... At least is the Venezuelan girl pretty?

—You have no idea...

—All young women are pretty. There are very few exceptions. Especially if you're already an old man no one pays attention to. At a certain age, you become a creep just for looking a woman in the eyes, and when even one gives you the time of day, and worse, she's a beautiful young woman, you feel like you've been chosen by God. It's like being on your second or third drink. The euphoria doesn't let you think that what comes after is all downhill...

—Something like that.

—But put yourself in Isabel's shoes. You surely wouldn't have tolerated it if she had an affair. Look, she's already past forty and is still very beautiful. That's against the rules, and it shows. She's elegant, cultured; she has green eyes that smile even when she doesn't want to...

—No, I wouldn't have forgiven her. But I already told you, I completely lost my head. I didn't think about the kids either. At first, they blamed her, until they found out the truth and hated me. But things have gone back to dialogue again. Every other day, I go back home, we have dinner together...

—Isabel will forgive you. Your kids will too. A few more months, and you'll be canceling the apartment lease. You'll move back to Bethesda again, and before you know it, Miss Pérez-Soto will call you, and her voice will resonate in you again somewhere below the shoulders.

I COULDN'T FORGET DAWSON ISLAND

AFTER PASSING BY THE RESIDENCE OF THE AMBASSADOR of Chile, the Sheridan Circle and Dupont, he stopped by the embassy headquarters. For some reason, for some time now he had convinced himself that if he didn't stop there for a moment, if he managed the difficult feat of indifference, the bad memories wouldn't come back to haunt him. That's why he passed by quickly and without looking.

But this time he stopped, and once again the past opened the door of the sky-blue Chevrolet Malibu, stepped in, sat down, and looked him in the eye. There it was, the same red brick building at 1732 Massachusetts Avenue. The same Chilean flag, with the same colors as the United States flag but with a single star, like Texas, now represented the exact opposite. Now it represented fascism, which proves that patriotic symbols protect no one from anything and, in reality, represent nothing more than a tribal, fragile, and therefore fanatical sentiment.

Letelier remembered that on September 11, 1973, the phone had rung at his house at 6:22 in the morning. He woke up startled. He had barely managed to sleep three hours. He knew something bad was brewing in the barracks, and he was the minister of defense.

Isabel answered. Her sleepy face and alert eyes listened for a moment, and then she said:

—It's Salvador. Something serious is happening.

Orlando dressed quickly and left. Outside, there was no guard. Only the driver was waiting. Isabel ran to say goodbye and begged him to be careful.

By 7:30, he was at the ministry, right across from La Moneda. The entrance was full of soldiers. At first, they didn't let him in. Then someone shouted, "Let the minister in." As soon as he entered, he felt a rifle pressing into his ribs.

Ten soldiers took him to the basement. After a few hours, they transferred him to an infantry regiment south of Santiago. There, he was hooded for days, subjected to absolute blindness. He couldn't see, he couldn't know what had happened exactly, what was happening with the country and his family, and much less, what would happen to him.

They transferred him to Punta Arenas, the southernmost provincial capital of Chile. A small, very Nordic-like town at the southern tip, due to the cold and the neatness of its streets. The Nordic pathology, the obsession with order and control, always looks admirable.

Soon they took him further south, to Dawson Island, along with other prisoners. To reach hell, they were made to walk on ice and under the freezing wind for over six kilometers. No one could escape from Dawson Island. Any attempt was doomed to certain death by freezing. Dawson was one of the many concentration camps of the new fascist regime. There, the prisoners were tortured for years. No one knew under what charges. Neither the soldiers nor the officers had the slightest idea, other than that thinking differently was a crime against God, the homeland, and the family. The democracy was always the real problem for the champions of freedom.

In Santiago de Chile, Orlando Bosch and other Cuban comrades were bored to death due to the permanent state of siege that had ended nightlife. Much further south, life on Dawson was even more difficult, even for the soldiers, who tried to combat boredom with the creative orders of their officers. What could be more fun than watching someone suffer?

Every now and then, the soldiers would make the prisoners fetch water from the river to drink, and every now and then, the prisoners would find their water containers soiled with excrement. It was very amusing. Every now and then, when the wind and freezing rain reached their maximum intensity, the prisoners were woken up at midnight to line up in the open air. Every so often, they would stage a mock execution. Once, Letelier refused to have his eyes blindfolded.

—I don't need any blindfold. I want to see your faces when you shoot.

When the officers ran out of ideas, the soldiers contributed their own:

—I bet you don't know what your little wife is doing right now so we can give you a second spoonful of lentils. Did you know she's a slutty bitch? Bet you didn't know, cuckold!

A UN human rights commission described the concentration camp management as "savage sadism." As in hundreds of other prisons and concentration workshops across the continent, the killers were the jailers. The prisoners made their captivity slightly less miserable through solidarity.

One of them, the deposed Minister of Mining, Sergio Bitar, told me:

—Orlando used to sing us tangos and boleros when the soldiers allowed him to play an out-of-tune guitar.

Bitar had graduated from Harvard and, together with Orlando, participated in impromptu English classes in the refrigerator-prison of Dawson.

MARCH

From the Southern Cone to the Northern Patio

On March 12, 1976, the *New York Times* reported on 17 Cubans executed in Angola.

—The news caused some impact—said CIA agent John Stockwell—but like so many other stories, we made it up to give our citizens something to be outraged about.[128]

In the CIA's bombing campaign over several towns in Angola, Cubans from Miami, like El Mono Ricardo Morales, had participated. The Cuban exile had become internationalized from the very first day, as much or more than the Revolution itself, which had supported Angola in its struggle for independence and against South Africa's apartheid.

—Look at this marvel, Michael—said Virgilio Paz Romero, shortly after arriving in Chile.

He held an automatic Colt 45 pistol, weighing it as if it were made of gold.

—This beauty was used in a special strike by the Cuban Nationalist Movement.

—What strike?

The Cuban responded with his familiar smile.

—What do you plan to do with it? asked Townley

They agreed it had to disappear, *just in case*. Paz Romero disassembled it and threw the pieces in different areas of Santiago.[129]

Townley had known Virgilio Paz for years. When the long-awaited September 11th arrived (it had been two years already, but it felt like yesterday), everyone had gone out to celebrate in a caravan of cars through Miami Beach. Finally, after three endless years, the Chilean dictator, irresponsibly elected by the Chilean people, had been overthrown by General Augusto Pinochet, a defender of the homeland and liberty—the homeland and liberty of the corporations of the North and the oligarchies of the South.

In Little Havana in Miami, there was a wave of joy. Some cars passed by the bar honking their horns. Townley had received the news right there, and he celebrated with the customers, mostly strangers, with lots of rum and many shouts of freedom. Then he went to a supermarket and bought cheap champagne. He took it to Mariana. On the kitchen table, he shook the bottle moderately and uncorked it, leaving a mark on the ceiling, as she would recall in her memoirs.

Two years later, in 1975, the Bay of Pigs Veterans Association awarded the Medal of Freedom to General Pinochet. Because of this incident, in April 1976 the Kennedy Library returned the flag of the 2506 Brigade, known for its participation in the failed invasion of the Bay of Pigs. The brigade sued the library. The Americans were the only ones who didn't have things entirely clear.

After the civic-military coup, some collaborators, real or imagined, received the long-awaited compensation for so much effort. The leader of Patria y Libertad, Pablo Rodríguez, became a respected journalist, an unconditional informant for the new government, and, as he himself said, a convinced defender of the free market. Other members of the group joined the DINA, the new intelligence agency. The influence market of the Chilean state, as in all other cases across the continent, was open to unconditional aspirants with a desire to advance.

Without a second thought, Townley and Callejas packed their bags to return to Chile. Townley attempted, once again, to place himself at the service of the CIA. This time in a more logical and effective way. He contacted Cuban exile groups in Miami. Some acquaintances worked in a car repair chain who, in turn, knew members of Patria y Libertad. Not by chance, the head of the DINA, Colonel Pedro Espinosa, had in his files some of these Cubans,

El exilio del terror 173

which allowed Townley to integrate into his team in Miami, not in Santiago.

The CIA always had a preference for individuals who weren't clear about what they wanted from life. What was always clear was the psychological profile of the candidate to be inducted into the sect of the national state. Like in other, older sects, they had complex and well-defined procedures for evaluating and deciding the admission of the candidate. Townley fit in perfectly. Or almost, because he hadn't managed to get into university, one of the most important evaluation points among national candidates. He was someone who, if he strayed from the agency's plans, did so to fulfill the agency's objectives. Especially when it came to resorting to methods that, if discovered, would have resulted in a heavy moral, budgetary, and even existential blow to the agency. If the idea was to eliminate someone, it was trusted that the chosen one would make brutal decisions that could not and did not need to be ordered by any secret bureaucrat or politician. Like planting a bomb to kill someone instead of eliminating them with a simple and inconsequential gunshot.

Although Virgilio Paz nearly softened her on the three-day trip from Miami to Mexico, Mariana Callejas still held some reservations and a visceral rejection toward the Don Juan of the Caribbean. Years earlier, she had thrown him out of her Miami apartment for his habit of chewing tobacco and for his anti-Semitic comments. Now, after being accommodated in the Lo Curro mansion in Santiago (and after a few days of putting up with his Cuban cigars, his long monologues about Cuba, and his complaints about the lack of nightlife under Chile's new regime), she sent him to dine in the basement, where DINA had its laboratories. As always, Townley tried to mediate in the new domestic conflict, with little success.

—It's sad to see a man dominated by a woman—Paz said as he went down the stairs, venting his anger in a controlled manner, resorting to macho humiliation.[130] But Townley did not have macho complexes, but rather a squire's complex. An Oedipus complex, as his critics would say.

Four months later, in that same mansion, in that same Lo Curro basement, Townley, Paz, and other DINA agents would torture the diplomat Carmelo Soria, while on the third floor Callejas, recently awarded for a short story in the El Mercurio contest, participated in one of her habitual literary gatherings. Every now and then, Callejas tried to mask the diplomat's cries of pain. Soria was murdered hours later and dumped by the side of a road on the outskirts of Santiago. Two months later, Townley and Virgilio Paz would participate in the terrorist attack that would kill Orlando Letelier and Ronni Moffitt in Washington.

Although Paz would admit to his involvement in these especially aggravated assassinations, and although a judge in the United States would sentence him to the minimum penalty of twelve years in prison, he would, as in other cases, be released a few years later.

Half a century earlier, in 1944, George Junius Stinney had been convicted in an express trial and then executed in the electric chair for the murder of two girls. The girls were white, and George Junius Stinney was a 14-year-old Black boy, accused of an impossible crime. Later, too late, when no one cared anymore, his innocence was proven.

The cases of Virgilio Paz and George Stanley are not exceptions to the rule, but further proof that justice is blind—and stinks like a goat.

—Justice is like a snake—Archbishop Óscar Romero would say shortly before being assassinated in El Salvador—; it only bites those who are barefoot.

Óscar Romero would be assassinated in the middle of a sermon calling on soldiers to stop the massacre of the people.

—No soldier is obliged to violate the laws of God—the conservative clergyman accused of communism had said.

The killer, Sergeant Marino Samayor Acosta, a mercenary from the death squad Los Angelitos, received one thousand colones for the job. Decades later, it will be confirmed that the order had been given by Major Roberto D'Aubuisson, a fascist by conviction, organizer of several death squads, and founder of the Arena party. The assassination was carried out with the knowledge of the CIA. The investigations were obstructed by powerful servants of justice, such as Colonel Oliver North. The same story as the rape and execution of the four American nuns seven months later, accused of being sympathizers of the poor, of Liberation Theology, and consequently, of the new Sandinista regime in Nicaragua.

—Nicaragua is closer to Texas than Texas is to New York—President Ronald Reagan would reason, in front of television cameras, to justify his economic and logistical aid to the Contras, as if it were a matter of national security.

By then, Luis Posada Carriles had already escaped from the Caracas prison and had received refuge in El Salvador. Protected by the dictatorship of Napoleón Duarte, he was received and recommended for re-entry into the CIA by the Cuban agent Félix Rodríguez, who boasted of having killed Che Guevara in a heroic but non-existent battle in Bolivia. Rodríguez, a close friend of the CIA director and future president, George H. Bush, one of those responsible for diverting ten million dollars from Colombian drug money to the Contras, boasted of wearing Che Guevara's watch as a war trophy.[131]

In El Salvador, finally readmitted by the CIA, Posada Carriles worked on supplying illegal weapons to the Contras in Nicaragua, despite the fact that the International Court of Justice and the U.S. Congress itself had concluded, somewhat belatedly, that it was a terrorist group, funded in multiple ways by the White House and its official sects with international jurisdiction.

AT IPS

Orlando Letelier discussed the new data arriving at the IPS offices. During Allende's government, inflation declined until the final stage of Washington's plot, when it went from two to two hundred percent. Other data pertained to the opinion of Americans and did not show a significant change. The citizens held a quite different view from that maintained by the White House, the CIA, Miami, and the Latin American oligarchy. In October 1973, one month after the coup in Chile, a survey had offered them to choose between two options:

The overthrow of Salvador Allende in Chile was:
1. a good thing because the president was a Marxist.
2. a bad thing, because he had been elected democratically.

19 percent had answered A, and 31 percent said B. Half the population had no idea about the coup in Chile or where that country was located.

—Interesting data, especially for academics—said Joe—. Irrelevant for everything else. A few days ago, I received something from the same Congress that's neither secret nor classified, but strategically will never make it to the major newspapers. The Democrats are more interested in the Allende case and plan to grill Kissinger with questions, but his advisors have already given him a golden rule: don't get tangled up in the web of Human Rights. When, suddenly, you have the most left-leaning Congress in history, what you need to do is dig up old corpses that always resurface.

—National security, the fight against international communism… Those things. They never fail.

—Exactly. As if imperialism and private corporations weren't an international issue.

—Specifically—interrupted Orlando— not everything falls on deaf ears. Here in the United States alone, there are 93 non-governmental committees in solidarity with Chile.

—None secret. None supported by the CIA.

—That's precisely what hurts the fascist dictatorships in the South. What we're not considering is that they won't just sit back and do nothing either.

—Pinochet and his people have launched movements that pass as popular and spontaneous organizations "to combat communist propaganda," they say.

—Typical *astroturfing*—said Joe—. Here it's a multi-million dollar business. Pseudo unions created by the same companies, street protests against some popular uproar...

The pot banging protests were invented by the CIA in Chile—I recalled— as protests by housewives against the government, and they reused them in Guatemala, in Brazil, and in other disobedient countries, long before the left adopted them as their own. It was acknowledged by David Atlee Phillips himself in his memoirs. In the southern countries, inoculated rebellions were always products of imagination, dating back even before the freedom fighters of the Colombian province of Panama, with the aim of dismembering that country to make more productive and civilized use of the future interoceanic canal. Later, the same strategy was perfected thanks to planted articles in the oligarchic press, thanks to the logistics and the always abundant money of the CIA.

—They still are—said someone I haven't been able to identify— but the Latin American oligarchy and its armed arms, the armies, don't find it hard to be creative on their own.

—At this moment—said Michael— in Chile, fake news campaigns have been launched against you. In fact, three. One, circulating the alleged discovery that during Allende's government, you introduced a shipment of illegal weapons into the country.

News that (I was able to verify later) were not only false but also concealed that there was, during the same period, a shipment of illegal weapons introduced to Chile by the US Embassy through diplomatic mail. To remove the constitutionalist General René Schneider, the CIA contacted Generals Roberto Viaux and Camilo Valenzuela to assassinate him and then blame Allende's followers. The most effective formulas are basic and repetitive.

On October 21, 1970, a diplomatic shipment containing weapons, grenades, and ammunition had arrived at the Arturo Merino Airport in Santiago. US Colonel Paul Wimert, a friend of General Schneider, was tasked with picking up the weapons and delivering them to General Viaux. The CIA agent, Henry Hecksher, handed Wimert $250,000 to invest in the assassination of his friend. Less than 24 hours later, General Schneider was ambushed while driving his car. An official CIA report would later acknowledge that the agency had provided weapons and, after Schneider's assassination, had given the killers $35,000 ($260,000 in 2025 value) "to maintain secret contact, the goodwill of the group, and for humanitarian reasons."[132]

The same strategy had been used in Guatemala. In June 1954, from modern Lockheed Lightning planes, the CIA bombed the British ship Springfjord in Puerto San José with Napalm. Shortly after, it was discovered that it was a shipment of cotton and coffee from the American company Grace Line, but the friendly dictator, Anastasio Somoza, informed the press that, aside from the weapons found, there were photographs of a Soviet submarine that was transporting them, bound for Guatemala. Similarly, when they spread the rumor that the training camps in Guatemala were for communists supported by Cuba and not for Cuban exiles trained by the CIA before the Bay of Pigs invasion. The then-president of Guatemala, General Miguel Ydígoras Fuentes, had handed over the Helvetia ranch in Retalhuleu to the CIA to house and train five thousand Cubans in exchange for a larger quota in the sale of sugar to the United States. To explain the strange movements in the area, the Guatemalan government spread the rumor that Cuban communists were organizing somewhere in the country to launch an attack against the homeland and the freedom of its citizens.

By then, the disinformation campaign had already spread throughout South America. The CIA agent Philip Franklin Agee, then assigned to Ecuador, reported on the purchase of opinion in the major newspapers of Colombia, Ecuador, and Peru (such as El Comercio and El Tiempo) to accuse Cuba of a nonexistent shipment of arms and money to that region. The plan, Agee confessed, was to prepare public opinion before the invasion of Cuba.

Fifteen years later, in the small IPS office in Washington, the three men continued to bombard the future president of Chile with hard facts. Those things wouldn't be of any use to him, because the truth almost never serves any purpose.

—What are the other two campaigns against me?—asked Letelier.

—Well, according to the press—said Joe— the alleged plan to bring weapons into Chile, organized by you, was set up to be presented as a scheme discovered by the Allende government.

—With what purpose?

—To blame the CIA. Allende planned to portray himself as the victim of an international conspiracy.

—Very creative...

—A farce about a farce to prove that Pinochet's enemies had staged a false farce... Do you follow?

—Another weapons shipment, according to these reports, would have been authorized by you to arm Allende's guards, who were going to organize various terrorist acts.

—Anything else?

—Yes. Apparently, you are preparing a terrorist act to plant a bomb on a LAN Chile plane. No, don't laugh. What's left for the last piece of news? Wait, here's the information... Let me see. Here. You are accused of living in a luxurious house in Washington.

—Does my house seem like a millionaire's home to you?

—Not at all. What I can't testify to is the last accusation… According to a rumor circulating in the Chilean press, you have participated as an actor in a pornographic film.

—Ah, man—said Letelier, exchanging a smile for a look of discouragement.

After a few seconds of silence, he tried to catch his breath:

—Well, let's move on to something more serious. How are the opinion polls in the United States?

—One last thing first. Some committees in favor of the dictatorship, like the American-Chilean Council, have been accused of being founded and funded by William F. Buckley and Marvin Liebman. The Department of Justice is considering declaring that the money they receive from the Chilean government is illegal.[133]

In his attempt to maintain a strong dose of optimism, Letelier observed:

—The favorable opinion of Americans toward our cause is an important piece of information, I think. The last vote in Congress was in our favor. 49 senators against 31 voted to stop providing military weaponry to Pinochet's government. That's a considerable majority.

—Yes… A good piece of news that worries me—said Joe.

Letelier looked at him and reached for his pack of cigarettes. He was determined to keep the group's morale as high as possible, even at the cost of denying a considerable part of reality. No one said anything for several seconds.

—In a few days, we have Michael and Ronni's wedding—said Joe, changing the subject just as Michael stood up to get a coffee—. I'll have to dip into my savings.

Almost at the same time, in Union City, New Jersey, Guillermo Novo received a call from Felipe Rivero in Miami. They had to assist Michael Townley in another operation, this time against a famous target that would put them back on the map for good:

—Listen, kid—Rivero told him— make sure President Pinochet understands that we're the best here. That would be a slap in the face to the other movements of La Causa.

Guillermo Novo, the eldest of the Novos, became the main contact with the new regime in Chile through Mario Arnello Romo, a member of the Nazi party in Chile during the 1930s, founder of the National Party of Chile in the 1960s, and in the 1970s, ambassador to the OAS and the United Nations.

When questioned by the FBI, Arnello Romo confirmed his friendship with Guillermo Novo, whom he recognized as the new leader of the fight for freedom in the United States, even more important than Orlando Bosch, who at the time was drinking rum in Santiago, asking for more donations from Miami, and fantasizing about emulating Che.

A Che without his libertarian arm. A Che of market freedom.

Raymond Molina in Buenos Aires

ON MARCH 15, THE LEGAL ATTACHÉ OF THE U.S. Embassy in Argentina, Robert Scherrer, sent a secret cable to the FBI director about a meeting held by one of his informants with the Argentine general Dalla Tea at the home of the son of financier Jorge Antonio. By then, and for a few years since 1970, due to President Nixon's frustration with the CIA, the FBI had regained some international jurisdiction, lost when its main rival was created in 1947.

From that meeting, it became clear that the Argentine generals wanted to secure Washington's cooperation with the imminent coup d'état. Two of the promises mentioned were the liberalization of the economy under a dictatorial regime like Chile's and, consequently, an increase in repression against unions and social organizations.

Another secret FBI document, dated the following day, reported that Raymond Molina, a member of the 2506 Brigade who participated in the failed Bay of Pigs invasion in 1961, had met with General Carlos Dalla Tea in Buenos Aires two days prior, on Sunday the 14th. At the request of a third party, Molina had been contacted by the U.S. Ambassador to Argentina, Robert C. Hill. Another document, this time from the CIA, noted that U.S. Congressmen Strom Thurmond and Jesse Helms had traveled to Buenos Aires with former CIA Deputy Director Daniel Graham and Cuban exile Raymond Molina on Friday the 12th.

Despite some minor inconsistencies in the details, what became clear was that during this meeting, General Dalla Tea revealed to Molina the Argentine army's plans to carry out a coup d'état between March 17th and 18th. Among the topics discussed was how the U.S. press would report on the coup to facilitate its recognition.

—For that, it's necessary for us to address some unions that have expanded their power too much, said General Dalla Tea—; the current government of Isabel has taken control of too many private industries, and they must return to private control to encourage investment.[134]

The president was not suspected of any leftist tendencies—quite the opposite—but it was better to remove the intermediary. Especially considering the possibility of significant growth in the left wing of Peronism, among the followers of Cámpora.

On Tuesday, March 16 at noon, by order of General Della Tea, the son of businessman Jorge Antonio met with the same Cuban at the Sheraton Hotel to discuss a media plan in support of the coup led by General Jorge Rafael Videla. The idea was to inform Molina's associate, the general and CIA lieutenant Daniel Graham. By then, Graham had already returned to Washington. He did not want to be in the country during the reported events. According to the same FBI document, General Rafael Videla insisted that Mr. Graham be contacted from a third country to be consulted on the media aspect of the coup.[135]

The informant confirmed that the Argentine military had completely neglected the public relations of their imminent coup, beyond the contacts and instructions in various Argentine embassies.

—It is absolutely necessary—Raymond Molina clarified to them— that a well-prepared public relations program be carried out in the United States to counteract the unfavorable reaction that a military coup against a constitutionally elected government would produce.[136]

A secret cable from the Intelligence Division on March 15 confirmed these meetings and added: *"After the coup, the junta would establish contact with ITT* to take control of the Argentine telephone company."[137] The International Telephone & Telegraph Corporation (like IBM and other American megacorporations) had been collaborators with Hitler's regime and active participants in the coups against João Goulart in Brazil and against President Salvador Allende in Chile.

Shortly after, in June, Ambassador Hill attempted to neutralize Henry Kissinger's statements in Santiago, about Washington's support for the new Junta in Argentina. Kissinger's statements had been made at the Hotel Carrera, a luxury hotel where, as in other hotels of the same category, hundreds of newborn children of imprisoned and disappeared parents waited to be exported to the European and American markets. 700 children were registered as born in the most expensive hotels in Santiago (born in the absence of their parents) such as the Hotel Montecarlo, El Conquistador, the Sheraton, and the Carlton House. The market for little humans reached the number of twenty thousand kidnapped children.

—Kissinger will ruin your diplomatic career—Kissinger's assistants warned the ambassador—. Perhaps a group of leftist guerrillas will assassinate a member of your family.

Another urgent document dated March 16 (classified as secret *"because it would reveal the FBI's interest* in an international matter"), reported that General Daniel O. Graham, who had traveled to Argentina with Senator Jesse Helms, after meeting with the Cuban

Raymond Molina, had been able to confirm the existence of a coup plan in Argentina, scheduled for the following week, information that had been relayed to Ambassador Hill.

The future mayoral candidate for Miami, Raymond Molina, stated in the official records of Washington:

—It is absolutely necessary to carry out a well-prepared public relations program in the United States to counteract any negative reaction to the military coup against a constitutionally elected government.

Raymond Molina—wrote Ernest— had run as a candidate for representative for the state of Florida in 1968, but was not elected. As a member of the 2506 Battalion organized, funded, and trained by the CIA, he had participated in the failed Bay of Pigs invasion seven years earlier. He had been captured by the revolutionary government and released two years later. A secret report from December 3, 1968 linked him to the far-right John Birch Society and to the smuggling of weapons and whiskey from Colombia and other Latin American countries through his own company in Miami, Americana Sales.[138]

Like most organized groups in Miami and Union City, Molina fought against Fidel Castro's dictatorship Castro supporting any other type of dictatorship on the continent that protected the right to private property above any other right, including the right to life. In not a few cases, directly participating in plots and attacks against innocents who were always categorized as combatants. The list of notable figures is long.

The promises were fulfilled. During the Argentine dictatorship, a third of the disappeared were factory workers organized in unions, largely workers from the industrial north of Buenos Aires, where the large transnational corporations were located. Several sectors of the economy were privatized, while, to compensate, private debts were nationalized.

Two decades later, in the summer of 1997, despite several accusations and trials for bribes, Raymond Molina announced his candidacy for mayor of Miami at the Versailles Restaurant. The most famous restaurant on Calle Ocho, founded by the Cuban Felipe Valls, became a mandatory stop for anyone wanting to win an election. The Versailles was the political baptism site for the Bush dynasty, Bill Clinton, John McCain, Ron DeSantis, and Donald Trump. Everyone had lunch there to secure the same votes. Everyone praised the Cuban coffee, the churros, and the ropa vieja.

Few months later, Molina took refuge in Panama, where he stayed for some time. In the U.S., he was accused of overseeing vote buying and not paying rent for his offices.

—I don't give a damn about the State Attorney's Office—he defended himself—. They're all full of shit!

In October 2008, Molina assaulted the former governor of Puerto Rico, Carlos Romero Barcelo, for daring to criticize President George W. Bush. Romero ended up with a piece of his glasses lodged in his eye. A judge sentenced Molina to therapy to learn to control his impulses and alcohol abuse.[139]

In 2020, Molina marked "non-Hispanic" on his voting card.[140] He lost the Republican primary race to represent Miami in Congress. His rival, María Elvira Salazar, beat him by a margin of 69 percent.

—The citizenship test for immigrants in the United States—Hunter interrupted me— includes a hundred questions. Naturally, they're not very complicated questions. Even so, millions of people who inherited citizenship by being born in this country wouldn't pass it.

—Perhaps a similar test should be required to obtain voter registration. This wouldn't solve the country's serious problems, but it would certainly reduce the political power of the most fanatical ignorants to some extent.

—But, well, go on.

Elvira Salazar, also the daughter of Cuban exiles from the first wave, never distinguished herself from her rival, Molina, in terms of her ideas. On February 2, 2023, she reacted against the decision of the Argentine government to consider purchasing JF-17 aircraft from China. Even, as was the case with the Pulqui aircraft after Perón's overthrow in 1955, the congresswoman warned against the possibility of Argentina manufacturing its own planes:

—They're making a pact with the Devil that could have consequences of biblical proportions—she said in two languages, from her seat in Congress—. The United States isn't going to sit idly by, because you can't have an ally that manufactures and exports Chinese military aircraft and sells them to its neighbors… There are two worlds, the free world and the world of slaves. May the Argentines stay in the free world![141]

Months later, on November 30, 2023, Salazar introduced a bill to commemorate the two hundredth anniversary of the Monroe Doctrine.

—Evil empires like Russia, China, and Iran are invading our territory. So we must wake up and understand that this is our territory and that no other country is going to treat Latin America better than the United States… We are the most generous superpower in the world… This country has been a beneficial influence in the Western Hemisphere since the Spanish crown was expelled in 1810, and we must continue down that path.[142]

One day after the Argentine elections that crowned the far-right candidate, Javier Milei, Salazar congratulated her candidate and praised the country. Argentina has it all, even "one culture, one religion, and one race, completely homogeneous."[143]

—It reminds me of the idea that all Chinese and Black people are the same—Hunter told me—. At least Milei is a liberal, and liberalism is, by definition, the opposite of fascism. One stands for the absolute control of the state and the other for the destruction of this control.

—True—I said—. They're ideologically opposed, but history shows, to the point of exhaustion, that behind every great liberal there's a repressed fascist waiting to come to power. Or is it just a coincidence that all the liberals of today are the ones who supported the military dictatorships of yesterday? It's that their concept of freedom closely resembles that of slave owners. It's the freedom of enterprise, and what's more dictatorial than a large corporation?

THE CAN OF TUNA

AT THE BAR, A MAN WITH A CARIBBEAN ACCENT was telling his second or third joke.

—Listen to this one, buddy—he said, hitting the arm of his friend who was doubled over with laughter—. Yesterday, a Cuban arrived in the Keys, hidden in a can of tuna. The reporters surrounded the can that was still drying on one of those piers, let's say the Emma Carrero, and they asked him, they asked him in amazement, in amazement: "Hey, buddy, how is it possible to get into a can of tuna and sail all the way here?" Then, then the Cuban says... wait, wait, the Cuban says to them: "Well, the hardest part wasn't getting inside the can. The hardest part, the hardest part..." no, listen, "the hardest part," the Cuban said, "the hardest part was getting a can of tuna in Cuba, man!"

—What a load of crap!

They both burst into laughter, leaning on the bar like Muslims at prayer time, but with their foreheads against drops of rum.

In truth, it wasn't just the Cubans, I thought... Trying to clarify what I meant by that, I took the black pen and wrote a few words in the notebook, as if trying to untangle my thoughts with my own hands. I remembered other experiences.

Not a few who came from countries like Vietnam, like Guatemala—I wrote— *impoverished and corrupted countries, like the banana republics, or blocked like the disobedient republics, go on publishing* on their social media photos mocking the hunger of their brothers in their home countries, while posing in front of luxury cars they rent or pay for in installments, in front of tall glass buildings they'll never enter except as aspiring wage slaves or, at best, as tourists in their own cities. For these poor people, there's nothing like getting close to the shadow of a lion and licking its claws to feel important, to believe they're felines, even if they're just small rodents boasting about someone else's success, by someone else's definition of success. Like remoras and like pilot fish that cling to sharks for protection, while feeding on the parasites of their protector. Like the black slaves who defended their white masters when they whipped other bad blacks. Like Judas who sold out a rebel from below to the empire for thirty pieces of silver...

That's when it stopped me. They're going to kill me if I publish this, I thought. I marked that page with a cross. On the other hand, it wasn't an academic observation. Any publisher would reject this manuscript just for that paragraph, but more important than that was not to get distracted by marginal speculations. I looked at my agenda. I only had three months left of sabbatical, and I couldn't waste time or money in that city. Upon my return, a mountain of data and documents awaited me, which I still didn't know how to organize. I didn't know where to start, much less begin assembling the puzzle.

—Nothing that a beer can't fix—I told myself, and ordered another Heineken, as the two Cubans from the jokes stepped out into Florida's unbearable heat and unceremoniously got into a silver Jeep Wrangler.

For obvious reasons, I kept writing my initial notes by hand, in an unlined notebook: conversations, some small idea or reminder, clippings from old newspapers or copies of declassified PDF documents from the National Security Archive that kept piling up.

One of those notes that followed me even to the bathroom said (transcribed without corrections): "History is like an old play that's staged with different directors, with different actors, on different sets, in different centuries. But it's the same piece. The same comedy, the same drama, the same tragedy..."

It's still a curiosity—I think now— that the same people who don't believe in historical continuities but in absolute breaks are the same ones who first check in the analysis of a text if one paragraph is well connected to the next. It's no coincidence they're Anglo-Saxon academics. We Hispanics, as in everything, are more disorderly. Disorderly in writing, in living, in killing, and in dying. Even in killing and dying we're different.

TOWNLEY'S FIRST VICTIM

TOWNLEY NEVER HAD THE CHANCE TO carry out his master plan to assassinate the president of Chile. He managed to assassinate the painter Jorge Henríquez, on the night of March 20, 1973, though it wasn't a premeditated crime, unlike all the others that followed. You have to start somewhere, and it's always for a good reason.

At the time, the director of Channel 13, the priest Raúl Hasbún, had contacted Patria y Libertad to resolve the government's blocking of an illegal channel, Channel 5. According to those affected, the blocking was carried out by a government socialist antenna placed on the roof of the Electrical Services Directorate in the city of Concepción. Patria y Libertad turned to Townley, the crazy yankee.

At the time, the General Directorate of Electrical and Gas Services was in charge of radio frequency allocation. The priest Hasbún disagreed with the regulation of radio and television waves. Shortly before, he had traveled to Spain and the United States, from where he returned with new equipment for the pirate channel's broadcasts.

—Mr. Hasbún admitted to having brought in that equipment from the United States—said engineer Rodrigo Gutiérrez—. What he didn't admit, but I have no doubt about, is that the CIA provided it.[144]

Channel 13 of the Catholic University supported the illegal broadcasts of Channel 5 from Concepción. To remove the government's interference, the head of propaganda for Patria y Libertad, Manuel Fuentes Weddling, sought out Townley's knowledge of electronics. Days later, on March 14, Townley and two other collaborators settled into the Hotel Dorado. Only the electronics engineer Undurraga registered his name. On the night of Wednesday the 21st, they arrived in Townley's Mini Cooper at the Electrical Services building on Freire Street, number 382. To access the antenna, they entered with a key provided by María Inés Fuller, the owner of the adjacent property. According to Mariana Callejas, it wasn't this woman, but rather the channel's director, Carlos de la Sotta, who handed the key to her husband.

When Townley found the oscillator and the wave meter causing the interference, he decided not to destroy them. The devices were expensive and highly useful. It made more sense to steal them. But the painter Jorge Henríquez woke up and discovered the intruders. Townley subdued him before he could raise the alarm. He tied him up and wrapped him in tape so he couldn't open his mouth.

Under the pseudonym Juan Manuel Torres, Townley called the head of propaganda for Patria y Libertad, Manuel Fuentes, to report the success of the operation. Then he called the number 28 58 50, registered under the name of another notorious Nazi of German origin and member of Patria y Libertad, Manuel Katz Pride. All patriotic freedom fighters.

The next day, Mario, the painter's brother, went to visit him at the boarding house on Freire Street. He found him in his modest room, lying on the floor, nearly naked, tied up with a rope and a cloth in his mouth. The autopsy revealed that Jorge Henríquez had been suffocated with chloroform. He was 35 years old, with a difficult life and an even worse death.

The crime outraged the residents of Concepción, and the police hurried to solve it. It took them three months. When Townley found out he was on the suspect list, he fled to the border.

—At the *checkpoint* I was stopped by the gendarmes—said Townley—. It cost me two small bottles of pisco to cross into Argentina.

From Buenos Aires, I fled once again to Miami.

According to Mariana Callejas, the radio in Chile reported on the painter's death in Concepción as if it had been a fascist attack. Allende's regime intended to use the incident as propaganda against the opposition.

—Several times I was interrogated by Allende's political police—wrote Callejas in her memoirs twenty years later—. Without violence, I must clarify, without pressure. But interrogated.

The police had suspected her insistence on retrieving her husband's Austin Mini Cooper, abandoned in Concepción, but they let her go. On the flight back to Santiago, Callejas encountered Father Carlos de la Sotta, the owner of Channel 5 in Talcahuano. She recognized him, but he did not. After gaining his trust as a fellow passenger, the priest told her he had been detained and tortured by Allende's police.

—All because of some amateur intruders—said the priest— who came from Santiago to meddle in what didn't concern them.

—But didn't they come to help with the channel?

—Help?—said the priest, indignant—. We knew perfectly well where the interference equipment was. What help could those idiots offer!

The investigation implicating Father De la Sotta in the death of the night watchman will be interrupted, as if by a divine sign, by the libertarian coup on September 11, 1973.

COUP IN ArgenTIna

—To avoid another defeat in Africa—Kissinger told the president, in the Oval Office, on March 15 at 9:30 in the morning— we must strangle the Cuban regime. We must humiliate them. Otherwise, we'll have to step in and support a black government ourselves.[145]

Angola's independence, led by António Agostinho Neto, was supported by Cuba. The militias against the government of the newly independent country received covert support from Washington, the CIA, London, and South Africa's apartheid regime. As Nelson Mandela would acknowledge years later, Cuba's support not only made Angola's independence possible but also marked a decisive step against apartheid in South Africa and provided moral reinforcement for the rebels.

Nine days later, on March 24, 1976, frustrated by the success of Angola's independence revolution, Secretary of State Henry Kissinger told President Gerald Ford:

—We're going to have to crush Fidel Castro. We must humiliate him.

—When is the plan for?

—We'll have to wait until after the elections.

—Fully agreed— said President Ford.

Kissinger insisted. His logic was airtight and tolerated no timidness in his circle of friends. We are special, and we must win at any cost. God (if He truly exists) will forgive us for any miscalculation.

—If the Cubans do the same in Rhodesia—said Kissinger— their next target will be South Africa… That would create a massive uproar and force us to support a black government ourselves. All of which could cause racial tensions closer to home, in the Caribbean, where the Cubans would appeal to disgruntled minorities. Then, the demands could spread to South America and even to the United States.

—Sounds good to me—said the president.

El exilio del terror

—I will be giving a speech in Dallas—concluded Kissinger—about the need to increase our military budget.[146]

On March 24, 1976, the military coup took place in Argentina. Kissinger supported the Junta, even after the new president Jimmy Carter decided to reverse the unconditional aid from the White House to friendly dictatorships.

In Argentina, the problem wasn't having a government of Black people, but anything that resembled a non-aligned movement. In other words, in any case, the problem was always the possibility of losing control over other people's lives.

APRIL

Let Them Sink a Ship, or a Plane

In April, the Church Committee of the Senate published its report on the illegal activities of the CIA. The massive account of assassinations of foreign leaders, coups d'état, and manipulation of the press was summarized in six volumes. Shortly after, the renowned General Lyman Lemnitzer was named a member of President Ford's Foreign Intelligence Advisory Board.

Fifteen years earlier, Lemnitzer had been one of the most important generals in the preparation of the failed Bay of Pigs invasion. An operation that had been doomed from the start, according to the CIA, due to the egocentric, manic, and explosive nature of its recruited Cuban exiles. An internal CIA investigation, led by Jack Pfeiffer and classified on April 18, 1984, concluded that "the leaders of the major exile organizations that the Agency attempted to organize were basically selfish and egomaniacal; they were more concerned about their future positions in Cuba once Castro was overthrown than about working for the common cause."[147]

The report left a detailed profile of its members recruited in Florida: "The Cubans' concern for their macho reputation, their petty and childish rivalries, and their tendency toward impulsiveness were addressed in the Inspector General's report. The review of the WH/4 records makes clear the difficulties of dealing with the exiled leaders during the operation. The Agency's agent E. Howard Hunt, *has provided a clear account of the difficulties encountered in the Miami area when he and his boss, Gerard Droller, attempted to persuade a group of egocentric leaders that the anti-Castro effort would require more than grandiloquence to succeed. Similarly, one of the Cuban pilots who was among the first contingent sent to Guatemala to receive training, highlighted the political friction among the pilots in training, which ended with the resignation of almost a dozen of them.*"

At the training camp established at the Helvética Estate in Guatemala, officers reported various difficulties with their subordinates: "The Cubans made a problem out of everything; they were always complaining and threatening to rebel. One month before the invasion (just after some political leaders arrived from Miami), the group split into two political factions. The division was so radical that Lieutenant Colonel Frank Egan had to separate the two groups and move one to another camp... The Cubans didn't know how to work as a team; everyone wanted to be brigade commanders."[148]

However, this experience of the exiles with the CIA was foundational. Their psychological profile came from the tradition of the Copacabana Club and the lower-ranking batistas (written in lowercase). Their methods, the compote, the denial at any cost, and the preference for the use of dynamite and C4 plastic explosives were perfected by the Agency.

One afternoon in 1962, the U.S. Joint Chiefs of Staff, chaired by General Lemnitzer, approved the proposal to carry out a series of attacks in the United States that could be attributed to Cuba. The document was not far removed from the plans carried out by a faction of Cuban exiles from Miami, such as Orlando Bosch, Luis Posada Carriles, El Mono Morales Navarrete, Virgilio Paz, Dionisio Suárez, and the Novo Sampol brothers, among many others.

In his youth, General Lemnitzer had served in the violent occupation of the Philippines, where sportive execution methods and torture techniques, such as *the water cure*, became infamous, and left behind hundreds of bitter, if not acidic, pages by Mark Twain. His last mission, during the Bay of Pigs invasion, was less successful. Like everyone who participated in one of the greatest national traumas, he never got over it. In Washington, he was known for carrying around an awkward and ridiculous M16 rifle everywhere, fearing that someone (or rather some group of ghosts, long deceased) might ambush him around a corner. His ever-pristine 5.56 mm could fire twenty rounds with a single trigger pull.

On March 13, 1962, the Department of Defense and the Joint Chiefs of Staff approved the document titled *"Justifications for US Military Intervention in Cuba."* General Lemnitzer, then director of the committee, sent the summarized report to Secretary of Defense Robert McNamara. The revenge against Cuba was going to be devastating, but a good excuse was needed to launch the final assault. The plan included the intervention of military and paramilitary forces for a "legitimate provocation." One of the proposals assigned CIA agents the mission of posing as university students on a fake flight to South America, which would be shot down by friendly fire in the Caribbean and immediately attributed to the terrorism of the Havana government.

The document, with the meticulous signature in the form of a logo *LLLemnitzer*, continued with a list of other necessary actions leading to the next and definitive invasion of the cursed island:

"Start false rumors (many) through fake media; Send friendly Cubans to fake attacks on the Guantánamo base; Fake capturing them inside the base; Initiate riots and protests in the area; Detonate bombs inside the base; Fake a sabotage by setting fire to a plane from the base; Set ships on fire; Capture the fake attackers and hold funerals for the nonexistent victims of the attacks… Thus, the United States can respond by destroying Cuba's military infrastructure. The strategy of 'Remember the Maine' will be used in many ways: we will blow up a U.S. ship in Guantánamo and blame Cuba. We will explode one of our drones (unmanned) in Cuban waters, near Havana or Santiago, which will allow us to "rescue" the nonexistent crew. The publication of a list of dead in the U.S. press will cause a wave of national outrage. We can also create a communist state of terror in Miami, in other Florida cities and even in Washington. This terrorism campaign could target exiled Cubans. We could sink some of those boats with Cubans coming to Florida. That would have great publicity… such as placing plastic explosives in strategic points, followed by the arrest of Cubans and fabricated evidence implicating Havana in the attacks. The same must be done in some neighboring country to blame the

Cuban government, like the Dominican Republic... Harassing commercial planes with adapted MIGs and F-86s, piloted by our personnel and painted with the colors of the Revolutionary Air Force, will provide additional harassment. The attack on our ships will also be very useful... A fake commercial plane bound for Jamaica, Panama or Venezuela could also be shot down and blamed on the Cuban government... The diverted plane should send out a distress call, saying it is under attack, just before the signal is cut off. This communication will be recorded by various controls across the Hemisphere, which will then 'inform us' of the incident. This way, no one will say that the United States is trying to convince anyone of anything."[149]

The recommendation, unanimously approved by the command, included the bombing of commercial planes and the assassination of American citizens in the streets of New York and Miami. The alibi was called Operation Northwoods (part of a larger strategy called Operation Mongoose) and it guaranteed Washington the automatic and democratic support of the population to resolve the problem.

There was only one problem. President Kennedy rejected the idea, just as he had rejected General Curtis LeMay's proposal to drop an atomic bomb on Havana. As in the days of President William McKinley (when he was pressured to send the provocation of the USS Maine to Havana in 1898), not a few understood that the nation now also needed "a man in the White House." Like McKinley, Kennedy was also assassinated.

The practice of so-called false flag operations to blame the aggressed for some aggression has always been a classic of the genre in all imperial expansions, from Andrew Jackson to John Wayne, from the crossing of the Appalachians to deprive the Indians of their lands to the war against Mexico to take half of its territory or the war against Spain, which was actually against Cuba, to prevent its true independence, which the island rebels were on the verge of achieving in 1898.

"No," said Kennedy. "I will never authorize this type of operation. Forget it."

Due to this unexpected refusal by the president, General Lyman Lemnitzer was not confirmed for a second term as Chairman of the Joint Chiefs of Staff. In November of that year, adding to his frustration with the new president, he was transferred to the NATO Allied Operations Command. In France, he made a few friends, though many found the Yankee's habit of being armed even to go to bed a bit exotic.

In 1962, General Lemnitzer was warmly welcomed by the then head of NATO, General Adolf Bruno Heusinger. Like other NATO officers, Heusinger had been one of Adolf Hitler's trusted officers. He was decorated by both Hitler and Washington with two little bronze medals.

In 1975, President Gerald Ford had chosen General Lemnitzer to join the Commission on CIA Activities in the United States, tasked with investigating whether the secret agency had ever violated the law.

The patriot exiles from Cuba would have more success a few years later, when they managed to assassinate American citizens, like Ronni Muffett, and then shoot down a commercial plane full of passengers in the beautiful waters of the Caribbean, and later, when they introduced various types of plagues to the largest of the Antilles, such as hemorrhagic dengue, which would leave extensive crop losses and hundreds of thousands seriously ill in Cuba—all for the homeland and freedom.

The Best Way to Eliminate an Undesirable

On April 9, Holy Friday of 1976, Michael Townley was euphoric. Everything was going perfectly. The Andrea Project had yielded excellent results. The production of sarin gas had been a complete success, and the new equipment continued to arrive at their dream laboratory.[150] Upstairs, some women were filling out 150 fake IDs to send them to Argentina. "Seems like they're having a huge surplus of dead people over there," explained one of them, "and they need to report them."

—General Pinochet is more pragmatic. When an undesirable reported coffins with two bodies, the general reminded him that saving is the foundation of wealth.

There were minor details left, like some issue with the title of the house in Quetropillán, in Lo Curro. The real estate agent René León Zenteno had refused to illegally transfer property titles to DINA and was eliminated with Townley's sarin gas, placed in his house on Avenida Holanda, northeast of Santiago, not far from Townley's laboratory."

Everything had taken just over a year. Michael, Mariana, and their children had moved to the new house at Via Naranja 4925, in Lo Curro, north of Santiago, on January 24, 1975. Quetropillán had three floors, a pool, two servants, and a secretary. It was a spacious 580-square-meter construction on generous land to develop ideas as inspiration dictated. Colonel Espinosa sent twenty soldiers to clean the house, the pool, and the gardens. They had also been provided with a cook, Delia, and a butler, Don José, two poor and hardworking peasants freshly arrived from the cold south.

In the surrounding area, the regime had begun building an exclusive neighborhood for its collaborators. Quetropillán had been chosen by Townley, paid for by the DINA and registered under the false names of two merchants to serve as a secret laboratory. The idea had been born long before by Colonel Contreras when he met with Townley at the headquarters on Belgrado Street to confirm the death sentence of Orlando Letelier in the United States.

At that time, Contreras had informed Townley that the new government needed a secret laboratory. A bunker that looked like a luxury residence, protected by army guards. The chosen mansion was located in an exclusive neighborhood, not too far from the center of Santiago, but difficult for ordinary people to access without a car and without a reason to climb up to that modern three-story castle. Its windows were boarded up, and the wooden doors were replaced with metal ones.

The DINA was interested in working with chemical and biological weapons, and Townley was the ideal candidate. When he wasn't tirelessly working in his laboratory, he was traveling, coordinating various assassination plots of Operation Condor or purchasing electronic equipment in Europe and the United States.

One of the geniuses identified to work on the new project, the Chilean Sidney Gottlieb, known by the alias of Hermes, was the chemical engineer Eugenio Berríos. At that time, he was researching sarin gas and other deadly gases.

—Do you know what's the best way to eliminate an undesirable?—Berríos asked Mariana Callejas, with a smile. Berríos considered himself a genius and was always laughing, Callejas would recall in her memoirs.

His face smiled, but his laughter was one familiar to psychiatry. A psychopath is not distinguished from others by their moral judgments, because they have learned what should be said and what is better kept silent, how to act so as not to draw attention from lesser people. The difference is only perceptible through a magnetic resonance scanner or through their resounding successes.

—There's no better way to eliminate an undesirable than with a little drop of golden staph—he answered himself and smiled again.

This bacteria was one of the regime's favorites because it left no traces, and if it did, it was impossible to attribute them to poisoning or intentional contagion since, in normal doses, it is found everywhere.

One day Callejas was alarmed by screams coming from the ground floor of the house. It was Berríos shouting euphorically: "It works, it works!" With Michael, they had tested a new bacteria with which they managed to slowly kill a donkey. The chemist could hardly contain his joy.

—He was a very cheerful man. It was contagious.

Berríos wasn't alone in his experiments. The DINA and Contreras himself, who had done postgraduate studies at Fort Benning, had drawn inspiration from various CIA experiences, such as Project MK-Ultra, experiments with LSD and sarin gas, all thanks to the assistance of Hitler's scientists. Also, as the CIA itself practiced, the funding was to be mixed: on one hand, with state money, and on the other (to give the operations greater discretion) with money that didn't require reports or accountants, money coming from drug trafficking.

Contreras and the CIA's deputy chief, Vernon Walters, knew that Townley was the ideal person to function as a liaison between the DINA and the Cuban paramilitary groups operating in the United States and in Europe itself. Three months earlier, Townley and his Miami associates had managed to leave diplomat Bernardo Leighton and his wife as two vegetables for the rest of their lives in Rome. Townley, Callejas, Virgilio Paz, and Francisco Franco's secret police had coordinated with Stefano delle Chiaie the assassination of the Chilean diplomat in Rome in October 1975.

—The old man didn't want to die—joked Pinochet, when he met in Santiago with delle Chiaie, that short man with bulging eyes who, his acquaintances said, instilled fear just by opening his mouth.[151]

The Italian, protected by Francisco Franco until his death, was no stranger among the generals of the Southern Cone. One month after the attack on Leighton and his wife, he met with General Pinochet and Lieutenant Contreras at the Ritz Hotel in Madrid, when the Chileans attended the funeral of the Generalissimo. Beyond the bloody attacks attributed to him in Italy, he had participated in the massacre at Ezeiza airport upon General Perón's return to Argentina in June 1973. Four years later, with Carlo Cicuttini, he would collaborate again with Spanish Falangists for another of his masterpieces, this time titled "Massacre of Atocha." The CIA also participated in this terrorist attack in Madrid, in which five people died and many others were seriously injured. Three years later, the CIA, one of their Nazi war criminals, Klaus Barbie, and delle Chiaie himself participated in the Cocaine Coup of Luis García Meza in Bolivia.

Though he lacked any ideological knowledge, Townley, the Yankee rejected by his father, his in-laws, and the CIA, was no less than the Italian. One of his most celebrated strikes was the car bomb that killed Chilean General Carlos Prats, also in Buenos Aires, on September 30, 1974—because the most important things in Latin America always happen in September.

Michael Townley was determined to show who, truly, was Michael Townley.

Vendettas in Miami

—Neither tradition nor new methods had anything to do with any of the three R's.

—*The Three R's*—Hunter mocked—. What's that? A pizzeria? Two Milks, Three Romero's, Four Cheeses... You know my favorite seasoning is basil, but it's not quantifiable. There's only one.

—None of these cases from the Miami-Caracas-Santiago axis ever had anything to do with a revolt, a rebellion, or, even less so, a revolution. From any angle you looked at it, it was the same tradition as the Cuban mafia from the Batista era, adorned with new speeches and watered with lots of rum... But let's get to the facts.

—Well, I'm all ears.

On April 13, 1976, an employee of the Piranha Boat Company yacht factory, located at 9970 Banyan Street in Perrine, south of Miami, found the boss, Don Ramón Donestévez, slumped over his office desk, in a pool of blood. Someone had shot him once, behind the left ear.

The scene showed all the signs of a political crime. Donestévez, an anti-Castro activist and fighter, had a large American flag behind his executive chair, as if he were an important government official. To the side, several copies of the Spanish-language newspaper he owned, the *Nationalist Olive Green*, which he distributed in a jeep, dressed in military attire and accompanied by people armed with rifles. Donestévez claimed that his criticism of other exile figures, such as Rolando Masferrer, Jorge Mas Canosa, Carlos Prío, and Manuel Artime, had earned him mortal enemies, so he had to carry a weapon even to count little sheep.

In front of Donestévez's body was a note in his handwriting and signed *Zero*. He still seemed to be breathing. The paramedics who took him to Miami's Dade General Hospital detected a pulse, though very weak. The ambulance arrived at 10:15 in the morning. Fifteen minutes later, the patient had died.

—Why do you mention the left ear? Is it relevant or can we leave it out?

The detail of the bullet behind the left ear was for the consumption of the Cuban community, which surely hadn't forgotten that just on April 12, 1972, after receiving a warning note signed as *Zero*, engineer José de la Torriente had been executed with a shot behind the right ear.

—And this one, why?

—For not having contributed to the cause as expected.[152]

Héctor Díaz Limonta, a member of the invasion battalion of Playa Girón and the same Group Zero, was strangled in Union City. The secretary of the Christian Democratic Movement, Ernesto Rodríguez (agent amMOP-1, for the CIA), was executed by a gunshot in Miami. The same story as other exiles, like Arturo Rodríguez Vives, who was also executed in his apartment at 2304 Amsterdam Avenue in New York. Arturo Rodríguez had been prosecuted for a plan to blow up several embassy offices that had commercial relations with Cuba, but since then, "he had retired from political activity," according to Cuban informants in Miami.[153] A year later, Luciano Nieves met the same fate, for being too timid an anti-communist. They were either executed or sent to execute. According to the extensive report from the U.S. Senate, published in March 1976,

> *"Cuban Action is a terrorist group composed of members of the Insurrectional Movement for Revolutionary Recovery (MIRR), which should not be confused with the patriotic Chilean MIR (Revolutionary Left Movement). This MIRR is the antithesis of patriotism. In the name of this group, (Juan Felipe de la Cruz) a 26-year-old young man traveled to Paris in August 1973. The powerful bomb he was preparing exploded in his hands, killing him instantly. His body disappeared among the rubble of the Hotel Abren Ville, where he was staying on the outskirts of Paris. Cuban Action had sent him to France. He was a terrorist, but also a victim of the bosses who took no risks."*[154]

For many years, countless activists of the Cuban exile (like Ramón Donestévez, who self-defined as combatants) had been arrested multiple times for carrying explosives on their yachts or storing them in their residences. On December 19, 1975, customs in Miami had seized Donestévez's yacht Luciano Nieves, with 75 people aboard. The late Donestévez had charged 400 dollars per head to take them to Cuba. The yacht's name was a tribute to another anti-Castro exile, also executed three years earlier in the parking lot of the Variety Children's Hospital in Miami by his comrades, due to methodological differences in the war against communism. In April 1976, Brigade 2506 of Bay of Pigs veterans machine-gunned several Cuban fishing boats, killing at least one fisherman. The New York Times headline read: "Investigation into Cuban fishing boat reveals no suspects."[155] In reality, it was two fishing boats, El Ferro 119 and El Ferro 123. The president of the Bay of Pigs Veterans Association, Juan Pérez Franco, told the Miami News that, "as Cubans and Bay of Pigs veterans, we support any action against Castro's communism. We congratulate those commandos. They represent all free Cubans."[156]

—I'll have to read it, because I'm already lost with so many executions.

—For some reason, all of that was quickly forgotten, even though each of the executions took place not far from here. Not far from the political and media center of the world.

—What remains is what the media repeats—said Hunter—. If there's no film, no newspapers, or TV channels repeating it a thousand times, it doesn't exist. It never existed.

The yachts loaded with weapons and bombs came and went freely throughout the Caribbean. After all, it was "our lake." Of course, every now and then, there was no choice but to apply the law of the Land of Laws. By the time the *Luciano Nieves* broke down shortly after leaving the port of Miami, Donestévez had already violated his ban on leaving Crandon Park County and was detained by the Florida Coast Guard.

Meanwhile, the vendettas among the Cuban exiles in Miami and New Jersey grew each year. Many were executed by snipers or apprentice mercenaries, but the favorite method was bombs, especially dynamite and the white plastic explosive, C4, in the good old days provided in large quantities by the CIA.

—Wasn't it easier to shoot someone in the back than to plant a bomb?—said Hunter.

—Of course it was easier. But more important than killing, eliminating, and suppressing was educating, persuading, teaching, intimidating. A bomb always has its place in the media and in people's fear. Killing someone with a gun may be much easier, but it doesn't qualify as terrorism because it impresses few when the victim is not someone well-known or close. After a successful explosion, donations from big businessmen increased.

On one occasion, Jerry Luack and Newton Porter, two explosives experts from the Miami Police, responded to a complaint from Donestévez himself. Someone had placed a package with several cylinders of dynamite in his yacht factory. Luack and Porter managed to disarm the dynamite circuit one minute before 8:55 a.m., the time marked on the detonation clock. The clock activated the detonator, made the expected metallic noise, but the dynamite had already been disconnected. Donestévez didn't forget the incident. Six months before his death, Rolando Masferrer, businessman and leader of a faction of Miami exiles, died when his car flew into the air. Parts of his body were found a block away.

Masferrer was the director of the *Libertad* newspaper in Miami and of the Nationalist Verde Olivo weekly. His reputation and ten million dollars had brought him from Cuba years ago, on one of his yachts. He had been a senator under Fulgencio Batista and was accused by the revolutionary government in Havana of having massacred two thousand Cubans in the Sierra Maestra. After the Revolution, he had participated in various attacks on the island, such as the explosion of the French ship in Havana that took 101 lives. Shortly after, he met with President John Kennedy himself, but Kennedy dismissed him for his fanaticism. The philanthropist Howard Hughes, one of the richest men in the world, had provided his ranch for organizing attacks against the island. By then, Masferrer's network of political and financial influence was, at the very least, enviable.

In Miami, his weekly Libertad competed with Donestévez's publication, though this detail may be considered irrelevant. More importantly, Masferrer considered exile leaders like Orlando Bosch communists and was himself assassinated for being considered a communist. The Cero group claimed responsibility for his murder and justified it because the director of the Libertad and Verde Olivo Nacionalista newspapers had become a divisive figure in the Cuban community, leading to suspicions that he could be an agent of Fidel Castro.[157] Commandos Cero, responsible for several executions in Miami, that same month had received credit (in common agreement by its main authors, Michael Townley and Virgilio Paz) for the attack that left former Chilean Senator Bernardo Leighton and his wife paraplegic in Italy.

On October 31, 1975, the same day the car bomb ended Rolando Masferrer, Verde Olivo Nacionalista hit the streets with his photo under the initials R.I.P. As was known, the Revolution had sentenced him to death in 1959, so Miami's radio and television reported that Fidel Castro had organized the attack. Neither the Miami police, the FBI, nor the CIA bothered to translate these articles. None had any doubts that it was another settling of scores in the capital of terrorism.

The lists of those condemned to death continued circulating through the streets of Miami. Almost all the names, except those self-implicated for publicity reasons, had been classified as traitors. Often, they were warned with a note taped to their front doors. The Miami police made progress in investigating those responsible for the wave of killings, but they failed to incarcerate the masterminds. The first Latino mayor of Miami, Puerto Rican Maurice Ferré, tirelessly supported the freedom fighters of Cuban exiles in South Florida. He supported the creation of "Orlando Bosch Day" to honor the hero annually on March 25th. Ferré also contributed thousands of dollars to the terrorist group Alpha 66, arguing that the organization had been accused of terrorism outside the United States, not within it. In 1983, he visited Orlando Bosch in the Caracas prison.[158] Along with ambassador and lobbyist Otto Juan Reich, he pressured the White House for his release. From the same prison, Luis Posada Carriles would escape with the help of money sent by magnate Jorge Mas Canosa to bribe the guards.

Of course, there are rules for everything, and certain values are respected. The executions of Torriente and Donestévez were the only ones that broke the unwritten rule of not eating meat on Good Friday or killing Christians during Holy Week. Journalist Emilio Milian also suffered an attack days later, already outside the protection of the week in which Jesus was executed.

Milian was known for his radio program *Habla el Pueblo* and had spoken out against the Havana government and against the terrorist attacks by Miami exiles. A bomb planted under his car blew off both of his legs and left him half-deaf and half-blind. Five years later, Cubans Gaspar Jiménez and Gustavo Castillo would be found guilty of the attack by a U.S. jury, but they would not be imprisoned because they were already incarcerated in Mexico, for kidnapping a Cuban consul in that country.

The Cubans of Miami, regardless of their rank within the CIA, the FBI, or their own obsessions, never ceased to be under threat from their own comrades. One of the CIA's most active assets in Latin America and founder of Alpha 66, Antonio Veciana, would face an attempt on his life on September 21, 1979, just before 7:00 PM, as he was about to enter his home. The former agent always took a different route home from work but always had to return to his house. Two strangers shot at him from a car. A .45 caliber bullet lodged in his stomach and the other in his head. In his memoirs, he would acknowledge his suspicions of other CIA agents. His daughter, then a journalist for The Miami News, could only (or only wished to) suspect Fidel Castro, the only person she knew and the only thing she had heard about all her life.

According to a Cuban informant of the FBI, Dionisio Suárez, one of the participants in the execution of Orlando Letelier, before settling as an exile in Miami, had personally executed in Cuba more than seventy Batista supporters accused by the Revolution of participating in the torture and disappearance of undesirables.[159] The figure might have been an exaggeration, but it wasn't the first time witnesses in Miami identified anti-Castro exiles as having participated in what they later pointed to as evidence of the brutality of Fidel Castro's communist regime.

In 1977, during the trial for the assassination of Letelier and his assistant, Suárez, known as El Mono Ricardo Morales, was protected by law as an informant.

—Suárez has immunity—complained prosecutor Eugene Propper—; he can stand before the Grand Jury and tell them it was he who planted the bomb that killed Letelier and Moffitt, and then walk out the door as if nothing happened. I've tried to get him for one of his many crimes, but it's practically impossible.[160]

THE CHURCH COMMISSION AND THE PARALLEL STATE

DESPITE PRESIDENT GERALD FORD'S order to maintain discretion, on Wednesday, April 14, the Church Commission published its investigations into Operation Mockingbird. In six books, the commission summarized, recorded, and detailed some of the CIA's: inoculation and manipulation of the press in the United States and around the world; programs of kidnapping, torture, and assassination of citizens and foreign leaders; planning and execution of coups d'état in various countries; illegal experiments with hard drugs in different parts of the world, using undesirables.

The Commission revealed the constant monitoring of the private lives of various social leaders, professors, anti-war activists, politicians, and actors. Although, henceforth, anyone accused of paranoia would be labeled as such, the very list of those spied on is paranoid. With the collaboration of distinguished volunteers (like Walt Disney or the National Students Association, invented by the NSA in 1947 and funded by the CIA until 1978), state agencies spied on and collected private data on any dissident in the United States: Albert Einstein for his socialist ideas, his defense of Black people, and his criticism of atomic bombs. Martin Luther King, for a letter admitting to being a socialist and, above all, according to Edgard Hoover, for his dangerous speeches on racial equality and integration. Marilyn Monroe for her trips to Europe. Arthur Miller for being Monroe's husband and for his uncomfortable interviews. Frank Sinatra, for being suspected of being a communist. The Beatles for their criticism of the apartheid in Jacksonville. John Lennon for his pacifist songs. The conservative Daniel Ellsberg for leaking the Pentagon Papers. His psychiatrist to gather private and personal information that could destroy him...

The very members of the Church Commission and the Pike Commission investigating these abuses were spied on, and information about their private lives was filed away for discretionary use. Starting in 1973, at the request of the U.S. military, all U.S. citizens who opposed the Vietnam War were recorded by the NSA.

The scandal forced President Ford to issue a decree prohibiting the secret assassination of foreign leaders. The decree was amended by President Ronald Reagan in 1981 to restore the freedom of action and espionage for agents fighting for the freedom and security of the homeland.

In 1971, a group of dissidents and anti-Vietnam War activists broke into an FBI office in New Jersey, proving they had been spied on and recorded to neutralize them through fear and extortion. No major press outlet wanted to publish their findings. The CIA and its parent organization, the NSA, did not moderate their actions thereafter, but quite the opposite. On March 12, 2013 (months before Snowden's revelations), the Director of National Intelligence, James Clapper, was questioned by the U.S. Congress. Senator Ron Wyden asked him:

—Does the NSA collect any kind of information on U.S. citizens?

General Clapper responded categorically:

—No, sir. They are all foreign.[161]

The NSA documents, revealed by former CIA employee Edward Snowden, left no room for doubt: while Clapper was being questioned in Congress, by that point in 2013 the NSA had already intercepted and stored three trillion communications from U.S. citizens and foreigners. According to the documents leaked by Snowden, from December 10, 2012, to January 10, 2013, the program Fairview (Fair View) alone had collected and stored 200 million phone calls, emails, and online chats.

Just in case—and in the name of freedom.

TOWNLEY DEMONSTRATES THE VIRTUES OF SARIN GAS

THIS MONTH, HE HAD TO REPORT ON THE PROGRESS with sarin gas. At DINA's secret headquarters, located at 8630 Simón Bolívar Street in La Reina, the effectiveness of the gas was confirmed. For the occasion, Colonel Manuel Contreras and several high-ranking DINA officers attended. The session began with two Peruvian detainees, blindfolded and handcuffed. No one knew the names of the prisoners who were placed against a wall.

Michael Townley put on a mask, like the ones that appeared in magazines during the Cuban Missile Crisis, and approached the prisoners. He took a spray from his pocket and applied it to one of them, who fell to the ground, asphyxiated almost instantly. Then, the same with the other, as confirmation of the experiment.

The gas spread in the air triggered alarms when two of the collaborators, Díaz Radulovich and Troncoso Vivallos began to feel ill. The collaborators survived, but the two Peruvian prisoners continued to writhe on the ground for a considerable time, so they had to be given a cyanide injection to finish the successful experiment.[162]

THE LITERARY GATHERINGS OF MARIANA

"POLITICS DIDN'T COME UP IN OUR CONVERSATIONS—wrote Callejas in her memoirs— because we were all satisfied with the state of things, and those who weren't, said nothing."

Unlike the ivory tower of Jorge Luis Borges and Adolfo Bioy Casares in Buenos Aires, Callejas' had some foundational issues. The first crack was domestic. The second, third, and fourth were more political cracks that, for the writer from the Andes, were earthquakes.

One April night, Mariana Callejas went down to Michael's office and heard her own voice speaking on the phone with a writer friend. She waited a minute behind the door and then flung it open. Townley turned off the recorder, but it was too late.

—Too late—confirmed Mariana—. You know? I can't keep living with you under these conditions.

Furious, she ran to her room and began packing a suitcase with clothes.

—What are you doing?—asked Townley, worried, like a child about to be abandoned.

—I'm leaving—she said.

—You can't go anywhere—said Townley—. You don't have any money.

—I have a mother. I have sisters...

Callejas knew that neither her mother nor her sisters would understand her, because she wasn't going to tell them anything. Townley knew that Mariana wouldn't leave. Even if she had reasons to be furious, her packing of suitcases was a classic feminine move in the art of domestic pressure, and most likely, Mariana wouldn't even step beyond the front door, let alone at that hour of the night.

Her children were perplexed by the situation and refused to pack their suitcases.

An Example of Fascist Democracy

ON THURSDAY, APRIL 22, 1976, THREE DAYS BEFORE the first free elections after half a century in Portugal and two years after the

Carnation Revolution, Adriana Corcho Calleja, wife of the advisor to ambassador Crescencio Palenzuela Páez, noticed that someone had left a suitcase near the embassy elevator.

—Be careful with that,—Adriana said.—I don't like it at all.

The bomb exploded shortly after, minutes before 5:00 p.m. Adriana Corcho and the diplomat Efrén Monteagudo died on the spot, while five others were severely injured. The bomb, hidden in the abandoned briefcase, followed a known pattern: six kilograms of plastic explosive activated remotely by a beep or a timer.

Hours later, a crowd gathered in front of the Cuban Embassy, on Fontes Pereira Avenue in Melo. Later, another crowd gathered in front of the United States Embassy, chanting, "Out, fascists! Punishment for the terrorists!"

The attack had at least two symbolic motivations. One was in retaliation for Cuba's support of Angola's independence, achieved five months earlier. For a decade, Angola and the Cubans had faced off against the dictatorship of Portugal in Africa, against Angolan colonial forces, South Africa's apartheid, Israel's which trained counterrevolutionaries and supplied weapons, as in Central America, and the CIA's flights, among whose ranks were several collaborators from the Cuban exile in Miami.

A second motivation, it was speculated, was to avenge another historical frustration. The *New York Times* the following day reported, on page 3, the appearance of pamphlets in the streets of Lisbon commemorating the upcoming 15th anniversary of the Bay of Pigs invasion, led by a thousand Cuban exiles recruited by the CIA. The pamphlets read: "Before your eyes, you have an example of fascist democracy."[163]

Ambassador Francisco Astray Rodríguez blamed the CIA for the attack. Washington denied it. Explosions against Cuban diplomats continued. Five months earlier, on November 18, 1975, a dynamite explosion had destroyed the car of the Cuban ambassador in Mexico, Fernando López Muino. The driver, Alberto del Río Aguilera, miraculously survived. A year earlier, other bombs had wrecked the

Cuban consulate in Mérida, Yucatán, and another bomb had blown up the offices of Cubana airlines in Mexico City. The same story had been repeated in Panama, in New York, and in other Cuban embassies further south, such as the one in Lima, Peru.

—It's just that the damn Revolution seems like a cat with seven, with a thousand lives,—said a skinny man, leaning on the bar at the corner of Eighth and 20th Avenue—. No matter how many times they crush her, she always survives.

I would have liked to talk to El Guajiro, but I concluded it wasn't wise. Next to him, two men gestured with enthusiastic movements.

—She doesn't just survive—clarified the one who had just invited—she is reborn, that's what you mean, Guajiro, like a snake, because we've killed her several times and she still won't die. That's what she is, a zombie, buddy.

—Yes, that's it, reborn—confirmed El Guajiro.

In the background, a flag with the thirteen white and red stripes of the East India Company, with a circle of stars in the left quadrant. The first flag of the new Anglo-Saxon country.

—The Betsy Ross flag—the bar owner explained to me, after the three men at the bar had left—. Actually, the new States were twelve, because the Carolinas were a single state. One of the stars is Cuban. That's why Cuba's flag has a single star.

THE CIA, EL MERCURIO, PINOCHET AND THE FINAL SOLUTION

SINCE THEY HAD ARRIVED IN THE UNITED STATES, Orlando's activities had multiplied. Isabel had a companion visa, so she wasn't allowed to work in anything that was paid or part of an established job. After some time, she founded the Chilean Human Rights Committee and a group called The Touchstone Gallery, where she was able to restart her work as a sculptor alongside other artists. Her green eyes will never stop seeing the world through tragedy. One of those deepest moments that began her descent into hell was the morning of the coup.

Letelier was still parked on Massachusetts Avenue, staring at the windows of the red brick residence of the Chilean ambassador which he once occupied with Isabel and the children. Other dreams, other violent ways of waking up. He knew he was running late, that he had to leave those old memories behind and head to the IPS offices. Nothing better to cure nostalgia and the remorse of memory than focusing on new projects, on new battles.

—The children woke up to the roar of planes and explosions at La Moneda—Isabel told him a year after that day when everything ended and began at the same time—. Francisco was scared. He knew you were there, with the president. He knew your office had been bombed.

Isabel could only scream at the children:

—Get out of there. Stay away from the windows.

She called the Ministry of Defense, but no one answered. When she realized something terrible had happened to Orlando, she began calling all the ministries and everyone she knew. All in vain.

The next day, she went to General Pinochet's residence. She knocked, but no one answered. The residence was a large, three-story mansion, a traditional home of Santiago's upper class. As she was about to leave, one of the general's servants appeared.

—The general must not be disturbed while he's eating—he said.

Isabel managed to organize the other wives to intercede with some international organizations. Secretly, they contacted the Red Cross and Amnesty International, but when they were discovered, they began to receive threats.

The most important media, the same ones that had conspired against Allende, like those run by the magnate Agustín Edwards, consolidated a state of paranoia in favor of the Junta, the kidnappings and disappearances.

The same day of the coup, rumors began to spread, carefully planted by the newspapers *El Mercurio*, El Día, and Las Últimas Noticias, about "a macabre Plan Z" by Allende's government to exterminate all Chileans who didn't think like him, particularly the Carabineros and the generals of the National Army, who would be executed in a public square on Independence Day, a week before the coup.On September 18, El Mercurio reported the discovery of "a plan for the mass assassination of military officers, political leaders, and opposition journalists, without forgetting their families" by the Marxist government of Allende. The rumor, whose source was attributed to the Naval Intelligence Service, was so effective that it even included the assassination of President Allende himself by his most radical followers.

Fortunately, according to this rumor, the coup had aborted the communist monstrosity, which not only touched nerve fibers reminiscent of Hitler's "final solution", but as a method, it bore the mark of the CIA in Operation Peter Pan. All of which justified the interruption of a century of democracy in Chile, the suspension of the constitution and individual rights, the kidnapping, torture, and death of thousands of suspects of thinking differently, the sale of tens of thousands of newborn children, and the exile of hundreds of thousands of dissidents.

This theory made General Gustavo Leigh Guzman, a member of the first Junta, and decades later the spokesperson of the Military Junta, Federico Willoughby, laugh. The CIA also dismissed it in a secret report as a fabrication typical of psychological warfare.

Decades later, the same journalists who had spread the rumor would admit that it had been a fabricated story. Of course, nothing can be done, nor is it advisable, against a rumor that satisfies the deepest fantasies of believers.[164] The military officials who would later recognize the falsity of this story would also justify it as part of psychological warfare—and in war, anything goes.

Four years later, the FBI agent assigned to Buenos Aires for the Southern Cone, Robert Scherrer, left the office of the head of the

DINA, Colonel Manuel Contreras, and began talking to several military officers in Santiago. According to Scherrer, President Salvador Allende had not taken his own life to avoid being captured by the enemy. He had been executed by Captain René Riveros, at the time a modest lieutenant with a spirit of progress and self-improvement.

Later, the version that the president had committed suicide with a gun gifted by Fidel Castro was too attractive not to be used as a way to crystallize a fiction about one of the most important events in South American history up to that point. For a few days, Scherrer had shared coffees and beers with different officers in Santiago, and had concluded that the blond Captain Riveros had become a celebrity in that military circle for being the man who had ended the life of the socialist dictator. General Baeza resigned, objecting to the manipulation of history and the invention of Allende's suicide, but the new leader of the country, General Pinochet, refused to accept his resignation. To calm his protests, he named him chief of Investigations, so he would stop meddling with that case.

MAY

The Internal Struggles of Santiago

In May, the Joint Command (a paramilitary branch of the Chilean Air Force, known as FACh) reached the conclusion that some of its members were spies for the DINA. Both organizations hated each other due to military jealousy and frequent jurisdictional overlaps, as when the DINA sent Rolando Otero to kill Pascual Allende in Costa Rica while the aviation command was doing the same with Orlando Bosch. They hated each other even more when both missions failed due to betrayals and internal disputes among the Cuban leaders of Venezuela's secret agency.

In Colina, Guillermo Bratti and the FACh's communist informant, Carol Flores, were executed in El Cajón del Maipo. The DINA and the FACh resolved their differences in a meeting between Colonel Pedro Espinosa and Commander Roberto Fuentes Morrison, which took place in a forest with both groups armed for war among the unpainted trees.

Pinochet knew that an army is a pyramid more rigid than those of Egypt, but to govern millions of undisciplined citizens, a strong dose of conflict and division was always useful. A general without wars is like a firefighter without fires, so, since Latin American armies were not prepared for war with any other army, according to John F. Kennedy, the internal enemy had to be invented.

Both factions of the repressive apparatus of the new Chilean state kept General Pinochet displeased, though only in appearance. The tradition of Christian-military displeasure was, by far, a mandatory style, part of the etiquette even at high society parties, even when the teetotaler Pinochet had allowed himself the indulgence of two whiskeys and went to threaten the U.S. ambassador with his red face (as reported to Washington by the ambassador) but still without the usual signs of alcohol-induced joy. Perhaps for that very reason, the revolutionaries insisted on being photographed with broad white smiles behind their dirty beards.

—Statistically speaking—said Hunter— the beard has been revolutionary.

—And the mustache, fascist.

In May 1976, Ambassador David Popper sent Washington a profile of Pinochet. "Pinochet, like the vast majority of officers—the memorandum said— comes from a middle-class background and is a product of the barracks and military quarters. Throughout his life, he has obeyed orders and given them. He expects everyone around him to do the same, and they do. The President is a rough man, a tough head. He is certainly not brilliant. He struggles to deal with contrasting points of view."[165]

General Augusto Pinochet, celebrated by his supporters for his intelligence, honesty, and moral rectitude, akin to bishops and military men, had at least two nicknames: Pinocho, for his closest associates, and Daniel López for others, a fake name used by the general to transfer twelve million dollars to his personal accounts at Riggs Bank in Miami, which, at least for the Latin American division of that bank, made him the most respected military man among many other clients with false names.

RITOQUE

AFTER EIGHT MONTHS OF CONFINEMENT in Dawson, Letelier looked like a ghost of bones and skin. No one wanted him to die there, not even Pinochet, so he was moved north, to Ritoque, another makeshift concentration camp. For Orlando, it was another tragic irony. Together with the Central Unitaria de Trabajadores, Salvador Allende had built Ritoque and Melinka an hour from Valparaíso so that working-class families could have a summer retreat near the exclusive Valparaíso.

—*Exclusive* is a word that defines it all, isn't it?

—Absolutely... In Ritoque, prisoners were beaten without reason, a technique designed more to destroy their mental health than their physical integrity. Other techniques involved taking the blindfolded prisoners to the beach, sometimes naked, and then beating them with wet sacks while setting dogs to chase and bite them as if they were runaway slaves escaping their masters. The regime's sadistic creativity never rested. It was like a desperate need, akin to an addiction.

For a moment, for Letelier, escaping the intense Antarctic cold after eight months was a form of relief. Everything else remained the same. The desperate need for military amusement, that infinite hatred from those above reaching those below—and passing further down—had ceased to be creative and was merely repetitive. One of his colleagues, journalist José Tohá, former Minister of the Interior and Defense, was confined there in Ritoque and executed shortly after.

—Are you a faggot, asshole?—a soldier asked him.

Orlando didn't answer.

—No?—insisted the patriot soldier—. Well, too bad for you, asshole. Did you know your little wife is a shameless whore? Here and in Santiago everyone knows it—everyone but you, of course. She leaves your kids alone to go asking for favors at the barracks. Didn't you know that, asshole?

Ritoque was under the command of Colonel Jorge Espinoza Ulloa and Admiral Toribio Merino and Ernesto Eberhard, who were subordinates of the Minister of Justice Miguel Schweitzer and informants of journalist Gustavo Lorca, from Patria y Libertad. Homeland, Liberty, Justice... Espinoza owed his fame to the heroic act of organizing the country's largest concentration camp in a football stadium, the same one that would continue to host international events just a few years after the Coup.

GaTHerInG WITH STeFano DeLLe CHIaIe

168 KILOMETERS FROM RITOQUE, AS EVERY Thursday, a literary gathering took place at Quetropillán, the laboratory mansion of Lo Curro. As per tradition, the meeting featured a distinguished guest. Jorge Luis Borges almost made it, but for some minor detail, Mariana had said.

This time it was the Italian Stefano delle Chiaie. The screams of the prisoners bitten by dogs on the beach at Ritoque could not be heard, just as the screams of diplomat Carmelo Soria in the basement of the house would not be heard during another pleasant Thursday gathering two months later.

The attendees didn't know him from the newspapers and much less from books, but Callejas had assured them that he was an immensely important figure in Italy's patriotic movements. He didn't tell them that he was a recognized fascist leader, a collaborator of Francisco Franco's secret police, and, for the past two years, an international agent of the DINA. Among his achievements were his involvement in the Ezeiza massacre upon General Perón's return to Argentina, the attack that killed Chilean General Carlos Prats in Buenos Aires, and the most recent one that left former Minister Bernardo Leighton and his wife in a vegetative state in Rome.

The meeting did not go as planned. Literature was the least discussed topic. The Italian launched into a speech against the Jews, and Callejas had to interrupt him. She touched the Star of David hanging around her neck and said:

—Please, don't spout your antisemitic rhetoric at my table.

Stefano looked at her with a smile:

—This isn't your table—he said—. It's Andrés's table.

—Andrés? Who is Andrés?—someone asked.

Callejas didn't respond. She simply glanced at her husband, alias Andrés, but Townley returned a look of reproach.

More Literature: Borges, Sábato, Videla

ACCORDING TO A SECRET CIA REPORT dated June 2 and only declassified in a minor section, the writer Haroldo Conti was abducted in Buenos Aires by the Forces of Order in the early hours of May 5. He was seen at a detention center but never reappeared. Neither alive nor dead.

Months earlier, he had received the Casa de las Américas prize from Cuba, for his latest novel. The new regime accused him of distributing Cuban propaganda. Though known within a small circle of intellectuals, his case was one among thousands, so his disappearance went unnoticed.

Less discreet was the disappearance of some foreign politicians. On Tuesday, May 18, Senator Zelmar Michelini and the President of Uruguay's Chamber of Representatives Héctor Gutiérrez Ruiz were abducted in Buenos Aires. Both had been living in exile in Argentina since the coup d'état in Uruguay three years earlier, from where they had denounced human rights violations in their country. El Toba Gutiérrez Ruiz was abducted from his small store, the 33 Orientales, on Callao Street.

On May 19, Juan Raúl Ferreira and his mother, the wife of Wilson Ferreira, sought refuge in the home of Raúl Alfonsín.

—You can't go anywhere now—Alfonsín told them— Stay here. The guest room has a double bed, if you don't mind.

At midnight, Juan Raúl went for water to the kitchen and saw Alfonsín sleeping on the couch.[166]

That same Wednesday, May 19, 1976, a few weeks after the coup d'état in Argentina, the priest Leonardo Castellani, the president of the Argentine Society of Writers, Alberto Ratti, and the writers Jorge Luis Borges and Ernesto Sábato, met at the Casa Rosada with General Rafael Videla.

Minutes before lunch, the general's image advisors achieved the photograph they planned to distribute worldwide. Two hours later, the second most important event occurred: the statements of the celebrated writers.

—The general made an excellent impression on me—said Sábato—. He is a cultured, modest, and intelligent man. I was impressed by his broad-mindedness and culture.

—He's a true gentleman—said Borges.

—Well, they screwed us all—Osvaldo Bayer will say in Berlin and Julio Cortázar in Paris, looking at the same photograph.

The statements, somewhere between complicit and forced, concealed the conversation the six men had over the table. Esteban Ratti asked General Videla about the writer Haroldo Conti, who had disappeared two weeks earlier, and handed him a list of ten writers who had disappeared under similar circumstances. Borges, more occupied with counting immortal syllables, would take a few years (which meant countless centuries on the unpredictable walls of infamous history) to understand what was happening. Without the presence of his mother Leonor, already in his eighties, he would become a late and insignificant critic of the dictatorship. Sábato, more reserved and less daring that noon (despite the artist's ability to perceive the immeasurable depth of the human condition), would eventually become the president of the National Commission on the Disappearance of Persons after the fall of the military regime.

After two days of detention and torture, on his birthday, Michelini was killed. So was Gutiérrez Ruiz. The leader of the progressive wing of Uruguay's conservative party, Wilson Ferreira Aldunate, managed to escape to London. His son, Juan Raúl Ferreira also escaped. He landed in Washington, and Orlando Letelier opened the doors of IPS to him, days before being assassinated.

The bodies of Michelini, Gutiérrez Ruiz, and the couple Rosario del Carmen Barredo and William Whitelaw Blanco were found on Friday the 21st, showing signs of torture. Rosario and William had long since renounced armed struggle to pursue politics, but this detail was irrelevant. Their three children, the eldest four years old and the youngest two months, were also kidnapped alongside their parents. After a denunciation campaign in Italy's *Corriere della Sera* and in the *Buenos Aires Herald*, the three children reappeared a week later, on Saturday, May 29th.

Tens of thousands of other kidnapped children in the countries of the Southern Cone (some ripped from the wombs of their dead or tortured mothers) would not be so fortunate. Thousands were taken to luxury hotels before being sent to Europe and the United States, where they were sold for a hundred thousand dollars each.

ROLANDO OTERO, THE MISSING LINK

ROLANDO OTERO HERNÁNDEZ arrived at Miami International Airport from Chile on May 20th and, hours later, fled to the Dominican Republic. He was accused of detonating bombs in several federal offices, a bank, and two buildings of the national post office in Miami, a few months prior. One of the bombs exploded at the entrance of the FBI offices. Another, hidden in a tape recorder, injured two secretaries of the local police. Another, a package of dynamite, blew out fifteen windows of the offices on 11th Street of the police department that had initiated an investigation into the previous attacks. Another, in the men's bathroom on the sixth floor of the building of the Criminal Justice Department that had initiated an accusation process against him. Another, in a Miami bookstore. Another exploded in locker 5030 of the same Miami airport, where Otero himself had left his fingerprints.[167]

Otero Hernández used to call radio stations in Florida to claim responsibility for the attacks in the name of El Cóndor. According to investigations, he was also linked to the bomb that exploded at La Guardia Airport in New York on December 29 of last year, which killed eleven people and injured dozens more, although this explosion, like many others, was never clarified.

—What they want is to crucify me—he had declared to the Dominican press.

Otero had previously fled to the Dominican Republic on January 5, but the authorities asked him to leave the country, citing fears of a new wave of bomb attacks, like the one that followed the arrest of the fugitive member of the Cuban National Liberation Front from Miami, Humberto López. From Santo Domingo, Otero flew to Caracas of Posada Carriles, Orlando Bosch and El Mono Morales Navarrete. Shortly after, he was granted safe passage to Santiago de Chile.

In Chile, the authorities decided that it wasn't worth adding another problem with U.S. justice, especially for a minor case, so they allowed his extradition. Otero left Chile at 9:50 p.m. on Braniff Flight 978, escorted by FBI agent Robert Scherrer. They arrived at Miami International Airport at 7:00 a.m. In addition to the previous charges, the FBI accused him of bribing agent Robert Scherrer during the flight.[168] He was charged and convicted for multiple bombings, along with other anti-Castro individuals like Antonio de la Cova, Gary Latham, Blas Jesús Corbo, and Miguel Ángel Peraza, editor of a Cuban magazine, accused of planting bombs in bookstores and at the University of Miami.

In July, Otero's defense managed to have his trial transferred to a court in Jacksonville, to avoid negative publicity in Miami that could harm their client. There was no need to record his fingerprints because Otero himself had already done so on March 8, 1974, when he applied to join the police. Back then, he had failed the entrance exam. He tried again on the 27th of the same month. According to the FBI, the fingerprints from his application matched those found on a newspaper vending machine and in a phone booth at the Miami airport that had exploded months earlier.

His way of pronouncing the word *joke* also matched the recording of an anonymous caller who had phoned the airport on October 17 at 5:58 a.m. to report the bomb that would explode in minutes:

El exilio del terror

—*This is no* joke—someone had said—. *We have placed some bombs in the complex.*

—He pronounced the *J* like a *Y*—said Mrs. Simpson, an operator in Charlotte, North Carolina.

—Other people of Hispanic origin may mispronounce that word—argued the defense attorney, Tom Alimón.

Agent Morris *Bud* Haddock collected pronunciations of the word *joke* from other Hispanics, but none matched the fossilized pronunciation in Otero's lexicon. For both the FBI and the Miami police, the biggest obstacle to clarifying each case of terrorism, intimidation, conspiracy, and settling scores lay in the absolute silence of Miami's Latino community on the matter and their refusal to cooperate with any investigation.

Finally, on August 10, they managed to get three accomplices from the latest series of bombings (Cirro Orizondo, Manolo Revuelta, and businessman Héctor Serrano) to testify against their comrades in exchange for immunity for their own crimes. A fourth informant, Antonio González, testified against Otero but didn't manage to get on the list of those granted immunity by the justice system. The fifth informant was (as before against Orlando Bosch and against other comrades) El Mono Ricardo Morales Navarrete, CIA employee, client of the FBI himself, and at that time head of Venezuela's secret police department. El Mono, who used to visit Otero's apartment in Miami, confirmed to FBI agent Robert G. Ross that Otero was one of the perpetrators of the latest bombings at the airport and federal buildings. For some strategic reason, this last piece of information was leaked in the Miami Herald on October 6.

On October 13, it was revealed that Otero had a bigger plan: to blow up the Turkey Point nuclear plant, located seventy kilometers south of Miami.[169]

—All evidence suggests that these terrorist acts are the work of frustrated Cuban activists—declared Attorney General Jerome Sanford.

—I remind you that my client was trained by the CIA to be an expert in demolition— argued his lawyer, Tom Almon—. I mean, when it comes to time for the decision, this court must maintain an open mind, a flexible criterion.

The clues, evidence, and witnesses that identified Otero in each charge accumulated throughout the trials. After claiming responsibility for the attacks in various confrontations, he denied it in court. Like the other accused, Otero pleaded not guilty. Like other more recognized names (such as Orlando Bosch and Posada Carriles), he oscillated between avoiding self-incrimination with a confession before the law and not relinquishing credit in the press and urban legends about his heroic terrorist actions.

—This is a circus— protested Otero when he was declared guilty—. The court wanted to crucify me. It's clear that this was all a political trial.

His lawyers pointed to El Mono Ricardo Morales as a key element of the verdict, but Otero appeared before the press with a new theory: the bombs were planted by communists to implicate the Cuban patriots of Miami.

—There are thousands of infiltrated communist agents— Otero told the *Miami* News—. Some of them could have planted all those bombs.[170]

During his trial in Jacksonville, Ciro Orizondo, one of his friends and roommates, would testify in favor of Otero. According to the Miami News on October 18, 1976, on page 4, Orizondo stated in court:

—Otero is a fervent anti-communist. I myself have seen him shed tears upon hearing the United States anthem…[171]

During the trial, on July 22, the same network of patriots had planted a bomb in the Mercedes Benz of the Chilean embassy in Colombia, as punishment for the mistreatment Otero had received in Santiago. The bomb did not explode. On Saturday the 24th, they had better luck with another bomb at the Chilean pavilion at the International Exhibition, leaving six people seriously injured.[172]

In 1976, Otero was acquitted by the same court in Jacksonville. A few months later, his case would be reopened in the Fort Walton Beach court. He would be sentenced to 45 years of probation, but a few months later he would be released on parole.[173] In 1982, he would be charged with drug trafficking. By then, cocaine trafficking had already become a very common source of income for freedom fighters.

IT'S NOT JUST IDEAS; IT'S SOMETHING DEEPER

RONNI AND MICHAEL GOT MARRIED ON the Memorial Day holiday, Monday, May 31, at her parents' farm. The Karpens were a Jewish family. The Moffitts, Irish Catholics. They had much in common. They had met at the IPS. The infatuation was immediate and overwhelming. Not by chance, they shared the same worldview. The triumph of Salvador Allende in Chile, six years earlier, had been one of the happiest moments for both. In the same measure, Pinochet's coup had marked them in a way they could not even imagine at the time.

One of Ronni's closest professors, John Marciano from the State University of New York at Cortland, witnessed the wedding and the premonitory poem by Pablo Neruda that Michael read to celebrate the occasion:

Rise with me
and let us go together
to fight hand to hand
against the spiderwebs of the wicked,
against the system that distributes hunger,
against the organization of misery.
Let us go,
and you, my star, beside me,

newly born from my own clay,
you will have already found the hidden spring
and in the midst of the fire you will be
beside me

Letelier and the Moffitts clicked from the very first day they met. All three thought the same way...—I wrote, and immediately crossed out the last sentence. No, that wasn't it, I thought. You usually get along better with people who share the same ideas, but that's not a requirement. Not for friendship, and much less for love. It's something else, I thought, or wanted to think. I looked out the window, searching for an explanation. Ideas are not the cause, but the consequence of something deeper. But what? Then I completed the paragraph:

More than thinking alike, they felt alike, which is what really matters. Thought is a derivative of deeper feelings. Sometimes they align, other times they don't, but they always orbit around that which different people hold in common, that invisible thing that cannot be clarified or formulated using pure critical analysis. Yes, it's the deeper feelings.

For a century, Jews and Irish Catholics were not welcome here. After World War II, the story reversed itself, and the memory of pain and injustice was forgotten. Surely, not for everyone. Especially not for Ronni and Michael. The same, perhaps, for someone as different as Letelier.

The same in other human galaxies. Someone like Townley, a perfect political illiterate, falls in love with a woman like Mariana Callejas and, in no time, shares the ideas of individuals as distant as Eugenio Berríos and Orlando Bosch. It's just a matter of time and context. Callejas was a typical species of the hyper-ideologized militant. Like Ronald Reagan's advisor, Jeane Kirkpatrick (also a proponent of bombing all rebellious nations), had gone from socialist militancy to extreme right-wing activism. A case for psychologists, rather than sociologists and political analysts. A typical case of the convert, of the fanatic with Torquemada syndrome...

It's not the ideas. It is that *something more*, much deeper than ideas, which are often very simple. The rest depends on the setting, the theater, the director, the actors, the century in which *Julius Caesar* or *Romeo and Juliet* or *The Seagull* is performed. The play is the same. The passions too.

—When *The Seagull* premiered, the audience booed it—said Hunter—. The uproar at the end of that October night in 1896 was so intense that Russia's most famous actress lost her voice. The failure was so great that even Chekhov stopped writing for the theater.

—Which is to say, an extension of the play into the real world...

—Assuming there's anything that has nothing to do with fiction.

Threats

Isabel received a call:

—*Are you Mr. Letelier's wife?*

—Yes...

—*No, you are Letelier's widow*—the voice in Spanish had replied before hanging up.

The calls had been made from Caracas.

A letter written in red ink addressed to Letelier warned: *"if you don't stop meddling in politics, we will kill you."*

One of his IPS coworkers looked at him, concerned:

—If they're threatening me, it's because I'm doing something right—Letelier said.

Letelier was convinced that Pinochet could not and would not dare to kill a minister of Allende in Washington, as the young Chilean Juan Gabriel Valdés would acknowledge years later, at the time working at IPS just months away from earning his doctorate from Princeton University.

Pinochet needed his biggest ally, and Washington wasn't keen on a scandal of that nature. On the other hand, Letelier had decided not to report the threats. During the Vietnam War, the FBI had already infiltrated the IPS with 62 informants, deeming the institute too far to the left in its criticism of Washington's foreign policy. At night, agents would go through the trash and reproduce written letters by reading the discarded typewriter ribbons. Months earlier, following the domestic espionage scandal of President Nixon and amid the Senate investigation into the CIA's infiltration of the press, the FBI had admitted to these practices against the IPS before a House committee.

A few months later, Gabriel Valdés himself would recommend Uruguayan Juan Raúl Ferreira to join the institute's team. At the time, his father, Senator Wilson Ferreira Aldunate, and his wife, Susana Sienra, were dodging agents of the DINA and the rest of Operation Condor in Europe.

JUNE

IDEOLOGICAL PATRIOTISM

IN JUNE, MICHAEL MOFFITT BEGAN WORKING AS AN ASSISTANT TO ORLANDO LETELIER at the progressive institute in Washington. He traveled with him to Amsterdam, where the IPS had its international headquarters, also focused on the study and activism against the war in Vietnam and against apartheid in South Africa. The IPS had emerged in Washington in the early sixties as a response to the RAND Corporation, the powerful ultraconservative think tank partly funded by the Pentagon, its main client. Among the academic members of the IPS were Jack O'Dell and Noam Chomsky. Since its involvement in the leaking of the Pentagon Papers by Daniel Ellsberg in 1971, most of the mentions the institute received in the press were negative references about its lack of—how to say it?—ideological patriotism.

—Ronni and I care a lot about Orlando—said Michael—. He has his issues, of course. I think he hasn't been able to get rid of the young Venezuelan woman who caused him problems some time ago. It's not that he loves her, but he desires her and hasn't decided to stop answering her calls.

—One day Orlando will be president of Chile—said Michael—. I don't think there's anyone in the entire Chilean dissent capable of bringing the opponents of Pinochet so close together. The only problem is that, by now, Pinochet must know it.

On June 16, the U.S. Congress passed the law promoted by Senator Ted Kennedy and the union leader Douglas Fraser, which reduced economic aid to the regime of Augusto Pinochet. Shortly after, Fraser, as president of the autoworkers' union, would lead the way for the Carter administration to save Chrysler from bankruptcy in 1979 in exchange for a wage reduction for its workers. A similar story would repeat three decades later, in 2009, when the administration of Barack Obama nationalized the largest bankrupt automakers and reprivatized them once they were rescued from financial chaos. All for the ideological homeland.

In Santiago they knew that Senator Ted Kennedy was a friend of Orlando Letelier. That same day, Isabel Letelier received another call:

—*Are you the wife of Orlando Letelier?*

—Yes, said Isabel, and immediately regretted it.

The caller doesn't ask. On the other hand, responding to a harasser is acknowledging them some form of power.

—*Not anymore*—said the voice, repeating the pattern of harassment and threat from other times— *Now you are his widow, you know.*

Despite his youth and his particular intellectual preparation, Michael Moffitt was an activist of action. In Washington, he had helped in the approval of the Thomas Harkin-Kennedy law prohibiting the expansion of military aid to Pinochet's regime. Later, Moffitt himself would prove that this cut of aid from Washington had been compensated with a five hundred percent increase in assistance from private banks in his country, the United States.[174]

Nothing new, but an academic is obligated to prove it.

Let him leave and never return

A HONK WOKE HIM FROM HIS MEMORIES. He was badly parked. He stopped contemplating the red brick residence of the Chilean embassy and continued down Massachusetts Avenue. He passed the Sheridan Circle roundabout and headed for the next one, Dupont Circle. His memories also traveled from the frozen prison of

Dawson Island to the office building of the IPS, where he was headed at that moment, like every morning.

One day before the first anniversary of the CIA coup in Chile, on Tuesday, September 10, 1974, the mayor of Caracas, Diego Arria, landed in Santiago of Chile. That same day, he met with Pinochet, who needed to secure allies in South America, in addition to the unconditional support from Washington. Above all, a crucial ally like Venezuela, due to its oil exports to the country.

The conversation did not go as the general had imagined. Arria conditioned the shipment of oil on Letelier's release.

—I deeply dislike that you bring up that subject—said Pinochet—. One thing has nothing to do with the other.

Arria did not respond. He looked at him for a moment, and the general said:

—Anyway, I was planning to release him at some point.

On Monday, September 16, they transferred Letelier and Osvaldo Puccio to the Tres Álamos concentration camp in the capital. At that time, Puccio was a 22-year-old young man, who had the misfortune of being in the Casa de la Moneda on September 11, 1973, with his father, Allende's secretary. At 5:00 AM the next day, they were transported to the Arturo Merino Benítez International Airport, handcuffed and escorted by soldiers. When the prisoners boarded the plane, the pilot blocked the guards from entering.

—No one can enter the plane armed—he said, pointing to an imaginary line—. From here on, I am the captain.

When the aircraft left Chilean territory, the captain announced:

—I am pleased to inform you that among the passengers, we carry two prisoners of the regime, until just a few minutes ago.

The passengers applauded enthusiastically.

Below, from the airport windows, Isabel watched the plane leave the country and breathed a sigh of relief.

Upon landing in Caracas, Letelier was surrounded by journalists. He remembered that it was advisable not to make political statements just days after being released, so as not to harm the release of other prisoners, so he merely said:

—It's like starting to live again.

In Chile, this statement didn't sit well. Neither this one nor any other. The newspapers tirelessly repeated it as proof of the betrayal of the homeland by Allende's minister. Betrayal of the ideological homeland. "Is this the loyalty they have toward the military and toward Chile?" another detainee from Dawson, Sergio Bitar, would recall, citing it as the most repeated comment.[175]

—Let him leave and never come back—said Pinochet, on September 11, 1974.

After a prudent silence, Letelier began to speak. Nothing makes fascists more nervous than someone who thinks differently being able to speak.

A few days after arriving in Caracas, a young woman known for her elegance went to visit him. Orlando couldn't get her out of his head for over a year.

—She caught me on the best day of the worst moment of my life.

A month later, Professor Saul Landau offered him a job at the Institute for Policy Studies in Washington. At the time, the salary was below the national average, but Letelier considered that the IPS would help him project the resistance in exile, and Washington was a safer city for his family. He knew that, sooner or later, he would break the promise of silence he made before being expelled into exile. He knew he was the leading figure of Allende's government who had survived the planned catastrophe.

Five days after Landau's proposal, Letelier picked up the phone and returned the call. His wife, Nina Serrano, answered the phone.

WeLCOMe, MISTer KISSInger

On June 7, 1976, Secretary of State Henry Kissinger landed in Santiago, Chile. Several human rights advocacy groups asked him to intervene with Pinochet to somewhat alleviate the violations of freedoms and guarantees of Chilean citizens.

A few days later, without applause and without television cameras, Guillermo Novo arrived, invited by DINA. At the airport, Michael Townley stepped ahead of the immigration officers and let him pass without being checked. A sign of power and status in protocol was to skip the protocol.

On the way to the apartment assigned to Novo, Townley apologized for the treatment given to Rolando Otero, who had generated so much controversy in Miami.

—I understand—said Novo—. To be honest, our biggest problem wasn't the treatment of Otero, but all that publicity against us. Why the hell didn't they just put a bullet in his head and be done with it? Why didn't they make him disappear, man?[176]

Two years earlier, on July 22, 1974, Ambassador David Popper had decided to bring up the issue of human rights in Chile during a meeting discussing military aid from Washington to Chile. Present at the meeting were Chile's Minister of Defense, Oscar Boinilla, and U.S. Secretary of the Army, Howard Callaway. Secretary of State Henry Kissinger sent a cable to the embassy without diplomatic ambiguity:

—Tell Popper to stop messing around. That he no longer attends those damn social science conferences.

Popper was left speechless but not crushed. Kissinger's order leaked, and the *New York Times* published it on September 27 on page 18. According to this newspaper, some groups in the United States protested, citing the latest revelation that the CIA had funneled eight million dollars of the time, from 1970 to 1973 alone, not for national defense, but to make the presidency of Salvador Allende intolerable, unbearable, and painful for the common people, for the population of that country that no one could locate on the map or, worse, that everyone preferred to ignore.[177]

Now, just hours after landing in Santiago, Kissinger shook Pinochet's hand and confirmed his goodwill:

—In the United States, as you know, we sympathize with what you're doing here. We want to help you, not undermine you. You did a great service to the West by overthrowing Allende.

To the West, to the constellation of Orion, and to the Paradise where lions eat grass and know nothing of sex.

Three years earlier, on September 12, 1973, before the cameras of U.S. television, the same Secretary of State, after three years of planning the removal of Allende from Washington, had put on a stone-faced expression to declare:

—We have never had any contact with those who have perpetrated this military coup in Chile.

Exactly one year later, while Orlando Letelier was flying to Caracas, Kissinger took credit for his release. More than that, he complained that the former Chilean minister had not made any statement thanking him for his release. Although no document or even the slightest hint would ever emerge to suggest Kissinger had intervened on behalf of Letelier's release, he once again declared without fear of lying, relying on the eternal confidence that the verb created the world:

—Mr. Letelier doesn't know the meaning of truth—he said— or he has no sense of gratitude.

As I was saying, on June 7, 1976, Kissinger landed in Santiago to attend the VI meeting of the OAS. His arrival was covered by the Chilean press as if it were the coming of the Messiah. A caravan of official cars took him to the luxurious Hotel Carrera, the same hotel that at the time was part of the network hosting newborns kidnapped from imprisoned or disappeared parents, waiting to be adopted by foreigners with high purchasing power and a better understanding of freedom.

The Secretary of State stayed in Suite 1122, which comprised five rooms and three bathrooms. His entourage occupied the entire floor below.

Cuba was excluded from the VI Conference, as the OAS charter requires its members to have democratic governments. Mexico self-excluded in protest of the particular definition of democracy by the Washington-backed organization.

The next day, Kissinger met with Pinochet and his advisors.

—I must admit, I was moved by the reception the people gave me—said Kissinger.

—This is a country of warm, freedom-loving people—said Pinochet—. That's why they didn't accept communism when it tried to take over the country. You know, we're part of a long-term struggle. It's just another phase of the same conflict that erupted in the Spanish Civil War... During the Vietnam War, I met American soldiers. I told them I trusted they would be able to defeat those little men... Unfortunately, in Chile, we don't have the millions needed to defeat communism.

—You know, General—said Kissinger— we're with you. Mr. Allende sympathized with communism. Now we support you, but we can't do much to prevent a certain reduction in arms sales to Chile, because our Congress is determined to obstruct everything. The usual excuse is Human Rights, which many say are a problem here.

Pinochet finished listening to his translator and suppressed one of his well-known bouts of rage.

—Slander from the ideologists of what they call human rights...—said the general, with his effeminate voice, almost as effeminate as that of his most admired man, General Francisco Franco—. A real racket that is.

—General—insisted Kissinger— I must inform you that when I speak this afternoon at the OAS meeting, I will support a resolution that some there want... But I will talk about Cuba. My speech will not target Chile. I believe you are a victim of the leftist groups of the world, and your greatest sin is having overthrown a government that was heading toward communism.

—We are trying to return to institutionalization—said Pinochet— but we are constantly attacked, not only by the socialists, who don't matter, but also by the Christian Democrats. It seems they carry weight in Washington, don't they? Not with the Pentagon people, obviously, but they have access to Congress. How do you allow that in a free country? Gabriel Valdés has some influence. Orlando Letelier too.[178]

—Christian Democrat?—said Kissinger—. I haven't seen one there since 1969, as the song says.

—We have paid our debts—continued Pinochet, more focused on what he had to say than on what he had to hear—. This year we are going to pay $700 million in debts and interest.

The U.S. Congress had managed to block the long-awaited delivery of the F-5 fighter jets, which were supposed to make the Peruvians of General Juan Velasco Alvarado pale in comparison.

—Anyway. We are one step away from a war with Perú, and they are blocking our weaponry. How do they explain that?

Shortly afterward, the two men and their translators were escorted by a caravan of motorcycles and cars to another location. The wives of Pinochet and Kissinger met at a reception hosted by the Brazilian embassy. Everything went perfectly, until the journalists arrived and asked Lucía Hiriart to move so they could photograph Mrs. Kissinger. Lucía turned to her husband and ordered:

—Let's go, Augusto. This place is full of rude, classless people.

The Chilean president's subsequent meetings with other foreign representatives did little to improve his sudden bad mood, but Pinochet was only interested in Washington.

The previous year, former President Richard Nixon had approved new military aid and $85 million for Chile. Senator Ted Kennedy considered this excessive and introduced a bill to limit this generosity, which was approved by Congress. As has been the tradition in Washington, the White House, now led by former Vice President Gerald Ford, approved $15 million in aid for Chile's Ministry of Defense and $90 million for food assistance. But Congress was not convinced, and on June 22, it approved another cut to aid, proposed by Senator Ted Kennedy, a friend of Orlando Letelier.

Pinochet and Chilean officials boiled with anger, blaming Letelier and even the former Social Democratic President Eduardo Frei for the loss of Washington's unconditional support. Civilians don't know how to do anything effectively.

—If it were up to the civilians, we never would have won the War of the Pacific.

Hours later, the head of the DINA, Manuel Contreras, gave the order to eliminate former president Eduardo Frei Montalva and former chancellor and defense minister under Allende, Orlando Letelier. The man chosen for the task was Michael Vernon Townley.

During his only visit to the United States, a year after Letelier's assassination, on September 6, 1977, Pinochet would declare to The Washington Post:

—I can swear that no one in the Chilean government planned anything like that. Letelier was detained in Chile, and it was I who gave him his freedom and authorization to leave the country freely.

The problem wouldn't be Letelier's assassination, but the way it was carried out. The first, planned. The second, unforeseen. Probably because of the latter factor (which would end with the dissolution of DINA and its replacement by a new repressive agency) was why the former conservative president Eduardo Frei was able to live a few more years. He died in 1982 while being treated in a hospital for a minor issue. Years later, an autopsy would find traces of mustard gas in his remains. A specialty of Michael Townley and the engineer Eugenio Berríos.

—The virtues of these chemicals—Townley had said, and Berríos had approved with a nervous chuckle— are that they leave no traces, or are very difficult to prove as the cause of any death.

Eugenio Berríos had been informed of Letelier's assassination, as well as that of Carmelo Soria a few months earlier in Chile. The smiling chemist of death was aware of many more things. After the return of Chile's monitored democracy in 1990, the perpetual commander-in-chief of the armed forces, Augusto Pinochet or his new enemy by then, Colonel Contreras, would take him out of the country. In 1995, he would be found on a beach in Uruguay with two bullets to the back of his head. By then, it had been discovered that the austere and honorable dictator had multimillion-dollar secret accounts abroad and his son was implicated in cocaine trafficking.

The Condor Spreads Its Wings

SEVEN MONTHS BEFORE KISSINGER'S CELEBRATED VISIT on October 6, 1975, at 8:20 p.m., the Chilean Bernardo Leighton Guzmán and his wife, Ana Fresno, had been shot just before entering their home in Rome, a few blocks from the Vatican. Leighton was not suspected of being a leftist. At one time an admirer of the Spanish dictator Francisco Franco, he had founded the National Falange Party of Chile, which later became the Christian Democratic Party. The problem was that Leighton had been an opponent of Augusto Pinochet's government.

For Miami's Zero Group, a branch of the Cuban Nationalist Movement of Orlando Bosch, the man "had become a Marxist." That was enough to warrant elimination. According to the FBI and all the later published memoirs of the actors of the time, such as Mariana Callejas, the Cuban Virgilio Paz had actively participated in the attack ordered by DINA.[179] Leighton and his wife survived but were left as vegetables for the rest of their lives.

More important than that was the message, the example, the lesson. The attack was organized by Michael Townley, who had hired Stefano delle Chiaie and other local neo-fascists. Before the assignment, Townley had been tasked with locating the exiled Chilean Carlos Altamirano, with the same purpose.

Leighton was shot in the head, which left him unable to continue his work opposing Pinochet and his enemies, the socialists. His memory and speech problems made him an insignificant opponent, except as an example, which is why Pinochet authorized his return to the country in 1978. His wife was left paraplegic.

Like many traditionalist politicians in Latin America, Bernardo Leighton shared with the head of the DINA, Manuel Contreras, a deep admiration for the dictator Francisco Franco and for National Catholicism. According to Colonel Manuel Contreras, the great mission of civilization was to "eliminate enemies wherever they are found, people like Letelier, who harm our countries."

On October 29, 1975, Contreras organized in Santiago the first meeting that would give birth to Operation Condor, which he defined as "gentlemen's agreements." From the beginning, the CIA was informed of the meeting and the objective of the largest terrorist group in the continent's history, which, moreover, had the support of several governments, including that of the world's greatest superpower. That year, the head of the DINA flew twice in secret to Washington to meet with different CIA agents. The first meeting took place days after the founding of Operation Condor. According to a classified CIA publication (dated June 12, 1982), Contreras coordinated the illegal purchase of weapons produced by a company run by CIA officers Edwin Wilson and Frank Terpil. The purchase was for 1059 Colt Cobra pistols, a weapon easily concealed in clothing and later widely used by undercover police.

Since early 1976, the U.S. Congress had prohibited the sale of arms to Chile due to public evidence of the dictatorship's genocide, the DINA processed the purchase with fake passports.[180]

The second and third transactions were with the agency's number two, Deputy Director Vernon Walters. The first meeting, in August 1975, confirmed an understanding between the two, as Walters had learned to speak Spanish fluently, and both were convinced of their divine mission on Earth. The second meeting was shortly before Walters' retirement on June 2, 1976. On Tuesday the 29th, Townley met with Bernardo de Torres, Armando López Estrada, Héctor Durán, and General Juan Manuel Contreras Sepúlveda.

—Mr. Letelier—said Waters—is a danger to the national security of the United States. His goal is to establish a parallel government of Chile abroad.

Despite the documentation to the contrary, the Pinochet government would tirelessly claim that they had nothing to do with Letelier's death. It had all been the work of the CIA and their agent, Michael Townley. It was even possible that Letelier's own communist comrades had executed him under orders from the Cubans in Havana.

Make it look like the reds from Argentina did it

But let's go back to the Miami connection-Santiago. When in June 1976 Guillermo Novo landed in Chile, Townley went to receive him at the airport. He took him by the arm and had him skip the usual immigration checks. It was a custom with special guests, so they wouldn't leave a record of their entry into the land of freedom.

They hadn't even gotten into the car that would take them to Lo Curro when, on behalf of DINA, Townley proposed a new mission: to kidnap the manager of the Dutch United Bank in Buenos Aires to raise funds. It wasn't that the government of Chile lacked money for such important matters, but there was a certain percentage that had to be reported. The rest, at discretion, was what mattered most in terms of intelligence.

This bank, Townley reminded him, had several infiltrated agents from Argentine intelligence, who collaborated with DINA in the bombing that ended the lives of General Carlos Prats and his wife, two years earlier. According to the FBI (though not even the most revisionist press would ever record it for generations to come), these infiltrated agents could predict any movement, even that of the bank manager himself.

In August, members of the Italian commando Alfa, the same one that had participated in the heist of the century in Nice a month earlier, were seeking a country to take refuge in.

—It wouldn't cost me anything to arrange for you to go to Chile—Townley told them in Buenos Aires.

Townley had traveled to Argentina to accelerate the operation at the Dutch Bank.

—Either proceed with the kidnapping—he told them— or return the six thousand dollars that Guillermo Novo sent you from Miami.[181]

Despite being a double foreigner, as both an American and a Chilean, Townley could boast an enviable reputation in Buenos Aires, before the new military regime of Rafael Videla made things much easier. Two years earlier, on the night of Saturday, September 28, 1974, he had been the long shadow that slipped into the garage of General Carlos Prats on Malabia Street 3305, facing the botanical garden, to place the bomb under the gearbox of the small Fiat 125. Shortly after midnight on Sunday, when Prats and his wife Sofía Cuthbert were returning from a comradeship gathering, the car exploded in their faces. Both died before paramedics could arrive. The attack was commissioned by Brigadier Pedro Espinoza Bravo to the head of the foreign department of DINA, Commander Raúl Iturriaga Neumann.

Michael Townley was not a Chilean creation. Many years earlier, he had been a member of the Cuban Chicago Junta group, dissolved on November 21, 1963, one day before the assassination of President Kennedy.[182] Since 1969, he had been under the surveillance of CIA agent David Atlee Phillips, while trying to prevent Chile's elected president, Salvador Allende from taking office. When this plan failed, Phillips tasked Townley with creating two paramilitary groups: Order and Freedom and Communal Protection and Sovereignty.[183] Townley was one of those in charge of the well-known harassment campaign against General Prats, who would eventually resign to be replaced by the apolitical General Augusto Pinochet. Prats was assassinated in Buenos Aires shortly afterward.

His killers never confessed. Townley and Mariana Callejas were not far from the scene at the time of the explosion that took the Prats. The FBI would conclude that, one way or another, Townley was the perpetrator. Although Townley would admit to several murders, he would never accept responsibility for that one and, for some other never-confessed mystery, he would always refuse to talk about it in every trial and even in the only interview he gave to a television channel in the 90s, when he was already a man protected by the FBI.

—With the collaboration of Argentine intelligence—Townley had told Novo on the way to Lo Curro in Santiago—the Cuban Nationalist Movement can kidnap the manager of the Dutch bank in Buenos Aires and demand a ransom that will outrage the public. We'll make the press blame the leftist guerrillas. We've done it before, and it's worked. Sometimes it's the Montoneros, and sometimes it's their enemies, the Anti-Communist Alliance of Argentina. Three years ago, they kidnapped the manager of Esso, Victor Samuelson, and it made the front page of every newspaper. That's what we want. Front pages. No one would suspect the Chileans. Much less the Cubans. This is the easiest part but of extreme importance, since the new Junta in Argentina is on our side.

The idea of the most spectacular robbery of the century, European-style, excited Guillermo Novo so much that he offered to contribute six thousand dollars, money that, once he returned to Miami, he sent to Townley through a friendly pilot from LAN Chile. Virgilio Paz put the money in a box and headed to Buenos Aires, where he invented a leftist terrorist group called, with little imagination, the Red Group.

Townley, on the other hand, was not as confident about the success of the operation. Latin Americans lacked the rigor and consistency to replicate the feats of European paramilitary groups. Not even a simple robbery that, just one month later, his friend Albert Bert Spaggiari would carry out at the Société Générale bank in Nice. A multi-million-dollar robbery for which he would be admired and never convicted.

CHaoS Has no name

BY 1976, MIAMI HAD SOLIDIFIED ITS REPUTATION as the capital of terrorism in the hemisphere. In second place was Union City, in New Jersey, from where the rest of the Cuban exile paramilitary commandos operated. The series of bombings and extrajudicial executions had become an unstoppable tradition for local police and even the FBI itself.

But their authors were beginning to realize that, while the attacks and executions solved internal problems and secured more donations from Florida's business community, the original goal of overthrowing the island's government had diluted into grandiose promises, resounding failures, and a growing carnival of terror that was decimating their own ranks. The main leaders, Orlando Bosh and Luis Posada Carriles, could not organize the chaos. Nor did they have ideas organized by any rigorous theory or concrete plans for rebellion in Cuba. It was less of a revolution, but they understood that their figures were suffering a dramatic decline.

According to their comrades, few things could worry Bosh more than a tarnished image, so he claimed responsibility for any attack that occurred in the Caribbean basin (the lake that the American Empire protected for the glory and development of all, according to Henry Ford's journalist, Samuel Crowther).[184] Bosh saw himself as a Che Guevara of the business world and even recommended following some of his tactics to create a historical mystery around his own name. Like the CIA agents themselves, who secretly admired El Che, neither Bosh nor Posada Carriles went to the front lines of their battles. Nor did they sign or acknowledge their actions, like the Argentine, except within their secret organizations, as, by the way, was the tradition and modus operandi of the mother of those same groups, the CIA, and the father, the Cuban mafia of the Batista era, the Meyer Lanskys, and the Santo Trafficante Jr.

For that reason, on June 11, in the Dominican Republic, a group of Cuban exiles founded a new organization called the Coordinación de Organizaciones Revolucionarias Unidas-CORU. Within a few days, the group planned different attacks in each of the countries in the region that had any connection with the Cuban government. Various bombs exploded in airline offices in Costa Rica, Colombia, Guyana, and Barbados. From then on, the chaos became better organized, but the results remained the same.

The series of bombings also continued the regime of terror that the Dominican dictator Rafael Leónidas Trujillo had practiced for decades, since the US Marines trained and installed him in power before withdrawing from the island due to the Great Depression and so Franklin Roosevelt could boast of his new Good Neighbor Policy. Trujillo not only massacred tens of thousands of Haitian immigrants but also managed to impose the peace of terror in the Dominican Republic and in the Caribbean countries. He ordered the kidnapping, torture, and systematic disappearance of tens of thousands of dissidents, like Columbia University professor Jesús Galíndez, to car bombings, such as the one that killed Colonel Ramón Armas Pérez and two young men in Caracas and left President Rómulo Betancourt, his defense minister, and his wife seriously injured. President Betancourt lost much of his vision and was nearly deafened. All in the name of the struggle for freedom and against communism, it goes without saying.

Apart from Washington and the successful transactionalists, Trujillo was a friend and ally of other fascist dictators, like Anastasio Somoza in Nicaragua. He supported the dictatorship of Fulgencio Batista in Cuba and the Italian mafia in Havana. When the revolution of Fidel Castro and Che Guevara began to gain followers in

Cuba, Trujillo spared no help to the friendly regime, sending planes, weapons, and money to prevent its fall.

Once the Batista regime fell in 1959, many of his collaborators were executed, others expropriated, and the rest fled or remained in Miami. Rum, bombs, and the conviction of possessing immunity and special rights were never foreign to the tradition that governed the Caribbean. The CIA capitalized on these human resources as before, during the Banana Wars and the massacres of the protectorates in the Backyard, was capitalized by the Creole generals, the Marines, and the American businessmen.

A bit of rum and a lot of TNT, sugar, brothels, and tropical casinos continued to be part of the culture of the ruling classes of the Caribbean, though in Miami this tradition became democratized and expanded to the poor exiles, especially after the Mariel Crisis of 1980.

Within a few years, several groups dedicated to planting bombs in the United States and the "backyard" were founded. For every bomb that made the headlines in newspapers and on television, the paramilitaries received donations from other Cuban exiles, usually successful businessmen. Dozens of paramilitary intelligence groups were founded, organized, and funded in this way. Although some called themselves combatants, none ever participated in any combat, except for the fiasco of the Bay of Pigs invasion and with the almost divine and infallible support, at least in faith, of Washington and the CIA. All of them insisted, repeated, and managed to crystallize in the major press of the North that Guevara was a cold-blooded killer. El Che, the one who led his own battles, which is why CIA agent David Atlee Phillips admired him while hating him for interfering with his professional efficiency.

The chaos of paramilitary groups in Miami and Union City was widespread. Perhaps for the same reason: as the CIA itself reported fifteen years earlier, while training the Cubans who were going to liberate Cuba in the Bay of Pigs invasion, the problem was that everyone wanted to be generals and ministers. They were "ego-maniacs, concerned about their macho reputation, with their petty and childish rivalries... Everyone wanted to be a brigade commander."[185]

Omega 7, a group that boasted of mocking the FBI with several bombs at Cuban consulates in the United States and for the assassination of other Cuban exiles, one of them shot in front of his nine-year-old son in New Jersey, had an unsurpassed image of itself. Another group, Alpha 66 was founded by CIA agent Antonio Veciana in Puerto Rico. Alpha, after the Greek letter that in the Bible signifies the beginning of everything, and the number 66 because it was the number of the hotel room where the founding members gathered. Shortly after, the group established operational bases in Miami and the Bahamas. Police officer Thomas Lyons and detective Raul J. Diaz from Miami defined this group as terrorist, but its members never ended up in any prison where, in the land of laws, human rights are respected. Nothing like Guantánamo, where the fight for freedom continues.

The *November 30 Movement* was another Cuban group derived from another CIA failure to counter the failure of the Bay of Pigs invasion, called Operation Mongoose, founded on November 30. The Cuban National Liberation Front was created by a group of Cubans led by Francisco Castro Paz, recruited by the CIA to invade Cuba, first, and to engage in sabotage against the island when everything else failed to achieve the expected results.

The Cubans of Miami blamed all their failures on Washington and the CIA, while the CIA blamed Miami's Cubans for theirs. One of the new groups, perhaps the most recognized for its museum in Miami and its Veterans Club, as well as its influence on Florida politics, will be Brigade 2506. Naturally, it will be another child of the CIA, like the Mujahideen and later the Taliban in Afghanistan, the Contras in Nicaragua, the drug-trafficking dictators of the Backyard, Osama bin Laden in Arabia, or ISIS in devastated Iraq.

Despite intense training in Guatemala, all members of the revered Brigade 2506 were captured in Cuba just hours after the 1961 invasion began and, later, exchanged for food. One of their moments of glory was when their leader, Manuel Artime (a close friend of the powerful CIA agent Howard Hunt) managed to shake hands with the First Lady, Jacqueline Kennedy, upon the battalion's triumphant return to Miami. Several members of Brigade 2506 continued working for the CIA in various plots against Cuba or its government from Nicaragua and Costa Rica. As in 637 other occasions, their members failed in the obsessive plan to assassinate Fidel Castro.

They had better luck in the assassination of Ernesto "Che" Guevara in Bolivia, after the government and the Bolivian army lost several battles against Guevara's poorly armed and underfed rebels. The ambush against this small group was possible thanks to the collaboration of a peasant, the satellite regime of General René Barrientos, Nazi criminals like the German Klaus Barbie, and the Cuban Félix Rodríguez, all sent by the CIA to protect the sanctity of private companies like Standard Oil Company and Gulf Oil Corporation, but in the name of a supposed fight against communism.

Félix Rodríguez was a partner of Luis Posada Carriles in the support that the CIA provided to the Contras of Nicaragua, in the financing through illegal arms to Iran, in dealings with the drug trafficking of Pablo Escobar in Colombia and later with the Guadalajara Cartel in Mexico. Besides participating in internal vendettas that ended in the assassination of DEA agent Enrique Camarena Salazar (who had uncovered the CIA's links to drug trafficking in the Backyard), Félix Rodríguez became in 2005 the chairman of the board of the Bay of Pigs Museum in Little Havana in Miami.

In Florida and New Jersey, various groups with the same objectives and methods proliferated, such as Operation Eagle, Cuban Secret Government, Cuban Power, and Young Cubans. Many derived from the groups organized by the CIA to invade Cuba. All failed unanimously, with or without Washington's support.

"The Cubans have no guts," explained the famous CIA agent David Atlee Phillips. "They're all cowards."[186]

However, the Cubans on the island seemed to contradict Agent Phillips' theory. Quite the opposite. Hence the great frustration of the world's most powerful military.

Among CORU's first successes were the assassinations of various Cuban officials in Mexico and Argentina. That same month, the CIA was informed of the upcoming attack, this time against a commercial flight from Cuba, likely in one of those insignificant islands.

The Organized Chaos with a Single Name

As I noted before, Orlando Bosch and his new family were deported from Costa Rica for attempting to assassinate Salvador Allende's nephew. The new failed attempt against Allendito was added to another one planned by the DINA in Mexico by the Cubans Virgilio Paz, Guillermo Novo, and Dionisio Suárez, in collaboration with the Chilean Mariana Callejas and her husband Michael Townley. This attempt also failed.

Bosch had arrived with his wife and six-month-old daughter in Santo Domingo on Saturday, June 12, 1976. The Dominican Republic continued to live in the shadow of Rafael Trujillo, mentor of then-President Joaquín Balaguer Ricardo. Since 1966, Balaguer had built his own resume, adding thousands dead, others tortured and disappeared, shortly after the invasion by the U.S. Marines. In his favor, reviews from major international media praised his commitment to liberalism and economic openness. Since neither reason stood on its own, they resorted to a single word: freedom. Who is against freedom?

—The Dominican President—Bosch confessed to journalist Blake Fleetwood, words that would later be published in the article "I am going to declare war"—allowed us to stay there to organize actions. It wasn't like we were going to church every day, right? We were there to conspire, to plant bombs.

El exilio del terror

But the main idea was to take it up a notch, after two decades of attacks with no results and historical fiascoes, like the invasion of the Bay of Pigs. Roberto Carballo, leader of the Bay of Pigs Veterans Association, Avbc for the FBI, and three other Cubans had received a visit from CIA agents, who informed them of the Agency's disagreement with the series of random attacks, lacking a concrete action plan. This setback did not result in a break with the CIA but led to communication and funding difficulties, which amplified the criticism from Cuban exile organizations directed at the CIA and the U.S. government.[187] Not only had they failed them in the Bay of Pigs invasion in 1961, but now they were left with limited resources to fight alone for freedom. However, the limited resources were not that limited. Fifteen years of bombings and multiple executions of their own members in the United States and the Caribbean basin had built them a reputation that attracted donations from major businessmen. To these donations, one had to add the growing influence on the politics and libertarian ideals of American conservatives.

But the CIA was right about one thing: if they wanted to leverage all those resources, they had to organize the chaos. Carballo and other members of the Avbc participated in the founding meeting of CORU, alongside other groups from Miami and Union City. This two-day meeting (promoted and facilitated by the CIA) took place in Bonao, a town in the center of the Dominican Republic, with the aim of coordinating new actions. Clearly, it was the right place. The government sympathized with the cause, and, as in the days of Trujillo, the conspirators based themselves in the heart of the Caribbean.

According to a secret FBI report, the meeting took place on Saturday, June 12. One of the attendees was Gaspar Eugenio Jiménez-Escobedo, an employee of the Florida East Coast Railway that connects Miami with Jacksonville. Jiménez-Escobedo himself was included in Miami's death lists signed by the anti-Castro group Cero, but that was just a detail. The main organizers were the Cubans Frank Castro, Luis Posada Carriles, Orlando Bosch, and Guillermo

Novo, with financial support from the powerful banker Guillermo Hernández-Cartaya, a Bay of Pigs veteran and connected to the CIA, money laundering, and drug and arms trafficking with Colombian cartels. Also participating were known CIA collaborators and members of the veteran clubs of the failed Bay of Pigs invasion, such as the former police officer of Fulgencio Batista, Armando López Estrada.

Years later, when Hernández-Cartaya found himself entangled with U.S. law, he would call in special favors. The federal prosecutor told journalist Pete Brewton that a CIA officer had approached him, explaining the situation of the accused:

"The officer told me that Hernández-Cartaya had done many things for which the U.S. government was indebted to him, and he asked me to drop the charges against him."[188]

Mysteriously, all charges related to CIA actions (except for minor tax evasion offenses) were dismissed in court. According to some U.S. investigative police officers, the idea for the creation of CORU may have come from the CIA, under the direction of George H. Bush, to unify and regain control of the Cuban organizations that had gone rogue and were acting on their own.

In short, I'll summarize, because I don't have all the time in the world. The June meeting in Bonao was attended by representatives of several well-known groups in the Cuban exile community, such as Alpha 66 from New Jersey, Abdalah from New York, the 2506 Brigade of Bay of Pigs veterans, the FLNC from Miami, F14 from New York, Omega 7, and Acción Cubana led by Bosch himself.

It was the founding meeting of CORU, which confirmed Orlando Bosch as spokesperson and leader. The Cuban Ricardo Morales Navarrete, one of his greatest personal enemies, would summarize the moment years later in an interview for the Miami television program En 1 Hora:

—We managed to unite all the terrorist groups—he said, uncomfortable in his chair—... or activists, under one name, CORU.

—It was a great meeting—Bosch confessed to Fleetwood—. We managed to reunite all our action groups after seventeen years. The most important things were planned there... It was no longer enough to plant bombs in embassies and police offices. We had to think bigger, about more impactful attacks.

According to a Miami publication at the time, it had been decided that something more impactful would be "to strike Castro's planes in mid-flight." At the founding meeting, a list of 50 bombings was drawn up for the following months.

—The fate of Cubana was already decided—stated El Mono Morales—. It wasn't just a commercial airline. Despite its limited resources, Cubana's planes had been used to transport materials that ended up in Angola's independence, months before the meeting in Bonao.

—Have you seen the new flag of Angola?—someone asked at the meeting.

—A half gear crossed by a machete. The African version of the hammer and sickle.

—Plus a single star. Che's star.

—All on a red and black background.

—Couldn't be more ridiculous.

More accustomed to the professional protocols of the CIA than to the Caribbean murmur, El Mono Navarrete added relevant information:

—Cubana is suffering from a lack of resources—he said— which is why they've had to lease three DC-8 aircraft from Canada.

The Cuban Guillermo Novo, implicated in the attack against Letelier in Washington, denied several times having been at that meeting. Even so, he assured:

—In that meeting, no mention was made of the operation against the Cubana flight. In the summer of '76, I was in New Jersey.

No mention was made of the operation against Cubana flight 455. It was only agreed to plan attacks against Cuban aircraft and to eliminate Orlando Letelier. In one year, CORU detonated fifty bombs in New York, Miami, Mexico, Panama, Venezuela, and Argentina. The agreement was that they would take credit for the killings anywhere but in the United States, because the FBI was putting too much pressure and had too much information on the Cuban exiles.

—Why don't they go investigate Cuba, boy?

—We will enter Cuban embassies, assassinate their diplomats wherever they are, and hijack and blow up Cuban planes until Castro begins to negotiate with us—said Bosch, convinced, trembling, with his prominent lower lip losing strength each year—. This is a global war. There are no civilians or innocents. Everyone is a combatant and must be treated as such.

As Frank Castro would later claim to the Miami *Herald*:

—The United States has betrayed the *freedom fighters* around the world. They trained us to fight, brainwashed us, and now they imprison Cuban exiles for what they had taught them to do in the early years.[189]

One of the attendees of the Bonao meeting, another ex-policeman of Fulgencio Batista, another member of the 2056 Battalion of Bay of Pigs and ex-CIA agent, the drug trafficker Armando López Estrada met on June 29 with Bernardo de Torres, Michael Townley, Héctor Durán and General Juan Manuel Contreras Sepúlveda to coordinate new and more exciting attacks. López Estrada had been implicated in a failed plan to assassinate President Kennedy in Florida and was now part of Operation Condor. One of the fifty thousand victims of the international network would be Orlando Letelier. According to López Estrada, the CIA, under the direction of George H. Bush, had facilitated the Bonao meeting to orchestrate the chaos of the multiple terrorist organizations that had proliferated out of their control since the sixties.

A year earlier, on June 10, 1975, the CBS television network had revealed the CIA's Operation Chaos, which, with the use of Cuban mercenaries, managed to violate another of the laws that prevented it from spying on U.S. citizens. Among their targets were feminists, the anti-Vietnam War movements, teachers, and journalists, always so radical and dangerous.

—We were trained to plant bombs,—López Estrada will defend himself in front of CBS cameras in a report titled "The CIA's Secret Weapon", exactly two years later, on June 10, 1977— we are trained to kill. Everything we know we learned from the CIA.

Exactly the same thing was said, as if he had memorized the same book of poems, by the Cuban Rolando "Musculito" Martínez*Musculito*, recruited by Howard Hunt and involved in the internal espionage scandal of Watergate. Like Richard Nixon, Rolando was also pardoned by President Ronald Reagan in 1983 and, years later, ended up working in a real estate company in Miami. He died in 2021, shortly before turning one hundred years old, surrounded by his grandchildren.[190]

CORU was responsible for more than fifty bombings in 1976 alone, such as a machine gun shooting at the Cuban embassy in Bogotá, the assassination of a Cuban official in Mérida, Yucatán, the kidnapping and disappearance of two employees from the Cuban embassy in Buenos Aires, the bombing of a Cuban Airlines office in Panama City, and the assassination of former Chilean ambassador Orlando Letelier and his assistant in Washington, D.C., the detonation of a bomb at the Guyana embassy in Port of Spain, as revenge for the Guyanese government's decision to allow Cuban planes to refuel at their airport.

At the meeting in Bonao there was a foundational agreement, but also a group that refused to sign it. It was the Cuban Nationalist Movement, known in New Jersey as Omega 7, whose representatives argued they would sign the agreement once they finished a pending task with the Chilean government in the United States.

Five years later, in front of Miami television cameras, El Mono Morales would admit:

—The bombing of a Cubana plane had already been decided before the foundational meeting of CORU. With Orlando García Vázquez, we were in charge of the project, and Venezuelan

President Carlos Andrés Pérez knew about it. Not only did he know, but he wanted us working there, in Caracas, to deliver a hard blow to Guyana. We had to destabilize the government of Arthur Chung and achieve a victory by reclaiming the Essequibo... President Carlos Andrés Pérez made a pact with us, and when you make a pact with terrorists, you become a terrorist. But I don't regret anything. If I had to kill 273 instead of 73, I'd do it again. Let them suffer as we suffered.[191]

No one will ever know who was the true mastermind behind the founding of CORU. It was clear that its goal was to bring together all these groups outside the CIA's control into an organization that would coordinate terrorist attacks more effectively and with better publicity. According to NSA secret agent, Perry Fellwock, CORU was an organization made up of former Cuban CIA agents, "a result of the fanatic passions of gusano businessmen, *now allied with Chile's secret police.*"[192] According to the CIA and FBI, confirmed by the Cuban lawyer of Venezuela's Disip, Rafael Rivas, the last meeting was attended only by the leaders: Luis Posada Carriles, Orlando Bosch, Guillermo Novo, Frank Castro, Armando López Estrada, and the attending members of the Brigade 2506 of the Bay of Pigs. There, it was decided to divide the hemisphere into three different areas: South America, North America, and the Caribbean. It was agreed that any of the three groups could operate in the Caribbean countries, which functioned as meeting points and pivots.[193]

In the following months, the press would report a series of bombings targeting airlines, consulates, and other sensitive locations. To the dismay of some CORU members, certain politicians in Washington had attributed those attacks to the communists.

Before the major success of the bombing that brought down the Cubana plane in Barbados with 73 people on board, CORU had several prior failures, which were valued as professional experience. Members and mercenaries of the libertarian organization placed a bomb in a suitcase for Flight 455 bound for Jamaica. The bomb exploded before the staff could load it onto the plane. On August 18, another bomb exploded in the offices of Cubana de Aviación in Panama.

THE WANDERING CARIBBEAN

A FEW DAYS AFTER BONAO, the government of the Dominican Republic suggested that Bosch leave the country, due to his growing notoriety.

—I told them they were all cowards—Bosch would later recall from the Caracas jail— I told them the Dominicans were afraid of Castro. Thanks to these incompetents, I had to return to Costa Rica. There, to make up for the damage done by unjustly arresting me, President Daniel Oduber Quirós, another incompetent, gave me three fake passports. One from Peru and two from Costa Rica.

With one of those passports, Bosch returned to safer territory, Nicaragua, although the last member of the dynasty, Tachito Somoza, was struggling with the rise of Sandinismo. Bosch, his young wife, and his infant daughter continued their routine of being expelled from one country to another. His international fame did not match his privileges. It was there that he began receiving calls from Orlando García to join the team in Caracas. By then, the career of Orlando García, like that of Luis Posada Carriles, had been more successful than his. Even that of El Mono Morales Navarrete. Posada Carriles had risen through the ranks of Venezuela's secret police while supplementing his income with the trafficking of Colombian cocaine to Miami. For many years, he had been a prominent and feared officer in Caracas' intelligence. Meanwhile, Orlando García was an advisor to President Andrés Pérez. He used to run with him in the mornings, until he got tired. El Mono, in a matter of months, had become the head of Division 54 of Disip, the division responsible for foreign affairs in Venezuela.

Humiliated by his own allies, Bosch waited in Costa Rica. There, he received a visit from Argentine businessmen linked to the new dictatorship in the South. The calls from Orlando García and, later, those from El Mono, caused him not only great distrust but also unease. He could be betrayed again or, alternatively, saved by a couple of traitors. One of them remained alive only because he hadn't placed enough C4 under his car, or he had placed it half a meter further forward than he should have, or he had adapted his car's chassis with some reinforced boat plating.

That noon on July 2, 1974, El Mono had left his apartment at 801 NW 47th Avenue in Miami. Thirteen minutes later, at 12:50 pm, on Flagler Street and just before reaching the corner of Dairy Road, his brand-new Chevy Impala Custom soared into the air. It had been an act of revenge for his testimony before the jury that had convicted Orlando Bosch for the attack on the Polish ship in 1968. The bomb coincided with Bosch's parole and his escape to Venezuela, where Posada Carriles was waiting for him.

—This is the second time this year they've tried to kill me—said El Mono to The Miami *Herald*.

—Who was behind this new attack?—asked reporter Frank Greve.

—I can't tell you—said El Mono—. I'm not going to tell you it was Doctor Bosch.[194]

Now, two years later and two thousand kilometers further south, El Mono was calling him on the phone, as if nothing had happened. He wanted to use him for something in Panama or Guyana, with the commitment not to carry out any actions in Venezuela.

In reality, the plans were more ambitious than Bosch, the official leader of Coru, imagined. It was about a more formal association with the powerful government of General Pinochet in Chile, with the collaboration of the secret police of democratic Venezuela and other friendly dictatorships in the south. In other words, several levels above what the Cuban exiles were accustomed to, following the defeat of the Bay of Pigs fifteen years earlier. Around that time, the director of the DINA, Colonel Manuel Contreras, had embarked on a tour across the continent to coordinate repressive actions. Contreras wanted to do everything personally and in private, to avoid any form of documentation.[195]

The Cuban Rivas Vásquez took note.

"CUBANS DON'T HAVE BALLS"

WHEN ON JULY 9, 1971, FIDEL CASTRO arrived in Chile, CIA agents David Atlee Phillips and one of his Cuban agents, Antonio Veciana, had everything prepared for a new attempt to eliminate the Cuban leader. At a press conference, a fake journalist was going to aim a weapon disguised as a microphone. At the last moment, the Cuban mercenaries got scared. One claimed to be suffering from peritonitis and the other feared that a cousin from Castro's secret service might recognize him. The operation was canceled at the last minute. Furious, David Atlee Phillips said to Antonio Veciana:

—Cubans don't have balls; they are all cowards.

He immediately ordered the elimination of Rodríguez and Medina.

—How much does it cost to kill a man in Bolivia?—asks Phillips— A hundred, two hundred dollars? You're not short on money. Invite them to a meeting and pay someone to kill them. We can't afford to let them stay alive under any circumstances. They're a risk. We can't allow the State Department to be exposed in any way. Can you imagine if either of these men implicates you, now that you're a member of the U.S. diplomatic corps in Bolivia?

—But that was the risk we were taking—said Veciana— even if the plan had been successful and Fidel Castro were dead now. The assassins could have been arrested...

Philips, furious, responds.

—Arrested? There's no way they were going to survive. I didn't tell you before, but that had already been decided.

The same procedure had been applied to the assassin of President Kennedy, when Lee Oswald was killed shortly after being captured.

JULIO

1976

we are all one under God

At 6:05 pm, before the nationwide televised fireworks show, NBC journalist John Chancellor announced the closing of the celebrations of the 200th anniversary of The Glorious 4th of July:

—John Adams said: "the purpose of government is the happiness of society." *It's also the purpose of the media.* With this in mind, NBC presents Paul Anka with a special performance of "Happy Birthday, America."

I paused for a moment here. Was it Adams or Jefferson? That morning, the filtered coffee from El Cristo Restaurant had gone cold. On the little table on the sidewalk, the cool morning air still lingered. Across from Calle Ocho, at El Pub Restaurant Comida Cubana, people were lining up and leaving with German pretzels. Above, hand-painted, it read, "where yesterday's Cuba lives today." I recalled a phrase by Borges and jotted it down, not to include it in this investigation, which is more academic than poetic: "one doesn't miss a place; one misses a time." Or something like that.

—Should we add some churros?—the waiter interrupted me.

—Of course,—I replied—. Why not?

Few things reminded me more of my childhood in Montevideo than Cuban churros. Nothing quite like the churros from Parque Rodó on Sunday afternoons.

I picked up my notebook and my pen to refocus on my work. "*The purpose of government is the happiness of society*" I read. It was Jefferson, not Adams, who had written: "*The care of life and happiness is the only legitimate object of government.*" Not only had it been attributed to Adams, but they had removed that bit about "*the care of a society"* as the only legitimate purpose of government. It would have sounded too socialist.

Countries are epic poetry. In prose, when they get serious. In verse when, in their anthems, they become emotional and passionate. *Society* (I read, in an online dictionary); from the Latin societas, association, union… More than obvious, but just to be sure, it's always good to consult multiple sources.

It was impossible not to think again about the collective obsession with something that is lacking. *Union, United, The Union is strong, Latinos United, We are United*. As the country's war shield says, *E pluribus unum* (Out of many, one), the ancient recipe-poem by Virgil for making good pesto: in a mortar, mix cheese, garlic, vinegar, olive oil, and herbs, and crush until you make one from many. That must be where the fantasy of the "melting pot" comes from. The verse contains the Masonic number of letters: thirteen. Thirteen colonies, thirteen stripes on the flag of the East India Company.

Let's go back to 1976, to July 4th. That evening in Florida, already night in the foundational North, millions of screens projected the red and blue colors of Pepsi and the red and white of Coca-Cola and Dr.Pepper.

Let Us Be the One. "Let us all be one," repeated the slogan of the ABC network for that year. The decade was determined to leave racial segregation behind, although in its ad filled with young, beautiful, and happy blondes, only two Black men appeared, spotted in nearly invisible fractions of a second.

The conservative reaction of the eighties was incubating with the segregation between the super-rich and the rest of the happy society. Your faith must be strong, unshakable. After all, in Vietnam, in Africa, and in Cuba they were worse off. The hit TV series Dallas, Dynasty, Rich Man, Poor Man (the equivalents of fairy tales in monarchical Europe and soap operas in the Backyard), never stopped bombarding the national fantasy about the mysterious, democratic, and meritocratic happiness of the rich, which then spilled over to the colonies in the form of movies and magazines.

These same colonies that had to pay the bill for the euphoria and waste. Laughter and smiles above; pain and suffering below. Below and to the south of the new happy South of Texas and Florida.

Let Us Be the One, says again the perfect voice of the successful ad.
Sponsored by Dr. Pepper—another voice, less solemn, as if it were two different things—. *Sugar-free soda, too good to be true!*
Halloween certifies that we do everything for you. McDonald's.

Finally, somewhere in Virginia or North Carolina, the national anthem plays. Everyone stands and places a hand over their heart:

O say, does that star-spangled banner yet wave
O'er the land of the free, and the home of the brave?

Oh, does that star-spangled banner still wave, over the land of the free and the home of the brave? The verses written in 1814 by the lawyer of slaveholders and a slave owner himself, Francis Scott Key, reveal the classic Puritan divorce between preaching and reality. Reality is what we want it to be. If it isn't, we pray until it becomes what we want it to be or until we see what we want to see. Why does an anthem sing of *the land of the free* in a country founded and settled on slavery, in a union where slaves were the majority of the population in some of its states? It was still half a century before slavery would at least be declared illegal, and yet everyone was already proud of the freedom in the land of the free. What does *the home of the brave* mean when only a few could carry arms and the police were the slave militia? Why is *dictatorship* never mentioned when slavery is discussed, and, on the contrary, the word most abundant since the country's founding is *democracy*? Democracy, freedom, equality, justice…

The next verse of the anthem explains it all:

No refuge could save the hireling and slave
From the terror of flight or the gloom of the grave:
The star-spangled banner, triumphantly waves
O'er the land of the free and the home of the brave.

The land of the free, of *the free race* of the slaveholding democrats. The land of the free whites, of the freedom of the masters, turned into free entrepreneurs and free corporations after the Civil War.

A thousand miles further south, Anita Bryant, Miss Oklahoma and official sponsor of the Florida Citrus Commission, was interviewing witnesses on the beaches of Florida who confirmed the virtues of Acme Brand Orange Juice, anytime, not just for breakfast.

Anita Bryant was a well-known anti-gay activist from the group "Save Our Children" in Miami. Historians will recognize that Bryant and her admirers not only succeeded in reversing laws against workplace discrimination but also introduced a new strand of evangelical activism into politics, a fundamental part of the new conservative wave called the New Right, which would end up destroying the degenerate hippies who smoked marijuana while singing about love, peace, and minimal consumption. Those traitors, activists against the Vietnam War and against the friendly dictatorships in the Backyard who wanted to destroy America and our freedom.

Over time, Anita would recognize that her successful activism began when her nine-year-old daughter announced that God would help her. The powerful senator from North Carolina, Jesse Helms, gave her his full support in her crusade to *save the nation's morals*. Days later, the senator traveled to Buenos Aires to lend his support to the new president of Argentina, General Rafael Videla, known for his deep Christian values and his fight for the salvation of the West.

PRAYING COSTS NOTHING

—WHAT NOSTALGIA...—said Hunter—. That chapter reminded me of Anita Bryant and my younger years. I liked Anita. I dreamed about her once or twice. I was afraid that Miss might drag me to hell. Years later, I remembered her when the Bridget Ziegler scandal broke.

—Bridget Ziegler?—I asked—. Wait, let me take notes.

— Ziegler, one of the founders of that conservative group that emerged a couple of years ago here in Florida, Moms for Liberty.

—Now I get it. *Mommas for Liberty.* Daddies for the Fly. Whenever someone calls themselves Liberty, they lose all my trust. They're going to end up shifting the semantic field of that word to overlap, or fall below, the field of fascism. It's only a matter of time.

—They went after the rights of gays, lesbians, and trans people for being immoral. The same old "Save our children" story. Well, turns out that Bridget Ziegler, who made it to the Sarasota County School Board not far from here, had to admit that she participated in orgies in the middle of an investigation against her husband for sexual assault.

—Her orgies don't bother me.

—Me neither. Maybe if they invite me, I'd join. The problem is the old moralist discourse, always obsessed with and legislating other people's sexuality.

—I'm going to end up thinking religions are monuments to everyone's ego. For some reason, when people don't believe they're chosen by God, individuals feel they are His favorites. Like a jealous son with his father. When they get into trouble or something doesn't go their way, they kneel and tell the Creator of the Universe what He should do. As if God doesn't know about all the misfortunes and suffering He has thrown at His favorite animals.

—When God doesn't listen to them, they don't say it's punishment.

—No, it's a divine test, like Job's. When God reveals Himself through a butterfly or a rhinoceros perched on the petitioner's shoulder, or a disease is cured, they attribute it to a miracle. Those who don't believe haven't been enlightened by the truth. More than that: they become automatic enemies. Why would God do me a favor while someone slaughters a hundred, a thousand, ten thousand children somewhere in the world? What kind of God is this who, on top of it all, enjoys sending unbelievers to hell?

—As Andrea's pastor told me—said Hunter— we men can't understand God's decisions…

—Then, what's the point of all this theology, all these Sunday sermons, and all the threats from His spokesmen on Earth? From the center of the Universe, everyone assumes God is bored and dedicates Himself to condemning human animals to hell. After terrifying half the population with the eternal flames of hell, pastors put on a constipated face and pray for infinite love…

—Praying is cheap. Thinking costs a little more.

AMONG ALL THE FORMS THAT DESERVE SILENCE

Settled in Caracas with two sticks of dynamite on his desk, Orlando Bosch called Guillermo Novo in New Jersey.

—He asked me to come to Venezuela—Novo admitted—. He told me that there we could have all the guarantees of the government, that the president Carlos Andrés Pérez was a friend of the Cuban cause… He was staying at the Hilton hotel, paid for by the government. He told me that there was interest from Venezuelans for anti-Castro belligerent elements to get closer. But I didn't go to Caracas because the individuals around the government of Carlos Andrés Pérez didn't offer me any guarantees… Not even him as an anti-communist activist.

On July 5, 1976, the older brother of the Novo Sampol brothers, Guillermo (by then a rival of Orlando Bosch in the leadership of the action groups in Miami and Union City) sent a letter to General Pinochet proposing the establishment of a parallel government for Cuba: "an anti-Castro government with its corresponding army."

This alliance would ensure the Chilean government an expansion of the areas of action for DINA and the Condor Plan, with experts experienced in assassinations and terrorist attacks in the Caribbean, Central America, and even the United States, if necessary. For the Batista group, this alliance would provide aid and protection for several of their fugitive leaders, such as Rolando Otero, accused by the FBI of detonating eight bombs in public buildings in Miami six months earlier, and of transporting C4 explosives in Chilean diplomatic suitcases. After each attack commissioned by DINA or their own leaders, the Cuban exiles could freely return to Chile. In fact, this alliance had begun de facto a couple of years earlier, with the granting of asylum to Orlando Bosch, not because he was being pursued by Havana but by U.S. justice.

But not everything went as planned on either side. Due to multiple bombings in the United States, the FBI began pressuring the Chilean government to deport or otherwise remove from the country some of the Cubans accused of terrorism. One of them was Rolando Otero, who not only wandered around Santiago for weeks awaiting a response from the government, but when DINA tasked him with the assassination of Luis Pascal Allende and a woman in Costa Rica, he decided to fly from Lima to Caracas where he sought the help of El Mono Morales for the operation, which displeased the Chileans.

"Any response you wish to give us regarding the case of Rolando Otero—the letter from Guillermo Novo to GeneralPinochet continued— can be sent to us through Major Eduardo Iturriaga who is under the orders of Colonel Manuel Contreras… *We pray to God that*

He preserves your health… Respectfully yours, Guillermo Novo Sampol, 2nd National Commander of the Cuban Nationalist Movement."[196]

In their investigation of the Letelier case, FBI agents Carter Cornick and Eugene Propper will focus on the phrase where Novo Sampol slips in his complaint to the Chilean government for not supporting some members of the Cuban exile in the manner they deserved, despite the fact that the Cuban Nationalist Movement had supported Pinochet's government "in all ways, public and private, that deserved to be mentioned and those others that deserved silence…"[197]

—A code of silence, standard of the mafia—said Propper.

THE QUEEN REPRESENTS FREEDOM

ON JULY 6, 1976, AT 10:00 AM, a day after a bomb exploded at the Cuban Embassy at the United Nations in New York, the Queen of England and her husband, Prince Philip, descended upon Philadelphia. The following day, the Queen inaugurated the construction of the Bicentennial Building with the motto engraved on a massive bell: Let freedom ring loudly.

—It was incredible to have seen the Queen…—confessed a man on television cameras.

Later, the monarch visited Washington, where she gave speeches as part of the program celebrating the 200 years of independence of the Thirteen Colonies, titled *The Path to Freedom*.

On July 8, Orlando Bosch's freedom fighters detonated a bomb at the Cuban Embassy in Spain. On the night of July 9, while the Queen enjoyed a banquet aboard the Royal Yacht off Manhattan, another bomb exploded at Jamaica Airport. The explosive, intended to bring down a commercial Cubana flight, detonated in a suitcase shortly before being loaded onto the plane. The perpetrators, members of the Coordination of United Revolutionary Organizations of the Cuban exile, added another failure to their record, but also gained the necessary experience to achieve success three months later against the same airline, managing to throw dozens of bodies into Bridgetown Bay.

The incident occupied five inches on the inside pages of Sunday newspapers. The Queen and Prince were unaware, and that same night, at 11:30 on Friday, they flew to New England. The next day, in Boston, Elizabeth II gave another speech, this time in the street. The experience was almost as exotic as when she was received by an African ambassador who resembled a gorilla.

—We are not two nations divided by a common language—said the Queen, with that Anglo-Saxon fondness for sophistry and paradox.

Everything under control. The Bicentennial Celebration Committee proved it had learned from experience. More than two years earlier, on December 16, 1973, the two-hundredth anniversary of the Tea Party had been celebrated with actors dressed as Indians throwing sacks of tea into Boston Bay to recreate the courage and rebellion of the patriot colonists against the British Empire. The celebration went off protocol when a group of misfits threw gallons marked with the logos of Exxon and Gulf Oil into the bay to protest the abusive profits and environmental impact of the oil corporations. The press and respectable people were outraged by these acts that deviated from the agenda, and protocol was restored in the rest of the Revolution celebrations.

The *Boston Globe* of March 11, 1975, on its page 18, recalled this unpleasant incident caused by followers of the new Tea Party, who claimed that corporations were the new *Tories*, that is, the abusive British conservatives from two centuries ago.[198] In December, the *Washington Post* published a survey of visitors to the exhibition at the historic Faneuil Hall Market, where the most famous revolutionaries gave speeches against the abuses of England. The exhibition was funded with 1.3 million dollars by Sun Oil Company, Rouse

Company, and Honeywell Information Systems. In total, seventy thousand people responded to questions about the most important issues of the decade leading up to the American Revolution.

1. *Would you have paid the taxes or boycotted the British?*
2. *Would you have joined a guerrilla group against the empire?*

Seventeen percent responded as the *revolutionary patriots* had responded two centuries earlier.[199]

But let's return to July 7, 1976. While the Queen finished her gin, that is, the second of her four daily doses of liquor, an excited woman answered in front of CBS cameras:

—The Queen represents freedom and the dignity of a true leader.

That same day, while in Ireland the paramilitary group loyal to the queen, *Ulster Freedom Fighters*, murdered a Catholic couple in their home, the CORU managed to detonate another bomb at the offices of Cubana de Aviación in Barbados. On July 11, the same group of Cuban exiles detonated another bomb at the offices of Air Panama in Colombia. To the outrage of their organizers, these news stories went unnoticed due to the massacre of seven people at the California State University bookstore (attributed, as per protocol for such cases, to an individual with mental health issues) and the massive Democratic Convention that the following day would confirm Jimmy Carter as their candidate for the November elections.

From the land of freedom celebrating its bicentennial, the queen traveled to Canada to inaugurate the Montreal Olympics. The organizing committee was determined to purge any political reading, following the tragic events in Mexico in 1968 and in Munich in 1972. Several African countries withdrew in protest over the presence of the New Zealand delegation, whose government was complicit in the apartheid regime in South Africa.

While in Ireland bombs and deaths were being distributed on both sides, the bombs of Bosch and Posada Carriles, unchallenged, multiplied across the Caribbean. The assassinations and settling of scores among friends and enemies in Florida, New Jersey, and New York also continued.

Anne, the queen's daughter, competed in the equestrian category. She was exempt from the humiliating gender test that other participants had to undergo.[200] She couldn't win because her horse stumbled over an obstacle, and the British team had to withdraw from the competition. In 1987, the princess will be named Princess Royal for life and, a year later, a member of the International Olympic Committee.[201]

Cubana 615

On June 21, in a document marked with a warning note due to the "sensitive source" involved as "a reliable businessman," the CIA recorded the plan of a group of Cubans led by Orlando Bosch to blow up Cubana Flight 467 with two bombs planted at the Panama airport.[202] The bombs exploded before the plane took off, but this did not discourage the Freedom Fighters. There are no declassified documents suggesting that the CIA attempted to prevent this or any other attack where the life of a high-ranking official was not at risk, as was the case with Henry Kissinger.

Shortly afterward, there was another attempt. From Trinidad and Tobago and with fake passports, the journalist Freddy Lugo and the photographer Hernán Ricardo Lozano, an apprentice at the magazine Visión, arrived on a PanAm flight to Norman Manley Airport in Jamaica. At that moment, in an apartment in Caracas, Orlando Bosch and Posada Carriles were awaiting news from the Venezuelans, but the grayish-blue phone remained silent.

From time to time, Bosch's young wife, Adriana Delgado, would appear with her seven-month-old daughter Karin in her arms, asking if they wanted her to serve them anything. Bosch, Adriana, and

Karin had arrived from the Dominican Republic shortly after the bomb that ended the lives of Orlando Letelier and Ronni Moffitt in Washington. Venezuelan President Carlos Andrés Pérez offered him a monthly stipend of 500 dollars in exchange for staying out of political activities in Venezuelan territory. Without thinking twice, Bosch accepted the first part of the generous offer.

Lugo and Lozano had met at the José Martí Association in Caracas. Lozano had previously met Posada Carriles at his private detective agency, called Investigaciones Privadas Comerciales e Industriales S. A. Thanks to this contract, he had secured an international mission in Buenos Aires to disappear two Cuban diplomats. The mission had not been too difficult, as those distant southern countries were already part of Operation Condor and acting there did not pose a significant risk.

Finally, they manage to send their luggage to Havana. One of the suitcases contained C4. With friendly smiles, the suitcases entered a tiny window and disappeared from their sight. The two looked for the window closest to the Cubana flight, but the flight had been slightly delayed. After a few minutes, they began to get nervous. Lugo went to the Cubana counter and asked if there was any delay. The employee confirmed:

—Yes, it's delayed.

—Do you know when it arrives?

—Not exactly, but we've been informed it's undergoing maintenance. It hasn't left Havana yet.

—Damn it.

Shortly before departure, the pilot had noticed that the navigation system was not functioning properly. It wasn't a problem for an experienced pilot, but he decided to order an inspection of the system, and the technicians took over twenty minutes.

—Almost two hours now—confirmed Lugo.

The explosive in Lozano's suitcase had been activated shortly before leaving Puerto Rico. Bosch had calculated the exact moment of the explosion, which was meant to coincide with the normal flight schedule to Havana: two hours, 45 minutes. There was no other way. The detonator could only be programmed with a timer, which was essentially the time it took for the acid to spill over the tensioner and detonate the C4. Neither Lugo nor Lozano were going to be there to detonate the plastic device, and due to the distance, it also couldn't be detonated with an electronic signal, like those Michael Townley so enjoys.

—There's a safer way to detonate C4 on a flight—Orlando Bosch had said—. There's a barometric detonator that only activates when the air pressure changes due to altitude. But at this moment, we don't have that detonator. Not yet.

Hernán approached the Cubana counter and asked again about flight 615. The employee confirmed that the plane had just left José Martí Airport and, in half an hour, would be at Manley.

The two Venezuelans approached gate number one and could see the luggage cart waiting for the Havana-bound plane.

—Twenty minutes and…—Hernán said.

—It could be thirty—corrected Lugo—. It's not a precision clock. Sometimes it's delayed by ten minutes…

—And sometimes it's early. I don't know what we're doing here. We should be outside, as far away as possible.

At that moment the cart with all the luggage exploded, shattering the windows. Airport security closed all entrances.

Classified CIA documents, one dated October 18, mention that last June, Orlando Bosch and Luis Posada Carriles planned to blow up a Cubana flight from Panama. According to the FBI, on that occasion, the bomb did not detonate. Another attempt ended in failure when the bomb planted on July 9, on a flight from Jamaica, exploded prematurely.

In Caracas, Luis Posada Carriles, Morales Navarrete, and Frank Castro met once again to finalize the details for the second attempt. A Cubana plane was going to fly, sooner or later.

THE BEST WAY TO GET RID OF AN UNDESIRABLE

LIKE EVERY THURSDAY NIGHT, on July 15, 1976, Mariana Callejas hosted several artists and writers at the Quetropillán mansion in Lo Curro for another of her highly anticipated gatherings. The Lo Curro gatherings were among the few legal ones in Santiago, a city under permanent curfew. The poet and suspected opponent of the dictatorship, Nicanor Parra, was among the attendees at least once, but he almost ended up in a fight with a painter who called himself Cisternas and never returned. Some young writers attended for the abundance of food and whisky. Others, for the growing prestige of Callejas, a promise of becoming the Silvina or Victoria Ocampo of Chile. The previous year, she had won the short story contest organized by the newspaper El Mercurio. Not a few considered that the story "Do You Know Bobby Ackermann?" was truly deserving of an award, even if it wasn't given by the major media group that promoted and supported the coup. The story, a tale about the son of a Jewish man from New York murdered by a gang of Puerto Ricans, had all the ingredients that fascinated the Anglo-Saxon world that, in turn, fascinated the upper class of Chile and Argentina. A taste that, inevitably, would be adopted by those below due to the prestige overflow of the most widely distributed literary publications of the time.

On the cold night of July 14, one of the attendees heard a muffled scream. Callejas downplayed it, and the conversation about Borges' metrics and the superiority of Enrique Campos Menéndez over José Donoso continued as it had been.

Shortly after, one of the attendees went to the bathroom and took the wrong door. He went down some stairs and found himself in a strange lab that contrasted with his idea of the house. Before he could digest what he had seen, Callejas appeared and, with a smile, told him it was the wrong way. The two went back the way they came. An hour later, the same scream was heard again. This time, no one paid attention. It was part of the mysteries of a house filled with literature.

The screams, more like moans, came from the basement, where members of one of the brigades of DINA, specialized in kidnapping, poisoning, and assassination, the Mulchén Brigade, kept Carmelo Soria tied up. Mulchén was one of the brigades closest to the Townley family and was familiar with the basement of the literary mansion in Lo Curro. It competed in sadism with other brigades, such as Purén and Caupolicán, responsible for torture and rape at the traditional Villa Grimaldi estate. The Spanish diplomat had been kidnapped 24 hours earlier as he was about to enter his home. From there, they had taken him, blindfolded, to the basement of Quetropillán.

Carmelo Soria had been a Spanish Republican and communist who had to take refuge in Chile after the Civil War in Spain and the triumph of Francisco Franco. Years later, he became a supporter of Salvador Allende and, after Pinochet's coup, used his status as a diplomat and UN ambassador to secure political asylum for several dissidents persecuted by the regime.

While upstairs the poets and painters poured themselves more wine, in the basement the DINA agentsDINA began interrogating him, but Soria was in no condition to respond coherently, so the agents tortured him further and without haste.

The sessions ended the next day with Soria's body showing no signs of reaction. Townley administered one of his specialties, a dose of sarin gas. Colonel Pedro Espinosa ordered Colonels Juan Morales Salgado and Guillermo Salinas Torres to dispose of the body that same night. No historical record will ever know what was going through the mind of each officer who ordered the kidnapping, torture, and disappearance of a dissident, nor of those who carried out the order without a second thought.

The records will also shed no light on what women like Mariana Callejas were thinking, the writer who dedicated herself to exploring the inner world, the woman who had a son, her eldest, who had turned out to be a socialist—something inexplicable, like when a very macho father ends up with a gay son. Maybe she thought it was just a phase of youth, like her own in Israel.

—One day, shortly before September 11, 1973, dawned—her mother recalled, in her 1995 memoirs, in other words— he drove in his old Citroneta to the industrial belt of Vicuña Mackenna, to offer his support to the workers in the factories…

One of those factory men (a worker), in front of a group of other factory men, said to the young idealist (as his mother called him):

—Go home, kid, save yourself, because none of us are getting out of here alive.[203]

A distant cry of pain interrupted her memories. When the artists had already left Quetropillán, Mariana collected the glasses and arranged the chairs and cushions.

In a closet, she found a tape recorder with its wheels still spinning.

—Why are you recording my gatherings?—she reproached Townley.

Townley murmured something that Callejas couldn't quite decipher, then headed to the lab. Ever since he started working for DINA, he hadn't rested. He would often stay up until 3:00 a.m., trying to discover the perfect weapon.

It will never be known whether the break in Carmelo Soria's spine was due to the punishments in the basement of Quetropillán or when the agents decided to eliminate him, taking him to the San Carlos Canal in Parque Metropolitano. They threw him over a cliff in his own running car, not far from where lovestruck couples with some means often gaze at the center of Santiago. A bottle of pisco was found in the car, but the radio was missing.

The government reported it as a traffic accident. Chile's independent press gave the accident meaning, reporting on a possible romantic infidelity by the diplomat. The Cuban Virgilio Paz, the Chileans Fernando Lario and Raúl Iturriaga Neumann, the biochemist Eugenio Berríos, and Townley himself were responsible for the accident.

According to Mariana Callejas, the chemical engineer Eugenio Berríos was a kind and cheerful man. He always wore a smile on his face.

"On one occasion," recalled Callejas, "he said there was no better way to get rid of someone undesirable than with a drop of golden staph."

Weeks later, on August 4th, Carlos Godoy, the son of the former rector of the University of Chile and a relative of Carmelo Soria, would disappear. Nine days later, on Friday the 13th, the former Chilean president and political opponent of Salvador Allende, Eduardo Frei, went to dinner with the poet and diplomat Óscar Pinochet de la Barra, who had served as ambassador to the Soviet Union during Frei's presidency, to Japan during Allende's government, and for a few months under General Pinochet himself. Just before leaving his friend's house, a neighbor knocked on the door and entered the house.

—Some individuals have been working on your car, he said, and left again, pretending to be out for a stroll.

The police managed to detonate the plastic bomb. The next day, Frei received a call:

—This time you got away. Next time you won't.

On August 22, former Brazilian president Juscelino Kubitschek died in a car accident near Rio de Janeiro. On December 6, another former president, João Goulart, passed away. Ousted in the 1964 coup, Goulart had exiled himself in Argentina. The official report on his death at 57 claimed the Brazilian had suffered a cardiac arrest in his apartment in the province of Corrientes. Although the reasons for his death were questioned, the Argentine military dictatorship prohibited an autopsy, just as it banned photos in the press of the thirty thousand attendees at his funeral.

A few years later, Eduardo Frei Montalva, Salvador Allende's rival in the last elections and a silent enemy of Pinochet's dictatorship, died in a hospital in Santiago from a mysterious staphylococcus aureus bacterial infection.

The best way to get rid of an undesirable.

BOMBS AND MARCHES FOR FREEDOM

ON JULY 23, AN OFFICIAL FROM CUBA'S NATIONAL Fishing Institute was killed in an attempted kidnapping of the consul in Mérida. Later, the CORU would detonate another bomb in Guatemala, in retaliation for Mexico's decision not to release two of its members involved in the Mérida attack.

On Saturday, July 24, at 4:00 AM, the New York police arrested three Cubans: George Gómez, aged 28, Armando Santana, 25, and Alfredo Chumanceiro, 22, while they were placing powerful pipe bombs containing TNT and C4 at the Music Academy located at 126 14th Street in Manhattan. That same night, a music festival featuring artists from the island was scheduled to take place. According to the police officer in charge, Albert Sulzer, there was enough explosive at the entrance to blow up the entire front of the building.

The newspapers reported that the perpetrators were members of the far-right group Omega 7.[204] The concert announcement had caught the attention of this Cuban cell: "Down with the blockade against Cuba." For Omega 7 and for the press, this alone proved and condemned the involved artists as pro-Castro, pro-communist, and, by logical deduction, terrorists who deserved death or mutilation.

Outraged by the arrest of the three Union City residents, on August 15, Cuban groups in Union City organized a march to raise funds in support of the heroes who attempted to blow up the New York Music Academy along with its potential occupants. The march was held under the slogan of the Cuban Nationalist Movement Cuba above all, which many identified with the Nazi slogan Germany above all adapted to a higher cause. Three of the Omega 7 members had received a $50,000 bail each, something their lawyers were unable to reduce to make it affordable for the accused.[205]

For this reason, solidarity collections were organized. New Jersey was accustomed to this kind of Freedom March. In January 1974, hundreds of protesters had marched down Bergenline Avenue in solidarity with Guillermo Novo, a well-known car dealer from Union City, who had been convicted in Canada for planting a bomb at the Cuban consulate, which the Canadian police managed to thwart in time.

The march had been organized by the Committee for the Freedom of Cuban Patriots and by the alternative government of Cuba.[206] Similar marches were repeated with the aim of pressuring authorities and raising funds for the cause, such as the one on November 12 of the same year.

The one on Sunday, August 15, 1976, filled Bergenline Avenue with 350 protesters and extensive coverage in the state press. It was approved and promoted by Mayor William Musto, who also offered them the baseball stadium, where several speakers repeated the same speech denouncing the insensitivity of the American people towards the cause for the freedom of Cuba.

"I don't see why I shouldn't approve this march," the mayor had declared to *The Jersey Journal*, two weeks before. "Cubans have always been very orderly in their political activities. In fact, we will make appropriate police protection available for the event."[207]

On March 26, 1982, Musto would be sentenced to seven years in prison for extortion and million-dollar frauds, thanks to the testimony of one of his collaborators, Bob Menéndez. On May 11 of that year, Musto was reelected as mayor, defeating the young Menéndez at the polls, but he had to hand over his position to his wife. Four years later, Menéndez was elected mayor of Union City, beginning a meteoric career. In 1993, he became his district's representative in Washington, and in 2006, he was elected as a senator.

—The success of U.S. foreign policy lies in its democracy—Menéndez will declare in Congress on January 19, 2021—. Public servants, such as senators, have the duty to defend democracy, the Constitution, the rule of law, and Human Rights.

For decades, Bob Menéndez, senator and chairman of the Foreign Relations Committee, will be accused of corruption. In 2023, the FBI will raid his residence and seize three kilos of gold, an undeclared luxury car, and half a million dollars in cash hidden throughout the house. Petty cash, compared to the bribes and donations received (such as the vulture funds from Paul Singer that will cost Argentina over ten billion dollars) in exchange for special favors. In October 2023, he will be charged with conspiracy and fraud, but he will refuse to resign from his seat and his legal immunity.

AUGUST

Letelier and Kubitschek must be neutralized

On August 6, the Chinese Embassy in Asunción hosted a reception attended by Paraguayan officials and diplomats from various countries. Among them were the intelligence chief of Alfredo Stroessner, Colonel Benito Guanes, and the U.S. ambassador, George Landau.

Colonel Guanes was aware of Deputy Director of the CIA Vernon Walters' trip the previous June. At one point, Ambassador Landau took Guanes by the arm and discreetly led him to a corner of the room.

—I received a call from General Walters—said the ambassador—. It seems there's been a problem with the passports of the two Chileans traveling to Washington.

—What kind of problems?

—Nothing serious, but the State Department has decided to suspend their visas. So they'll have to use their own Chilean passports. I don't think there will be any issues if they use their own passports.

The ambassador informed him that this same information was going to be sent to "my friend, Colonel Contreras."

On Tuesday the 24th, he dined with General Enrique Morel, the military attaché of Santiago in Washington, and several American collaborators. One of the attendees, whose name will be redacted in the declassified documents, reported that he had met with Contreras in the past month of July. The head of the National Information Service, the Brazilian colonel Joao Batista Figueiredo, mentioned in writing that Orlando Letelier and Juscelino Kubitschek needed to be neutralized because they supported the candidacy of Jimmy Carter, considered a threat to the security of South America.[208]

By then, the DINA already had the plan fine-tuned. Only a few details remained to be resolved.

TO KILL AND WHOM TO KILL, THAT IS THE QUESTION

THE FIRST THING TOWNLEY DID WAS TO CONTACT FIVE CUBANS FROM HIS PERSONAL LIST: GUILLERMO NOVO, Ignacio Novo, Virgilio Paz Romero, Dionisio Suárez, and Alvin Ross Díaz. The five agreed.

Shortly before, Townley had participated with one of them in an operation that had added another success, more experience, and confidence among several valuable collaborators. On August 9, the CIA sent him to Buenos Aires along with the Cuban Guillermo Novo. Although Novo was on parole for the attack on a Cuban vessel in Canada, he was able to accompany him to Argentina to interrogate two Cuban diplomats who had been kidnapped by paramilitary groups from that country. After the interrogation, Crescencio Galañega Hernández, 26 years old, and Jesús Cejas Arias, 22 years old, disappeared forever. According to a witness who did not reveal his name, their bodies were thrown into the foundations of a building under construction.

Like many members of Operation Condor, on August 23, Townley obtained a fake passport in Paraguay under the name Juan Williams Rose. When they went for the U.S. visas, Ambassador George Landau raised objections. But Landau received a visit from the right-hand man of the Paraguayan dictator, Stroessner, who informed him that the visas had been requested by Pinochet for a special meeting with the Deputy Director of the CIA, Vernon Waters, in Washington. Shortly after, the visas were assigned to the fake passports. Just in case, the ambassador copied the passports and sent them to General Vernon Waters for authentication, but Waters responded that he did not know who these Chilean agents were. Landau urged immediately to deny entry to the United States to the men who had been granted the visas.

On August 3, 1976, Harry Shlaudeman informed Henry Kissinger about potential assassinations of international figures. At the Department of State, officials discussed how the U.S. government should proceed, and several key advisors recommended a direct and forceful response to Chile against any assassination that could spark an international scandal.

On August 23, Kissinger signed a cable addressed to the embassies of Uruguay, Paraguay, and Chile. The ambassadors were informed of the CIA reports about planned and directed assassinations inside and outside the territory of Operation Condor members, with instructions to collaborate with their counterparts. Washington was aware of the planned assassinations of "prominent figures" and remained concerned about the impact on international opinion.

The following day, August 24, the U.S. ambassador to Chile, David Popper, opposed participating in Pinochet's passport request. Popper knew that Pinochet would take the precautionary measure as an insult and that it would undermine collaboration with his regime, but he had few alternatives. The U.S. ambassador to Uruguay also hesitated. He considered that ignoring such a warning would endanger his life and suggested transferring the entire responsibility to Kissinger's office in Washington.

On August 30, the Undersecretary for Inter-American Affairs, Harry Shlaudeman, sent a memorandum to Kissinger requesting permission for the U.S. ambassador to Uruguay, Ernest Siracusa, to meet with high-ranking officials of Operation Condor: "We must avoid a series of international assassinations that could cause serious damage to the reputation of our countries."

But Kissinger and the CIA did not share these concerns.

BOMBS and ArTICLes

On August 28 *The Nation* published Orlando Letelier's article titled "The Chicago Boys in Chile." On page 137, Ronni and Michel recognized Orlando's voice in the printed words:

"Economic policies are conditioned by the social and political situation in which they are implemented and, at the same time, they modify it. Therefore, economic policies are always introduced to *alter social structures.*

It is curious that the man who wrote a book titled Capitalism and Freedom, *arguing that only classical economic liberalism can sustain political democracy, can now so easily separate economics from politics when the economic theories he defends coincide with an absolute restriction of all rights and all democratic freedoms. One would expect that if those who restrict private enterprise are held accountable for the effects of their measures in the political sphere, those who impose "unrestricted economic freedom" should also be held accountable, especially when the imposition of this policy is inevitably accompanied by massive repression, hunger, unemployment, and the perpetuation of a brutal police state.*

The violation of human rights, the system of institutionalized brutality, the control and drastic suppression of all forms of dissent are discussed (and often condemned) as a phenomenon only indirectly linked (or even completely unrelated) to the classic unbridled "free market" policies that have been implemented by the military junta."

A few pages later:

"Repression for the majority and 'economic freedom' for small privileged groups are two sides of the same coin."[209]

—Orlando is the ideal candidate to be the next president of Chile—said Ronni.
—That's exactly what worries me—insisted Michael.

His former assistant, General Augusto Pinochet, likely thought the same. The political and intellectual stature of Letelier was growing rapidly. He worked at IPS, taught at American University, and had managed to get the Dutch government to withhold a major investment from the mining group Stevin in Chile. He had just received an offer for a book with an advance equal to what he earned in a year at IPS. There was no figure in exile with more recognition and acceptance. He also had the support of many senators in Washington; he often lunched with Ted Kennedy, Hubert Humphrey, and George McGovern. The feminist activist Angela Yvonne Davis and other figures from social movements often visited him at his home in Bethesda.

But Letelier and the exiles from the fascist dictatorships of Latin America had a notable weakness: they wrote articles, gave lectures. They didn't plant bombs in embassies, theaters, or airplanes.

The DINA also took note of this danger.

KILL THE FUTURE PRESIDENT

COLONEL PEDRO ESPINOSA SHOWED UP ONE NIGHT AT THE HOUSE IN LO CURRO. He lived seven blocks away. He didn't get out of the car and asked to speak with Michael Townley. The decision to eliminate the undesirable Letelier came from higher up. There were only two people above Colonel Espinosa in the chain of command: Contreras and Pinochet.

Michael Townley knew (or believed) himself to be the fourth link in the chain. He went down and spoke in the privacy of his boss's car. Mariana Callejas had given birth to their son on June 6, so she had asked Townley not to travel so much. But Townley couldn't refuse an order from the man he called "My colonel," especially when it involved the biggest operation since his entry into the DINA.

—We need to neutralize the traitor— said Colonel Espinosa.

He had discussed it with *Mamo* Contreras. The idea was for all the leads in Letelier's assassination to point to the Cubans. Letelier was mentioned in the U.S. press as a Marxist. He worked for IPS, which had been portrayed as Marxist in the media. In other words, these backgrounds were reason enough for the Cubans in Miami to want him dead.

—What's the plan?

Colonel Espinosa's instructions were clear, though never entirely rigid. He was a military man and knew that the reality of combat is full of unforeseen events and exceptions to the rules.

—Your job— said Colonel Espinosa— is to contact the Cubans. They already know and trust you.

—I'm not so sure about that— said Townley, somewhat skeptical and based on experience.

—Trust me, they need allies— said the colonel with a confident smile.

—What's the plan?

—First, we'll send you to Paraguay to get a passport and an emergency visa.

—Why the urgency?

—It's orders. Letelier must be eliminated in September. It's national month.

—I know better than anyone. Carlos Prats, Bernardo Leighton...

—That time the Cubans turned out to be excellent partners... On the other hand, it must be before the elections that Jimmy Carter could win and before the UN General Assembly. In Washington, you'll receive help from a Chilean officer. You will organize everything, but the Cubans must carry it out. Do I want this last point to be crystal clear? Understood?

—Yes, it's clear. Have you already thought about how we will neutralize the target?

—One possibility is for a woman to take him to a hotel and poison him. We know the man has weaknesses for women, and we already have the proven ingredient. That's why we've been paying you all this time.

—I've had successful results.

—Without a doubt, and we are very grateful for that.

—We can't trust a woman with a Cuban accent—said Townley—. He would be suspicious from the start.

—That's true—confirmed the colonel—. Like a CIA agent who speaks Spanish with a Yankee accent. We're not the naive Argentines who sent Cuban women to Perón. He slept with them, and they were left with nothing. We'll send a Chilean woman posing as an exile, in case it's decided that this is the best approach. For my part, I prefer an accident. In that, your friends can help a lot. They have experience. But here comes the second condition…

—Go ahead, Colonel.

—They must ensure that Letelier is alone at the moment of the accident. We need to contain any collateral effects. Any other person involved could trigger an investigation beyond what's anticipated. I mean, something with international implications. The general doesn't want more problems than he already has. Neither do we. Do you understand what I'm saying?[210]

—Understood, Colonel.

TWO FAKE PASSPORTS, ANOTHER MISSING LINK

TWO DAYS LATER, MICHAEL TOWNLEY and Captain Armando Fernández Larios flew to Paraguay. Townley exuded confidence, but Fernández Larios couldn't stop thinking about his father, Air Force Colonel Alfredo Fernández.

—Sit there—his father had told him days before—. I want you to look me in the eyes.

Alfredo was a stern man of few words. He had studied in Washington, D.C., where his son was born in 1950. Decades later,

Armandito had returned to the United States, this time to study at the School of the Americas in Georgia.

—What's wrong?—asked Armando.

—Leave DINA—his father said—. Go back to the army. You're a soldier, not a secret agent.

—No—said Armando.

—Listen, son—the old man insisted, with less patience—. I know you better than anyone. I know about your loyalty to your superiors, but one day you'll end up in jail, and none of them will protect you. Only I could protect you, but by then I'll be dead.

The old man died a year later. At the time, Armando didn't pay much attention to his father's words. Just old man's talk, he thought.

As Townley and Fernández Larios flew to Asunción, Augusto Pinochet called the Paraguayan dictator Alfredo Stroessner to expedite the passport process.

—These are two officers of the Chilean army—said Pinochet—. They must be in New York in a few days to investigate some irregularities in the state copper company Codelco.

Shortly after, the Paraguayan presidential advisor, Conrado Pappalardo, contacted U.S. Ambassador George Landau to process the visas for the Paraguayans Juan Williams Rose and Alejandro Romeral Jara as quickly as possible. Landau, an Austrian more patriotic than George Washington, as naturalized immigrants often are, had in his later years been influenced by the uncomfortable issue of Human Rights.

—The two officers—Pappalardo told the ambassador— need to urgently meet with the CIA Deputy Director Vernon Walters in Washington.

Vernon Walters had retired in July. After a delay of weeks, Pappalardo authorized the two visas for Townley and Fernández Larios, but he suspected the urgency and the two men, so he made copies of their photographs.

Finally, Townley and Captain Fernández Larios did not use their new Paraguayan passports. The U.S. ambassador to Paraguay canceled their visas at the last minute.[211] Later, the photographs taken for the passports with false names and the confession of a disgraced Cuban in Jacksonville would be the clue that gave the FBI the key to solving the murder of Orlando Letelier and Ronni Moffitt.

THE CAPTAIN AND THE DANCER

—Here are the tickets—Colonel Pedro Espinosa told him—. The hotel is also paid for. In Washington, you'll share the room with Luisa.

Captain Fernández Larios took the tickets with the shyness that characterized him, and the colonel warned him:

—You lay a finger on her and I'll kill you.

Captain Armando Fernández Larios and the dancer Luisa Mónica Lagos became, from then on and for several days, Romeral Jara and Liliana Walker. They entered the United States as a couple on their honeymoon, but their job was to gather the necessary information so that Townley and the Cubans could eliminate Orlando Letelier with the fewest possible errors.

Luisa Lagos had chosen the false surname Walker because it was the first thing she thought of when asked. Walker had been the only man she had ever fallen in love with, a musician who, like her and all her friends, was a supporter of the Popular Union and had voted for Salvador Allende in the last elections. After the coup, the musician, Pata Walker, was identified as a member of an underground group. He was known to hate DINA and was quickly arrested by its agents.

After Pinochet's coup, things had gone from bad to worse for her shoemaker father. The same for her. She worked as a bar dancer and as decor in some TV programs. Luisa began to mix her vocation with tips she received for special favors to her clients.

Once, a military officer hired her for an easy and fun job. She only had to accompany him to social gatherings. She didn't have to do anything else because the officer was very polite and only asked her to let him show off her beauty and youth to shut up those who doubted his masculinity.

—Little by little—she confessed years later— I realized I really liked luxury and living beyond my means.

So she began working in the biggest military brothel in Santiago. According to some testimonies, Pedro Espinosa was one of the administrators.

During Henry Kissinger's visit to Santiago last June, Luisa's mission had been to gather as much information as possible from the delegates of the ambassadors of the OAS for propaganda and extortion purposes. She wasn't the only woman assigned to this intelligence operation. Among the various repressive agencies that had emerged after the 1973 coup was the Women's Brigade, much more effective than the police's single women\'s squad for intelligence purposes. The Women's Brigade had been created with failed television actresses who still maintained the sensuality of firm muscles and the unsatisfied anxieties of success and money. After a fake casting organized by a journalist from Channel 7, another dozen dazzling young women with dreams of stardom had been recruited. The operations center was located at the El Sauce motel on Gran Avenida.

During the OEA meeting, the Women's Brigade worked full-time. The most common tactic was to seduce or, rather, let themselves be seduced by some distinguished visitor, make him drink as much whiskey as possible, and take him to the most ancient confessional in human history. The reports never revealed any valuable information, but the Women's Brigade remained active, waiting for its first big success.

On August 24, Colonel Espinosa called Luisa to say:

—Get dressed, you're going to the United States.
—Me? To the United States?
—Yes, but only for a few days. We have a mission for you.
—To the United States?
—New York. Washington. You'll stay in very nice hotels…
—But I…
—No, don't worry, you don't need to know a word of English. You'll only work with Chileans and Cubans.
—Why me?
—Well, everyone knows you have a special talent for attracting womanizing men.
—Me?

Luisa Larios was 23 years old. Her biggest dream had come true. It was something indescribable, like being in love.

SEPTEMBER

THE SENSUAL ART OF KILLING A MAN

COLONEL ESPINOSA INTRODUCED HER TO HER COMPANION and fake husband shortly before going to the airport. Neither Luisa nor Captain Fernández Larios knew each other or spoke much during the trip to New York. She found him a bit childish, a military man incapable of disobeying an order from his superior, but with an insistent gaze. From experience, she knew the captain imagined himself in her bed in a hotel room they hadn't even reached yet. On the one hand, not doing so would mean obeying a superior's order, and on the other, it felt like breaking the natural laws of any military man. On September 7th, Luisa and Fernández Larios met their first contact.

Michael Townley had arrived weeks earlier, on August 22nd, also under a false name and thanks to an A-2 visa issued by the Embassy in Santiago. In the end, he hadn't used the Paraguayan passport but another one under the name Hans Petersen Silva. In one pocket of his jacket, he had smuggled into the country part of the bomb he intended to use. In the other pocket, as a plan B, a small bottle of Chanel No. 5 perfume containing an organophosphate compound. That is, sarin nerve gas, enough to paralyze all the passengers and crew of the airplane had it accidentally opened.[212] A similar bottle would appear in the photograph that, on November 30th, would report the mysterious death of Renato León Zenteno, the real estate agent who refused to illegally transfer the property of Lo Curro.

At the airport, Townley (identified as Andrés Wilson) rented a car from Avis Rent a Car and headed to Virgilio Paz's apartment, in Union City. After crossing the Brooklyn Bridge, he stopped at a corner, where he saw a poster advertising an event featuring Orlando Letelier, alongside the famous singers Joan Baez and Piru Seenger. He got out, read it, and tore the poster down as if he genuinely felt something against those names.

—Up to six dollars a ticket, for sale at 156 Fifth Avenue... They say it's to support the return to democracy in Chile, but they're stealing it all, those corrupt bastards.

—Are you thinking of going?—asked the captain—. It's a place where information will be abundant...

—I don't know—answered Townley—. No, better not. Someone might recognize me.

They crossed Midtown Manhattan, not far from 156 Fifth Avenue, and shortly after, they passed by Madison Square Garden. On 33rd Street, they went straight into the Lincoln Tunnel and, within minutes, emerged in Union City. He dropped the couple off at the hotel and, from a payphone, called Virgilio Paz.

At a restaurant (likely on Bergenline Avenue and 43rd Street, later renamed Celia Cruz), Townley met with the Cubans.

—This is a big mission, very big—he told Paz.

The mission would require the participation of other Cubans, such as Guillermo Novo.

—But where, man? We're not interested in going back to Europe so soon.

—No, this time it's right here, in Washington.

The next day, at the entrance of IPS, Luisa Lagos managed to speak with Orlando Letelier, but the suspect preferred not to continue with the Chilean stranger's seduction game and said he had to leave for a meeting. In reality, he had to be in New York for the Madison Square Garden event.

—An elegant man—she reported—. Few words, but attractive.

If he had seen her on some television program years ago, there was no way he could recognize her. She worked as a dancer, as a background figure. She kept her voluminous hairstyle, her thin eyebrows, and her thick eyelashes, like almost all the young women of that time. For a few years she believed that everyone recognized her when she walked the streets of Santiago, but the truth slowly dawned on her, like the realization that only money remains and is real.

—Well, she wasn't entirely wrong—said Hunter—. There's nothing more real than a belief... Well, go on, go on.

Luisa did her job: she paid attention to every kind of detail to report back to the captain, such as the color and model of the car the minister used.

The sarin gas in the Chanel No. 5 bottle was meant to be sprayed on Letelier's pillow, like the poisoned toothpaste sent to eliminate Fidel Castro and the African leader Patrice Lumumba.

From that day on, Captain Fernández, Townley, and Paz began to track every move of Letelier. They knew he would be in New York that same day. Townley had a plan and its possible variations, from the use of sarin gas to a bomb in the hotel room the diplomat had reserved on 44th West in Manhattan. The seduction time given to Lagos was minimal, if not impossible. To make matters worse, Letelier had traveled with his wife Isabel, so any plan involving Letelier's room was ruled out. On the other hand, none of these options seemed to meet one of Colonel Espinosa's conditions: not to cause the death of other people that could trigger a larger investigation ultimately implicating the Chilean government. By "other people," they meant any American citizen.

—Captain Fernández tried to seduce me—Lagos would admit years later. But Colonel Espinosa's threat was still fresh in his memory, and he didn't dare touch one of his favorites.

—To be honest with you—the captain said then— I don't understand how a man like Colonel Espinosa, who says he cares for you so much, sends you on a mission to assassinate a man.

—For what?—asked Luisa.

—To kill a man—confirmed Captain Fernández.

STATELESS BY DECREE

On Friday, September 10, Orlando Letelier came down early from his room at the Algonquin Hotel. In the lobby, a journalist stopped him.

—General Pinochet has just revoked your citizenship—said the journalist.

Decree 588, signed by General Augusto Pinochet Ugarte and his sixteen ministers, declared the Chilean minister stateless, citing his "publicity campaign" against Chile, which "constitutes a grave attack on the essential interests of the Chilean State." For this reason, "such ignoble and disloyal behavior severs the national from his Homeland and the State, making him deserving of the maximum and shameful moral sanction contemplated in our legal system… The evidence clearly and irrefutably shows that the aforementioned individual has, from abroad, attacked the essential interests of the State."[213] The decree mentioned Article Six of the 1825 Political Constitution of the State, without acknowledging that the fundamental rights of that constitution had been violated by the dictatorship itself.

—At least now I know I have one more year to live—said Letelier—. For now, this is my punishment.

He went up to his room and rewrote the speech he planned to give that evening. Then he wrote a note to be published in the *New York Times*: "When democracy and human rights are restored in Chile, no one will question the nationality of any Chilean, not even those who are in power today."

At eight in the evening, just before the anniversary of Pinochet's coup in Chile, seven thousand five hundred people filled Madison Square Garden. Letelier himself introduced Joan Baez and Pete Seeger. After listening to "Gracias a la vida" by Violeta Parra and other protest songs that had become popular in the United States, Letelier took the stage:

—Tonight, here, there are many who have been imprisoned by the Chilean dictatorship. There are parents of sons and daughters who have been killed by Chilean fascists. If some of us were freed, it was due to international pressure on the military junta; it was because of their support and efforts for the restoration of Human Rights in my country... Tonight we have with us several ambassadors and representatives from governments in Europe, Asia, Africa, and Latin America. We are particularly pleased to have with us Ambassador Dinh Ba Thi, Permanent Observer to the United Nations for the Socialist Republic of Vietnam. To all of them, our recognition... We also have members of the National Council of Churches of the United States; representatives from United Auto Workers and several other unions; many community leaders, particularly from the Black, Puerto Rican, and Chicano communities; and representatives from Amnesty International, which has played such an important role in securing the freedom of hundreds of Chilean political prisoners... Today, Pinochet has signed a decree stating that I am deprived of my nationality. This is an important day for me. A dramatic day in my life when the actions of the fascist generals against me make me feel more Chilean than ever. Because true Chileans are, in the tradition of O'Higgins, Balmaceda, Allende, Neruda, Gabriela Mistral, Claudio Arrau, and Víctor Jara, and they (the fascists) are the enemies of Chile, the traitors who are selling our homeland to foreign investments. I was born Chilean, I am Chilean, and I will die Chilean. They were born traitors, live as traitors, and will forever be known as fascist traitors... Exactly two years ago, I was freed from a Chilean concentration camp and expelled to Venezuela. The day I arrived in Caracas, Joan Baez was giving a concert in the largest stadium in that city, and she dedicated her songs to the struggle and suffering of the Chilean people. This was my first encounter with the expressions of solidarity that I knew existed but had not yet witnessed. There, in that stadium Venezuelan, was this extraordinary woman with her guitar, with her voice full of emotion and feeling, bringing her message of human solidarity with the

Chilean people to thousands of Venezuelans... More than two thousand Chileans have disappeared at the hands of the DINA, Pinochet's private secret police and the cornerstone of his regime. Those concerned about human rights in Chile realize that the efforts to free political prisoners, as important as they are, may not be enough, because the DINA arrests a number of people every day that is always greater than the number of people who are freed... The solidarity of the American people in favor of the restoration of human rights and democracy in Chile must continue to grow. This solidarity is paramount to us. We will never rest until we achieve the overthrow of the fascist regime in Chile. At that moment, when we are building a new democracy, we will count on your support to uphold the hard-earned achievements of the Chilean people and to stop once and for all the reactionary forces that, from within and outside Chile, destroyed our democracy... The words of Salvador Allende have a stronger meaning now than ever. In the final moments of his epic struggle, he said: "I have faith in Chile and its destiny. Other men will overcome this dark and bitter moment in which treason prevailed. Keep in mind that much sooner than later, great avenues will open where free men will pass to build a better society."[214]

The speech lasted twenty minutes.

—This guy has more balls than Maceo...

The original idea of Townley was to spread sarin gas in Letelier's car or office. But he changed his mind. In any case, it would be speculated as a natural death. The newspapers would say that the Chilean dissident suffered from heart problems or had been under stress from overwork.

A more significant publicity stunt was necessary.

ENEMY OF FREEDOM AND OF WARS

On September 10, Townley met with Guillermo Novo and José Suárez at the Bottom of the Barrel restaurant in Union City. Novo, for his part, had reserved a room at the Howard Johnson motel. Townley was reported to the FBI as "the blond Chilean" named Andrés Wilson, also known by the nickname El Flaco.

—He's a Marxist—said Townley, referring to the target.

The Marxist label was a catch-all that worked for anything. Even for mercenaries without a defined ideology, because they felt more comfortable on the other side. Maybe that was their ideology. Like many others, José Suárez had been a colonel for Fidel Castro until he defected and was hired by the CIA for the Bay of Pigs invasion in 1961. He later became the leader of the Cuban Nationalist Movement. His friends knew him as José Blood Pool, for his brutality.

—Eliminate an enemy of freedom.

—We have other jobs. We won't be able to go to Europe again.

—This one is right here.

Townley went into the details. The success of the operation would be the final test of a solid alliance between the government of Chile and the Cuban government in exile.

—We agree—said Novo—. But there are details that are not clear to us. What we want is for an agent of the DINA to participate in the operation, and here there aren't many options.

Captain Fernández Larios and the dancer Luisa Lagos reconstructed Letelier's movements from his home in Bethesda to the IPS in D.C.

One morning, the captain called the IPS. Since Letelier was not in his office, he requested his address to deliver some extremely urgent documents. Someone provided it to him. At the indicated address in Bethesda, he saw a car with the Chilean coat of arms. He got out, climbed the stairs, and knocked on the door. Inside, someone told him that Orlando would be away for twenty days. Townley received from Fernández Larios a sketch of Letelier's house and office, as well as information about the cars of Letelier and his wife.

Augusto Pinochet had ordered that, in this case, the DINA should ensure by all means that the trails of international investigations would not point to his regime. Hence the importance of the participation of the Cubans Dionisio Charco de Sangre Suárez and Virgilio Paz, alias Don Juan to the women who knew him in his international travels.

—Before leaving for Washington—admitted Callejas— Michael told me that his mission was not to participate directly in anything, that the Cubans were going to take care of that. But I didn't believe in the Cubans. My relationship with them had been, from the very beginning, unpleasant.[215]

He was not only referring to his contacts in Miami to assassinate diplomats in Mexico. Or in Argentina. Or in the United States. Since his years at the University of Miami, when Callejas was still an idealist, as his eldest son still was, he had participated in the protests against the Vietnam War in Florida. The Cubans threw eggs and tomatoes at them. Being against any war made those students automatically anti-American. Killing their own and others with bombs or executing them in an ambush for thinking differently did not. That, they must have considered it very American and very patriotic.

Perhaps they were right.

The Cross and The Brothel

On September 12, Townley reserved a room at the Chateau Renaissance motel, in North Bergen, north of Union City. Then he met with Guillermo Novo and Dionisio Suárez in the Avis car to discuss the final method. The only remaining option was a bomb in the minister's car.

Townley and the Cubans knew that the chances of clarifying a bombing, even for the FBI, were less than ten percent. The material evidence was usually destroyed in the attack itself and, above all, the combatants could be far away by the time the first alarms sounded.

Townley remembers one of Colonel Espinosa's conditions and decides that the Cubans would handle the execution of the plan.

—Wait—interrupted Guillermo Novo—. We won't do anything if a DINA agent does not participate as well.

After several hesitations, Townley agrees to take charge of the explosives to leave the detonation to the Cubans.

—You will also have to place it in the car yourself—Suarez clarified—. We will take care of the rest.

Though this part wasn't planned, on the other hand Townley maintained the option of being far, very far away when the bomb would be detonated. Despite an old partnership of mutual suspicion, none of the three was willing to risk another failure.

At a Radio Shack, they acquired most of the devices needed for the detonation. That same day, at the Chateau Renaissance motel, they assembled the detonator. The motel had thick red curtains and golden cushioned beds.

—This looks like a brothel.

—It probably is, despite that cross above the bed. It reminds me of my grandmother.

—The brothel or the cross?

Two days later, in Union City, Novo and Suarez handed Townley the C4. The next day, Townley and Virgilio Paz began to follow Letelier during his routines in Washington. At the insistence of the Cubans, Townley facilitated a visit to the Naval Attaché of the Chilean embassy, Admiral Ronald Mc-Intyre Mendoza. Novo and Suárez protested the treatment that the Chilean government had given to Rolando Otero, whom they labeled a traitor, and informed them of the cancellation of the assassination of a Chilean journalist in Mexico.

For FBI agent Carter Cornick and prosecutor Eugene Propper there was little doubt: this meeting confirmed the assassination operation of Letelier as a gesture of goodwill to revive the relations of the Cuban Brigade with the Chilean government.[216]

After the return of democracy, Mc-Intyre would be elected senator of the Republic of Chile, a position he would hold for almost the entire 90s.

A Good-For-Nothing to the Rescue of Civilization

On September 18, the day of Chile's independence was being commemorated. That same night, Townley and his team headed to Letelier's house at 5818 Ogden Court in Bethesda, and found his light blue car parked in the driveway, outside the garage.

There were several cars parked all the way to the cul-de-sac where the neighborhood street ended, because Letelier and his wife Isabel had organized a gathering with many guests.

—There must be fifty people, at least. The son of a bitch is pretty popular. Some will be journalists, others *researchers*, as the communist conspirators are called.

Townley managed to catch a glimpse of Letelier. His face, his figure momentarily brought him back to the Chile of the years before the coup. He was one of the most well-known men at the time. He had been Pinochet's chief, was adored by the left, especially when he left his diplomatic position in the United States to return to Chile to join a government that was already under attack. He was in the newspapers, on television… and now he was, as his secretary Michael Moffitt said, the future president of Chile.

In contrast, he, Townley, always said he had little idea or interest in politics, though he had been born and raised with the conviction that a Marxist was an enemy, a traitor to his country and the human species. His wife Mariana held the same position. When someone asked her about her political stance, she would say she was a Feudalist. A dialectical, sarcastic, nihilistic dodge typical of Jorge Luis Borges, whom she admired so much. But far from unrealistic.

In Valdivia, during the few years of Allende's government, Townley had dedicated himself to building a luxury yacht that he planned to sell in the United States for a profit so favorable it would allow him to build another, and then another. But then the coup came, and he could no longer continue his project and had to work as a mechanic in the upscale neighborhood of Las Condes.[217]

When he offered to collaborate with the CIA, the only thing he knew for sure was that he could either focus on his business or take a stand for the good of Chile. He had chosen the latter. Apparently, the exact moment when his indignation (according to the shared memory of Michael and Mariana) had finally awakened him was when, one night, he was walking down a street in Santiago with Mariana. At one point, they saw an old man sitting on a dark street (according to their memoirs, which would be published in 1995 under the title *Siembra vientos*), and the couple approached the poor man with the intention of consoling him.

—Look at that man—Mariana said to Michael—. He's so lonely. Let's keep him company.[218]

According to the same memoirs, the poor elderly man, who was protesting alone while hitting a can, was confronted by the police under Allende's government.

It was then that Callejas and Townley saw how the officers mistreated the poor old man, and that changed everything. The fault lay with President Allende. The country was beginning to sink into chaos, he said, as was typical under socialist governments.

"*I was starting to notice that corruption was taking over Allende's people*—wrote Mariana—. It wasn't possible to blame Yankee imperialism."[219]

Mariana couldn't bear that act of brutal violence by Allende's government and joined the fascist party Patria y Libertad, first, and then DINA shortly after.

—We weren't suffering. We had the dollars from the sale of our house, a business in Miami and the alimony that my ex-husband sent for his older children...[220]

Callejas' narrative, a writer later awarded in Chile, didn't differ much from the dominant press's narrative against Allende's government:

"Class hatred was fostered. The maids and gardeners didn't get, after all, the houses of their employers. The hatred between the dispossessed and the rich floated in the air like a stench."[221] Besides her usual clichés: *"we were absolutely perplexed"*, *"I raised the alarm..."*[222]

In February 1971, the CIA had given the green light to accept Townley as a "valuable asset." However, Townley was never accepted as an agent, something he hid from Callejas until the end. With few known exceptions, the CIA only recruited agents with university degrees, whatever they were, and Townley hadn't finished high school. This rejection, shortly before flying to Allende's Chile, must have been another blow to his self-esteem, damaged since he could remember. Anyway, as an asset, he had his value, both for the CIA and DINA. Politically illiterate, convinced of the importance of the fight against Marxism but without any idea of what it was about, with no time or desire to investigate, he was unscrupulous and had personal fixations, something like a functional psychopathology, well concealed. Holder of a U.S. passport, not only could he enter and leave the United States without a visa, but he also spoke Spanish flawlessly. He spoke Spanish so well that he didn't even sound Chilean, one of his employees in Peru would have said.

Michael Townley was a man with very low self-esteem. Having married an older woman might spark psychoanalytical speculations about some Oedipus complex, but this would be unfair or, at least, a minor detail. The truth is that all his life he spent trying to gain recognition from his father, the successful businessman, representative of Ford in Chile, which also didn't come when he married

Callejas, and neither his family nor hers approved. At the peak of the good times in Lo Curro, in Santiago, he worked late into the night in the laboratory for Colonel Espinosa and General Contreras, whom Townley called "My colonel" and "My general," something that even Callejas herself found annoying. One night, speaking with his mother-in-law in the United States, he told her that the Chilean government had promised him the rank of Major. He had blind confidence in his superiors. He once described Colonel Espinosa as someone whose subordinates would jump out of a plane without a parachute if he asked, because anyone could trust blindly in the colonel.

—Major Michael Townley—said Michael Townley.

—Don't pay attention to him, Mom—corrected Mariana, taking the phone as if it were Colonel Espinosa himself—. How could you think that someone without a military career would be promoted to a higher rank in the Chilean Army?

NOTHING LIKE A GOOD BOMB

NOW, TOWNLEY HAD THE RESPECTABLE MR. LETELIER, ANOTHER DAMN INTELLECTUAL, WITHIN SHOOTING DISTANCE. HE COULD HAVE KILLED HIM RIGHT THERE WITH A BURST OF BULLETS, AS THE CUBANS HAD SUGGESTED, BUT HE WAS CONVINCED THAT EVEN MORE IMPORTANT THAN ELIMINATING AN UNDESIRABLE WAS THE WAY IT WAS DONE.

—There's a shooting here every day—had said Townley, a few days before—. Every day someone dies for a minor reason in Washington, New York, Chicago… It's reported on the news, and people forget it in minutes. A bomb is something different.

Virgilio Paz knew it. They all knew it and practiced it, but they cared more about their copyrights than the reasons of their allies.

—As you say—said Virgilio Paz, who barely knew Letelier by name. Paz wanted to finish that job as soon as possible to focus on something bigger.

On the way back to the motel, Townley took care of all the technical aspects that, not without modesty, he considered extremely simple, something even a child could do. All that was needed was to combine TNT with C4, a plastic explosive, as easy to handle as gray modeling clay. Neither of them posed a risk of explosion while being handled.

—They're both very stable materials—he said—. Especially the C4. It looks like gray modeling clay for kids. See, you can hammer it without danger.

—We know, but you better stop playing with that.

—You can shoot it, and the plastic is so reliable it won't explode in your face. All it needs is a detonator.

—Close the damn package already, kid—said Alvin Ross.

Ross Díaz didn't know what made him more nervous, the TNT, the C4, or the suspicious Clint Eastwood-like cowboy calm that Townley always boasted about. He, Ross Díaz, also had participated in the failed invasion of Playa Girón and knew that even with an almost zero chance of failure, something could always go wrong, very wrong. His dream was to kill Fidel, the dictator who had taken away his casinos in Havana, but since all attempts had failed, he had to accumulate small successes elsewhere, like small investments that one day would lead to the grand prize. Some earlier failures, even before the Bay of Pigs (like the bazooka with which he himself had almost killed Fidel Castro and ended up taking the life of some fool who was in the car behind) had served as lessons. In all cases, the escape plans never failed.

José Dionisio Suárez had also participated in the Revolution against Batista. He had been a guerrilla for Fidel in the Sierra Maestra and had executed several accused by the revolutionary tribunals that he himself had been part of on some occasions. Ross Díaz hated him without even knowing him and, had they crossed paths somewhere on the outskirts of Havana, he would have shot him once or twice, as they say real men did. In 1961, the CIA recruited all of them, including José Suárez, who missed the first flight to the training camp in Guatemala because he arrived late to the airport. The CIA assigned a number to each of the fifteen hundred recruits, and the group adopted the name of one of them, number 2506, who died during training and was remembered that way. A number.

Now, disillusioned with Fidel, failed with the CIA, they all devoted themselves to selling used cars in Miami and, in their spare time, painted or assembled bombs and planted them wherever necessary. Not a few, like Fernando Acosta, Agustín Barres, Edgardo Buttari, Manuel Artime, Silvia Odio del Torro (daughter of Amador Odio), the boss of Batista's mafia, Santo Trafficante, supplemented their income with drug trafficking.[223]

Had they not also learned this from the CIA? Were the CORU, the DINA, and the DISIP not reflections of the mother of all conspiratorial agencies?

Acronyms for Freedom

I WROTE THIS LAST LINE AND COULDN'T HELP BUT OVERHEAR the conversation of two women and an elderly man at the next table. Like when you discover a word and immediately start hearing it everywhere.

They weren't students. Or they were Ph.D. students or professors. They whispered, as one always does in a library, as if that were less distracting than shouting. More so when I noticed they were talking about *FDR*.

Once I was in the Academic Freedom committee meeting and, at one point, I lost the thread of the discussion.

—Who's FDR?—I asked.

—What?—answered the new professor in the biochemistry department—. FDR! Franklin Delano Roosevelt!

—Oh F-D-R…—I said, relieved— Why the hell do you always have to talk in acronyms? Does it tire you so much to say the full name?

—Do you never say JFK to refer to Kennedy?

—No, never. That's an Anglophone nonsense. I recognize CIA, DINA, FBI, USA because they've already replaced the full names. I don't even have a problem with JFK, because of the damn movie, or with ADHD because it's a trendy psychological label that applies to a fifth of students these days with concentration issues, but it pisses me off when I'm trying to figure out what the hell you're talking about. If you can't speak Spanish, at least you could speak English when you're in a meeting with a Hispanic. Or can't you? Out of kindness, I say. You save ten milliseconds with your acronyms and make people like me lose several minutes. The same goes for those damn books. They save a millimeter of paper and waste the reader's time, forcing them to flip to another part of the book to figure out what the hell HLID is…

—Please, don't start with another one of your *rants*—someone scolded me.

—At least a diatribe isn't an imposition—I doubled down—. I'm saying this in case you want to understand something outside your bubbles. Honestly, I hate this obsession English speakers have with acronyms. *"UF students with SPTX can apply for a RMNI before getting DS in a term of BPT from IT. Also, LGBTQ people who were advised by AI to complete DTXC and not PRA can get either SI or WI credits in BA and BS programs in COAS or DCOB towards their MA or PhD. ABD can apply too. IMRIs are also welcome. Regarding the new policy about the use of N-word and B-word by AI ChatGTP we understand it is just BS, not meaning Bachelor of Science. We disagree with ISA… FDR during the WWII predicted JFK presidency followed by LBJ, something which was suggested by an NSA document declassified by FOIA at GMU* with the collaboration of NYU researchers." Why don't you just say the damn words? Is BS for Bachelor of Science or Bullshit?

—Lol, WTF!

—What the Fuck or Whiskey Tango Foxtrot, in its military use?

WHAT MATTERS IS THE PSYCHOLOGICAL EFFECT

AT THE HOME OF THE FUTURE PRESIDENT OF CHILE, the gathering seemed lively and no more guests were arriving to celebrate Chile's independence. Michael Townley looked at Virgilio Paz. Neither Alvin Ross nor the Novo brothers had wanted to travel to Washington for a minor mission. With Paz and Suárez, it was enough.

Paz's indifferent face seemed to confirm that the moment had come. He was playing with his cigar because he couldn't light it. Townley took the package and got out of the car. He walked several meters and leaned against the Chevy Chevelle, which, at that hour of the night, had lost its sky-blue color. He waited a moment to confirm that no one had seen him and then slid underneath the car to attach the C4. Although it wasn't something common for him, he was very nervous, especially when placing it on the left beam of the chassis. He trusted his tools, but even the smallest accident could blow up in his face. Any mistake and the super stable plastic could stop being stable. He embedded the detonator, moved his hands away from the little devil, and breathed a sigh of relief.

Mariana had written a wonderful story about that moment, Townley remembered. He was Max (he couldn't call him Juan), the main character who specialized in car bombs. If he remembered correctly, the story was called "A Small and Joyful Park" and Max was a sensitive man, capable of feeling compassion for a dead bird. When it was published, some would know that Max was Michael. Michael Townley. Not a failure. Not someone who wrote about history after it had already been made, but someone who made history.

The story was still unpublished, but it was certain it would win another award in Chile or Argentina and then would be turned into a Hollywood movie, superior to Mission Impossible or that cheap SWAT series that, for some reason, is so popular in Miami and even beyond, in the South.

—*We have two kilos of C4* for this job—says Max or says Mariana in the story—. You see, it's important. Two kilos for the gentleman. It can't fail. But the precise work has to be done by you, otherwise the danger is tremendous, you know. But what about the machine guns, says Max—the Max in the story— if the man lives as peacefully as you say, they can get him when he leaves his house, like usual. No, Max, they say, what we're looking for is the psychological effect. A shooting is just a shooting, people are already used to it. It has to be something big, so others like him, the enemies, will learn.

When Townley came out from underneath the Chevelle, Virgilio breathed a sigh of relief.

—I thought you'd never come back—Virgilio complained.

—Good work always takes a little longer.

A Savior's Call From an Enemy

President Joaquín Balaguer was not comfortable with Orlando Bosch conspiring nearby, so he asked him to leave the country. When the Dominican agents went to his apartment in Santo Domingo to arrest him, they found Bosch soaked in patriotic Bacardí, completely out of his mind. Since his repeated failures, he had increased the amount and frequency of his rum infusions. Still under the influence of Bacardí, Bosch insulted General Neit Nivar Seijas, a strongman since the days of Trujillo.

As a solution, it was agreed to expel Bosch and his family to Nicaragua. The destination seemed like common sense, but it didn't work either. Although Somoza was another traditional ally of Washington, he also didn't want him in his national territory.

On September 7, Orlando Bosch managed to detonate a bomb at the Mexican embassy in Guatemala City. Despite the success of the operation, the last of the Somoza presidents, Somoza Debayle, felt uncomfortable. He was in trouble with the Sandinistas and the Democrats in Washington and didn't want Bosch there. He informed him that he had 72 hours to leave the country.

Bosch, his infant daughter, and his Chilean wife decided to return to the distant cold of Pinochet. Cold for its unbearable winters and even colder for its endless curfews that had ended the nightlife of that country. Almost at the same time, he received a call from Ricardo Morales Navarrete, his greatest enemyafter Fidel Castro. From the personal phone in his office at Disip (number 6616804, and by special request of Orlando García), El Mono invited him to return to Venezuela, this time at the request of President Carlos Andrés Pérez.

—When I heard his voice—said El Mono Morales— it was like hearing the voice of a ghost from the past.

Bosch also distrusted him. El Mono had sold him out to the FBI and had cooked him in court after the attack on the Polish ship in Miami, in 1968. When Bosch got out of the Florida prison, he hunted him by land and sea until he managed to place an explosive in his car. The explosion shattered the car, but El Mono emerged unharmed. The dynamite had not been placed in the right spot, which was a shame for the paramilitary leader of Miami, after so many years of experience.

After that attack, which El Mono tried to downplay in the press, through the CIA and Luis Posada Carriles (head of Venezuela's secret police and, in turn, also a CIA agent), El Mono Morales managed to flee to Caracas. Shortly after taking an Israeli Counterintelligence course, according to La Gazeta on Friday, June 25, he was naturalized as a Venezuelan citizen in record time worthy of the Guinness Book of Records. Months earlier, he had been named an agent of the Foreign Counterintelligence Division of Disip. In record time, he was promoted to Chief Commissioner of Division 54, directly by order of the Minister of the Interior Octavio Lepage Barreto.On September 6, an internal Disip document recorded that El Mono had been appointed commissioner by order of Rafael Rivas Vásquez. That same day, the new president Carlos Andrés Pérez designated him as Head of Division 54, that is, the division in charge of counterintelligence. Years later, Bosch's defense lawyer, Raymond Aguiar, would say on Venezuelan television:

—That man's meteoric rise is unparalleled in Venezuela.

In early September of '76, El Mono contacted Cuban Frank Castro, who was then in Managua, and asked him to intervene with the Batista government to expedite visas for Orlando Bosch and his family. The visa was granted without delay and without the proper process, as it should be.

On September 17, El Mono called him again, this time while passing through the Dominican Republic. Bosch grew suspicious once more. Beyond the mutual hatred they harbored, Bosch had already been in Venezuela in 1974 and had been arrested by the very same Disip and then deported for a bombing at the Panamanian embassy. This was despite the fact that Posada Carriles was already a prominent and feared chief of the secret police under Rafael Caldera's government. These were the times when the secret police was combating leftist subversive activities. Naturally, under the direction of Posada Carriles himself, the repression extended to other activists who had never taken up arms, let alone detonated a bomb.

In 1974, the false passport granted to Bosch by the Venezuelan government came with the promise that he would not engage in attacks on Venezuelan soil, to avoid violating his conditional freedom granted by the United States, which was merely a formality. Deported once again, Orlando Bosch came into contact with Dionisio Suárez and Guillermo Novo, both tasked with targeting Allende's minister, Orlando Letelier.

Now, the idea was similar, but El Mono's invitation was far less subtle. At stake was the prestige and future of the recently founded CORU, and both El Mono and Bosch knew what would dominate global headlines in the coming weeks.

THE STRATEGIC AMBIGUITY OF CARLOS ANDRÉS PÉREZ

ACCORDING TO EL MONO MORALES, THE NEW PRESIDENT OF VENEZUELA knew about the assassination plans for Allende's minister since June 1976, just as he knew that the perpetrators of the Washington bombing were the feared brothers Guillermo and Ignacio Novo Sampol.

—Letelier had been sentenced to death in May—confessed El Mono on Miami television.

Posada Carriles had resigned from the DISIP in 1974, just as the new president took office. Carlos Andrés Pérez was seen as a communist sympathizer, despite only being a member of the Socialist International. In any case, his first term was very different from the one he would face in 1989.

During the sixties, Venezuela was one of the few Latin American countries not under a military dictatorship promoted by Washington and major international corporations. Like Uruguay and Colombia, Venezuela was a liberal democracy. Like these countries, the CIA had also infiltrated the press and the Venezuelan police under the doctrine of National Security and the fight against subversion, both of which emerged before leftist guerrilla movements were founded or gained strength in those countries.

Venezuela was different in one aspect. By 1974, it was one of the few countries in the world that had not felt the global recession caused by the oil crisis. Quite the opposite, and for the same reason. By the time Andrés Pérez assumed office as the first candidate sold by an advertising agency, like any product, the price of oil had already tripled since 1970, and during his administration, it went from ten dollars a barrel to over 25.

As Minister of Interior Affairs under Rómulo Betancourt, he had earned a reputation as a hardliner against armed leftist groups, but his economic policies were no different from those of any other progressive candidate. He completed the nationalization and state control of oil, extended various labor rights, supported workers' unions, created food subsidies for the most needy, and put oil revenues to work in agricultural projects, massive aqueducts and highways, and generous scholarships for studying abroad. As in the dream of right-wing liberals, in Venezuela the state did not collect taxes. There was no VAT. The government distributed and invested the wealth derived from oil, as in some Gulf Arab states. Private companies also benefited from this boom, which later led to an increase in debt due to excessive and unfinished public works. When Andrés Pérez is elected for the second time in 1989, like Carlos Saúl Menem in Argentina, he will take up the privatizing banner of the Washington Consensus and the IMF as an economic solution to the social problems created by those very creditors in the previous decades. The privatization of lands, mines, oil wells, and public assets of neocolonies was the most effective and widespread way to continue being owners of foreign resources that once belonged to the empire of the time.

Unlike Carlos Menem, the new Andrés Pérez would not have a day of glory, despite the aid and soft credits from Washington to appease the social explosion of 1989. His first presidency had been full of euphoria. The economy was overflowing. In January 1976, he had been appointed vice president of the Socialist International, whose president was the chancellor of West Germany, Willy Brandt. Just this new title had made the blood of Luis Posada Carriles and his comrades boil. Even more so when the political agility of Andrés Pérez, like a José Figueres of South America, allowed him to dance with world leaders of all ideological stripes, including Panama's Omar Torrijos and Cuba's Fidel Castro.

As is textbook for the FBI and the CIA, Luis Posada Carriles, the merciless CIA agent and head of Venezuela's secret police for years, knew that all enemies have some personal weakness. When homosexuality was a civil death sentence, these agencies began looking for any hint in this direction, which is why, later, the vindication of gay pride had strong political implications, as it nullified, at its root, one of the most effective instruments of extortion. Obviously, the greatest possibilities always lay in weaknesses related to women. The discovery and blackmail of Martin Luther King's affairs aimed to make the depressive leader attempt suicide again.

"Your end is near—said a letter accompanying the recording he received with his voice and that of a woman in a hotel— neither your titles nor the Nobel Prize will save you; you're finished. The Protestants, the Catholics, and the Jews will know you for what you are—a dangerous beast. The same goes for all those who have supported you... Only one way out remains for you, and you know very well what it is."[224]

The report from the United States Senate intelligence committee, published in April 1976, revealed that these were not just practices of the CIA, when the territorial jurisdiction belonged to another government agency:

"The FBI pressured universities to deny Dr. King honorary degrees and to prevent the publication of articles favorable to his figure while simultaneously promoting unfavorable ones. The FBI threatened to hand over recordings allegedly made with surveillance microphones in Dr. King's hotel rooms to journalists. They also mailed him one of these recordings. According to the Chief of the FBI's National Intelligence Division, the tape was intended to provoke a divorce from his wife to attack his moral standing. The recording was accompanied by a note that Dr. King and his advisors interpreted as a threat: the recording would be made public unless Dr. King committed suicide. The FBI also made preparations to promote someone 'to assume the leadership role of the Black people once King had been completely discredited."[225]

For FBI director J. Edgar Hoover, King's speech on equality and racial integration was proof enough of his danger, which justified any action to maintain *"the existing social and political order"* and thereby save Western Christian civilization.

In the case of Andrés Pérez it wasn't so easy. He had married his cousin Blanquita, but that was known and accepted. Years later, he had had an affair with his secretary, but by 1976 it wasn't a consummated relationship. It seemed clearer that he had a somewhat inflated ego. As soon as he became the president of a country that didn't know what to do with so much money, he began traveling abroad like no other president had done before. His meetings and interventions in the most diverse countries started to bestow upon him the image of a global leader. He had the means. In international meetings, they had to ask him politely to let other leaders speak. Andrés Pérez knew everything and had a solution for everything. Once he began by saying, "I'll be brief," and then spoke for four hours.

Everyone knew that only one name in Latin America overshadowed the dazzling star of the Venezuelan president: Fidel Castro.

"Venezuelan politics is a permanent discussion between caudillos and friends," said former president Rómulo Betancourt.

Years earlier, Andrés Pérez and Posada Carriles had confronted the Venezuelan guerrilla, which was assumed to receive some form of economic and moral support from Cuba. Posada Carriles, as supervisor of Venezuela's secret police and as tradition dictated, had extended this struggle to the rest of humanity based on his personal impulses and convictions, often ordering and directing the torture of civilian suspects or sources of information.

Andrés Pérez was different: he was a born politician and didn't refuse to shake hands with or invite the most diverse leaders in the world, including Fidel Castro. With his victory in the 1973 elections, Andrés Pérez, the DISIP, and Posada Carriles lost their ideological coherence and personal sympathy. Posada Carriles resigned from his position, but, as expected, the structure, tradition, and personal protection of the DISIP continued unchanged. Only this time, the president became a dangerous enemy, much like John F. Kennedy had been for the CIA.

Now, if it was already difficult to fight Fidel Castro, it would be much more difficult to fight him with a new front open, with Andrés Pérez as president of the country and head of the secret police, which Posada Carriles no longer wanted to be part of but still depended on in many ways.

It is very likely that both Posada Carriles and the DISIP focused on exploiting the personality clash between Andrés Pérez and Fidel Castro. To achieve this, there were two options: first, to create or amplify the conflict of influence between the two leaders in the region; second, to attribute to Andrés Pérez an action against Castro's Cuba.

For some reason, President Carlos Andrés Pérez still wanted Posada Carriles there, working with a team of known Cuban agents from the CIA and other secret police forces on the continent. Years later, Bosch's lawyer, Raymond Aguiar, would vehemently claim that Carlos Andrés Pérez wanted to eliminate the influence of the Havana government in the small republics of the Antilles. When things went wrong, he simply washed his hands of it and denied everything, even the fact that El Mono had been part of the DISIP or any office of the Venezuelan state.

It wasn't easy to corrupt Andrés Pérez with money, because money wasn't what attracted him the most. Nor did he lack it. He was determined to go down in history as a different kind of revolutionary, a democratic revolutionary, loved by God and the Devil. He loved being surrounded by the people when they chanted his name, and he always bid them farewell with his favorite phrase, "let's get to work," a gentler phrase than the more famous "go to work, lazy bums" of Latin American oligarchies. He probably loved even more to surround himself with great world leaders and influential national figures. Perhaps without realizing it, this led him to make more wealthy friends than poor ones, considering that the poor are always more abundant and in a liberal democracy, they are the ones who vote the most.

The president's weakness was clear. Just as this had led him to glory, it was also destined to lead him to hell. A process that, inadvertently, had already begun that same year.

Bosch in Caracas

FINALLY, ORLANDO BOSCH CONTACTED LUIS POSADA CARRILES to ensure that El Mono's proposal was reliable and, above all, to guarantee that he would be safe in Venezuela. Rather, it was a desperate act of faith in search of confirmation. Posada Carriles gave his word. He assured him that he would be safe there. Moreover, he offered him a place within the DISIP.

According to the CIA, Orlando Bosch entered Venezuela with a false passport under the name of Pedro Antoni Peña on September 13. Other sources indicate that the arrival was after September 17. In any case, it was not an illegal entry, as the government of Andrés Pérez would later claim, but rather an agreed and facilitated entry by the DISIP and the Venezuelan government itself. According to the CIA, "Bosch was received at the airport by García and Luis Clemente Posada,"[226] that is, by Luis Posada Carriles and Orlando García Vásquez, the chief of El Mono Morales.

By then, Bosch already had in mind the attack on a Cubana airplane.

"I have fought in many places," said Bosch, though others would question his definition of *combat*. "Our struggle is not one of words. It is one of blood. We have brought mourning to the families of our enemies, and we will continue to do so."

Once he arrived in Caracas, Orlando Bosch was accommodated at the luxurious Caracas Hilton Hotel, paid for by the DISIP and under the name of Carlos Paniagua. The adjoining room was occupied by another of Bosch's historical enemies, Orlando García Vásquez, now the chief of police for President Carlos Andrés Pérez. As if Bosch's discomfort wasn't enough, El Mono had also checked into the same hotel.

Shortly after, the DISIP assigned him an office, and Posada Carriles ordered a security lock to be installed, not on the outside but on the inside. No one would ever know what was concocted behind that door. Except for a few details. For example, all the secret services of the time knew that Orlando Bosch maintained contact with Dionisio Suarez and the brothers Ignacio and Guillermo Novo, who, at that moment, were in a motel in the United States, less than an hour from the Capitol and the White House.

Posada Carriles was the one who ordered El Mono to go to the international airport in Caracas to pick up Orlando Bosch. When El Mono managed to spot Orlando Bosch's profile in the crowd, he recognized his worst enemy. Years later, he would recall:

—I saw a man defeated, physically and in every way.

He took him out to eat at the restaurant La Estancia. From there, they went to the Hilton Anauco Hotel, assigned by the DISIP.

—I had to sleep next to my worst enemy, all because Orlando García Vásquez ordered it—said El Mono.

Aside from El Mono, Bosch, and García Vásquez, on the eighth floor of the Anauco Hilton Hotel, Gustavo Castillo was also staying, wanted by Mexico for the attack in Mérida that left one dead a few months earlier. At the time, he was patiently and meticulously preparing the bomb that would bring down Cubana Flight 455.

Letelier. First Attempt

On September 20, Letelier's light blue Chevrolet did not fly through the air as planned. Suárez, Novo, and Paz had no words to insult the gringo Townley, who was then on an Iberia flight to Spain. The expert had failed to detonate neither the C4 nor the TNT. Was it a premeditated mistake?

—He's a screw-up.

After a brief discussion, they decided to finish the job on their own. It was better than losing the entire investment over a stupid detail. They just had to make sure the medical beeper was working, something Townley had supposedly taught them. That night, they returned to the house in Bethesda.

Ronni and Michael were having dinner with Orlando and Isabel. The enthusiasm of the young couple had infected them. The dreams of youth are the true dreams. Everything else is just lessons and awakenings.

The kids were looking for something to watch on the many color channels that had them captivated. A voice announced the first episode of the new season of *Rich Man, Poor Man*. After the murder of the poor brother, Tom Jordache, the wealthy brother Peter Haskell, owner of Tricorp, must confront the killer Falconetti, who has been released. He had to be Italian or of Italian descent. "Tomorrow, September 21 at 9:00, on ABC."

Ronni Karpen was 25 years old, and her brief biography was summarized as her years at the University of Maryland and her activism against the Vietnam War, like Mariana Callejas in Miami. She had graduated in Education and immediately dedicated herself to creating Centers of Learning for students in need. At IPS, she met Michael.

When the kids had already gone to bed, Orlando stayed up talking with Michael about something that was beginning to worry him. He reminded him of the assassination of General Carlos Prats and his wife Sofía in Buenos Aires. In ten days, it would be two years since the attack. There were other cases, like Bernardo Leighton and his wife in Rome... All the attacks also targeted the wives of their victims, but this had to be just a coincidence of the indifferent cruelty of the freedom fighters.

Although the idea of some kind of aggression by the government of a Latin American country in the U.S. capital seemed unlikely, there was the case of the Columbia University professor, Jesús Galíndez, kidnapped by the regime of Leónidas Trujillo twenty years ago, later tortured and murdered in the Dominican Republic. Orlando had witnessed the executions in Chile and knew the fascist regime was capable of anything. In fact, little by little Letelier had become the leader of the Chilean resistance to the Pinochet regime. Only a fool wouldn't realize that he was number one on Pinochet's blacklist.

—The DINA has already killed other exiles—said Orlando—. It wouldn't be strange if they tried to do it again. It's very likely that they are spying on me all the time.

Letelier stood up and walked to the window. Outside, it was as dark as death, so he could only see the reflection of his face and, beyond that, his own thoughts. Then he returned to where Michael Moffitt was.

Two hours later, on their way back, Michael and Ronni found their car broken down. There was no way to start it.

—Take mine—said Orlando.

—Oh, no...

—No problem—insisted Orlando—. Just be sure to come back early tomorrow for the offices.

With no other option, the young couple returned home with the TNT and C4 strapped to the chassis of Letelier's Chevrolet.

—*Shit!*—said Suárez.

—Shit!—confirmed Virgilio Paz.

—We'll have to get up early tomorrow.

—What a charming couple—said Isabel, carrying two glasses to the kitchen.

A few hours later, Townley flew to Miami. He wanted to be as far away as possible at the time of the explosion. Later, he traveled to Madrid.

FINAL INTERVIEW

DINNER WITH HIS ASSISTANTS AND THE CONVERSATION about personal safety had stirred up several memories. The magazine *Playboy* had conducted an interview with him that had not yet been published, about that September 11th morning, three years prior. He would never know why an erotic magazine would publish his torture in the coldest prison of fascism, nor why it would interest their readers, as if there were a sinister connection between fear and desire, between the pain of others and one's own pleasure.

The children had already gone to bed. The television continued selling promises of happiness, all at a fair price and within reach of the true man and the true woman. Always more for less.

He remembered the morning of the coup again. He recalled telling the journalist that he had rushed to the Ministry of Defense early that day.

—Immediately, I felt a gun in my back. I was surrounded by a dozen soldiers.

From there, they took him to a room where he had to witness the execution of dozens of detainees in the central courtyard throughout the night. At five in the morning, he heard the soldiers outside saying:

—It's the minister's turn.

As they were taking him to the courtyard to be executed, there was a discussion among the soldiers. Someone had received another order. Finally, the one holding him said:

—You're lucky, you son of a bitch.

They transferred him to a cold cell on Dawson Island, near Antarctica. The new government didn't know what to do with him. Executing him or letting him live were two options with multiple benefits and side effects impossible to calculate.

A year later, as a result of international pressure, they sent him to Venezuela. There, the Institute for Policy Studies offered him the job of researcher. He was in the safest city in the world, at least politically speaking, but the institute had a clear history of resistance against the Vietnam War and the foreign policies of Washington. The press and television never rested in alerting the population to the danger of the IPS to democracy and freedom. Especially when, from the skies of the White House, millions of dollars rained down on journalists to reverse the growing resistance of the people against the Vietnam War.

—The IPS is a nest of radicals—some guy named Harvey had said.

—Yes, very radical—someone from another desk had responded—. They're against the Vietnam War and against the dictatorships we planted all over the world.

Orlando turned off the TV and went to sleep. In reality, for some time now, he only pretended to sleep.

THIS TIME IT CAN'T FAIL

THE NEXT MORNING, MICHAEL AND RONNI returned to Orlando's house to go to the IPS offices. At eight, Orlando, late and without having slept well, dressed hurriedly while telling Isabel to join them for lunch.

—I don't think I can, I have too much work—Isabel replied.

—You'll like the surprise—he insisted.

He called his assistant Juan Gabriel Valdés to tell him he would pick him up on the way to the office. Juan Gabriel told him he couldn't at that time, that his wife was going shopping and he would stay home to take care of the kids, that he would see him a bit later.

The three of them left the house in a hurry. Orlando lit a cigarette and adjusted his shirt collar.

—Do you want me to drive?—Michael said.

—No problem—murmured Orlando, the cigarette between his lips.

Michael went ahead and opened the passenger door for Ronni and sat in the back.

In fifteen minutes, the blue Chevrolet Chevelle Malibu had left Bethesda and entered Massachusetts Avenue.

Behind them was the gray Ford. José Suárez was discussing details of the bomb that last Thursday the 16th he had successfully detonated with Omega 7, on the Soviet ship Ivan Shepetkov, in the port of New Jersey.[227] Like Fidel, the damn thing didn't sink. It was left with a huge hole in its side, but it didn't sink.

—Shortly after noon, we called to claim responsibility for the attack. We weren't going to do all that work without getting credit. What the hell does it matter if the damn thing sank or not.

—No one died this time.

Because of that, the news didn't go around the world and donations didn't skyrocket like other times.

At 9:30, the blue Malibu passed by Letelier's former residence. Ambassador Manuel Trucco was just getting out of bed at that moment.

IN THE MIDST OF THE FIRE, YOU WILL BE WITH ME

SHORTLY AFTER NINE IN THE MORNING, Jorge Luis Borges was walking down Diego Portales Avenue in Santiago. In a few hours, he would attend a ceremony in his honor, with General Pinochet and the writer Mariana Callejas sitting in the third row.

—Yes, Neruda was a bad poet. He didn't understand the sonnet or the mysteries of meter. There were too many syllables, just like *One Hundred Years of Solitude* was at least fifty years too long...

Borges agreed with the CIA's literary criticism, not with the Swedish Academy's judgment. Even less with the opinion of the workers who bought his books at newsstands.

—Your books are also sold at newsstands—Antonio Carrizo informed him.

—At newsstands?—asked Borges, surprised—. My books at newsstands?

In Washington, the Chevy Chevalle took Massachusetts Avenue before entering D.C. At 9:33, it passed by its former residence, now occupied by the family of Pinochet's ambassador, and, seconds later, entered the Sheridan Circle, three minutes away from the IPS offices on Q Street 1901.

At that moment, a few blocks away, a meeting of LASA, the Latin American Studies Association, was taking place to prepare for the conference that would be held in Atlanta that year. Letelier had sent Juan Raúl Ferreira to report on the Uruguayan dictatorship.

At 9:34, in the Ford trailing the blue Chevy, Virgilio Paz pressed the two small buttons on the remote control. It was one of the devices that Townley had adapted and tested himself during the trip to Mexico, one of those used by doctors for emergency calls. The beep activated the C4 placed on the Chevy's chassis, right under the driver's seat.

Michael heard an electric sound and a flash behind Ronni's head. After a fraction of a second, the Chevy flew through the air, and its pieces scattered up to twenty-five meters. When it fell, it crashed into an orange Volkswagen that was parked. Ronni was thrown from the car and landed on the grass. Barefoot and unable to feel his legs, suffocated by the smoke, Michael managed to crawl out through a window and saw Ronni standing, as if nothing had happened to her.

The only one seriously injured seemed to be Orlando. He was leaning back against the driver's wheel. Michael patted his face:

—Orlando—he said—. Can you hear me?

Orlando didn't answer. He tried to put a hand on Michael but couldn't. His eyes moved slowly, and tears streamed down his cheeks. He was about to say something but faded in seconds.

—It was DINA!—shouted Michael—. Damn fascists.

Letelier died within minutes.

Ronni wasn't okay. The explosion had cut her throat, but Michael hadn't noticed because she was walking away. Until she fell to the ground.

Dana Peterson, a doctor who ran to help her, couldn't stop Ronni from choking on her own blood as she tried to push Michael away. Minutes later, the ambulance arrived. After a brief argument, Michael managed to get in to accompany her to the hospital.

At the LASA meeting, Juan Raúl Ferreira was still answering questions about the Southern Cone dictatorships. Around noon, the meeting was interrupted by a muffled commotion. Juan Raúl couldn't understand the fragmented information being exchanged in English. He grabbed a young woman by the arm and asked what was happening.

—They killed Letelier!—she said.

Juan Raúl ran to IPS.

—They also killed Ronni—said someone who had just entered the old building on Q Street.

Then, Juan Raúl looked at the desk across from his. It was Ronni's desk.[228]

A light drizzle had begun to fall. At the hospital, Michael Moffitt struggled to fend off the police harassment. He remembered the verses by Pablo Neruda that he had read to her on their wedding day. She, still in white, smiled radiantly, with a joy that couldn't be contained in her small body:

Rise with me
and let us march together
to fight hand to hand
against the webs of the wicked…
Amid the fire you will be
by my side…

—Why do you say Neruda isn't a great poet?—the journalist asked him.

—Do you remember any verse by Neruda?—Borges shot back, smiling at a television camera that pointed at him from eternity.

—Well—stammered Carrizo— I think with Neruda one can quote something...

—Let's hear it, which one?

—No, don't test me...

—I don't remember any memorable one—said Borges, fading slowly, with a faint smile.

—Borges, are you afraid of death?

—No, not at all. I just want to be forgotten.

THE MYSTERIOUS LABYRINTH OF INFAMY

THE BOMB WAS SET TO EXPLODE on Monday. Townley bought the newspapers, listened to the radios, and found no information confirming it. When it finally detonated on the morning of Tuesday the 21st, he was already in Miami. From there, he went to have dinner with his parents in Boca Raton.

In Union City two men conversed in front of two almost empty glasses of rum with two thick cigars between their fingers.

—Listen, boy. Something's still lingering in my mind...

Along Bergenline Avenue walked the last miniskirts of the year, while the sky couldn't decide whether to send rain, drizzle, or the first snowfall of the year.

—Well, tell me.

—What if the American rigged the detonator to fail on purpose, knowing we'd fix it?

—We'll never know...

—He seemed a bit reluctant to join the operation. Now, after all, it turns out it was us who planted the C4 and then detonated it. Isn't that what the Chileans wanted?

—We wanted the credit too, didn't we?

—Of course, boy! But betrayal is another thing. I can't stand the thought of them possibly using us.

At the same time, Jorge Luis Borges walked down Diego Portales Avenue in Santiago for the second time. He was about to receive an honorary doctorate from the Faculty of Philosophy and Letters at the Catholic University, the same one that had bestowed upon Chile and the Universe the proud Anglo-Saxon infamy of the Chicago Boys. Borges was an atheist, but he wasn't impressed by the mysterious designs of the hand that shapes and foreshadows the avatars of the chess pieces that, at the same time, entertained the musings of the Moor and the Jew in the labyrinth of a civilization already forgotten by the fictions of history.

María Callejas knew in advance of this historic visit and leveraged all her contacts to be included in the dinner with the Argentine writer. At one of the weekly gatherings in Lo Curro, a guest had said:

—They say Borges is politically illiterate.

—Very wise.

—He didn't care much.

—It's that a metaphor or a paradox are universal. The winner of an election is like the soccer champion lifting a trophy. Both are products of chance, a conjunction of the arbitrariness of fate that will erase the sands of the Persian clock on the ships of the inspired Anglo-Saxon over the undulating surfaces of the warm and never quite real southern seas.

—Whatever. In the 1973 elections, Borges told his mother he wouldn't vote. Surely he assumed a Peronist victory. Leonor, his mother, then 96 and bedridden, got angry. Leonor Borges hated Perón, almost as much as Evita. "If you want, I'll go and vote for you," Georgie told her. Borges himself admitted that Leonor had given him the envelope with the vote that Borges placed in the ballot box.

He never saw the ballot his mother put in the envelope. Out of political decency, though it was too obvious, he said he hadn't wanted to know what that envelope contained.

—So, he never wanted to know what he was voting for…

—That's what democracies are about, right?—someone said, adding another unanimous laugh.

—Is it true that he's still hurt for losing the Nobel Prize to Pablo Neruda?

—He doesn't care. Stockholm is full of communists.

—He's absolutely right when he says that even Neruda probably couldn't remember his own poems, because no one can remember them. I mean, they're not memorable. If someone read them and skipped a verse, Neruda wouldn't even notice.

—He also said that Neruda was a disciple of Lorca, but much worse than Lorca.

THE PATRIOTIC BUSINESSMAN

Days after the explosion at Sheridan Circle, businessman Edwin Wilson contacted three Cubans from Miami, who had traveled to Washington three days earlier, to negotiate the sale of explosives and timed pencils to the Libyan government, for a value of one hundred thousand dollars. Initially, the agreement with Muammar Gaddafi involved the purchase of explosive detection equipment, to clear paths of landmines, but some sources had reported the possibility that the deal could be extended to the export of C4 to eliminate dissidents. Wilson (like one of the contacted Cubans, had been a CIA agent until weeks before) owned an arms and explosives business, Consultants International, located at 1425 K Street, ten minutes from Sheridan Circle.

Bob Woodward, the journalist elevated to celebrity status by the Watergate scandal, reported that, aside from technology to detect explosives, "the promotional literature of Consultants International itself makes it clear that it can equip an army with patrol boats, parachutes, airborne accessories, and armored vehicles." The same company asserted in its brochures: "We can design weapon packages to meet each client's needs."

For some reason, the agreement scheduled between Wilson and the Cubans during a meeting in Genoa did not move forward.

—We know that the Libyan government has, in many ways, done things that could have stimulated terrorism—said President Ford, during a press conference.[229]

The attempt to link the Libyan government to the assassination of Letelier also did not prosper. Its greatest weakness was its lack of common sense.

Wilson will be arrested in New York, upon arriving from the Dominican Republic, six years and fourteen million dollars later, accused of illegal trafficking of explosives. The press will say that, over two decades of clandestine life in service to the CIA and the Marines, Wilson had "traded patriotism for business." From 1955 to 1976, he had been a CIA agent, participated in the failed invasion of the Bay of Pigs, in multiple attacks against Cuba, and in the creation of several fake companies with the purpose of continuing privately what had been a government plan.[230]

Private individuals don't do better, but their ideology isn't visible. Only their profits.

THE EMBASSY OF CHILE INFORMS THE PUBLIC

ON SEPTEMBER 21, 1976, THE AMBASSADOR of Chile in Washington, Manuel Trucco Gaete, issued a statement:

"My government categorically repudiates the outrageous act of terrorism that has claimed the lives of a former Ambassador of Chile to the United States and one of his collaborators.

The deplorable act only emphasizes the need to combat terrorism in all its aspects because it demonstrates the extent to which hostile elements will go to achieve their unspeakable objectives."

On behalf of my government, I urgently request that a complete and rigorous investigation be initiated so that all facets and circumstances relevant to this brutal act are investigated and the culprits prosecuted.

Terrorism and violence must be stopped before there are more innocent victims.

When asked for more details, the ambassador added:
—Letelier posed no danger to me. The man lived on an island of Marxists, with no significance in the United States.

September, Love

IN WASHINGTON, LETELIER'S ADVISOR, Juan Gabriel Valdés, had invited the Uruguayan Juan Raúl Ferreira to collaborate with the Latin American research institute IPS.

—September 11 was the anniversary of the Coup—said Juan Raúl—. The 18th, the national Fiesta *dieciochera*.

Pinochet always commemorated it with some memorable event. In September 1974, his predecessor, General Prats, exiled in Argentina, was killed. On October 5, 1975, Townley and his associates from Miami shot Bernardo Leighton and his wife in Rome, leaving them paralyzed. 1976 could not be the exception.

Ariel Dorfman learned about the attack on Letelier that same afternoon. He was in the offices of the Transnational Institute in Amsterdam, the institute founded by Orlando Letelier himself. His colleagues were murmuring in different languages or holding incredulous silences.

Ariel recalled the last time he had seen him. It had been exactly three years earlier, at a meeting at the Peña de los Parra, in Santiago, where Violeta Parra and Víctor Jara used to sing.

—The gathering—Ariel told me— had been organized by Fernando Flores in memory of General Prats. We worked together at La Moneda. Orlando, José Tohá, and their wives were also there. All the men present had been Allende's defense ministers. They knew Pinochet closely, could testify to his betrayal of Allende and his emotional and mental pettiness. Pinochet killed all three.

At one point, a tango started playing, and some guests went out to dance. Ariel remained in his chair. He knew he was terrible at dancing tango. His wife Angélica, on the other hand, was marvelous, but she almost always stood in solidarity with Ariel's clumsiness and shyness and stayed in her role as a spectator.

—Nor was I going to interrupt those three couples who had stolen the moment—recalled Ariel.

Orlando Letelier danced with Sofía, the wife of General Carlos Prats, Isabel with José Tohá, and Prats with Moy, Tohá's wife. The joy of that night was like the calm before a hurricane.

—At that moment—recalled Ariel— I couldn't realize that the three men dancing were united by the same fatal destiny: all three had been Allende's defense ministers. All three had been close figures to the military. All three were betrayed. All three knew too much. All three were killed by Pinochet.

A More Ambitious Gamble

As President Andrés Pérez denied any connection to the assassination of the former Chilean minister, the governor of Caracas, Diego Arria, interceded once again for Orlando Letelier, this time

El exilio del terror

to have his body sent to Venezuela. Isabel agreed to send what remained of her husband to Caracas. On September 29, Letelier was buried on the side of a hill overlooking the city. Andrés Pérez embraced the widow and gave a speech that no one remembers now.

A week earlier, on Thursday the 23rd, Orlando Bosch had arrived in Caracas with another fake passport, but in Immigration, everyone knew who the Cuban was. A few days later, a discreet charity event was held at a house in La Castellana or, more likely, at La Lagunita Country Club, a neighborhood similar to Lo Curro in Santiago, established by General Marcos Pérez Jiménez for the military and which quickly became an exclusive area. The cocktail party had been announced to raise funds for the refugee fighter whose name was not mentioned in the invitations but everyone knew or wanted to know.

In a report dated October 18 to Secretary of State Henry Kissinger, the CIA claimed that Bosch had offered Venezuelan officials to renounce acts of violence in the United States during the visit of President Carlos Andrés Pérez to the UN in November, in exchange for "a substantial cash contribution to Bosch's organization." The same report stated that Bosch declared:

—Now that our organization has done very well with the work carried out in Washington against Letelier, we are going to try something more.

According to classified CIA documents, the meeting took place at the residence of the Cuban surgeon Hildo Folgar between September 22 and October 5 (the most likely date being Saturday, September 25). The price per plate amounted to 5,000 bolívares per attendee ($1,118 at the time; $6,000 fifty years later). Other sources reported nearly a hundred attendees.

The funds raised that night clearly exceeded the two thousand dollars it cost to pay a mercenary from Honduras or El Salvador to Cuba or the United States, with all expenses included. According to the same classified CIA document dated October 14, "at the dinner, Bosch approached an official from the Ministry of Internal Relations along with García and proposed that the Venezuelan government *make a significant financial contribution to his cause; in exchange, Bosch pledged that Cubans in the United States would not stage any protests against the visit of Carlos Andrés Pérez* to the United Nations, scheduled for November, which the Venezuelan official accepted."

—Now that our organization has successfully concluded Operation Letelier—said Bosch at the meeting, and his words were recorded by the CIA informant— we are going to try something more.231

Orlando Bosch and El Mono Ricardo Morales lived for a time at the Caracas Hilton Hotel, near Los Caobos Park. Like Hernán Ricardo Lozano, Morales had begun working for the Venezuelan secret police thanks to the efforts of his CIA bosses. All were experts in explosives, but none had ever detonated one in their lives. As Posada Carriles said, the CIA taught everything, from patriotism to how to assemble and detonate a bomb, but that did not make them terrorists, just as soldiers who took courses on how to kill people were not terrorists. The knowledge was there just in case, but they never used it. The only one who would confess to being behind some bombings was El Mono Morales. Bosch and Posada Carriles also confessed at different times, but later denied it, especially in the few trials they had to face.

—We're going to hit a Cubana flight—said Posada Carriles, according to the CIA informant in Caracas—and Orlando has the details.

No declassified document would reveal that the CIA made any attempt to prevent the terrorist attack by their operatives.

Freddy Lugo and Hernán Ricardo Lozano, the two Venezuelans hired by Posada Carriles for his new private detective business, were the only ones who witnessed the incident. Was that spectacle really necessary, as if it were fireworks or a baseball game? For the same reason, they had been arrested during the first attempt to blow up another Cubana plane two months earlier. But this time the plan was a success. Lugo and Ricardo took the next flight back to Trinidad. There, the police arrested them.

They confessed. In Venezuela, the police arrested Bosch and Luis Posada Carriles, head of the explosives division of the DISIP. Both denied all accusations. Like in the bad translations of their favorite TV shows:

—I don't know what you're talking about—they said.

They knew nothing about anything. Although they didn't condone the acts published in the press, they also weren't capable of perpetrating such an abominable act. Bosch, Posada Carriles, El Mono Navarrete, and almost all the other collaborators agreed on one thing: Cubana 455 was a combat plane, and the 73 victims of Cubana were not victims. They were combatants, like all those who didn't think and feel like them.

IT WAS THE DINA

IN MINUTES, THE STREET WAS FILLED WITH AMBULANCES and police cars. Shortly after, Agent Carter Cornick arrived. When he saw Michael burned and screaming like mad "it was DINA," he thought he was talking about a woman. The FBI agent had no idea what was happening beyond borders.

Michael reached a payphone and hesitated. Then he called the IPS secretary to call Isabel. Agent Cornick wanted to talk to him.

—Tell her we're at George Washington Hospital, there's been an accident...

The FBI brought a dog to Michael to sniff him from head to toe. When Isabel answered the phone, she sensed the worst. In recent years, she had grown accustomed to the worst. She remembered what Orlando had told her hours earlier: "Come have lunch with us. I have news that you'll like."

She called the schools where her four children were, to have them let out early. Trembling, she opened her closet and grabbed a black jacket. Then she hung it back up and decided on a colorful dress.

When she arrived at the hospital, she saw a crowd at the entrance. She thought, or wanted to think, that it was something else.

—It's her; it's the widow—she heard or thought she understood.

They must have been talking about someone else. Maybe she didn't understand the hurried English. When she managed to get to the floor where Orlando was, she found Michael, as if he had just come from a fire. She hugged him. Michael murmured:

—They took my baby too…

Isabel can't fully grasp what has happened and asks to see Orlando.

—Your husband is dead—a nurse informs her.

Isabel insists on seeing him, but the healthcare women rely on protocol and say it's not possible. Mr. Letelier has died in an explosion, and his body is in very bad condition.

—I want to see him—Isabel insists—. I want to say goodbye to him, even if it's just to a hand.

—I'm sorry, but that's not possible.

Isabel keeps repeating the same thing until a nurse finally agrees.

When Isabel discovers Orlando's face, she sees his expression of pain, or sadness. She knows that look better than anyone. Orlando knew what had happened before he died, and that's why he had that expression. He knew Pinochet had done it again.

In the car radio as she drives her sons Juan Pablo and Francisco to the hospital, they hear something about a car bomb, but they know they're in the safest city in the world and that their father will be fine. 480 kilometers away, at the University of South Carolina, the eldest son, Cristian, has to leave a World Politics class where they were discussing the Cold War's *Détente* policy.

By then, at IPS, the employees had locked themselves in, waiting for another attack on the offices. At 2:00 p.m., when FBI agents, armed and with dogs that wouldn't stop barking, convinced them to open up, the interrogation began.

Landau and his team seized all the material from Orlando Letelier's office.

—We won't answer anything until our lawyer is present.

Due to the previous surveillance of IPS and other anti-war groups, acknowledged by the FBI before Congress, the IPS investigators measure their responses and distrust even their own shadows.

—Take it easy, guys—says an agent—. We're here to help you.

Half an hour later, another agent begins the interrogation:

—If you'll allow me, I'll proceed with the first question. Who do you think carried out this attack?

—The DINA.

—Can you spell that name?

—D-I-N-A.

—What's DINA's last name?—asked agent Carter Cornick.

At the hospital, detective Walter Johnson knows Ronni is dead and pressures Michael to provide some valuable information before the trauma of the attack silences details that might only be relevant to him. Night fell hours ago over Washington. Michael is released from the interrogation and walks down a hallway as if dragging his own body. In one room, a patient watches *Rich Man, Poor Man*. In the next room, another patient entertains his insomnia with *M*A*S*H*, Orlando Bosch's favorite show after *Mission Impossible*.

That night, Michael, still with the remnants of the explosion on his clothes and in his hair, with the memory of the smoke and the FBI dog sniffing him ingrained in everything he saw and felt, returned to the house in Potomac, where Ronni will never return. There, investigators will search every corner for any trace of explosives. Senators and all kinds of strangers will come to keep him company, as if that could lessen his pain in any way. When, finally, they leave him alone, he will take a shower and drink himself to sleep. Not for many hours. He wakes up several times until he finally gets up in the early hours of September 22.

One of the worst nightmares a person can have is waking up to the same nightmare as the day before. There were Ronni's clothes, books, and cooking pots. Michael didn't move anything for months. He didn't mow the lawn or clean the kitchen. For months, for years, he abused alcohol.

COLLECTIVE FANTASY, PURE AND HARSH REALITY

—Is it necessary to include that reference to the TV shows in the hospital?—complained Hunter.
—I think so—I replied—. In fact, I feel that it is.
—But there are no records of that detail. You yourself criticize additions that are impossible to verify.
—It's true, I hate things like "the plane was falling and the young woman ran her hand across her forehead to wipe away the sweat." It's also true that I didn't find any testimony of what movie the patients were watching at that time, but there's no doubt that those shows were the most popular at that very moment. In fact, *Rich Man, Poor Man* and *M*A*S*H* were being broadcast by CBS and ABC at 9:00 PM that same Tuesday, September 21st. Hospitals had televisions to alleviate the tedium of the patients, which wasn't much different from the tedium of office workers returning home.
—I don't know…—Hunter hesitated —. The point is that you need to shorten those thousand pages.
—I've already cut more than two hundred.
—You're still over by three hundred pages, thanks to your damn habit of expanding like a tsunami. If at least the patients had been watching *The Six Million Dollar Man* it would make more sense.
—That would be black humor.
—Alright, you're right, but…

—Besides, that show aired on Sundays. It doesn't cease to be significant, of course. By the late seventies, the future was over. That is, the fantasy of the future.

—With Ronald Reagan and The Terminator, the Orwellian dystopia was inaugurated. I was living in North Carolina at the time. I think The Six Million Dollar Man was very popular in Mexico too.

—In all the cities and towns of Latin America. Not in rural areas, where TVs and electricity didn't reach. It was called *The Nuclear Man*.

Hunter laughed. As was his habit when he was pondering something he couldn't put into words, he leaned back in his chair and stroked his Hemingway-style beard.

—I should have imagined it,—he said.

—A six-million-dollar man doesn't make sense in our cultures of the South. At least not as a hero.

—*Steve Austin, astronaut*—recited Hunter from memory, as if reading from the ceiling—. A man barely alive... Gentlemen. We can rebuild him. We have the technology. We can make him better, than he was. Better, stronger, faster.

—As I see it—I commented— the translation also avoided including that bit about "*We can make him better than he was.*" It wouldn't have made sense to us either... Although that sense of meaning is something that's created with just a few years of bombardment.

—How did it go in Spanish?

—*Steve Austin, astronaut. His life is in danger. We will rebuild him. We possess the technology to turn him into a cybernetic organism, powerful, gifted.*

—Interesting—said Hunter—. Either way, I'd cut those pop culture references.

—It's pure realism—I tried to defend myself—. If I don't include the dreams, nightmares, and hallucinations along with the hard, verifiable data, I feel like I'm losing a lot of reality. As if it becomes pasteurized, mutilated, McDonaldized. I prefer the vertigo of multi-dimensionality.

—Well, I prefer the brevity of Borges.

Borges and Pinochet

WHILE THE FBI INTERROGATED MICHAEL MOFFITT, in Santiago, General Pinochet entered the old Portales building, at 2855 Diego Portales Avenue. Waiting for him was the honoree, Jorge Luis Borges, leaning on his cane and trying to imagine what was happening. Which is, basically, what we all do.

At one point, Borges heard a high-pitched voice, like that of General Francisco Franco, directing measured but flattering words at him, as if they'd been memorized. "That must be General Pinochet", he thought.

Then they led him to a chair in front of a table. General Pinochet, Mariana Callejas, and a large audience fell silent. Someone adjusted the microphone for him. Partly relying on his memorized notes, partly improvising, Borges said:

—In this era of anarchy, I know that here, between the mountains and the sea, there is a strong homeland. Lugones preached the strong homeland when he spoke of *the hour of the sword*. I declare that I prefer the sword, the clear sword, to the furtive dynamite.

Thunderous applause. Callejas also applauded. She couldn't not do it.

—Here we have Chile—continued Borges—. That region, that homeland that is at once a long homeland and an honorable sword.

From the audience, Mariana Callejas must have recalled (with a memory that evades the interrogation of mirrors and is lost in the labyrinths of the vain mystery of a universe prefigured by a nonexistent god) one of her own stories, "A Small and Cheerful Park." On those pages, one day yellow or the fleeting dust of eternity, she had put to use her knowledge of how to make a bomb with dynamite and plastic explosive C4.

Those who knew him would say that the maestro regretted such sentimentality until the last minute of his life.

—They are using you, Borges—he recalled someone saying, someone he didn't remember and who, probably, never existed.

IT HADN'T BEEN THE PERFECT CRIME

Perhaps the perfect crime doesn't exist, that which fascinates so many consumers of real and fictional horrors, just as the squaring of the circle doesn't exist. But not few have tried it.

Thousands of kilometers away, with only a few hours' difference and with destinies forever intertwined, John Marciano, the professor of Ronni who attended her wedding months before she turned 26, attended her funeral. Ronni's mother said to him, not knowing what she was saying, as is common with everything spoken under the unbearable weight of grief, something others judge as incomprehensible frivolities:

—You never imagined you'd see me again so soon.[232]

A month before Letelier's assassination, the two mercenaries of the DINA had arrived in Paraguay to obtain false passports. The two would declare years later that the deputy director of the CIA, Vernon Walters, and the DINA had participated in the plot that ended Letelier's life.[233]

While Michael Moffitt, Isabel Letelier, and her children entered a cold and dark tunnel, Townley was having dinner with his parents. Vernon Townley, manager of Ford Motor Company in Chile must have felt for the first time that, in truth, his son wasn't a good-for-nothing but could actually stand on his own.

—Where did you say that was?—asked Hunter— In Miami?

—Close. In Fort Lauderdale, half an hour north of downtown Miami.

—I remember now. There must be a hundred cities that begin with *Fort*.

—They weren't defense forts. Back then, they were what military *bases* in foreign territory are today. They were Indian lands, people unfamiliar with the concept of private property that legitimized any dispossession.

—They are still called "defense" forts. They will never say it is to attack anyone.

—Like today, more or less, except instead of *fort* they are called *bases*, and instead of *dispossession* it's called *privatization*.

—Alright, alright. Let's get back to the facts. What did Townley do after having dinner with his parents? I don't remember that part of your manuscript.

Townley returned to Santiago and took refuge in the Lo Curro mansion. A few days later, the discomforts began. Colonel Contreras told him to leave for a while to the south of Chile. Not everything had gone so well. The enemies of freedom began to accuse the Chilean regime of having participated in the assassination of the diplomat and his secretary. General Augusto Pinochet found himself in a somewhat uncomfortable situation, which is why he decided to distance himself from the matter. Even Mariana Callejas began to suspect that her life, or rather her status, her way of life, was in danger after the last mission.

General Contreras called Michael Townley on the phone. He said he wanted to see him urgently. Shortly after, he was waiting for him in a car between two others.

—I trust my General—said Townley.

—*My General*...—Mariana replied—. Don't you realize that here you are the disposable piece? Anything, to wash their hands, your colonel and all the others will say you are a CIA infiltrator and you'll disappear in less than twenty-four hours. What we need is a lawyer.

El exilio del terror

Dragging his inferiority complex like a child about to be scolded, Michael went down and got into the first car. Colonel Contreras was in the second one. Michael and Callejas got into the third and from there they went to the pizzeria Nicos. Townley got out and entered the colonel's car. Soon after, Captain Fernández Larios, now a colonel, joined them.

—Both of you go to the south—Colonel Contreras told them—. A country house is waiting for you.

Townley received the news with displeasure. For ten seconds, Townley wasn't Townley.

—I'm not leaving Santiago—he said—. Nor do I plan to escape from Chile. The only things that have left this country are some documents about the activities of DINA. I have them in a very safe place.

Colonel Contreras understood the threat but chose to downplay it.

—The Department of Justice of your country and the FBI are after you—the colonel said—. If, under any circumstances, they manage to locate you, don't forget the golden rule: deny everything. If it's raining, say it's sunny.

Callejas wasn't entirely wrong. Everyone was replaceable. A year later, the diplomat Carlos Guillermo Osorio would be found by his wife lying in bed with a bullet to his forehead. Osorio, in his youth a member of the Nazi youth of Chile, had collaborated with Patria y Libertad and, after the coup, had been promoted by Pinochet to head of protocol. It was he who authorized and signed the false passports for Michael Townley and Armando Fernández under the names Williams and Romeral for their trip to the United States. The diplomatic passports had received A-2 visas from the U.S. Embassy in Santiago.

Both Townley and Osorio were a few ranks below Colonel Manuel Contreras, although ranks meant nothing in the new regime. Captains gave orders to colonels, and colonels ordered generals to shut up, as long as it wasn't General Pinochet.

The night before his death (which occurred a year later), Osorio had seen Contreras at a cocktail party.

—I don't know why he was so nervous— his wife, María Sordelli, would later recall.

Contreras had smiled at him. It was the smile of death. Shortly after, he had approached him with Colonel Enrique Valdés Puga to invite him to talk in his car. From there, they went to another celebration at the Military Club and, finally, dropped him off at his house at 2:00 a.m. Osorio was one of the implicated parties and, clearly, one of the key witnesses in the Letelier case.

At 6:00 p.m. on October 22, 1977, Osorio was found dead in his bed with a gunshot to the forehead and a revolver in his hand. Minutes later, General Carlos Forestier Haengsen informed the attending physician of the cause of death: cardiac arrest. It was later diagnosed as suicide.[234]

But let's return to that cold September night in 1976 in Santiago.

—Don't you realize you're in danger?—Mariana had told him.

Townley called one of his father's former employees at the Ford Company in Chile and one of the businessmen complicit in the coup, Federico Willoughby-MacDonald. Mr. Willoughby-MacDonald was very busy at the time and could do nothing to help the son of his highly respected friend, Vernon Townley.

The earthquake had been started by a journalist, a nobody named Jeremiah O'Leary, who had published the story in the Washington Star. O'Leary's article added details from notes collected by Orlando Letelier in a notebook found in his bag, such as a meeting with the future President Jimmy Carter, which never actually took place.

Shortly after, *El Mercurio* of Chile published photographs of the two conspirators wanted by the FBI, although under the false names from their Paraguayan passports. Those involved knew who they were: Armando Fernández and Michael Townley. Everyone else, including the FBI, had no clue.

Callejas convinced Townley to see a lawyer, who naturally confirmed the gravity of the case.

—The only solution I see—said the lawyer— is that you take refuge in notoriety.

—What do you mean?

—Well, make yourselves so public that the disappearance of Mr. Townley could become a national scandal.[235]

Callejas, more so than Townley, began speaking to some media outlets, but the doubts and limitations were many.

IT WAS THE COMMUNISTS

WITHIN HOURS OF THE ATTACK IN WASHINGTON, numerous journalistic rumors spread and took root in various countries. As on other occasions, the White House circulated in the major press the idea that Letelier had been assassinated by left-wing terrorist groups. One of the versions, likely initiated by FBI official Stanley Wilson, suggested that Letelier's death had been planned by his wife Isabel in coordination with the Chilean leftist group MIR, for both political and personal reasons, such as a possible revenge for his affair with the young Venezuelan woman.

Shortly after, agents Stanley Wilson and Joe Schuman interviewed one of their confidential informants in New York, who claimed that both Isabel and a faction of the MIR hated Letelier. He also informed them that the former secretary of the Socialist Party of Chile, Carlos Altamirano, was in the United States on the day Letelier was murdered to oversee the terrorist operation.[236] Other speculations indicated that the mayor of Caracas, Diego Arria, the same man who two years earlier had traveled to Santiago to demand the Pinochet government release Letelier, now wanted him dead for having been involved with a woman from his family.

Based on his intuition, Eugene Propper considered these theories to be rooted in fantasy, which allowed him to keep the investigation open for a long time, despite the high-profile failures of his team.

Pinochet did the same in Chile, ensuring that the press and public opinion viewed him as a victim of an international leftist conspiracy. As in the case of the nuns murdered in El Salvador in 1980 by the military and paramilitary forces funded by Washington and trained by the CIA. For years, the White House blamed Central American guerrillas not only for the necessary massacres carried out by friendly dictators but also directly held them responsible whenever an assassination turned into an international scandal.

—Clearly, these nuns were not simply nuns— said Jeane Kirkpatrick to the committee investigating the case— They were also political activists.

—The nuns were probably fleeing a roadblock— tried to explain Secretary of State Alexander Haig in his statement before a Senate committee.237

By the time the investigations proved the Salvadoran dictatorship's responsibility in the murder of the nuns, several years had passed. The White House never apologized for its tragic fantasies or for its terrorist allies, such as the Contras or the Atlácatl Battalion.

As the rumor of a connection between Letelier and Cuba and the affair between Letelier and Ronny Moffitt did not materialize, some variations emerged where Michael Moffitt was portrayed as a jealous husband who had decided to end the humiliating situation. In his trial, Michael Townley would testify that, had Ronni (the secret lover) not been so close to Letelier at the moment of the explosion, she would have survived.

The response from politicians in Washington was diverse. Senators like Edward Kennedy condemned the attack that took the life of his friend and his assistant. Others, like the ultra-conservative Democrat from Georgia, Larry McDonald, accused Letelier of being a socialist and, therefore, of supporting terrorism against the "law

El exilio del terror 361

and order" of the United States. According to McDonald, Letelier was primarily responsible for his own assassination.

—The CIA could have prevented this attack— he said in the chamber— if it hadn't been subjected to so much criticism from the IPS and from Letelier himself.[238]

The Republican representative from Ohio, John Ashbrook, blocked an initiative in the lower chamber to issue a condemnation of the terrorist attack. On September 24, the friend of General Rafael Videla and senator from North Carolina, Jesse Helms, defended the allied government of Chile.

—As I have pointed out before— argued Senator Helms— terrorism is often a tool of the left, used cold-bloodedly for their political ends. Leftist terrorists do not hesitate to kill their own comrades... Violence is a way of life in leftist Latin American politics: the MIR in Chile, the Tupamaros in Uruguay, the ERP in Argentina. The Institute of Political Studies here in Washington itself has a long history of dissent and participation in violent confrontations alongside revolutionary groups... For example, Tariq Ali is a member of the foreign branch of the Institute, the Transnational Institute; and maintains contacts with terrorist groups worldwide.[239]

Nothing new. It was part of a long tradition dating back to the speeches of Andrew Jackson accusing savages of unprovoked attacks, false flag attacks against other countries they sought to invade, to more meticulously planned accusations by the CIA during the Cold War or the false positives of paramilitarism in countries like Colombia. Each Latin American country reproduced the same practice at a national scale with the same objectives. Naturally, the press played a fundamental role, as since the invention of the printing press and the penny press in the United States in the mid-19th century, popular penny newspapers like The Sun.

A century later, in Chile, one of the most successful clandestine operations was Operation Colombo, through which over a hundred dissidents were eliminated while their deaths and disappearances were attributed to some leftist terrorist group. This operation was carried out by media conglomerates owned by Agustín Edwards Eastam, whose main newspaper, El Mercurio, not only participated in the coup against Allende but also continued to terrorize the population with false news about deaths attributed to the opposition to the regime. Another of its newspapers, La Segunda and La Tercera, denied the existence of the disappeared on their front pages or attributed them to the communists. A year before Letelier's assassination, on July 24, 1975, La Segunda of Chile reported the death of 59 Chilean terrorists killed in combat against the Argentine army in La Plata. On the same front page, and in the classic style of sensationalist tabloids, La Segunda reported the dismemberment of a man. All attributed to the enemies of freedom. In an adjacent column and on the front page, the same newspaper reported on a leave of absence by the Argentine president Isabel Perón, due to the flu and a deep depression over the wave of violence in the neighboring country.

The same strategy of attributing the torture, death, and disappearance of enemies to their enemies was already a tradition in the rest of the continent's countries.

Media Protection by Intelligence Begins

On September 22, *El Mercurio* (the newspaper of Agustín Edwards which, along with Ford, ITT, Pepsi Cola, and other companies promoted, funded, and supported the coup) published, with a classic genre of inaccuracy and semantic evasion:

Bomb in New York. Orlando Letelier dies in attack

It was impossible to attribute it to an accident, as Colonel Espinosa had requested. Further down, the statement from the Foreign Ministry: "*Chile* repudiates all terrorism" and "Government of Chile repudiates outrageous terrorist act." Years later, the same CIA will confirm that the order for the attack had come from General Pinochet's office.

The head of propaganda for Patria y Libertad, friend of Townley and Callejas and turned journalist after the coup against Allende, came to Pinochet's defense. The strategy was also textbook: confuse the general with Chile:

—This is a CIA plot against Chile—Pablo Rodríguez Grez stated.

—This government has nothing to do with the attack on Letelier—Pinochet will confirm two years later—. It's a very well-organized campaign, like all the propaganda campaigns of the communists.[240]

On February 1, 1977, journalists Timothy Robinson and Stephen Lynton leaked a significant part of the FBI investigation led by Propper and Cornick, much to their displeasure.[241] Despite media distractions, the investigation had made progress based on the initial theory of the IPS, Isabel Letelier, and Michael Moffitt, who, minutes after the explosion, had declared:

—It was the DINA. It was those damned fascists.

The greatest challenge for the FBI was proving this theory. Along the way, they encountered the decisive involvement of former CIA agents and anti-Castro paramilitary groups from Miami, mostly members of Brigade 2506, protagonists of the failed Bay of Pigs invasion. This did not surprise them either. The C4 used for the explosion, the method, and the location were a well-known tradition in Miami and Union City.

In March 1977, Professor Saul Landau published an article titled "This Is How It Was Done" accusing the press of distracting attention with alleged communist conspiracies to taint the investigation of the attack. In his article, he summarized the problem accurately:

"*An agent of the DINA* landed in the United States on September 13 last year and met with a group of Cuban exiles... After obtaining plastic explosive and a detonator, they headed to Washington. There they met with DINA agents, who posed as Chilean officials from the Embassy of Chile. *The agents informed the exiles about Letelier's habits, the description of his car, his departure times, the usual route to his workplace, the location of the parking lot, and the routine at the Institute of Policy Studies... When Letelier entered Sheridan Circle, a hand in the gray car following them pressed a button... Questions remain: Will U.S. authorities be able to point directly to Pinochet's government as the perpetrator of the terrorist attack? Will Washington's secret agencies acknowledge their role in the events and reveal the names of those who trained and supported the Chilean Junta?"*[242]

The version of events given by Professor Landau was correct. The problem was proving it.

THE CIA OF GEORGE H. BUSH

THE CIA DIRECTOR, GEORGE H. BUSH, was informed that DINA and its Cuban collaborators were responsible for the terrorist attack. "If the Chilean government did it—a secret report from October 23 noted—then they must have hired Cuban mobsters." The 2506 Brigade of the Bay of Pigs veterans in Miami promised to provide funds for the defense of any of its members implicated in the attack against Letelier.

Bush leaked another story to some members of Operation Mockingbird to cover up the role that the CIA and DINA played. On October 8, Jeremiah O'Leary published "The Left is Also Suspect in Letelier's Assassination" in the Washington Star: "The right-wing junta of Chile had nothing to gain and much to lose with the assassination of a peaceful and popular socialist leader." According to the October 11 issue of Newsweek, "The CIA concluded that the Chilean secret police were not involved." Newsweek went further, stating that the CIA had studied the files generated by the FBI and had concluded that Chile's secret police had nothing to do with the matter. The bomb was too crude and the association with DINA too

El exilio del terror

obvious to be taken seriously, especially when the Santiago regime was interested in expanding trade with the United States. Shortly thereafter, IPS revealed that this information had emerged spontaneously, and O'Leary ended up admitting that the unfounded information might have reached his office from Chile.

In December, Winslow Peck wrote an article in Counter Spy, archived by the CIA, in which he blamed the agency for contaminating the investigation with false rumors, such as the one stating that Letelier had died from a bomb he himself had built, intended for his wife's lover. Another version blamed Michael Moffitt, who allegedly discovered that Letelier and his young wife, Ronni, were lovers. The head of DINA, Manuel Contreras, would tell FBI investigator Robert Scherrer in Santiago that it had all been about Michael Moffitt's revenge, when he discovered that the now victims were lovers. In the plot, Isabel Letelier would have collaborated. Both Michael and Isabel were at the time pressuring the new government of Jimmy Carter to force Chile to facilitate the FBI investigation.

—What the CIA is hiding—said the repentant NSA agent, Winslow Peck— is the existence of a widespread network of far-right terrorists, infiltrated agents in the media, and corrupt governments… What American citizens must not know is that the bloody hands that killed this Chilean patriot and democrat along with the young American woman are firmly gripped, body and soul, by the secret power of fascism, forever entangled with liberal American democracy and its foreign policy.

The same Winslow Peck anticipates the investigations and concludes: "Orlando Bosch, leader of the terrorist worms, has accused Guillermo and Ignacio Novo Sambol of being the perpetrators of the attack against Letelier… The CIA trained the worms… now the DINA declares itself independent of the CIA, deciding its own attacks. The worms, trained by the CIA, recruited by Chile's DINA, also operate a vast network of far-right governments in Central and South America, with the secret police of Venezuela… To wash its hands, the CIA uses all its paramilitary and psychological warfare resources."[243]

Shortly after, it was discovered that Winslow Peck was Perry Fellwock, an NSA agent who had decided to reveal some secrets. So secret that before him, almost no one knew about the existence of the powerful NSA. Fellwock revealed the existence of the Five Eyes, the operation through which secret agencies like the CIA manage to bypass the legal prohibition of operating on U.S. soil by exchanging intelligence with other secret agencies from four other Anglo-Saxon countries, each spying on the citizens of the others and then sharing information.

Robert Scherrer, the South America expert on the team assigned by the FBI, contacted Colonel Manuel Contreras, to obtain true or false information, which always serves any investigation.

—For now, I can only give you confidential information—says Colonel Contreras.

—Which one?

—From what we know, Michael Moffitt's recent wife, tragically killed in the attack, was Orlando Letelier's lover. Michael was a cuckold. He knew it and was willing to avenge the betrayal. So...

Scherrer dismissed this version. It was too naive.

—Who would sit in a car that had a bomb ready to explode, even if it was in the back seat?

U.S. right-wing groups and media also collaborated. One of them was Gaeton Fonzi, author of The Last Investigation (1993). Another, Virginia Prewett (collaborator of the far-right group Inter-American Security Council, collaborator with the CIA, with agent David Atlee Philips, and with the Cuban terrorist group Alpha 66) attacked journalists who suggested that Chilean generals were involved in Letelier's assassination. According to Prewett, Letelier had been sacrificed by the leftists, to shift global opinion and change U.S. policy against Pinochet's regime.

Chile's Ministry of Foreign Affairs agreed: it was all a Russian smear campaign. The newspaper La Tercera published that "far-left terrorists" wanted to link Letelier's death to his loss of citizenship decreed by the Chilean government shortly before. According to El Mercurio, Letelier and Moffitt were heading to the Chilean embassy with a bomb that exploded prematurely.

The young prosecutor Eugene Propper had no idea about national or international politics. His entire career had been spent behind street crimes. The more he listened and read, the less he understood, so he decided to enter the CIA offices at any cost. His youthful inexperience helped him. After several failures, he managed to assert his status as an FBI investigator in a case with international ramifications within the mysterious CIA offices by the Potomac River.

The CIA director, George H. Bush, finally agreed to a meeting. The first thing that caught Propper's attention was a biblical verse stamped on a wall at the entrance of the building:

AND YOU SHALL KNOW THE TRUTH, AND THE TRUTH SHALL SET YOU FREE
John 8:32

On the seventh floor, right at noon, the director of the agency himself was waiting for him. They received him in a small lunchroom. The CIA director and future president of the country, George H. Bush, offered him a glass of sherry. Shortly after, he refused to collaborate with the investigation, claiming that the Agency had no jurisdiction over U.S. territory and, on the other hand, he did not want to disrupt the collaboration they were receiving from Latin American secret agencies. He didn't even inform Prosecutor Propper that the embassy in Paraguay had issued visas on fake passports for the suspected DINA agents, information that had reached the hands of the CIA deputy director, Vernon Walters.

"Explain, Tony," said Bush, while sipping Spanish sherry and reaching for the hors d'oeuvres cheese served on a white tablecloth in a windowless office in the CIA headquarters in Virginia. Anthony

Lapham, from a family of bankers in California, was one of the agency's top lawyers. He had refined manners and rarely said more than necessary, even under the influence of alcohol.

—The problem is that in the past we have collaborated with the Department of Justice, and sooner or later, they have ended up taking one of our informants to trial.[244]

—This case involves people who acted abroad—argued Prosecutor Propper—. It's your jurisdiction.

—Well, that's true—admitted Lapham—But we still haven't determined if this is a matter of National Security.

The CIA never informed Propper that the embassy in Paraguay had issued visas on fake passports for the suspected DINA agents, information that had reached the hands of the CIA deputy director, Vernon Walters. Instead, they leaked to the press the meeting that their director, George H. Bush and lawyer Tony Lapham held in private in their offices. As is a tradition of the CIA, those who leak classified information are hunted down, but the agency often practices this kind of leaking for propaganda purposes or to distract public opinion.

Propper was caught off guard with a backhanded blow to his investigation when the following Sunday he read in the *Washington Post* a detailed report of his visit to the CIA offices. On October 11, 1976, NEWSWEEK reported that "after studying the FBI reports *and other investigations on the case, the CIA has concluded that the Chilean secret police was not involved in the death of Orlando Letelier.*" According to the same magazine, the CIA had reached this conclusion because the bomb used in Washington was "too primitive to be the work of experts and because this assassination occurred just as the Chilean government was trying to improve its relations with the United States." On Monday the 12th, the New York Times confirmed that the CIA had ruled out any possibility that the Chilean government could bear any responsibility for the assassination, which was more likely an action by the leftists themselves to create a martyr for their cause against Pinochet. On November 1st, the

Washington Post confirmed that the CIA director, George H. Bush, had informed the Secretary of State, Henry Kissinger, that the Chilean Junta was not involved in the attack.[245] In a memorandum dated October 6, 1987, Secretary of State George Shultz would acknowledge that "we have known for a long time that the secret police and the intelligence service of Chile were behind the brutal assassination of Letelier, perhaps the only indisputable case of terrorism in Washington DC supported by a state."[246]

On March 2, 1978 (through his usual contact, journalist Jeremiah O'Leary), the FBI leaked to the Washington Star the two photographs of Townley and Fernández Larios taken in Paraguay for the fake passports they never used. Hours later, in Chile they identified the photos of Juan Williams Rose as a well-known American from Lo Curro and Alejandro Romeral Jara as Colonel Armando Fernández Larios.

Although shortly afterward the FBI was already convinced of the authorship of Michael Townley and the DINA in the attack, on October 25, the famous TV journalist William F. Buckley, a known sympathizer of Pinochet, also participated in this disinformation campaign: "U.S. investigators believe it is unlikely that the Chilean government would risk such an action given the respect it has gained with great difficulty over the past year in many Western countries that were previously hostile to its policies."

According to Donald Freed, Buckley had been providing disinformation for the government of General Augusto Pinochet since October 1974. He also revealed that William Buckley's brother, James Buckley, met with Michael Townley and Guillermo Novo in New York City just one week before the assassination of Orlando Letelier.

OCTOBER

THE FIRST PIECES OF THE PUZZLE

ONE OF THE FIRST TO ARRIVE AT THE SCENE while the smoke from the explosion had yet to dissipate was a 29-year-old lawyer, Eugene Propper. The rain complicated the evidence collection, Propper would recall, who, along with FBI agent Carter Cornick, was assigned to the case hours later. Since 1972, the FBI had jurisdiction in investigating crimes involving diplomats or former diplomats like Letelier. The case was dubbed Chilbom.

On September 23, they received a call from a chief of the secret police in Venezuela.

—We know who the perpetrators of the attack are—said the voice.

—Who is this?—asked Cornick, as Propper took notes.

—It was the Novo brothers.

—Do you know their names?

—Guillermo and Ignacio Novo. Check the archives—Propper nodded.

—How did you get this information?

—I was told by Orlando Bosch.

It was the voice of El Mono Morales. The Novo brothers were residents of Union City and two of the few leaders of the Cuban exile community who had not participated in the Bay of Pigs invasion. The elder, Guillermo, was beginning to challenge Bosch's leadership, and internal suspicions and rivalries continued to grow.

El Mono was one of the most reliable informants for the CIA, the FBI, and the DEA, and he never missed an opportunity to maintain his prestige with new revelations. He wasn't as interested in whether the information helped solve a case, but rather in ensuring that the official agents could never prove he was wrong or that he had provided false information. On the contrary, it made them more dependent on him, granting him more power, immunity, and protection.

—Do you want to know how the Cubans got to Venezuela?—asked Cornick—. The CIA put them there.

The CIA agent for Latin America, Jack Devine, flatly denied it, accusing the FBI agent of being "full of crap." The CIA never denied it again. Their own declassified documents would confirm it time and time again.

Cornick began with the latest available information. An FBI telegram from September 1976 confirmed that Bosch had an agreement with the Venezuelan government: if he didn't commit terrorist attacks in Venezuela, he could reside freely and raise funds for his organization. This agreement was broken when he and Posada Carriles blew up Cubana Flight 455. The FBI had also recorded the founding meeting of CORU, where José Suarez assured that before moving their attacks outside U.S. territory, the MNC had to finish another job, this time for the Chilean government.

The investigation was plagued with failures and risks that the young agents had never taken before. Propper admitted he must have been crazy when he agreed to attend a secret meeting of an anti-Castro group in Miami blindfolded.

—Don't worry—one of the Cubans told him—. If we wanted to kill you, we wouldn't blindfold you.

THE HAPPIEST DAY

FRIDAY, OCTOBER 1ST, WAS SUPPOSED TO BE the happiest day of María González's life. She had arrived at Havana's José Martí Airport with her big smile and mingled with her nineteen teammates. It was her first time boarding a plane and her first time leaving the country. She was the youngest in the group but not the smallest.

As the twenty athletes walked toward Cubana's D-8, someone ran up to the group, which had already started climbing the stairs.

—You can't go, María—said the coach—. We just saw in your passport that you're not yet thirteen.

—I'm a few days away—said María—. I turn thirteen in February.

—I'm sorry, María, but you can't compete if you haven't turned thirteen.

María began crying desperately.

—You can compete in the Olympics…

As often happens, the happiest day of her life was about to turn into the saddest. Or rather, one of the saddest.

The coach led her back to the airport waiting room, and María returned to her parents' small apartment in Havana's La Víbora neighborhood. She threw herself on her bed and cried for four days and four nights. Every day, the radio announced the results of the Caribbean championship. The television showed moments when her teammates defeated their opponents. Each day, the number of gold medals won by Cuba's unbeatable fencing team increased. Young María smiled and cried at the same time.

The city, the entire country, was already preparing for a well-deserved welcome for the young heroes.

They think the Revolution gave them superpowers

—Today I went to see the fencing team—said Orlando Bosch.

—Are they good?—asked Posada Carriles.

—They're snobs—said Bosch—. They think the Revolution gave them superpowers. They won, but that's it. After receiving their gold medal, a Black woman sent a greeting to Comandante Fidel. They're not athletes; they're fighters.

—How's that going?

—Almost ready. Black Joe spent an entire month studying the flights, transit times, and cleaning routines of Cubana's planes in Barbados. There's nothing more to adjust. The abuse ended, and the trampling began.

—Well, we're caught. I just hope the black guy doesn't chicken out halfway through.

On October 26, an FBI report will claim that the attaché of the U.S. Embassy in Caracas, Legat Joe Leo, had helped Hernán Ricardo obtain a visa to enter the country last year. On October 25 and September 30, he had received phone calls from Ricardo. He personally knew Posada Carriles and, up until October 24, communicated daily with the chief of Section 54 of the DISIP, El Mono Morales.[247]

The plan was that, after bringing down Cubana's DC-8, Hernán Ricardo and Freddy Lugo would be picked up by Joe Leo at the Holiday Inn and taken immediately to the port of Bridgetown, where a boat awaited to take them out of Barbados.

Bosch (Doctor Panyagua for Lugo and Ricardo), almost instinctively, as a kind of longtime tic, touched his right side. He verified that he hadn't forgotten it. It was his old and most faithful friend, a Walther P38 from World War II, a chubby German girl with fifteen bullets that never left him alone.

POSADA CARRILES SELLS OUT BOSCH

A FEW DAYS LATER, TAKING ADVANTAGE OF THE SILENCE of his apartment in Caracas, Luis Posada Carriles dialed a number from memory. Someone, a young woman with a Cuban accent answered, and he asked to speak with The Boss. He knew that from the moment the secretary picked up the phone, the recorder in Virginia had started rolling.

As in February of last year, he once again requested his reintegration into the CIA as a special agent. As usual, The Boss neither said no, nor yes, nor maybe.

Every time I ask you
When, how, and where
You always answer me
Perhaps, perhaps, perhaps

He waited for his interlocutor to speak and then asked and asked again. Once more, Posada Carriles offered significant information in exchange for his reinstatement. The Boss knew that his former agent had a long track record of providing *quality information*. Both the Agency and its collaborators understood the unspoken codes of no contract: in what, for some mysterious reason, is called *intelligence*, there exists a sensitive market for information, and relationships are based on the credit rating assigned by those above to those below. The information about Orlando Bosch's plan to kill Kissinger in Costa Rica was highly useful, though nowhere was Bosch formally accused of the plan. It was enough to have him jailed and then deported from that country so he could continue his filibustering work, William Walker-style.

Posada Carriles knew he couldn't trust The Boss either. *Trust* was a forbidden verb (trust, not even your own shadow), but he had to play the same card again, hoping for a different outcome. So he told him: *a group of Cuban exiles already had a plan ready and fine-tuned to bring down a Cubana flight with the usual materials: TNY and C4 plastic explosive*, concealed in a Nikon camera case and a Philips radio, enough material to blow up a bridge. As in the first attempt, the two Venezuelans chosen would carry false passports and present themselves as businessmen in the photographic equipment industry.

Why had Posada Carriles leaked this information against himself, against his own comrades, and against his own objectives? The fact was neither new nor surprising to The Boss or anyone, but the answer is a matter of speculation. It's likely that Posada Carriles calculated that the CIA wouldn't stop the plan but would reintegrate him into its ranks and its payroll once the veracity of the information was confirmed. They would be foolish if they decided not to make use of that valuable asset. The CIA was not and is not an agency that collaborates with any form of justice. In fact, its record of obstructing FBI investigations is long and dark. Its mission is not to uphold legality, much less to exercise any moral principle, but to achieve political objectives, even if it means protecting anyone who offers even the slightest advantage.

According to a classified document from October 18, this CIA source had already informed at the end of June about the attack on a Cubana flight. The only thing that can be confirmed is the first part of the speculation. The second, about whether they did anything to preserve the asset, will remain in the shadows. More like in the darkness, considering subsequent events.[248]

WALKING ON CLOUDS

ON OCTOBER 4, ORLANDO LETELIER'S AUNT, María del Solar, received a brief call.

—María, María, María...—said a mocking voice, just before hanging up—. Talking to the FBI won't help you at all. Your legs will be scattered across the streets of Washington, just like little Orlandito's.

That same day, in Cuba, they were finalizing the last details to welcome the athletes who had won all the gold medals they had contested in Venezuela.

In Guyana, the families of the medical students awarded scholarships to study at the University of Havana, for other reasons, were also living moments of joy and were organizing parties, not to welcome their children but to wish them luck in a new stage of promise and youthful dreams, which are the truest dreams.

In a modest neighborhood of Georgetown, among invited and uninvited guests who kept arriving, Raymond Persaud's father calculated that the yard was big enough to hold eighty people, but they were short on chairs.

—The church!—he said to Charles Persaud—. Let's go borrow chairs from the church.

Raymond, his father, his siblings Kenrick, Sharon, Trevor, and 11-year-old Roseanne, hurried to get the chairs from the church. Within half an hour, the yard began to fill with the church chairs. Standing, the guests welcomed them like a long-awaited refreshment.

The Persaud family was happy and anxious. In less than 24 hours, their son would be flying to Cuba. Raymond was going to study medicine.

—Doctor Raymond Persaud—joked the father, with feigned solemnity.

Raymond, the little genius of the family, was 19 and had started practicing Spanish even before receiving acceptance from Havana. It had been Plan B, after the recent high school graduate*high school* had discovered that studying in his language in Canada or the United States was too expensive for the family's means. His father wasn't poor; he was the director of the Redeemer Lutheran School in Georgetown, but the savings weren't enough. When Raymond discovered he could do it for free at the University of Havana with a scholarship from the government of Guyana, he didn't think twice. He and five other students from the country had been selected for the great opportunity of their lives.

The party and music ended late into the night. Almost without sleep, the Persauds were up early that same morning. They had to travel forty kilometers along the Demerara River to Timehri Airport. Seconds before getting into the family's red car, his mother told him:

—Wait. Stand there.

Raymond looked at the camera and smiled with the sun in his face. His pants and shirt, the same brown color, with four pockets and large lapels, made by a friend tailor especially for the occasion, his smile beneath a budding mustache, and a sun casting his shadow and his mother's, together for the last time, were captured for weeks in the darkness of the camera.

Falling from the Sky

Labor Day in the United States. An ordinary day in Barbados. Wednesday dawned sunny at 6 a.m. Raymond Persaud and his classmates landed in Trinidad. This had been their first flight, and the excitement of takeoff from Guyana was as thrilling as their first landing in a different country, even though the flight time had been half the duration of their father's trip from home to the airport. Minutes later, the group of students took off for Barbados.

In Bridgetown, Sheila Harris-Thompson had just finished packing her suitcases when the phone rang. Her husband answered, and a woman's voice asked to speak with Mrs. Harris.

—Good morning, Mrs. Harris—she heard a woman's voice say—; you must come to the hospital.

—I'm on my way to the airport. I leave for Jamaica at noon.

—Before that, you must stop by the hospital…

—Can you come with all your documents?

—What documents?

—The documents for your house.

—But you already have copies of everything…

—Please do as we say.

Three islands further south, Hernán Ricardo and Freddy Lugo arrived in Trinidad and Tobago on PanAm flight 443 from Caracas. In Port of Spain, Hernán Ricardo and Freddy Lugo boarded Cubana flight 455 to Barbados, with Havana as the final destination. Ricardo boarded with the package of explosives and an image of the Virgin Mary, which he touched like a talisman. C4 is odorless and undetectable by metal sensors. The Virgin Mary was also not suspicious.

On the same flight was Cuba's large fencing team, the six scholarship students from Guyana, and four Koreans. The young Cubans had won every single gold medal at the Caribbean and Central American Championship in Venezuela. Apart from having proven themselves the best, there had been some last-minute favorable circumstances, as if, suddenly, the stars had aligned. Initially, the Cuban Federation had canceled their trip to Venezuela but then had to reconsider the decision. In Venezuela, they had to share a bathroom in a modest hotel, and within a few days, they began collecting medals. As Orlando Bosch had said, perhaps they believed the Revolution had endowed them with superpowers. Apparently, they used them.

Given their age and having brought home all the gold medals, the young men spent the short one-hour flight chatting and restlessly moving from one seat to another. Some passengers must have been annoyed, while others may have remembered that age that feels so much like freedom, when the future promises more than it threatens. The latter is just a product of imagination; we don't know for sure, but it's hard to assume anything very different.

At some point, most likely halfway to landing in Bridgetown, Lugo took out the Philips radio filled with gray plastic, broke the small acid bubble that would slowly eat away at the wire and detonate the explosive in 45 minutes, and placed it under the seat. Two minutes later, Ricardo got up and went to the bathroom. He inspected the small receptacle and decided on a compartment near the floor, where the trash was deposited. He knew, from the field study conducted by El Negro Joe, that the stop in Barbados was too brief, so Cubana's cleaning service was done at the third stop, in Jamaica. He opened the Nikkon camera case and, like Lugo, broke the small bubble of the timer pencil embedded in the C4. Both the chemical timer pencil and the C4 were two tools that the fighters of Brigade 2506 from the Bay of Pigs had learned to use in CIA training camps, and after the failure of the invasion, they became recurring weapons in sabotage flights against Cuba's sugar plantations, mills, and ports.[249]

Before leaving, he urinated. When he tried to open the door, it wouldn't budge. Desperate, he started banging on it until a flight attendant told him not to get nervous, that they would find a way to open it, but Ricardo kept pounding violently, prompting the copilot to intervene and instruct him to slide the latch.

—I already did!—Ricardo nearly shouted, annoyed.

—Make sure you slid it all the way—the copilot insisted.

The door immediately opened. The copilot gave him a puzzled look for a moment, but Ricardo pretended to apologize, making everyone forget the incident for a few hours.

The plane arrived at Seawell Airport in Barbados before noon, as scheduled. Lugo and Ricardo went to a waiting room and were alarmed when they saw the fencing team had also disembarked. They asked an official who didn't understand Spanish. Coincidentally, a Cuban who overheard them acted as an interpreter:

—The flight to Jamaica leaves in a few minutes, but passengers must wait in the airport.

—Thank you…—said Lugo—. Cuban from Miami?

—Cuban from Cuba—replied the impromptu interpreter.

—Thank goodness!—said Ricardo, erasing any suspicion.

Ten minutes later, the twenty-five young men lined up again alongside 48 other passengers. The athletes' enthusiasm and restlessness hadn't subsided—it had intensified. From anecdotes about the championship in Venezuela, the conversation now turned to their expectations of returning home and their plans at the University of Havana. Some were thinking of pursuing architecture, others medicine. By then, they had already struck up a conversation with the six scholarship students from Guyana. Someone joked about the Spanish of the scholarship students while they wrote in their notebooks names, addresses, and all sorts of details to meet them again at the university.

They are all fighters

Eleven minutes after takeoff, at an altitude of five and a half kilometers, in the Douglas DC-8, the first bomb exploded under the seat of a nine-year-old girl.

—We have an explosion aboard... We are descending immediately!—reported the captain—. We have fire on board! We are requesting immediate landing! We have a total emergency!

The pilot managed to control the aircraft, which was starting to lose pressure while filling with smoke. With only one engine, he turned it to the right and headed back to the runway.

The airport activated the alarms. The control tower ordered the runway to be cleared, and all flights were diverted to move away from the airport while ambulances were on their way.

Captain Wilfredo Pérez shouted, this time in Spanish:

—Close the door!

The cabin began to fill with smoke. The passengers, in a panic, did not know it, but Captain Pérez was minutes away from solving the problem. They will never know. A second bomb, the bomb that Lozano had placed in one of the bathrooms, exploded, ripping off the tail of the plane, while a sudden and intense rain began to blur the horizon of Barbados.

The plane pointed skyward and ascended vertically. The control tower yelled at the pilot that this was a bad idea, unaware that the pilot had already lost control of the machine. Some passengers fell into the sea when the plane reached maximum altitude. It stopped for a moment impossible to pinpoint, as if suspended in mid-air, and then it fell into the sea like a lost arrow.

The flight of Cubana 455 was the first flight in the history of civil aviation to be brought down by a terrorist attack and the one that claimed the most lives in the hemisphere, until September 11, 2001.

As always, the rest died slowly

When nurse Sheila Harris-Thompson arrived at the designated office, she didn't hide her frustration at having missed the flight to Jamaica. A woman attended to her but didn't have time to take her papers, which required her signature. The phone rang, and shortly after, the woman told her:

—Well— Mrs. Harris, the official told her— it's lucky you didn't take that plane, because it just fell into the sea.

Sheila never knew the woman's name.

In Cuba, the father of one of the athletes, upon hearing the news, went to the mountains and stayed there all night. Another remained at the Havana airport for a week, convinced that his son would appear on one of the flights. The fiancée of one of the champions went up to her room and didn't come down for ten years. Among the victims was Lázaro Serrano, the boyfriend of Moraima Secada, a member of the renowned Quartet Aida (later Buena Vista Social Club) and aunt of Jon Secada. Another farmer refused the financial compensation won by a lawyer from the Canadian insurance company. In Guyana, tormented by the loss of his son and feelings of guilt, Raymond's father secluded himself in his library and didn't leave for a week.

In Miami, the land of freedom, the owner of the weekly magazine Réplica, the Cuban Max Lesnik, was one of the few who dared to denounce the terrorist act against Cubana Flight 455.

—Luis Posada Carriles and Orlando Bosch planned it all—Lesnik said years later—I denounced this terrorist act while the extreme right in Miami applauded it.[250]

The weekly magazine *Réplica* suffered seven bombing attacks until it was forced to close permanently in 2005. No one was ever arrested for these acts despite the fact that, according to researcher Ann Louise Bardach, an FBI agent reported that, without his knowledge, he had saved Lesnik from assassination many times.[251]

All in the name of press freedom, which doesn't exist in Cuba.

THE SAME PATIO, THE SAME CHAIRS

Around 3:00 PM, someone knocked on the Persauds' door. It was the cousin who worked at the Department of Foreign Affairs.

—What's wrong?

—I need to talk to you—said the cousin, tasked with bringing the tragedy to the house where the echoes of music and laughter from the early hours of that morning still lingered.

—Just speak, woman!

—Raymond's plane crashed...

—What do you mean it crashed?—the mother asked—Is Raymond okay? What are you saying?

—There were no survivors.

The neighbors could hear the screams of a woman. If someone's hands were cut off, they wouldn't scream with such pain. In five other houses not far away, the Persauds' story was being repeated. The young Jacqueline Williams, Seshnarine Ramkumar, Ann Nelson, Eric Harold Norton, and Rawle Thomas met the same fate as Raymond. In others, they received the news of the deaths of fathers, mothers, wives...

Within minutes, the same guests who had filled the party just hours before began arriving at the Persauds' house. The same guests entered the same patio and sat in the same chairs. Raymond's father couldn't process the events, the murmurs of grief from the crowd, and locked himself in his study. He didn't leave for a week.

Charles Persaud would spend his last 25 years obsessively and relentlessly writing letters to the U.S. Congress, demanding justice for his son. He would die of a heart attack while writing an investigative book about his son's case.

IT WENT OVER THE CLIFF WITH ALL THE DOGS INSIDE

SHORTLY AFTER THE EXPLOSIONS, Freddy Lugo called Orlando Bosch to report the operation's success:

—The bus went over the cliff with all the dogs inside—he said.

It was a cryptic message only Bosch and Posada Carriles could understand.

Minutes later, they took a taxi. The men had a Venezuelan accent, recalled the taxi driver who saw their faces in the rearview mirror. They were talking about something important and laughing heartily.[252]

The police in Trinidad arrested Herman Ricardo and Freddy Lugo. Ricardo, an employee of Posada's security agency in Venezuela, admitted that he and Lugo had planted the two bombs on the plane. He also acknowledged that Luis Posada and Orlando Bosch had planned the attack.

—It was a heroic act—declared Bosch, alongside Herman Ricardo, before a court in Caracas.

—The Cuban fighters carried out a revolutionary act regarding the plane—declared Ricardo Lozano in front of television cameras—. That should be respected just as Venezuelan activities were respected when they sought to overthrow the dictator Pérez Jiménez.

—It was a heroic action of the Cuban Revolution—insisted Orlando Bosch nervously shaking his right index finger, surrounded by journalists in a hallway leading to the court—. Because, as you know, war is a competition of cruelties. The struggle will continue, and so will the attacks in all forms and ways within our reach.[253]

Later, Bosch would deny everything whenever questioned about the incident, *"because that's illegal in the United States,"* and he would always justify it as *"an action against combatants, because everyone is a combatant."* Instead, he would implicate his comrades.

—Guillermo and Ignacio Novo did it— he would say in the interview with Blake Fleetwood in the Caracas jail— It was all planned by DINA of Chile.

Only eight bodies were recovered from the sea.

That same day, in Havana, María González waited in the schoolyard for the triumphant words of the principal. She had written her speech filled with praise and congratulations for her prodigal daughters, but when she appeared in the yard full of students, her face hinted that something was not right.

—There was a terrible accident—she said—. The plane carrying our team has crashed. There are no survivors.

At the funeral ceremony, each deceased student was represented by one of their classmates. For one day, María González was her friend Nancy Uranga, the blond girl who had substituted for her before boarding the plane. Nancy was much older than María. She was 22 years old and pregnant.

On October 15, after seven days of national mourning, one million people filled the Plaza de la Revolución. In his speech, Fidel Castro recalled that since 1959, 51 flights of Cubana had been sabotaged and hijacked. This would, for decades, remain the worst terrorist attack against a flight in the hemisphere:

"We cannot say that the pain is shared," he said. "The pain is multiplied."

"The terrorist is him," replied Posada Carriles, watching the images coming from Havana.

Orlando García, head of security for President Andrés Pérez, and Ricardo Morales Navarrete (both Cuban exiles), had attended Bosch's welcome cocktail in Caracas. According to a CIA document, both García and Morles mentioned that, during the massive gathering, Orlando Bosch had claimed responsibility for the Washington attack against Letelier, something he would tirelessly deny in public. After some time, the CIA began to feel uneasy about the number of uncontrolled attacks by their Cuban agents.

Journalist Fleetwood called from Caracas to prosecutor Eugene Propper, in charge of the FBI investigation Propper wasn't very optimistic about his chances of solving the bombing. Rarely were bombings ever resolved. After a few hours, Propper called the journalist again:

—The CIA had already informed everything to Venezuela's secret police… I think they're onto you. You're in danger.

—So, what should I do?—asked Fleetwood, with six hours of recordings with Bosch and Posada Carriles in hand—. Should I go to the U.S. Embassy…?

—No, quite the opposite—said the FBI agent—. I'm afraid you'll have to figure it out on your own and find a way to get out of there.[254]

Immediately after the bombing of Flight 455, Frank Castro flew from Venezuela to Miami. In an internal memo, the CIA identified him as one of the individuals involved in the bombing. Detained in Miami by the FBI, he admitted to having met with Orlando Bosch, the last time on September 26, but denied any knowledge of the bombing.

It didn't take much for the Venezuelan police to locate Orlando Bosch and Posada Carriles. Until recently, the hard part was arresting them, but since the surrender of comrade Orlando Bosch in February, Posada Carriles had not regained his position at the CIA. He had tried again last month, informing the agency of an imminent bombing against a Cubana flight by a group of Cuban exiles, but he hadn't succeeded this time either. Unlike the alleged plan to kill Kissinger in Costa Rica, this time the CIA didn't act with the necessary speed, but with calculated clumsiness, as it often does.

El exilio del terror

Without the invaluable protection of the CIA, Bosch and Posada Carriles, for months, had to rely on the networks of secret services from other countries, such as Chile or Venezuela, but this complicity had cracks. On Thursday the 14th, the Venezuelan police arrested Posada Carriles and Orlando Bosch.

On Friday, the detectives questioned Posada Carriles about the latest bombing of the Cubana plane. Posada Carriles answered without hesitation:

—I had nothing to do with that, kid—he said—. I would never do something like that.

—Do you condemn the bombing?

—I would never do something like that, but I don't condemn anything. Sometimes you have to respond to violence with violence.

—Even if innocents die?

—Those things happen. Sometimes innocent people pay for being in the wrong place.

Orlando Bosch repeated almost the same words.

—I would never be capable of such an act against innocent people. I'm innocent, but I don't condemn anything that leads to the downfall of the Cuban regime. The terrorists are them.

—So, you don't consider yourself a terrorist...

—Not at all, kid.

—How would you define yourself?

—I'm a combatant, a soldier in a relentless war. My enemy is the murderous regime of Cuba.

—Combatants face other combatants...

—In a total war, there are no civilians. I'm not a military man, I'm a doctor, and I'm a civilian combatant.

—Do you consider the passengers of Flight 455 combatants?

—They were in the wrong place... Yes, as I've said, in a global war, everyone is a combatant. The terrorists are Fidel Castro and his henchmen. They came to power through violent means and will be overthrown through violent means...

—We agree that Fidel Castro is a despicable dictator, but he came to power by returning from exile and taking up arms against Batista's dictatorship, and Batista was the strongman of the United States...

—I also took up arms against Batista! And now I take up arms against Fidel's Marxist regime. I have fought against God and the devil...

—And why don't you return from exile and organize a counter-revolution in your country? That would make you a true fighter. Setting bombs against non-combatant civilians, many of them teenagers, doesn't seem very heroic.

—Are you interrogating me or trying to brainwash me?

—The first. But a little brainwashing never hurts.

—The problem is your intelligence isn't sharp enough to manipulate mine. What you're aiming for is to make me confess that we planned that attack and others...

—So you're not going to confess?

—No.

Bosch looked his interrogator in the eyes and said:

—*Never*.

When President Andrés Pérez learned of Fleetwood's daring interview in the Caracas prison, he ordered his arrest, but the DISIP didn't manage to stop him from catching the next flight to the United States. Waiting for him was Prosecutor Propper, who asked for a copy of his recordings to use in his interrogation of Guillermo Novo. At the same time, President Pérez accused Fleetwood of being a CIA agent.[255]

There were no other suspects. There never were

FREDDIE LUGO AND HERNÁN RICARDO LOZANO were arrested in Trinidad and Tobago, after Ricardo called from Barbados to his girlfriend Mariloly, instructing her to contact Posada Carriles and Orlando Bosch. Also arrested were José Velásquez, José García, and Llano Montes, responsible for planting CIA articles in El Mundo de Caracas.

The investigations determined that they were not the masterminds behind the attack. In Lugo's agenda appeared the name of the deputy to the U.S. Embassy in Caracas, Joseph Leo, but Leo denied knowing Lugo and said Posada Carriles had likely given him the number. A classified CIA report dated October 18 reiterates that, at the end of June, a group of Cuban exiles led by Orlando Bosch had planned the explosion of a Cubana flight departing from Panama bound for Havana, information that Posada Carriles himself had leaked to the CIA to undermine his friend Orlando Bosch in an attempt to be readmitted into their ranks and payroll. The FBI confirmed the attempt. The detonator had failed, so they tried again on July 9 with another flight from Jamaica. That time, the bomb exploded on the ground due to a technical delay with the Cubana aircraft.

The commissioner of Trinidad and Tobago, with fresh memories of the bomb attack on the Guyana embassy by CORU, proceeded with professional rigor and isolated them, interrogating them separately. After two weeks without using any coercive methods, relying solely on questioning, he managed to get Hernán and Ricardo talking. Both admitted they worked for Orlando Bosch and Luis Posada Carriles, who would deny any link to the attack. Venezuelan police raided Posada Carriles' house in Caracas and found several items implicating them from the outset, such as the schedule of Cubana de Aviación for that day.[256]

An FBI document dated October 7, notes that Lugo's passport proves he had entered Barbados on July 9, two days before the bombs exploded at the West Indies Airways offices, another in the car of the company's general manager, and another on a boat anchored in the port of Bridgetown.[257] A secret CIA report addressed to Henry Kissinger recorded that Ricardo had traveled from Caracas to Port of Spain, Trinidad, on August 29, en route to Puerto Rico. In his visa application, he had reported being a correspondent for the magazine Visión, returning from Port of Spain to Caracas on September 1. The same document reported that on the same day, at 10:15 in the morning, a bomb had exploded at the Guyanese consulate. CORU claimed responsibility for the attack.

The FBI also included the Security and Intelligence Advisor to President Andrés Pérez, the Cuban Orlando García, as a participant in the attack. Also Frank Castro, who had flown from Caracas to Miami days before the attack. During interrogation, Castro admitted to having met with Bosch several times but denied participating in any terrorist plot.

Three days later, on Saturday, October 9, and based on information provided by U.S. agencies, HenryKissinger wrote a secret memorandum on "the suspicion that Bosch participated in planning the Cubana de Aviación crash." The memorandum was leaked by WikiLeaks in 2013 and later blocked on the internet.[258]

A CIA agent assigned to the case would later acknowledge in a New York Times article on July 13, 1998 that, from the beginning of the investigation, "Bosch and Posada were the prime suspects; there was no one else."[259] Nor was there ever.

For decades, in response to the demands from the governments of Cuba and Venezuela for the extradition of Luis Posada Carriles and Orlando Bosch, the U.S. government would deny the request. On the contrary, it would intervene to secure presidential pardons for them due to other terrorist attacks, such as the one in Panama, early release, or commutation of sentences until both, along with their collaborators, enjoyed a peaceful retirement in Miami.

Prison and a New Escape

IN MIAMI, THE CATHOLIC CHURCH ORGANIZED VIGILS AND PRAYERS FOR THE RELEASE OF ORLANDO BOSCH. The Venezuelan government twice offered the U.S. embassy the extradition of Orlando Bosch, but Washington rejected the offer. Bosch admitted to Venezuelan investigators that he had participated in the attack on the Cuban aircraft, but the government transferred his trial to a military tribunal, and Bosch was declared innocent, except for falsifying identity documents.

Bosch was held in a windowless cell in the old San Carlos barracks building. The monster, as he was known by other inmates, boasted of occupying the same cell once held by dictator Marcos Pérez Jiménez.[260] There, he dedicated himself to painting landscapes of Cuba, an artistic hobby he shared withPosada Carriles. The paintings were sold in Miami with some success, becoming an extra source of income.

On October 30, a member ofCORU traveled to Madrid, where he detonated two bombs to send a clear message: the imprisonment of Orlando Bosch did not mean CORU would sit idly by. No, sir. On November 6, 1976, a bomb exploded in the offices of Cubana de Aviación, and the next day another exploded in a bookstore with leftist literature.

The military court acquitted Posada Carriles, ruling that most of the evidence against him was null and void because it had been gathered outside Venezuela. A year after the attack on Cubana, a civil court in Venezuela ruled that the military court had no jurisdiction in the matter.

During the process, in 1977, with the help of the DISIP, Posada Carriles bribed the guards at San Carlos prison and escaped alongside Freddie Lugo. They then crossed half of Caracas to reach the Chilean embassy.

Even though the fugitives had participated weeks earlier in the assassination of General Augusto Pinochet's number one enemy in Washington, Orlando Letelier, Pinochet got rid of his two collaborators in the fight against communism and returned them to the Venezuelan police. In Santiago, the dictator and the new administration of Jimmy Carter were engaged in a reverse Cold War that would end with the defeat of the U.S. president. The most progressive Congress in U.S. history and a president with some hints of moral idealism had cornered the Chilean government, accusing it of participating in the terrorist attack against Letelier and his assistant Ronni Moffitt.

Lugo and Posada Carriles were returned to the Venezuelan authorities, much to the surprise and indignation of the exiles in Miami. It was an unforgivable act of betrayal, especially because it had not been committed by themselves. Posada Carriles held no grudge against the Chilean dictator.

—Pinochet was the best, the greatest dictator Latin America ever had—Posada Carriles confessed to Cuban journalist Ann Louise Bardach.[261]

He had to wait a few more years in prison until he could finally escape dressed as a priest and with the help of Jorge Mas Canosa, a Cuban millionaire businessman and CIA agent, participant in the failed Bay of Pigs invasion, president of the Cuban American National Foundation in Miami, and founder of TV Martí, both partly funded by the NED and the U.S. government. Posada Carriles was an old acquaintance of Mas Canosa. CIA records show that in July 1965, Mas Canosa had given him $5,000 to blow up a ship in Veracruz, Mexico, and any other Latin American country. Although a Cuban named Carballo offered to do the job for just $3,000, it wasn't about the money but the success of the operation, and Mas Canosa entrusted the task to another CIA comrade, Luis Posada Carriles. On July 28, 1965, he bought 125 pounds of Pentolite for just $375. On June 25, while processing a visa for Mexico with fake Puerto Rican papers, Posada Carriles informed Mas Canosa in Texas that he already had 100 pounds of C4. As was usual, most of these plans to blow up ships, planes, embassies, hotels, and assassinate presidents failed. But the notable inefficiency of the freedom fighters, despite unlimited resources, did not discourage the combatants.

A few years later, Posada Carriles escaped from San Juan de los Morros prison in Caracas, thanks to multiple assists from Miami. He managed to land in Santiago, Chile, seeking protection for his role in Letelier's assassination (a role he would both claim and deny numerous times), but Pinochet's regime was already too entangled with the FBI and Jimmy Carter, which is why they decided to return him to Venezuela.

Once again, Jorge Mas Canosa came to his rescue, arranging a private plane for him to travel to Costa Rica. Later, his journey extended to friendly dictatorships in El Salvador and Honduras. Canosa and the CIA handled the expenses, which were more like investments. In El Salvador, the Ministry of the Interior provided him with false documentation under the name Franco Rodríguez Mena. Another CIA asset who assisted him was the Cuban Otto Reich, tasked with overseeing CIA and Pentagon employees in charge of propaganda against the Nicaraguan government, which was planted in the press as if it were objective information, testimonials from victims of that government, or writings from Contra fighters themselves. With tens of millions of dollars funneled by the Agency, the goal was primarily to convince the American public of the danger posed by the Sandinista government, as polls indicated that the vast majority opposed intervening once again in Nicaragua.

—El Salvador is closer to Texas than Texas is to Massachusetts—said Ronald Reagan on a television broadcast, seeking public approval for friendly dictatorships and congressional funding for the Contras, shortly before the illegal arms sale to Iran scandal broke out, intended to supplement drug trafficking money in the fight against socialism in Latin America.

Much of this propaganda sold as journalism was handled by the *Office of Public Diplomacy for Latin America and the Caribbean*, founded by Cuban Otto Reich, until it had to be shut down in 1989 for misappropriation of Pentagon funds and accusations of fake news. Reich, after serving as ambassador to Venezuela and working as a professional lobbyist, would later reappear in the campaign to destabilize Venezuela and the subsequent coup against Hugo Chávez in 2002.

—If it weren't for my friends, like Jorge Mas Canosa, I would still be in prison—Luis Posada Carriles confessed to journalist Ann Louis Bardach.[262]

According to American *marine* Eugene Hasenfus, in Central America, Posada Carriles devoted himself to planning other forms of terror, from explosions of commercial planes to bombs in hotels and tourist locations in the Caribbean or any country that might have some connection to Cuba or Nicaragua. From businessman Mas Canosa alone, he received $200,000 as an advance for his sabotage operations.

—We Cubans were betrayed by the Venezuelans as well—Bosch said in an interview a year later—. When journalists asked me if I had identification from the DISIP, I firmly said no… But one day I will start talking.

Bosch will speak on many occasions. He moved freely through Venezuela with DISIP identification. The last attack on Cubana Flight 455 surprised many collaborators of Andrés Pérez's government, but Bosch claimed he had a pending meeting with him, scheduled for October 10. The Cuban plane incident upended everything, and the meeting was canceled.

—President Andrés Pérez is a traitor to democracy—Bosch told Fleetwood from his cell in Caracas— a traitor to the Cubans and also a traitor to the American cause. Some friends have told me that the Venezuelans brought me here only to betray me. I don't know. Maybe… I'm going to declare war on the Venezuelan government in the name of the Cuban cause. And if they want to put me on trial, they'll have to call the heads of the Disip, because I'm going to talk… Did you see how the offices of the Venezuelan airline yesterday blew up in Puerto Rico? My little Cubans did it, though none of them will claim responsibility for the attack.

Bosch didn't either.

In 1982, under the immunity of Miami, shortly before being executed in a luxurious bar, El Mono Morales Navarrete confessed in front of television cameras:

—I did it—he said, adjusting in his seat to emphasize his words. Me, along with others. Not Bosch.[263]

Bosch, as Posada Carriles and all who knew him would say, had a fixation with taking credit for all the major attacks. When he denied something, it was because the law was on his tail, but, like Posada Carriles, he did so with enough ambiguity not to kill the myth, like a wink to his comrades and, above all, to his donors, whom he called "the friends of the Cuban cause."

LUCKILY PINOCHET WASN'T A MARXIST

ON THE NIGHT OF OCTOBER 8TH, AMONG COFFEES and cigarettes, agent Carter Cornick transcribed his interview with a witness who remained anonymous in the report he sent to Propper:

—Michael Moffitt is a committed Marxist—said the witness, and Cornick typed the same words in his machine— but it's an intellectual commitment. He was never in favor of violence.[264]

The young woman accompanying him seemed annoyed by his words. She leaned her head forward a few centimeters in a gesture of disbelief.

—Luckily Pinochet isn't a Marxist...—she said, but this comment was more of political sarcasm and didn't qualify for the report— Not President Nixon, nor Mr. Kissinger, nor the owners of ITT who funded the coup in Chile, nor the newspapers nor the television complicit in capitalist massacres are Marxists, because if they were, they'd be suspected of being violent... Luckily we're capitalists, so our dead around the world don't make us seem like we're in favor of violence...

Carter Cornick didn't want to comment. He just waited for the young woman's indignation to pass so he could continue his investigation. He knew, from the courses he had taken, that you shouldn't argue with rebellious children to let their anger fade faster.

—*He was never in favor of violence*—Hunter read, and looked me in the eyes—. It sounds a bit cheesy. I'd remove it.

—Cheesy or not, it's in an FBI report—I defended myself.

—That's what everyone says. We mustn't forget that class struggle is a call to violence.

—The Pax Romana, the Pax of the slaveowners too—I said, unable to hide my annoyance—. In fact, all those *paxes* are the origin of violence.

—The story of the chicken and the egg—said Hunter.

—No—I said—. When I say "the origin of violence" I mean injustice.

—*Injustice*…—Hunter sighed— It's hard to define that in any objective way. But if we're talking about pure and simple violence, like someone coming to rob your house, rape your wife, kill your children, and shoot you…

—Are you talking about capitalist imperialism?

—I was referring to revolutions in the name of class struggle.

—Well, I believe in the class struggle. It's not a prescription but an observation. The problem is that the *class struggle* of the left has been demonized by the *class hatred* of the right.

—Right, left…

—Sorry, I forgot you were ambidextrous.

IF I'VE SEEN YOU, I DON'T REMEMBER

PERHAPS SHOCKED BY THE SCANDAL of the largest terrorist act in the history of the Caribbean, Carlos Andrés Pérez began to distance himself from the Cubans who, for more than ten years, had worked with and dominated the Venezuelan intelligence apparatus. In a statement intended to be made public, President Andrés Pérez assured the Cuban ambassador in Venezuela, Norberto Hernández Curbelo, that his government would do everything possible to investigate the case, starting by handing over Orlando Bosch, and that he hoped Cuba would also support Venezuela's anti-terrorist position at the next UN meeting, scheduled for the following month.

According to a CIA document dated October 14, three days after the bombing of the Cubana plane, on Saturday the 9thLuis Posada Carriles and Orlando García Vásquez led Orlando Bosch to the border with Colombia. Bosch crossed that same day. On October 12, agents of the DISIP, on the orders of the new director, General Raúl Jiménez Gainza, arrested his former boss, Posada Carriles. Among his belongings, they found a map detailing the daily route taken by Orlando Letelier from his home in Bethesda to the IPS offices in Washington DC.

That same day, New York Congressman Edward Koch sent a letter to the head of the Department of Justice, mentioning that U.S. intelligence services had detected the intention of Uruguayan military officers to send one of their own to assassinate him. The reason that had infuriated the Uruguayan military was the New York congressman's move to cut their financial aid, due to "the repression against their own people" and especially "the acts of terrorism perpetuated in Argentina against Uruguayan refugees."

The Uruguayan dictator, Dr. Aparicio Méndez, had decided to send Officer José Pons and Lieutenant Colonel José Nino Gavazzo, two members of the National Intelligence Service and participants in Operation Condor, to Washington. According to a later report written by Ambassador Harry Shlaudeman to Undersecretary of State Philip Habib, although they were two drunk blowhards, they were dangerous. The threats to kill Senator Koch, due to his criticism of the money sent by Washington to friendly dictatorships, could become a reality. For many Latin American military officers, the clear victory of Jimmy Carter in the November 2 elections could radicalize the position of the U.S. left, a situation that had to be stopped by eliminating another undesirable, as had been the case with Orlando Letelier.

José Pons and Nino Gavazzo (the colonel who laughed every time a victim tied by their feet and hands screamed in pain) did not receive their visas. This, at the military club, was taken as a humiliating offense. Thirty years later, on the occasion of President George W. Bush's visit to the first socialist president of Uruguay, the wives of the torturers convicted by Uruguayan justice will hand him a letter reminding the U.S. president of everything their husbands had done for the United States, for freedom, and for the salvation of the West, asking him to intervene against the government of Uruguay which, although constitutional and elected by vote, they will label as a regime for allowing justice to prosecute their husbands in "unfair judicial processes."[265]

Orlando Has The Details

Despite his repeated demonstrations of being a valuable and reliable asset since 1960, and despite his sale of insider information about his comrades since January 1976, Posada Carriles was not reintegrated into the ranks of the CIA. In a vulnerable position since his official resignation from SIDE after the victory of Andrés Pérez in the elections, shortly after the bombing in Washington, a classified CIA document recorded his words:

—Now that the world knows what we did in Washington, we won't stop. Our next target will be a Cuban airline… and Orlando has the details.

The CIA not only recruited individuals with a clear psychological profile, like Manuel Noriega, but it also never directly involved itself in the actions it planned, as in the death of Congolese leader Patrice Lumumba. It was the trigger, the great enabler. Others reaped the glory, except when some agents like David Atlee Philips,

El exilio del terror

Howard Hunt or Antoni Veciana retired and decided to publish their memoirs.

When it came to eliminating an individual or a world leader, the Agency not only ensured that the death was dubious, like an accident, a heart attack, or some more stubborn cancer, but it also made sure everything was done by third parties. For that of *do everything in a way that allows you to deny it*; if you're discovered, deny it against any evidence. It didn't take a genius. It was enough to be a son of a bitch.

After some time, some CIA mercenaries became just that—dangerous individuals better not to support directly and, in case they planned other attacks or assassinations, it was best to let them do it.

For the CIA and the FBI, from the beginning, Posada Carriles was involved in the plan against Cubana Flight 455. Orlando Bosch was too. Bosch would never admit it, though at different times he justified it because, according to him, the passengers were not innocent but combatants.

—In this war, there are no civilians—confirmed Posada Carriles, from his apartment in Caracas and from a TV studio in Miami, years later—. Everyone is a combatant.

On another occasion, after acknowledging his involvement and then denying it shortly after, he said:

—The bombing of Cubana 455 was the most effective sabotage against Fidel Castro.

It was El Mono Morales who arrested Orlando Bosch at the home of another Cuban naturalized Venezuelan, Suarez Quiñones, on Monday, October 11, by order of Orlando García Vásquez. According to El Mono, the team that planned the technical details of the successful attack on Flight 455 was made up of five agents from DISIP, two Venezuelans, and three Cubans, including himself. His old enemy, Orlando Bosch, couldn't take any credit, even though he had been indirectly involved in the attack.[266]

Bosch was locked up for a few years in the Caracas prison. The Monkey, no. Never. His status as a triple informant for the CIA, the

FBI, and the Disip protected him from any trial. Not from the vendetta that would end his life in Miami, though for less political reasons, months after his historic interview for En 1 Hora.

According to Luis Posada Carriles, Bosch never missed an opportunity to claim credit for any violent action that succeeded, even if his involvement had been rather marginal. For legal convenience, now battered by multiple failures and gallons of Bacardí rum, Orlando Bosch accepted his lawyers' advice and applied the simple CIA formula: evidence doesn't matter; always deny it, never admit it.

—I didn't give orders to García Vásquez—insisted The Monkey Morales—; I received them and carried them out.[267]

At Suarez Quiñones' house were Bosch and Gustavo Castillo, another explosives expert responsible for assembling the bombs that brought down the plane. Even though Orlando Bosch, The Monkey, and Michael Townley considered themselves part of an elite global group of C4 explosives experts, in reality, at that time there were more than a thousand Cuban exiles who were experts in explosives, because the CIA had trained them in the deadly plasticine. Perhaps a bit more knowledgeable or less egotistical than the rest, the American Michael Townley downplayed this specialty. According to Townley, even a child could learn how to handle C4 and set up the detonator correctly. C4 was so safe you could hammer it without any risk, Townley said. There was nothing special about it.

Of course, perhaps as the powerful CIA agent for Latin America, David Atlee Phillips, said, only a few Cubans had the guts to do something serious, which is why the recruitment of new agents and collaborators should focus more on the psychological characteristics of the candidate than on their ideological convictions. Among Gustavo Castillo's merits was the attempted kidnapping of the Cuban consul in Mérida, which had cost the life of the consul's guard.

WITH ALLENDE, THOUSANDS OF DISSIDENTS WOULD HAVE DISAPPEARED

ON OCTOBER 14, 1976, TWO YEARS AFTER Friedrich von Hayek won the Nobel Prize in Economics, one of his disciples, Milton Friedman, received the same award. At the same time, the admitted pedophile Daniel Carleton Gajdusek was honored with the Nobel Prize in Medicine for his research in New Guinea.

Friedman and Hayek visited Chile and celebrated the economic freedom of their theories forcibly applied in that country. Pure freedom without government intervention that produced prosperity. Prosperity. Always that about prosperity.

At the same time, Washington approved another $38 million in aid to the Chilean regime to promote the economic miracle of freedom and good example.

—I *prefer a liberal dictatorship to a democracy that doesn't respect liberalism*—Hayek declared to *El Mercurio*.[268]

Back in the United States, he confirmed:

—I can't say that during my visit to Chile I met anyone who said that individual freedoms under Pinochet were worse than during Allende's time.

When Friedman returned from one of his triumphant visits to Chile, he was met with a protest at the University of Chicago. Despite all the aid from London, Washington, and transnational corporations, Chile was moving from one economic crisis to another. Faced with the protests at the university, Professor Friedman, the newly minted Nobel laureate, defended his support for Pinochet:

—If Allende had been allowed to remain in power—he said— it is possible that in Chile, in addition to a terrible economic crisis, thousands of dissidents would have suffered unjust persecution, imprisonment, torture, and many would have been killed.[269]

TO UNDERSTAND THE DRUG TRADE, YOU HAVE TO BE PART OF IT

ON OCTOBER 15, *EL NACIONAL* of Caracas headline: "Orlando Bosch Arrested in Caracas" during a raid on a property of Cuban exiles.

Other newspapers reported that, *"in the DISIP investigation into the sabotage of the Cuban plane, Luis Posada, Oleg Gueton Rodríguez, Celsa Toledo, Francisco Núñez were also detained, and other documents and equipment related to the sabotage were found in a research office in Florida"*

The same newspaper, on April 8, 1978, headline: Homosexuals Endanger State Security, citing former ambassador Francisco Herrera Luque who denounced Ricardo Morales Navarrete as the author of the theft of documents from the Venezuelan embassy in Mexico and identified him as one of the major drug traffickers. In the interview for Miami television, El Mono Morales not only claimed involvement in the attack on the Cubana aircraft but also admitted to having been a drug trafficker.

—Because to understand the drugs that the communists traffic—he justified—, you have to be a drug smuggler...

The government of Trinidad and Tobago detained two Venezuelan citizens suspected of participating in the terrorist act in Barbados. Among the primary suspects were Luis Posada Carriles, Oleg Gueton Rodríguez, Celsa Toledo, Francisco Núñez, and Orlando Bosch, who at the time was carrying a fake Costa Rican passport. Also arrested was a former CIA agent and former head of Operations for the DISIP, Luis Posada Carriles, after the police raided a private detective office he had in Florida.[270]

In reality, Orlando Bosch was never captured. The DISIP agent, Fredy Romero, went to look for him. With a photo of Bosch in hand

and his name on the back, he found him at the corner of Cine Junín. He was waiting and did not resist.

When Bosch's old enemy, El Mono Navarrete, took him to his apartment, he handed him four thousand bolivars and told him to leave, but Bosch decided to stay. At the time, El Mono Navarrete, aside from being the Chief of Division 54 of the DISIP, was in Venezuela on a CIA mission.

In a Global War, There Are No Innocents

ON OCTOBER 21 AT 11:00 AM, JOURNALISTS Hilda Inclán, Taylor Branch, and John Rothchild arrived in Caracas to report on the latest attack. Shortly after, they identified the head of Foreign Research of Venezuela's secret police, the Disip, as a CIA agent. El Mono Morales would deny it, deny knowing them. Hours later, he would eject the journalists from the hotel at gunpoint.

Ricardo Morales Navarrete had a long and dense file with the CIA, of which only part is known. All his comrades in Miami and Union City knew it. Andrés Pérez in Venezuela, Pinochet and the DINA officers in Chile also knew it. They didn't know, but they suspected, that for years El Mono had been selling information about his own comrades to the FBI and the CIA itself, a practice that was quite common among the rest of the aspiring leaders of the exile terrorist groups. A year before being assassinated in Miami in a drug-related settling of scores, El Mono would admit it on television: not only had he been a member of the CIA; he had also recruited many others, such as Orlando García Vásquez, who ended up on the Agency's payroll.

—You interpret the CIA as an organization defending democratic and Western countries...—journalist Francisco Chao Hermida would say during El Mono's final television interview in Miami.

—Of which I am a part—confirmed El Mono.

If the CIA's secret reports were filled with complaints about the exaggerated egocentrism of the Cubans recruited to invade Cuba, Morales himself also took every opportunity to mention that, after the failed invasion, he had participated in operations assigned by the Agency to the army of mercenaries led by the Irishman Mike Hoare and other Cubans, in support of the bloody and neo-colonial dictatorship of Mobutu Sese Seko in Congo. By then, in 1964, Mobutu had begun an extensive assassination campaign, a year before Che Guevara, known in Miami as The Assassin, arrived along with a hundred black Cubans, aiming to support the independence rebels.

On the other hand, El Mono's B26 squadron was composed of Cuban pilots from Miami, trained and financed by the CIA. The B26 squadron carried out heroic bombings from the skies of Congo, reported the Miami News. According to the same newspaper, El Mono Morales had assisted in Washington's fight in favor of South Africa's apartheid regime under the command of a certain Robertson and alongside the mercenary Michael Hoare, also known in Congo and South Africa as "The Mad Irishman." Hoare, who led the commando formed by Belgians and Cubans from Miami, claimed the title of being the first mercenary in the world to have defeated Che Guevara. Meanwhile, at the same time that it declared Nelson Mandela and his movement as terrorists, Washington insisted on defending the South African apartheid regime for being its great ally in the struggle for freedom in Africa.

—Can we abandon a country that has stood by our side in every war we've fought—President Ronald Reagan would question himself regarding South Africa's apartheid regime, in a CBS News interview in 1981—; a country that strategically is essential for the Free World in its mineral production, something we all need?[271]

Branch had interviewed El Mono Morales in Miami, in 1974.[272] Based on this interview and many others that followed over the decades, the most important conspirators, such as El Mono Morales, Guillermo Novo, José Dionisio Suárez, Luis Posada Carriles, Orlando Bosch, Frank Castro, Orlando García Vásquez, and Virgilio

Paz were trapped in an unsolvable contradiction: they could only operate effectively and with some semblance of security in secrecy or under false names, yet they were all obsessed with their own egos, desperate to be major historical figures, and consequently, they hated anyone who might cast a shadow or pose any competition, whether it was Fidel Castro, El Che Guevara, or any of their own comrades in exile.

From a psychoanalytic perspective, one could argue that they were like brothers who hated each other while competing for resources and recognition from the father figure. Naturally, they also hated the father (the power that had castrated them; the totem and the body represented in the wedding cake and in the central absence of all repressive superstition), embodied by the CIA and, by extension, by the most powerful country in the world, onto which they projected their feelings of grandeur and from which they absolved themselves of responsibility for every failure and defeat.

The CIA reports, even before the Bay of Pigs invasion, were no less psychoanalytic. They described their own recruits from exile as "egomaniacs, obsessed with their macho reputation, their petty and childish rivalries, their tendency to act impulsively... incapable of working as a team for a common goal," and entangled in political disputes; "everyone wanted to be a brigade commander."[273]

Some members of the same exile community laughed at Bosch's obsession with taking credit for any violent act, even those in which he had barely been a witness. Later, Bosch would deny everything in each interview, knowing that his followers applauded his ability to lie without hesitation. The strategy was always the same: when questioned by a judge or journalist about his involvement in each terrorist attack, his response was more or less consistent:

—I neither deny nor confirm.

—I am innocent, but I applaud the attacks, because in a global war, there are no innocents.

—If I told you I participated, I would be arrested, so I'll say I had nothing to do with it...

This strict ambiguity was also functional: the goal of a terrorist act is to attribute it to a group that seeks to spread terror and raise funds from sympathizers of The cause. The terrorist act is illegal, but it is nothing without publicity, just like any company trying to sell a product.

Three Inappropriate Journalists

LET'S RETURN TO THE CARACAS AIRPORT for a moment. The Miami NEWS OF OCTOBER 22, 1976, CONFIRMED THAT ONE OF THE JOURNALISTS EXPELLED FROM VENEZUELA, Hilda Inclán, worked for that newspaper. The day before, Thursday, October 21, at 11:15 AM, shortly after the plane that had taken her to Caracas landed, Inclán saw El Mono Morales approach and greet the Miami police officers who had traveled on the same flight. Later, she learned that the first officer he embraced was a Mr. Díaz, a Miami police officer and son-in-law of Ronaldo Martínez, one of those involved in the Watergate scandal, which led to the resignation of President Nixon, but not to the prosecution of the CIA officers and collaborators who organized the espionage in Washington.

—Mr. Morales...—said the journalist, trying to break through the airport security barrier.

—My name is Ramón Bravo—Morales corrected her, and he walked away.

When Inclán arrived at the Arauco Hilton, she was informed that, although her reservation for room 8-N had been confirmed, it had already been occupied, and there were no other rooms available.

That afternoon, Taylor Branch and John Rothchild also recognized Morales during a meeting with Miami officers. The journalists tried to contact him to get his response regarding his testimony against Rolando Otero in Jacksonville, and about the case that ultimately sent Orlando Bosch to jail, thanks to his testimony.

Taylor Branch recalled the many interviews he had conducted with Ricardo Morales. One of the phrases he remembered most was about Morales' experience with the CIA:

—The only thing I learned from them—he had said, visibly upset with his former bosses— was how to handle weapons and how to place plastic explosives, like the powerful C4, in embassies and airports.

Two years before the Caracas incidents, El Mono Morales had admitted in an interview with Taylor Branch that he had lost all idealism in Africa. His work and that of his Cuban comrades was to machine-gun the population they considered rebellious, like a firefighter hosing down a fire, or like a general of the Free World dropping napalm on a city in the middle of the night.

—The mercenaries had no problem burning entire villages and killing all their inhabitants—wrote historian Justin Podur of New York University later, referring to the most recent bombings in Africa.

The CIA loves those troubled souls. When he returned to Miami in 1965, El Mono Morales opened his own business as a Secret Agent, using the contacts he had made with the CIA and the persuasion techniques he had learned in just a few years, such as the use of C4 plastic explosives and the stone-faced denial of any accusation regarding illegal actions. He wasn't the first Cuban in Florida to open a similar business, needless to say. He also offered himself as an informant for the FBI, which guaranteed him immunity for his own crimes while sending one of his comrades, like Orlando Bosch, to prison, accused of doing the same in 1968: placing bombs here and there, driven by some ideological or personal reason. On several occasions, Morales assisted Bosch in the production of his bombs, sometimes packages with dynamite, other times gray plasticine packages. Sometimes it was just moral support. Later, Bosch himself would be betrayed once again by Morales, and by another of his comrades, Luis Posada Carriles, who needed to rejoin the CIA's payroll. By then, Posada Carriles was in a precarious situation, after the socialist Andrés Pérez became president of Venezuela.

In 1974, for the second time, Morales betrayed Bosch to the FBI, as they were both in Caracas sharing beers. Bosch was accused of violating his parole by traveling abroad to resume his political activities. He returned to Miami with Chilean bodyguards and several suitcases of money. Mysteriously, once in the United States, the State Department decided not to prosecute him. His case was dismissed. Shortly after, Bosch was welcomed by the regime of Augusto Pinochet in Santiago. From there, he traveled to several countries with the same mission as always: to plant explosives somewhere, against anyone, if it was for the cause of freedom.

In early 1976, Bosch was invited by Luis Posada Carriles and by El Mono Morales to work with them again, in Caracas. Although he was wary, his situation (that of his new Chilean wife and his newborn daughter) in the countries where he had sought refuge was very unstable. He accepted.

In Caracas, Bosch, El Mono, Posada Carriles, and other Cubans from CORU continued to be shielded by the delicate and strategic silence of President Carlos Andrés Pérez, who saw Fidel Castro and other regional leaders as marble statues casting too long a shadow. The Cubans in his secret police were just another card to play when the time came. When the time came (i.e., the terrorist attacks against Letelier and the Cubana airline flight), he denied them three times.

But let's return to the Arauco Hilton Hotel in Caracas. After several arguments over the room she had reserved, and after failing to find another hotel in the area, that night Hilda Inclán returned to the Arauco Hilton. The employees allowed her to spend the night in the lobby, but 45 minutes later, she woke up startled:

—Come on, come on—l Mono told her—Get up, right now.

Still not fully awake, Hilda Inclán began to follow Morales until she saw a bathroom. She hurried in and locked the door before El Mono could push it open. After a long wait pressed against the door, she heard the voices of Taylor and Rothchild and rushed out. The men had been forced to leave the hotel after Morales went to fetch both of them from their room.

Finally, they got lucky and didn't end up on a cliff. It's not that easy to make journalists disappear, especially when all three have U.S. citizenship. The three were taken to a car that drove them to the airport.

—Are you going to testify in Jacksonville?—Hilda Inclán asked on the way to the airport—I mean, in the Otero case, for terrorism…

Morales ignored the question.

—Don't you remember I interviewed you four times two years ago?—Taylor asked, as soon as they arrived at the airport.

—What are you talking about, kid?—Morales said—I don't even know you.

Twenty agents from the DISIP pushed the journalists down a hallway and then onto the plane. The journalists resisted and began informing the passengers about the situation, so the agents drew their guns and removed Taylor from the boarding line. After a scuffle and protests from the passengers, Rothschild managed to stay on the plane.

Inclán and Taylor were taken to a DISIP barracks, where they were held incommunicado for over ten hours.

—The lady is Cuban—said one of the agents—She must leave the country. The American stays.

Shortly after, both their visas were stamped as Revoked, and automatically, they became illegal immigrants, ensuring that those troublesome individuals wouldn't return to the country for a long time. Then, they were put on the 4:00 am American Airlines flight, heading to Miami.[274]

In March 1977, El Mono Morales would admit that the Number Two of Venezuela's secret police, who had deported the journalists, was him, El Mono Morales.[275] Number One was Posada Carriles, but everyone already knew that. Somehow, he had to claim the credit. Miami's B and C class had to know in which league that short guy everyone called, with pretended affection and hidden disdain, El Mono was playing.

He would deny it vehemently again later, when necessary.

EL MONO'S SKILLS

AS WE HAVE SEEN, FOR YEARS, Ricardo Morales had been one of the top chiefs of the Venezuelan secret police, under the control of Luis Posada Carriles. He had been expeditiously naturalized as a Venezuelan, which had allowed him to become a citizen of three countries. Undoubtedly, El Mono was the most enigmatic figure among all the Cuban exiles. Not the most dangerous, but the most enigmatic.

He had worked for Castro's secret police, which was nothing exceptional among the members of the Batista community in Miami. Nor were lies and betrayal something exceptional among the members of the community, but Morales' talent for playing dumb, for distracting, for lying and deceiving was, at the very least, exceptional. He had worked for the CIA in America and Africa in the early 60s. By the end of the decade, he had already betrayed his own comrades. As we saw before, the most notable case was the repeated betrayal of Orlando Bosch, whom he sent to prison in Miami for one of the attacks in which he himself had collaborated. As a collaborator and informant for the FBI, he had secured immunity for his own crimes. In Venezuela, he became an untouchable figure within the police and a high-ranking official of Disip. Like Posada Carriles, he befriended Bosch again and betrayed him once more, just as Posada Carriles had done, in exchange for CIA protection. During the investigation of the terrorist attack against Letelier in Washington and the bombing of Cubana Flight 455 in Barbados, he entered and left the United States as many times as he pleased, all while the detectives on the case kept close tabs on him.

"It's unbelievable," FBI agent Cornick eventually admitted. "El Mono is a real gunslinger. He works for us as an informant, and the first thing he does when he leaves here is spread the rumor that we were the ones who brought down the Cubana plane."[276]

Years later, in an interview for the Miami television program *En 1 Hora*, he admitted that Orlando García Vásquez had been one of the participants in the plan to bring down Cubana Flight 455. García had been one of the Cuban expatriates in Venezuela, thanks to his friendship with Rómulo Betancourt and his Foreign Minister, Carlos Andrés Pérez.

—I was the one who recruited Orlando García Vásquez for the CIA in Venezuela,—said El Mono Morales, who, in turn, had been protected by García Vásquez in Venezuela.

The recruitment, following the well-known ideological and psychological process (such as the chest straps of *lie detector machines* to rule out flaws, such as homosexuality and other character deviations), had been approved in March 1972 and confirmed a year later. One of the points in his favor, included in his resume, was being friends with the candidate Carlos Andrés Pérez, who at the time was still suspected of communist sympathies.

The journalist from the CIA's multimedia outlet La Voz de las Américas and collaborator with the Cuban exiles, Francisco Chao Hermida, asked him:

—Don't you feel any shame for having been a CIA man?

—Shame would be if I had been an agent of the KGB or the Cuban DGI.

—It's not shameful for you because you interpret the CIA as an organization defending the democratic countries of the West.

—Of which I am a part…

WHY DO THEY ALWAYS BLAME US?

—I DON'T KNOW WHY THEY ALWAYS BLAME US for all the terrorist attacks—complained Guillermo Novo.
—What do you think?—asked the prosecutor Eugene Propper.
—I think there's a bias against Cubans in Florida.
—I have nothing for or against you—said Propper—. The only Cuban I knew before all this mess was my Spanish teacher...
—Why am I a suspect in this case?
—Because another Cuban implicated you in the attack.
—How is that?—asked Guillermo Novo—. Who could do something like that?
—Orlando Bosch—said Propper, aware of the growing rivalry and power struggle among the paramilitaries of Miami and Union City, embodied in Bosch and the eldest of the Novo brothers.
—Bosch is a liar, a traitor to freedom—reported Propper—. Bosch is a hard-drinking drunk always seeking notoriety.[277]
—How do you explain the bombing of the Cubana flight?
—I believe that was a move, either by the CIA or Venezuelan Intelligence, to counter the influence Havana's intelligence was gaining among the university youth in Caracas. Through newspaper distribution, they planned attacks against the Venezuelan government... The bombing of the plane (and on this I agree with Mr. Morales Navarrete) was intended to try to halt the communist government of Cuba... Later, things exploded, arrests followed, and the mess got mixed up...

According to Orlando Bosch, El Mono and his CIA recruit, Orlando García Vázquez, had planned the bombing of Cubana 455, not with C4 but with two sticks of dynamite in a suitcase checked at the Timehri Airport in Guyana, placed in different spots, one in the bathroom, set to explode with a timer detonator during the flight between Trinidad and Barbados. In his memoirs, he stated: "Chao Hermida passed the information to Posada and one of his defenders, Raymond Aguiar, recorded a video in Miami *of El Mono, who confirmed the version he had given to Chao Hermida and, in passing, harshly attacked President Carlos Andrés Pérez.*"

In Venezuela, and at the direction of President Carlos Andrés Pérez, the official investigation into the attack was led by one of the main suspects, the Cuban Orlando García Vázquez, who trusted the report to another Cuban CIA operative, Antonio Veciana, with a copy to Washington, and gave his word to Carlos Andrés that he wouldn't speak further on the matter.

THE STONE IN THE HORNET'S NEST

ON TUESDAY, OCTOBER 19, THE UNDERSECRETARY of Intelligence and Research Harold Henry Saunders informed the Secretary of State, Henry Kissinger, of the accusations by Fidel Castro regarding the involvement of the Venezuelan Hernán Ricardo Lozano in the explosion of flight CU-455. Ricardo Lozano was one of the accomplices of Félix Martínez Suárez, another Venezuelan agent of the CIA. Saunders mentioned that, according to Castro, "for the moment we cannot determine whether the attack was directly prepared by the CIA or indirectly through Cuban exiles with the agency's assistance; we believe the first possibility is the correct one. The CIA was directly involved in the bombing of Cubana flight 455 in Barbados."[278]

Ricardo Lozano also worked sporadically for the DISIP, photographing suspects. When Posada Carriles arrived in Caracas, he supplemented his salary with a private detective firm he himself invented. According to a classified CIA report, the Venezuelan government was concerned that some of these connections might reach the headlines of the national press.

Shortly afterward, the U.S. consulate officer in Caracas, Joseph Leo, admitted to having helped Ricardo Lozano with some visas, although he claimed that the phone number found in his address book must have been provided by Posada Carriles. That same day, the U.S. Department of Justice summoned José Suárez and the Novo brothers to appear before a grand jury for an earlier case, the Letelier case. Suárez had planted an explosive five days earlier on a Soviet ship, in addition to participating in the bombing of the New York Music Academy on July 24.

On October 22, the Panamanian National Guard informed the FBI of the statements made by the owner of Pasco's SeaFood, located on the outskirts of Miami and not far from where the most notorious attacks were usually planned, at 1030 West 23rd Street in Hialeah. According to Mr. Manuel Cháves, Luis Posada Carriles, in association with Aldo Vera and Orlando Bosch, was behind the latest attack on the Cuban airline.

In turn, Pastor Manuel Espinosa accused Cháves of importing seafood from Cuba, which made his business an ally of the island's regime. These accusations were never proven but were a classic of the genre. One of the accused, Flavio Mora, president of Imperial Seafood in Panama, denied any kind of importation from Cuba, and the FBI found no evidence to support the pastor's accusations. Importing seafood from Cuba was a major crime, punishable. Carrying out attacks with C4 and raising funds from drug trafficking for the fight for freedom were justified.

For some reason, Pastor Manuel Espinosa, in just two weeks, had changed his open criticism of the armed groups of the Cuban exile into an accusation against a whistleblower of those same groups. During a press conference held by the pastor, he was accompanied the entire time by Armando López Estrada and Jorge "Bombillo" González. The former was a Batista policeman, a CIA employee, military chief of the Bay of Pigs Veterans Association, and founding member of CORU in the Dominican Republic. The second, military leader of anti-Castro groups based in Miami.[279] Bombillo had participated with Orlando Bosch in the 1968 attack on the Polish ship, which is why he was prohibited from possessing firearms. In February 1982, he would be arrested in Miami for the possession of a stockpile of pistols and AR-15 rifles, intended for the training of paramilitary groups in Florida.[280]

An FBI memorandum reported that in early November 1976, Dominican Republic Air Force Colonel, Juan Armand Montes, attended a meeting at the residence of a former senator of Fulgencio Batista in Santo Domingo. Among those who attended the meeting were Orlando Bosch, Luis Posada Carriles and others, who discussed several terrorist attacks, including the bombing of the Cubana plane.[281]

NOVEMBER

It was Unintentionally Intentional

—Look,—George H. Bush told Propper— I'm appalled by the attack on Letelier. Obviously we can't allow people to come here, to the capital, and kill foreign diplomats and American citizens in this way. It would be a dreadful precedent. As Director of the CIA, I want to help you. As an American citizen, too. But I also know that the CIA can't help in many situations like this. We have some issues... Tony, tell him what they are.

—The first problem—said Anthony Lapham— is that every time we've tried to help Justice, they've screwed us. They always promise that if we give them this or that information, they'll just use it as background, but then someone starts taking our source as a witness.

—I see—said Propper— but it's hard to believe there's no way for you to be involved in this case. If someone comes into the country from abroad and kills people here, in Washington, that must be your problem. Who's going to stop them from doing it again, right?

—If it's a national security matter, yes—said Lapham— but we still don't know if this is a security matter. First, we'd have to investigate the crime to know.

According to the *New York Times* of October 12, "*intelligence officials* [from the Ford Administration] said that apparently the FBI *and the CIA* had ruled out the idea that Mr. Letelier was killed by agents of the Chilean military junta... Intelligence officials said a parallel investigation was looking into the possibility that Mr. Letelier had been killed by members of the Chilean left, as a way to obstruct U.S. relations with the military junta."

On November 1, the *Washington Post* reported a personal leak from CIA Director, George Bush, according to which his agency believed that agents of the current Chilean military junta were not involved in the assassination of Letelier. According to informed sources, CIA Director George H. Bush, expressed this opinion in a conversation the week before with Secretary of State Kissinger.

I Didn't go either

—INFORMATION...—SAID THE MAN IN THE WHITE GUAYABERA, with an elbow on the bar— like people, like everything, is a market and, like everything in a market, it's bought and sold.

On the bar's TV, a woman dressed in red was saying that RCA ColorTrak was making television *"better and better."*

—Where did you get those ideas?—asked the FBI agent.

—What do you mean where, kid? I learned it from you right here, damn it.

A classified FBI report, dated November 5 and addressed to Secretary of State Henry Kissinger, summarized:

"Our confidential source from Miami, who in the past has provided reliable information, stated that the attack on Cubana de Aviación's DC-8 was partly planned in Caracas, Venezuela, during two meetings attended by Morales Navarrete, Luis Posada Carriles, and Frank Castro... On one occasion, Gustavo Castillo was also present. The first meeting took place in Morales Navarrete's apartment at the Anauco Hilton Hotel. According to Morales Navarrete, the same group had already attempted to bomb other flights in Panama and Jamaica... They are all members of CORU, *an anti-Castro terrorist group that has already carried out numerous attacks across the Caribbean."*[282]

Henry Kissinger, who had also been the target of a failed assassination attempt by Orlando Bosch in Costa Rica, was informed. He did nothing to facilitate the prosecution of any of them. Quite the contrary. Politicians, congressmen, and presidents who shared his ideology never tired of handing out pardons when some of them were found guilty of murder and terrorism by a court, whether national or foreign.

When Luis Posada Carriles was arrested in Venezuela, a printed map of Washington was found in his home with the daily route of Orlando Letelier to the IPS offices marked by hand. Later, El Mono Morales also admitted that he had worked on the plan that killed Letelier and his assistant's wife.

Posada Carriles vehemently denied it.

Investigate, from Here on Down.

On Monday, November 8, the CIA director, George H. Bush, flew to Miami and, in the afternoon, walked through Little Havana. He then met with the FBI agent in Miami, Julius Matson, and with the head of the anti-terrorism squad investigating Cubans in Florida. What had Bush come for?

—Just be careful with the boundaries you cross in the investigation—he said, kindly, with his classic smile.

—What do you mean?

According to investigator Donald Freed, Bush warned them:

—We would not look kindly upon you continuing your investigation above the level of ordinary Cubans.

The phrase was ambiguous and vulgar, to say the least. What did "ordinary Cubans" mean? That yacht owners didn't walk?

In the end, Bush's biographers, Webster Tarpley and Anton Chaitkina, will conclude, "some low-income Cubans were convicted in a trial in which Townley secured a guilty plea and received a lighter sentence than the rest. The material on Townley under his various aliases disappeared from INS files, and the July-August cable traffic records between Walters and Bush were deleted. There was undoubtedly obstruction of justice; there was undoubtedly a cover-up."[283]

Hours later, at New York's Kennedy Airport and just a few meters from the American Airlines counter, someone stopped flight attendant Elizabeth Ryden by grabbing her arm.

—Elizabeth—someone said—. Tell your little friend, that Larry Wack, not to stick his nose into Chile's affairs.

Ryden looked at him for a second. He concluded:

—Otherwise, you won't remain so pretty… Because… *booooom*! You understand me, don't you?

—Yes, yes—said Elizabeth— yes, I understand.

Someone smiled. Mission accomplished.

Shortly after, Elizabeth fell to the floor, screaming, in a panic attack.

The flight attendant, girlfriend of the FBI agent Larry Wack, was removed from her flight, fearing another attack on a commercial airline.

Larry Wack had been interviewing several Cubans in Union City, New Jersey, with the aim of clarifying the recent attacks in September. According to his colleague Propper, the procedure and the ability to gather information by the Cubans in Miami and Union City revealed a sophisticated military intelligence system.

The Cuban Nationalist Movement threatened Propper with death, a plan that was denounced by prosecutor Griffin Bell and lawyer Robert Fiske. Ignacio Novo also threatened the grand jury:

—If my brother Guillermo ends up in jail, rest assured that this will be a total war between the CNM and the Department of Justice… And if Washington dares to normalize relations with Cuba, well, guess what…? There'll be corpses everywhere.[284]

The motto of all CNM headquarters was "Save Cuba or sink the whole world."

A version of Cuba.

KILL IT once More

ON NOVEMBER 26, THE XIII CONGRESS of the Socialist International was held in Geneva. The vice president of the International was the president of Venezuela, Carlos Andrés Pérez, and his latest trade agreement to sell oil to the Soviet Union had gone down poorly among those who wanted to save Cuba or sink the rest of the world. To make matters worse, at that same congress, the former chancellor of West Germany, Willy Brandt, was to be elected president of the Socialist International.

Weeks earlier, Michael Townley had informed DINA of his unwillingness to operate outside of Chile for a while, at least until the Letelier case cooled down. To his dismay, Colonel Espinosa assigned him a new mission: to assist a group of two Argentinians and two Chileans from DINA who were going to assassinate some journalists in Paris.

—The enemies of Chile are resurfacing in Europe—said the colonel, in response to Townley's displeased expressions.[285]

For the Pinochet government, the end of the fascist dictatorships in Portugal and Spain was another clear attack against freedom. Two years earlier, the Chilean regime had hijacked the popular song, Libre, by Spanish singer Nino Bravo. Without asking permission and taking advantage of Bravo's death in an accident, they had turned it into the most recognized anthem of their Regime of Freedom, while the military used it during torture sessions against dangerous dissidents. Bravo had died four years earlier, and the song had been inspired by rebellion against Franco's regime, not the death of a young man shot by a guard from communist Germany.

True to his nature, Townley did not refuse a superior's order. According to the FBI, the two journalists on DINA's blacklist, whose names were never revealed, planned to found a socialist newspaper in Paris, which would undoubtedly be a tool for defaming Latin American dictatorships.

Less than two months after the murder of Orlando Letelier in Washington, Michael Townley and Mariana Callejas traveled to France. Callejas' new fake passport was issued under the name Carmen Luisa Correa Letelier. Shortly after landing in Paris, they were informed by the Chilean embassy that the French secret police had received leaked information and warned them that they would make the details of the plot public if it were carried out.[286]

—This means someone knows about our activities over the past few months—Townley warned Colonel Espinosa—. It's imperative that we return as soon as possible.

—No—said the colonel—. You can't come back.

—What are you talking about?

—We need to save the operation. You must go to Madrid. This can't have been leaked because we just decided it. Spain is slipping away. We don't know how the King could allow this...

—What is our role in all this?

—We know Altamirano will participate in the PSOE congress.

—Carlos Altamirano?

—The very one. The secretary of the Socialist Party of Chile. The one your friends from Patria y Libertad couldn't eliminate in time while Allende was corrupting this country. The same one you two and Virgilio Paz couldn't eliminate in Mexico. The same one who survived when the successful attack on Bernardo Leighton in Rome happened. The same one now strolls through Europe badmouthing Chile. The same son of a bitch who hates the freedom and the homeland that fed him.

—I don't understand. Please, speak more clearly.

—Kill him.

—How?

—*Kill him*—Colonel Espinosa emphasized.

—But how?

—That's your job. Contact the members of the Francoist Phalanx. They're everywhere. They know Alfa, they know everyone... Look through your contacts.

Townley and Callejas prowled around the hotel in Madrid where many of the congress participants were staying. Coming or going, they saw the newly elected president of the Socialist International, former German Chancellor Willy Brandt, and the Prime Minister of Portugal Mário Soares.

—François Mitterrand, congressman from France.

—Olof Palme, that was the Prime Minister of Sweden, until recently.

—This mission is madness—Callejas complained—. There must be security agents everywhere.

Townley managed to get Altamirano's room number, but it turned out to be fake.

One evening, they managed to sit at the next table in a restaurant where Altamirano was dining. Michael and Callejas began speaking in English, posing as tourists so that Altamirano's companions wouldn't stop speaking Spanish for fear of being overheard. They needed to take note of some place where the target might be alone in the coming days, but they reached no definitive conclusion. It was one of those cases where the Cubans could have helped with some prostitute. With or without the Cubans, it seemed like another mission destined for failure.

—We still haven't been able to find out where the target will be for the operation—Townley reported over the phone, fearing the call might be intercepted.

—It doesn't matter!—shouted Colonel Espinosa, in an unprecedented tone—. I don't care. Kill him. Just kill him once and for all!

—Yes, Colonel—said Townley.

But Townley had never executed anyone by his own hand. His entire career had consisted of preparing murders from a distance, at times when he was engaged in some innocent routine. Hence his fascination with explosives, timing devices, and poisonous gases like sarin, which he had carried to New York in a small Chanel No. 5 perfume bottle in one of his pockets to kill Letelier.

Townley and Callejas followed Altamirano to the airport. There, they had a brief exchange with the man wearing the black-framed glasses, as a ridiculous tribute from an admirer of the deposed Marxist. In the boarding line, they noted his next destination.

At the same time, the FBI was also taking note of one of his aliases, Wilson. But it wouldn't be until much later, when Rolando Otero, another Cuban frustrated by DINA's treatment in Chile, decided to identify the photograph of Wilson.

DECEMBER

Pragmatists, Kill That One Too

ON FRIDAY, DECEMBER 3, 1976, MIAMI POLICE were still on the trail of the killers of the Cuban Luciano Nieves. A year earlier, he had dined at the restaurant on 8th Street and 37th Avenue, the Versailles, owned by Felipe Valls. Miami's most famous restaurant, a favorite of Luis Posada Carriles and Orlando Bosch, had an eternal reservation for several successful businessmen to celebrate the death of Fidel Castro, which was the only guaranteed triumph any investor could bet on and any exile patriot could hope for as a concrete achievement, even if only an alien and inevitable one from nature.

Before he could stand up, someone had broken a chair over his back. His mistake had been supporting dialogue with Cuba. Ultimately, Nieves was executed in a hospital parking lot. The police concluded that Cubans Valentine Hernández, Jesús Lazo, Luis Velasco, and Héctor Carbonell (a member of another Cuban terrorist group called the Pragmatists) were behind the murder.[287] They disagreed with Nieves' lukewarm stance and that of the rest of the dialoguers. A decade earlier, the CIA had tried to recruit him, but Nieves showed little conviction and provided unreliable information, so in 1967 the agency decided to cut all ties with him.[288] Like in the TV series of the time, which almost all of them were fans of, they all claimed they didn't know what they were being accused of.

—I don't know what you're talking about—they repeated, like a bad translation of Hollywood movies into Spanish.

Valentine Hernández, the shooter who killed Nieves, was the only one found guilty. Immediately, as reported by the *Washington Post* on April 17, 2005, the press and the bars of Miami elevated him to the status of freedom fighter—for eliminating one of their own, from behind.

In 1992, Bill Clinton appeared at Victor's Café. By then, the timid left of the Democrats had hit their heads so often leaning to the right to gather funds and votes to return to the White House. The extreme right of Miami was pleased with the new rebel and promised him $125,000 of the time, in addition to the $150,000 the Cuban American National Foundation was set to receive as a prize from an earlier event, plus another hundred thousand from a local organization that preferred to remain anonymous. Within a few days, the generous visit of presidential candidate Bill Clinton had surpassed the generosity of one million dollars.

In August, Clinton and the powerful Cuban businessman Jorge Mas Canosa had lunch at the Versailles restaurant.

At the entrance, a sign warned:

"No Castro, No problem"

The Fight with the Drug Trade

In December, the CIA director, George H. Bush, received Panamanian General Manuel Noriega in his office. Jimmy Carter's victory had been a setback, but it was nothing that couldn't be resolved.

Noriega had been a loyal paid collaborator of the CIA since the 1950s, when he was recruited at the Military School of Chorrillos in Peru. The short, pockmarked young man had the profile the CIA desired: ambitious, unscrupulous, with psychological issues but consistent and predictable, meaning he had a low probability of betraying his superiors. At the time, Noriega had a registered CIA salary of over one hundred thousand dollars annually, which he supplemented with drug trafficking.

Five years later, plane accidents showed a clear preference for independentist heads of state. In Latin America, Ecuadorian president

Jaime Roldós, his wife, and seven other companions crashed on the hill of Huayrapungo. The official version closed the case by labeling it an accident, despite the investigations suggesting otherwise. His ally in the region, Panamanian president Omar Torrijos, also died in another plane crash two months later, on July 31, 1981.

After Torrijos' death, General Noriega became the new dictator of Panama, yet another friendly dictator. Besides his CIA salary, he supplemented his income with a share of his dealings with Pablo Escobar and the Medellín Cartel. The other portion was funneled to the Contra in Honduras, against Nicaragua. When Luis Posada Carriles escaped from Caracas prison, he was immediately reinstated on the CIA payroll to take charge of this group of freedom fighters.

—They are the moral equivalents of our Founding Fathers and the brave men and women of the French Resistance—said Ronald Reagan—. Because the fight is not between right and left, but between the righteousness of good and the crookedness of evil.[289]

As is a known pattern, friendly dictators always end up believing they merited their own power, until they are abandoned by God and by Washington. Noriega's problems began when he felt untouchable, especially due to his knowledge and documentation of Washington's and the CIA's maneuvers in the region. To make matters worse, during the 1988 presidential debates against Michael Dukakis, the vice president and presidential candidate George H. Bush repeatedly denied knowing his friend and collaborator, the pockmarked man with the beautiful women. In fact, he would accuse him of drug trafficking, and once elected president, he would order the assault on Panama in 1990 to bring him before U.S. justice, at the cost of hundreds of dead Panamanians in just a couple of days.

Due to a series of scandals over poor coverage of the attacks, the headquarters of Operation Condor in the region had to move from Venezuela to El Salvador.

Letelier's Briefcase

SHORTLY AFTER THE BOMBING IN WASHINGTON, the executive Samsonite briefcase of Orlando Letelier was taken to the FBI office. The briefcase contained irrelevant material, according to agent and prosecutor Eugene Propper. His notes, written in Spanish, were neither understood nor classified, despite his widow demanding a list of the items it contained.

A columnist for the *Washington Star*, Jeremiah O'Lary, published that the briefcase, with two locks, contained compromising material, which demonstrated the double life of the well-known diplomat, "*who carried it with him all the time to prevent the CIA from stealing it.*" The supposed secret information discovered in the briefcase referred to the letter from Salvador Allende's daughter, who was in exile in Cuba and still the president of the banned Socialist Party of Chile. In the letter, Beatriz Tati Allende informs Orlando of the possibility that the Party might send him a thousand dollars per month to support his activism against the Pinochet government. The funds had been approved by the offices of the Chilean Socialist Party, directed by Carlos Altamirano, then in exile in Berlin.

Copies of Letelier's briefcase were leaked to journalist Jack Anderson, who on December 20 published an article in the *Washington Post* titled "Letelier's Havana Connection." That same day, as always happens in print and local television news, a dozen other smaller newspapers reproduced the same article in different states.[290]

The proof, according to Anderson, was the letter sent to him from Havana by Beatrice Allende, daughter of the deposed Chilean president, in which she promised him money from the Socialist Party of Chile to support his activism against the Pinochet regime. Nowhere were executions or bombings against innocents mentioned. Nor were there ever any. The only clear thing was that, as with the Moffitts, as with many Chileans in exile, and even for General Pinochet himself, Letelier was the undisputed figure of the outlawed opposition. For many, he was the future president of Chile.

El exilio del terror

According to FBI agent Carter Cornick, a known associate of Anderson, the column was sensationalist, full of exaggerations to gain readers. Although it wasn't his intention, it complicated the investigation to the delight of those who wanted the public to lose interest in its resolution, considering that Letelier was a communist spy.

—Pure bullshit—Cornick complained—. Everyone knows Letelier didn't meet any of the requirements to be a spy. He was a public intellectual with a personality incompatible with that of a spy who follows orders... Besides, spies don't send letters through the mail or carry them around in a briefcase with aspirin and personal notes. Especially not someone who had already received several death threats in his mail.

—In fact—Propper added—, the letter doesn't mention anything Letelier had hidden. We all know he was a Marxist intellectual who worked for a socialist government and had friends in Cuba. That "secret missive" is yellow journalism. It only makes our work more difficult.[291]

One of the most notable stars of the nascent neoconservative reaction (and a CIA collaborator since his graduation in 1951), journalist William Buckley, didn't miss the chance to point out the communist tendencies of the victim, something the investigators weren't taking into account to solve the case. Buckley, besides enthusiastically supporting the Franco dictatorship in Spain and apartheid in South Africa, was linked to Pinochet's official press. He did not tire of repeating in the country's most important media that Letelier was an agent of Cuba and the Soviet Union.

Beatriz Allende committed suicide a year later in Havana, in the same way (it is assumed) her father, President Salvado Allende, did.

YEARS LATER

OTERO, THE LINK FOUND

THE FALL OF MICHAEL TOWNLEY BEGAN with the testimony of Rolando Otero in Florida, one of the least significant members of the paramilitary groups in Miami and Union City. After several failed trials against him, accused of the explosion of nine bombs in Florida, he was finally sentenced to 45 years in prison. Before the judge granted him parole a few months later, Otero had agreed to talk with FBI agents.

By then, Cornick and Propper were under pressure due to repeated failures to solve the murder of Letelier and Moffitt in Washington. Both had worked on several hypotheses, including those from Chile, about a communist plot, and the media's speculation of Michael Moffitt's revenge for his wife Ronni's alleged affair with the exiled leader and future president of Chile, Orlando Letelier. Both had found the Chilean connection hypothesis more credible from the first day, hours after the attack, when Michael Moffitt and other investigators from the Institute for Policy Studies had assured them that the perpetrators were from the DINA.

In May 1977, Cornick and Propper requested an interview with Rolando Otero in prison. Otero refused to cooperate with them, so they turned to the mediation of El Mono Ricardo Morales. El Mono visited Otero in prison and told him that the feds were investigating the Letelier case and that it might be worth negotiating for information.

—I don't know anything about that Letelier— said Otero.

—Neither of you have anything to do with that mess— El Mono had told them, but they could still get something out of the situation. Especially from Otero, who had just been sentenced to half a life term.

Otero was reluctant to cooperate, but the interview with the feds took place anyway. During the interrogation, he didn't cooperate. Most of the time, he remained silent. The FBI detectives focused on the possible emotions of a man who had recently been convicted of other crimes. Not just any man. Not just any crimes.

When, hours after the attack on Letelier, Cornick and Propper heard Michael Moffitt saying, "it was DINA, DINA did it," they thought he was talking about a woman. They barely knew where to place Chile on the map, but they had much more experience with Cubans from Florida.

Carter Cornick looked at a defeated Otero and said:

—The Chileans didn't treat you very well, did they?

—Neither did you— said Otero—. I no longer have any respect for the Chileans, but the U.S. government also used us and then abandoned us. The CIA betrayed us.

Cornick and Propper returned the next morning.

—Can we show you some pictures?—said Cornick.[292]

Otero shrugged.

When Cornick showed him the photograph of Juan Williams, Otero's gaze paused for a moment. Attentively, Cornick noticed on Otero's face that the photograph had not left him indifferent, nor was that face unfamiliar to him.

—Who is he?

—He's the captain I already told you about…—said Otero.

—The blond captain?

—Yes.

—The same one? Are you sure?

—It's him, only his hair was blonder than what you see in this photo.

—The same captain who interrogated you, in Santiago, alongside Major Torres?

—The same one.

The blond captain was not only Juan Williams Rose on a Paraguayan passport, but also Andrés Wilson on his Chilean ID, Hans Petersen on his Chilean passport, and Kenneth Enyart on one of his U.S. passports (identity stolen from the glove box of a Ford Escort belonging to one of the customers at a Miami auto repair shop), but also Michael Townley on his birth certificate from Iowa.

With years of experience in the technique of identifying common criminals by their photos, the detectives had no doubts: Otero was telling the truth.

The fate of the entire investigation and that of Michael Townley were cast.

THE BLOND CHILEAN

On August 28, 1977, Colonel Manuel Contreras called Scherrer at his office in Buenos Aires.

—I need to speak with you about a matter of extreme urgency.

—When? Where?

—Tomorrow, here in Santiago—replied the colonel—. I already have the ticket in your name.

—Impossible, Colonel—said Scherrer—. Your embassy takes at least three days to process an urgent visa.

Scherrer heard the colonel's nervous chuckle, who didn't take long to find the words he was looking for.

—You just come and will see that you don't need any visa.[293]

At the Pudahuel International Airport, a man received Scherrer and had him skip all the immigration checks. He was a blond man, perhaps "the blond Chilean" that Otero mentioned, thought Scherrer for a moment, and then: "No, impossible; the colonel wouldn't be so stupid as to send me the same man I'm looking for."[294]

The DINA learned of the identification of "the blond Chilean" by Rolando Otero, by then processed in Jacksonville. The internal scandal and the accumulation of leaks about their procedures would end with the dissolution and replacement of DINA by a new repressive agency. It was time to get rid of the crazy Yankee. But Scherrer couldn't identify the blond Chilean, known as Juan Williams.

—Juan Williams doesn't exist—concluded Scherrer after weeks of searching—. At least he's not Chilean. Williams and Romeral must have been fake names.

Juan Williamses abound in the history of the Chilean Navy, which was once as powerful as that of the United States, before the Marines realized that whoever dominates the seas dominates the world and decided to build metal ships instead of heroic wooden vessels. Perhaps because of the superior Anglo-Saxon race.

Someone else was behind those names.

Hours later Scherrer was in Contreras's office. The matter of grave urgency wasn't exactly what Scherrer thought and was interested in.

—I need to send 54 men from DINA to Washington—said the colonel—. Most of them with fake passports and not a few armed, as it should be.

—To begin with, your men should report the serial numbers of the weapons they bring into the country... What's the idea?

—Next week, General Pinochet must be in Washington for the signing of the Panama Canal Treaty that his new president, the crazy fruit vendor, will sign with the communist Torrijos. We are responsible for his security. There will be nineteen other heads of state invited for the occasion.

—Don't you think that's too many people?

—No—said the colonel—. What I need is that, just as you've arrived here without the corresponding paperwork, you don't hassle my men with all that unnecessary bureaucracy.

Scherrer must have looked at him like someone who's fallen into a trap.

—Needless to say—concluded the colonel— I don't want any of my boys to be arrested in Washington when they land to fulfill their diplomatic mission.

—Well, some paperwork will have to be done...

—Absolutely not. There's no time.

—Why not send fewer personnel? That would speed up the whole process.

—I'm sending all 54—said Contreras—. I owe each of them a reward for their invaluable service to the homeland. Many are retiring this year. Besides, the DINA will be replaced by another agency very soon. Actually, it's just a name change, but I want to retire without any issues.

Scherrer felt used, cornered like a beginner by a colonel who had high self-esteem and a generous perception of his own intelligence. On the other hand, receiving the 54 passports of the DINA's top agents for urgent processing was a kind of informational treasure.

In less than 24 hours, Scherrer sent him the 54 passports with U.S. visas. Contreras thanked him.

—There's still one pending matter—said Scherrer— and it's something that won't be filed away until it's resolved.

—I imagine, Bob—said the colonel.

—We're still investigating the Cubans regarding the attack in Washington.

—I can assure you, Bob—said the colonel—it's not as easy for us as it might be for the FBI. I have no record of whether Guillermo Novo spoke with the Minister of Defense or not. I don't ask those kinds of questions to our ministers.

They Have Abandoned You

In January 1978, Guillermo Novo, Virgilio Paz, and Ross Díaz called Michael Townley from Miami:

—We need twenty-five thousand dollars to move them. Things are getting tough here. The FBI is breathing down our necks.

Townley knew the complications such a transfer would entail, but he took a deep breath and went to see Colonel Contreras.

—If they want to come to Chile, let them come. But we won't give them a single dollar.

Months after the attack on Letelier, Pinochet removed Colonel Pedro Espinosa and, later, the untouchable Colonel Manuel Contreras as heads of the DINA. Before that, he had promoted him to General. Pinochet was upset that the DINA had failed to meet the first requirement of the plan in Washington: getting rid of the growing notoriety of Allende's former minister, but without leaving traces pointing back to Santiago.

Just as the FBI did in 1947, when it was informed of its replacement in Latin America by the new agency created by President Harry Truman, the CIA, the removed chiefs of the DINA also burned a large portion of the documentation generated since its founding. Photographs, reports, names of detainees and the disappeared were consumed in the fires of professional jealousy.

Michel Townley lost his bosses and protectors, even though neither Espinosa nor Contreras ever trusted the Townley Callejas couple, suspecting them of being CIA spies which, in turn, had been the driving force behind the coup against Allende and later a partner of DINA and Operation Condor. For Colonel Espinosa, the case could be even worse, as the gringo's wife could be a double agent for the KGB, very likely forced to marry the CIA agent. Trust was not precisely a known value. All these groups, like any neighborhood mafia, required loyalty from partners and members. Any form of betrayal was paid for with death.

When the FBI asked the deputy director of the CIA Vernon Walters if they had discussed Letelier in the second meeting with the head of DINA, Walters refused to answer. But the FBI learned that Walters had traveled to Paraguay that same month of June.

Pinochet denied any involvement in the assassination and refused to hand over Colonel Contreras when the U.S. justice system requested it. Twenty years later, already in prison, Contreras declared:

—What, Pinochet didn't know about DINA's plans? Come on! He was in charge of everything.

The CIA also lied to the FBI whenever it wanted. The same happened when Colonel Pedro Espinosa was implicated in the assassination of the young journalist from New York and supporter of Salvador Allende, Charles Horman, and one of his friends from Chicago, economics student Frank Teruggi. In 2014, Colonel Espinosa and U.S. Navy Captain Ray E. Davis would be found guilty of these political crimes.

Michael Townley was the first to fall and the first to admit to the attack. Later, the U.S. justice system issued an extradition request for Colonel Contreras, but Pinochet flatly refused it. He denied any involvement in the regrettable incident and rejected the possibility of any extradition.

For its part, the CIA's Cuban network, composed of Orlando Bosch, Luis Posada Carriles, Virgilio Paz, Dionisio Suárez, and the Novo brothers, barely knew Orlando Letelier before assassinating him. It was clear that the original idea had come from Pinochet and the DINA. The Cubans only took credit for the successful attack as a group, while each individual separately denied any responsibility.

On March 17, 1978, Eugene Propper, the U.S. prosecutor investigating the Letelier case, arrived in Chile and pressured the government to provide information. The result was a negotiation that concluded with the handing over of Townley and his expulsion from the country in April.

In protest and as a threat, Mariana Callejas sent a handwritten letter to Air Force Commander Gustavo Leigh:

"I have thought about it a lot. The Fatherland is not the Government. This Government may fall, but the Fatherland will continue. I may die,

but my children will know, along with the whole world, why their father is in prison. Nothing can stop what could be revealed now, only I can prevent it, but my husband was thrown to the lions, and I am waiting for new developments. "My last letter if my husband receives a long sentence and I see my home utterly destroyed, is the formula and a sample of Andrea, a chemical developed here with incredible precision and scientific sophistication, a lethal product that in case of war would be an absolutely effective weapon, but that here has been used to eliminate troublesome individuals because the results appear to be a heart attack."[295]

Callejas could not prevent her husband's deportation to the United States. With the vial of sarin intended for Letelier still in her hands, she handed over to the FBI all the information she had about the chemical laboratories of Pinochet's dictatorship.

When the U.S. prosecutor Eugene M. Propper, in charge of investigating the Letelier case, arrived in Caracas, the same Disip was responsible for explaining his presence in the country as an intelligence exchange against the terrorism that plagued the hemisphere. According to Propper, the government of Carlos Andrés Pérez hindered his investigations by denying him permission to interrogate Orlando Bosch and other terrorists detained in Venezuela, something an American journalist would eventually achieve through his own improvisation.

Propper managed to interrogate Rivas Vásquez and Orlando García. Both admitted in their statements that the government of Andrés Pérez had brought Cubans accused of terrorism in the United States to Venezuelan security agencies, although this tradition had started a decade earlier. In exchange, Rivas Vásquez secured the promise from the FBI agent to help his daughter obtain a scholarship at George Washington University.[296]

When the FBI finally managed to put Townley on a plane to Miami, Scherrer whispered in his ear:

"Your own people have betrayed you. They have abandoned you. You owe them nothing..."[297]

Townley looked at him. He glanced at Cornick sitting beside him.

Scherrer was a professional, and a good one. Within the next year, he would reveal to the world Phase III of Operation Condor and its assassinations of exiled dissidents on both sides of the Atlantic. For that, he had to go case by case with infinite patience. He knew that eroding a criminal's morale was a matter of time. Sooner or later, they would talk without even needing to lay a finger on them.

Mentioning the betrayal of their accomplices was a well-known strategy to make a suspect talk. Especially when they were part of a group that operated under the logic of a mafia. The same strategy had been used to get Rolando Otero to identify Townley in Jacksonville.

—I don't understand—said Townley, and he began to cry like a teenager abandoned by his first love.

Before Townley, the feeling of betrayal and abandonment had its effect on his wife, Mariana Callejas. On April 11, she left Chile. The newspapers in Santiago published her resentment:

—They used my husband—she declared—. I'm sure neither General Pinochet nor the high officials of the government know what my husband knows. Otherwise, they would never have expelled him from the country.

The press and diplomatic cables heated up over the potential consequences of the investigation into the attack in Washington.

—Intelligence services serve the government—clarified President Pinochet—. Any unpleasant situation is your problem. Not mine.

A year after Letelier's assassination, Pinochet declared to The Washington Post:

—I can swear to you that no one in the Chilean government planned something like that. Letelier was detained in Chile. I was the one who gave him his freedom.

Freud's borrowed teapot.

Father, ask God to heal my son

JOURNALIST BLAKE FLEETWOOD MANAGED to enter as a visitor to the prison where Orlando Bosch and Luis Posada Carriles were held, thanks to some improvisation. Fleetwood introduced himself as a journalist, to which Bosch couldn't resist. They talked for a few minutes with a table between them, and then Bosch showed him his cell. A Sony television stood out, saving him daily from boredom. Shortly after, Luis Posada Carriles appeared with a box of Cuban cigars and offered him one:

—The United States has an embargo with Cuba—said Posada Carriles—. But we don't.[298]

Years later, the first Latino mayor of Miami, Maurice Ferré, also visited Posada Carriles in prison. Not long after, the guards were bribed with part of the $28,000 that Miami's powerful media mogul Jorge Mas Canosa had sent. Another portion of the money had been donated by the board members of the Miami lobby, the Cuban National American Foundation, at a rate of $2,000 per member.[299]

Luis Posada Carriles walked across the prison yard dressed as a priest, holding a Bible to his chest. The scene was so believable that a farmer joined him in his hurried steps.

—Father—said the man—. I have a son who is very sick. Please, pray to the Lord for him.

—We can pray for your son as we walk—said Posada Carriles, while keeping his hurried pace.

The farmer's company made his charade more convincing. The two men walked away from the prison, worlds apart from each other. Years later, Posada Carriles would recall this scene unable to hold back his laughter. By then, the farmer's sick son must have been dead. Who knows. Either way, he found it amusing.

Three guards served three years in prison for collaborating in the plot. Posada Carriles fled to improve his resume of terrorist attacks in various countries, but never again did he step into a prison. A fishing boat dropped him off in Aruba, where he rested for a week. From there, a private plane took him to Costa Rica and later, he was brought to El Salvador, where his old friend from his training days at Fort Benning, Félix Rodríguez, awaited him. Rodríguez (linked to Fulgencio Batista's regime, the Anti-Communist League of the Dominican dictator Rafael Trujillo, CIA agent, participant in the failed Bay of Pigs invasion, murderer of Che Guevara in Bolivia, participant in the massacres in Cambodia and Vietnam, implicated in the Iran-Contra scandal-Contra, drug trafficking in various Backyard countries, and decorated with a Silver Star by the U.S. Army) admitted to being funded by a Miami millionaire, presumed to be Jorge Mas Canosa.

—One day I received a call from our benefactor in Miami—declared Félix Rodríguez— who had helped me greatly financially, to hide Posada Carriles.[300]

In turn, Félix Rodríguez had been hired by CIA agent Donald Gregg, advisor to Vice President George H. Bush, former CIA director during the most violent years of Cuban exile in the United States and future president of the United States.[301]

After Jimmy Carter was defeated in the 1980 elections, Posada Carriles' fortunes took an unexpected turn. His dream of being officially reinstated on the CIA payroll came true. The dictatorship of El Salvador provided him with immediate refuge. As defined by Ecuadorean President Jaime Roldós, the regime of José Napoleón Duarte was built on a mountain of corpses, but being a personal friend of President Ronald Reagan had its benefits. Years earlier, in 1980, the priest Oscar Romero had been executed for demanding that the military cease the violent repression against his poorest parishioners, and a few months later, four American nuns were raped and murdered on their way to Nicaragua, accused of being communists or belonging to Liberation Theology, which had the unfortunate habit of aligning itself too closely with the poor. The Ronald Reagan administration worked to obstruct the investigations of these cases, accusing the victims of being sympathetic to Marxism. Those responsible, Generals Carlos Eugenio Vides Casanova and José Guillermo García, retired to Miami, where they became respectable businessmen, unsuspected fathers and grandfathers in suits and ties. Finally, after a lengthy legal battle over other murder charges, both will be deported in 2016. Hundreds of other criminals and genocidaires will remain in Florida and will lead peaceful and honorable lives for the rest of their days. This will be the case for Orlando de Bosch and Luis Posada Carriles.

In the early 1980s, Posada Carriles began collaborating directly with Colonel Oliver North in supplying arms from Honduras to the Contras—freedom fighters, in the words of Ronald Reagan and terrorists in the eyes of the UN and the U.S. House of Representatives. Oliver North will be accused and convicted of lying to Congress in the Iran-Contras scandal, but he will be pardoned shortly after by President George H. Bush. As tradition dictates.

According to the FBI, Posada Carriles was responsible for planting at least 41 bombs in Tegucigalpa, Honduras, but these cases will remain open and never be resolved, as expected.[302]

I am a Christian, not a Murderer

ON THE MORNING OF SEPTEMBER 6, 1977, hours before meeting with President Jimmy Carter at the White House, the Chilean leader shared breakfast with the press.

Journalist Jeremiah O'Leary from the Washington Star asked him:

—Mr. President, I must ask you this: Did anyone in your government or the Chilean military have anything to do with the assassination of Orlando Letelier here in Washington?

General Pinochet leaned toward his translator and then replied:
—I am a Christian, not a murderer—he said, kissing his two index fingers in the shape of a cross—. I can swear to you that no one in my government planned anything like that.

Jimmy Carter received Pinochet at the White House. He informed him of the new U.S. foreign policy, which would be based on the defense of human rights. General Pinochet agreed and showed enthusiasm for the idea.

Hours later, a journalist approached Michael Moffitt.

—If President Carter is sincere about the new human rights policy—Michael said—why then does he receive Pinochet and not receive Isabel or me?

Zbigniew Brzezinski, Carter's National Security Secretary, had indicated to him that a meeting with Isabel and Michael would be completely inappropriate, "given the sensitive nature of the facts." When Isabel and Moffitt protested, they were linked in a possible romance. When Isabel was able to return to Chile for a few days, a journalist asked her:

—Are you going to marry Michael Moffitt?

—You really live in Fantasyland—Isabel said.

THE FALL OF MICHAEL TOWNLEY

ALTHOUGH COLONEL CONTRERAS HAD ORDERED him to deny everything, even when the processing of the fake passports in Paraguay had traveled to the United States, agents from the Department of Justice in that country managed to prove that Townley had called Guillermo Novo two days before the attack from his sister's house in North Tarrytown, a suburb north of New York. They also recovered the record of a call made from the bar where members of the Cuban Nationalist Movement used to meet to his sister's house, and the calls from the motel they stayed in south of Washington DC.

One of those calls (irrelevant to the FBI but significant for my notes of a book I may never write) was made to the well-known mercenary and arms trafficker Mitchell WerBell, then residing on a farm in Georgia. WerBell, son of an officer of the last tsar of Russia and OSS agent, was a CIA agent. Among his various collaborations was the CIA's failed 1973 coup in Panama against Omar Torrijos. He was a client of dictators like Rafael Trujillo in the Dominican Republic, collaborator of the Phoenix Foundation in the 70s, a libertarian project that aimed to take advantage of the post-colonial wave to found far-right libertarian micro-republics in former strongholds of English pirates, such as in the Bahamas. In his later years, he focused on illegal arms trafficking. One of his specialties was the design of silencers, highly demanded by snipers worldwide.

For Michael Townley, the execution of enemies with silencers was not as attractive as the noisy car bombings with plastic explosives, but it remained a tempting option if things did not follow their most logical course.

The FBI also located the receipts for the spy equipment purchases made by Townley in Florida. With this evidence on the table, they began to pressure him.

—For now—Cornick said—we already have Guillermo Novo and Alvin Ross in our hands. All that's left is to reach an agreement with one of them. The rats are starting to abandon the ship, you know what I mean, kid... Your friends are going to be charged not only for this conspiracy and murder case but also for cocaine trafficking.

Townley didn't need to have two obvious things explained to him. One was the advantage of becoming a protected witness, even while being part of the crime. The other was the tradition of betrayals within the Cuban exile. Considering the first premise, it was only a matter of time before one of them spoke first. If they hadn't already. Cornered, Townley decided to negotiate.

—Better to reach an agreement with the FBI—he later told Mariana Callejas— before the FBI does so with the Cubans.

The agreement consisted of providing information to the investigation into the assassination of Letelier, without including other activities of DINA, in exchange for a reduced sentence of no more than ten years in prison with the possibility of parole years earlier. Not bad for an international terrorist. Otherwise, he could receive seven years in jail just for each of his two entries into the United States with false passports.[303]

In August 1978, Townley received a letter from Peru accusing him of having negotiated with the FBI:

"You are a traitor and you are going to pay with your life. You can't hide. There will be no corner of this world where you can live in peace."[304]

At the end, a nervous signature:
Virgilio.

WITHOUT MONEY, THERE IS NO JUSTICE

ON JANUARY 9, 1979, THE TRIAL BEGAN against Alvin Ross Díaz and the brothers Guillermo and Ignacio Novo Sampoll. The three were found guilty of the murder of Orlando Letelier and Ronni Moffitt.

Guillermo Novo and Alvin Ross were sentenced to life in prison. Ignacio Novo received eighty years. Virgilio Paz Romero and Dionisio Suárez remained in Chile, under the protection of Pinochet.

In the reconstruction of the events, FBI agents asked Townley to place a bomb with C4 similar to the one used in Washington, which they placed in another light blue Chevelle. When the bomb was detonated, Agent Cornick couldn't help but be surprised. In both the reconstruction and the attack, the cars suffered identical damage, as if one were a copy of the other.

Ignacio Novo's wife published a plea in the Miami press:

"I, as the wife of Ignacio Novo, accused of perjury before the Grand Jury handling the case, and sister-in-law of his brother Guillermo, ask the exile radio stations, the Cuban newspapers, the 2506 Brigade, and the Cuban Municipalities in exile and in general, all Organizations, to make a joint effort and set a date for the first days of December of this year and call the people to a new marathon to raise the $100,000 needed for the defense of these Cuban patriots who risk remaining in prison for life if they lack an effective defense at the trial scheduled for January 8, 1978."

The Miami media mobilized for the fundraising with the slogan "For Legal Defense of the Fighters Guillermo Novo, Ignacio Novo, and Alvin Ross." The press, like the Miami Herald, described the accused as used car dealers from Union City "accused of multiple terrorist acts." Virgilio Paz was described as the Latin Don Juan, the ladies' man. According to the FBI, just like Alvin Ross, Paz is "an extremely dangerous individual," trained by the Pinochet regime in Chile.[305] The campaign was a fundraising success.

Alvin Ross, another veteran of the Bay of Pigs invasion, was also arrested by the FBI, after raising funds on his own through the cocaine trade and shortly before fleeing the country. His most recent attack had been a bomb at the offices of a company planning to send medical supplies to Cuba.[306]

Before the trial against Ross Díaz and the Novo brothers Sampoll, Judge Barrington Parker and Prosecutor Propper were threatened with death, so they could not walk without bodyguards. The jury members were chosen from 153 candidates. Anyone who had any knowledge about Chile or Cuba was eliminated. One of the selected jurors received a phone call from Ignacio Novo:

—I just hope your children's health remains very good.

Propper also received a call to his office:

—We're also going to blow off the legs of your damn judge. Sooner or later we're going to go after his family, and if we have time, we'll come after you too, even though you're just another lover of damn communist niggers.

When Michael Townley entered the courtroom, the Cubans began muttering insults in Spanish:

—Traitor.

—CIA agent.

—Faggot, son of a bitch.

Shortly before, Townley had sent a message to Michel Moffitt through Prosecutor Popper:

—Tell him I'm sorry about his wife. I'm not sorry about Letelier, but I am sorry about his wife.

—Go to hell—Moffitt had replied—. Tell him that if I had the chance, I'd cut him into pieces.

Just like Posada Carriles, Orlando Bosch, José Suárez, Virgilio Paz and the Novo brothers said that the 73 passengers killed in the explosion of Cubana Flight 455 were not innocent but combatants, Michael Townley justified the assassination of Orlando Letelier with the same argument:

—We are at war—he said—. Mr. Letelier was an important soldier in the ranks of Marxism-Leninism, a leader in a war that used the capitalist society of the Free World to attack Chile.

—Was Mrs. Ronni Moffitt a soldier too?—asked the judge.

—I regret that Mrs. Moffitt also died—Townley later told the officer evaluating him for parole—. But it's likely that the relationship between Letelier and Moffitt wasn't just professional. She must have been very close to Letelier, perhaps leaning over him, when the bomb exploded. If that hadn't been the case, she would be alive today...[307]

During the trial, Michael Townley testified that he had been sent from Chile to the United States to carry out the assassination alongside members of the Cuban Nationalist Movement, for which he was sentenced to ten years in prison. The Cubans denied knowing Townley and denied owning the cocaine seized in one of their cars.

The FBI classified them all, including Posada Carriles and Orlando Bosch, as dangerous terrorists.

During the judicial process, on October 27, 1978, five minutes before 10:00 PM, a bomb exploded at the Cuban Embassy mission to the United Nations on 38th Street and Lexington Avenue. The explosion shattered the building's windows and injured three people. Another warning bomb exploded at Avery Fisher Hall in New York. The attacks were claimed by Omega 7.

—Nothing new, declared Inspector Kerins. They've done this before when the embassy was on East 67th Street.

More recently, this branch of the Cuban Nationalist Movement had placed a bomb at Avery Fisher Hall in the Lincoln Center where a Cuban ballet group was performing. For years, Omega 7 had claimed other attacks using the same method: C4 bombs or dynamite and remote detonation, allowing enough time to flee the crime scene. This didn't rule out their second most used tactic: execution by a barrage of bullets, in the style of Al Capone and the Cuban Mafia from Batista's golden years. Last April, for example, Omega 7 claimed responsibility for the murder of Carlos Muñoz Varela, a 26-year-old Cuban exile who had organized tourist and family trips for other exiles to the island.

On February 4, 1979, the jury deliberated for eight hours.

—Obviously, they're screwing us, said Guillermo Novo.

The jury read the verdict, which unanimously found Alvin Ross and the brothers Guillermo and Ignacio Novo guilty on all charges. Ross and the Novos shouted:

—Long live a free Cuba!

Their family members confronted Judge Parker and yelled:

—Black son of a bitch!

On March 23, before sentencing and in front of Judge Parker, Guillermo Novo declared:

—The Cuban Nationalist Movement is an honorable organization, whose goal is the liberation of Cuba from the communist oppressor, the foreign oppressor. Its objective is the defense of Cuban culture and traditions, and of course, the defense of our Western Christian Civilization...

—This is not a political committee, Judge Parker interrupted. You are not here to give us a political speech.[308]

After three days of deliberations, on May 13, 1981, the U.S. District Court acquitted Guillermo Novo Sampol and Alvin Ross Díaz, whose 1979 life sentences for the assassination of Orlando Letelier and Ronni Moffitt in 1976 had been overturned in 1980.[309] This year, a federal appeals courtordered a new trial, arguing that the previous one was tainted by the misuse of testimony from the defendants' cellmates. They were only found guilty of lying to the grand jury. In June, Judge Parker reduced Ignacio Novo Sampol's sentence to perjury, but officials also released his older brother. Guillermo went to his parents' house south of Union City for two days before being arrested again by police.[310]

Michael Moffitt testified in the trial against Guillermo Novo Sampol and Alvin Ross Díaz, whose previous convictions for conspiracy, murder, and cocaine trafficking charges were also overturned by an appeals court.[311]

When the judge issued the final dismissal ruling, Novo and Ross looked at Saul Landau. As they were leaving, Ignacio Novo approached him and said in Spanish:

—Now we can finish off all these filthy communists.

Landau made a mocking gesture, and Guillermo Novo stepped forward, but was stopped by Agent Robert Scherrer. Scherrer moved his jacket aside to reveal his gun.

Novo added Landau to his target list.

In June, one of the Novo brothers, Guillermo, returned to jail on a perjury charge. Guillermo Novo's legal team, part of the Michael Young law firm, requested that his case be transferred to another judge for bail consideration. Procedural errors, such as the judge reading the pre-sentencing report about the accused, led the defense to argue that the judge could not remain impartial.

Judge Burlington Parker was also questioned for describing the crime against Orlando Letelier as the most monstrous cold-blooded crime he had ever faced in his career, which proved his bias in the case.[312]

The first petition was denied, but the life sentences were affected by a grant of bail. Guillermo Novo and Ross Díaz were released in 1981 after bail was paid, funds raised through exile businesses, benefit banquets in Union City, and charity programs in Miami.

On November 23, Miami's Channel 23, WLTV, organized a telethon to raise $100,000 to pay for the bail and lawyers of the Cubans accused of killing Letelier.

—I support the cause of the accused—said Joaquín Blaya, the vice president of Channel 23, a Chilean— We see this case in terms of justice, not driven by ideological reasons… We realized the need to hold this televised marathon after airing the program 'Forgotten Prisoners,' where we presented the cases of Orlando Bosch and the Novo brothers and received very high ratings.[313]

Suárez and Paz remained fugitives, protected by the Cuban community in Florida and New Jersey. Two days after the sentencing, three bombs exploded in New Jersey. One in Union City and another in West New York, targeting a place collecting medicine for Cuba. The other bomb targeted the New Jersey Cuban Program, a nonprofit organization working to help exiled Cubans.

At 8:45 that night, another bomb exploded at the Trans World Airlines offices at Kennedy Airport. Once again, there was a miscalculation, and the bomb detonated prematurely, while the luggage was being loaded, so the honorable organization failed to bring down another plane, this time a TWA aircraft. According to the FBI, Virgilio Paz and José Suarez were behind the terrorist attacks.[314]

Only three of the accused, Townley, Guillermo Novo, and Alvin Ross, were sentenced to life in prison for the terrorist attack that killed Letelier and Moffitt. All three ultimately spent fewer years in prison than a car thief. An appeals court overturned the ruling. Guillermo Novo Sampol was only convicted of perjury, for lying a little under oath. Soon after, the powerful Miami businessman in the food and media industries, Jorge Mas Canosa, hired him as his personal bodyguard. In 2000, he will be arrested in Panama alongside Luis Posada Carriles for a plan to assassinate Fidel Castro. Both will be pardoned once again.

Shortly after his trial, Michael Townley was also released, protected by the Witness Protection Program. He will live the rest of his life in Florida, far from Callejas and his children, under federal protection and with a fake name so his former Cuban comrades cannot locate him.

All, or nearly all, will retire in Miami or Union City, drowning their frustrations in rum and Havana cigars imported from Cuba.

In prison, Michael Townley dedicated himself to finishing high school and teaching English to Mexicans and Spanish to others. When on July 25, 1983, he was granted early release, Argentina issued an extradition order to have him tried for the assassination of the Chilean general Carlos Prats. But a judge in the United States rejected the request. Since then, Townley has lived in hiding, under the threat of Cuban exiles. Only in 1994 did he agree to give a lengthy interview to a Chilean television channel, first on a boat and later in a secret location in Florida.

THE COLD WAR WITHIN

IN JUNE 1977, PINOCHET REJECTED THE MILITARY AID PACKAGE FROM WASHINGTON. THE SAME HAD BEEN DONE BY FIVE OTHER DICTATORSHIPS IN THE REGION, FOR THE SAME REASONS: THEY REFUSED TO BE CONDITIONED BY THE HUMAN RIGHTS RHETORIC OF THE NEW U.S. GOVERNMENT. MANY WERE CONVINCED THAT CARTER WOULD NOT LAST LONG IN POWER, AND KISSINGER SEEMED TO CONFIRM THIS WITH HIS VISITS AND HIS OPEN SUPPORT FOR FRIENDLY DICTATORS. PRESIDENT CARTER HELD HIS GROUND AND CONTINUED

CUTTING MILLIONS OF DOLLARS THAT USED TO FLOW TO LATIN AMERICAN ARMIES SINCE BEFORE THE BANANA WARS. TO MAKE MATTERS WORSE, VENEZUELAN PRESIDENT ANDRÉS PÉREZ welcomed Carter's new Human Rights policy, which was understood by the DINA (and later by the DNI) as yet another masterstroke of hypocrisy from a politician of his race.

Amid this new Internal Cold War, investigators Carter Cornick and Eugene Propper managed to secure permission to travel to Santiago. One of their main goals was to secure the extradition of Michael Townley so he could be interrogated in the United States. It didn't seem like a very difficult task, given the suspect's nationality and the situation of the Chilean government.

Shortly after landing in Santiago, Chilean officers began speculating about Propper's beard. Hippie, communist, or Jew, which more or less amounted to the same thing.[315] The newspaper La Tercera denounced the "interference of American imperialism" and its attack on "national dignity." The former member of Patria y Libertad, Pablo Rodríguez, by then a respected journalist nationwide, accused Senator Ted Kennedy and Chileans advocating for human rights in Chile of attempting a coup against the legitimate government of General Augusto Pinochet.

On Thursday, June 22, 1978, General Pinochet and U.S. Ambassador George Landau attended a diplomatic cocktail party. Though the general rarely drank alcohol, that night he accepted two whiskeys on the rocks and a Coca-Cola. Alcohol and sugar do not mix well without some form of minor catastrophe. The ambassador reported to Washington the details of that evening:

With a red face and a slightly tired tongue, the general told him:

—You are causing me a lot of trouble, Mr. Ambassador.

—Well, we deeply regret that your government has not collaborated with us on certain issues.

—Tomorrow I will order the closure of the newspaper La Segunda...

—Why?

—They plan to publish an interview with an idiot who took something from The Washington Post... One of those editorials that your government plants in that paper from time to time. Such things will not happen here. What is it you're trying to achieve? A revolution in Chile? I will not allow it.

With the second whiskey circulating through his cardiovascular system, the general, more euphoric but still in control, pointed a finger at the ambassador of China, who was engaged in an animated conversation in another corner of the room.

—Do you see that gentleman, Mr. Ambassador?—the general asked—. Well, I can go talk to him at any time.

The ambassador did not respond.

—I mean it—the general insisted—. Chile can go talk to China at any moment. We are not married to you. In fact, if I want, I can go talk to the Russians. Believe me, they would take us seriously. They would do anything to mess with you.

—Excuse me, General—said the ambassador, trying to focus on Pinochet's Castilian, though this strategy is often a common tactic in the world of the U.S. legal system—. Allow me to ask to make sure I have understood correctly. Are you saying that Chile could become an ally of the Soviet Union?

—Exactly—confirmed the general—. Do not doubt it for a moment.[316]

Long Live Freedom of Expression in Cuba, Not in Miami

THAT SAME YEAR, THE PRESIDENTS Jimmy Carter and Fidel Castro decided to open a path for dialogue. It was one of the most violent years, but it was not the beginning of the controversy surrounding the *dialoguistas*. Several Cuban exiles had already been executed long before, accused of being traitors. In 1975, Valentín Hernández and

Jesús Lazo executed Luciano Nieves for speaking out in favor of dialogue with the island, as President Carter would later propose. He was executed in the parking lot of the Miami hospital where he had gone to visit his eleven-year-old son. On January 8, 1977, the two executed Juan José Peruyero, former president of the Bay of Pigs Association, for being labeled as too moderate in his anti-communist fervor and for criticizing the use of terrorism by his fellow members of Brigade 2506. He was shot six times in the back as he was about to enter his home in Miami. Similar to the attack suffered by CIA agent Antonio Veciana just before entering his house, some (typically family members of the victims) will attribute Peruyero's assassination to the government of Fidel Castro. Historians such as Cuban exile in Miami María Cristina García concluded that this, like others, were decisions made by members of the exile belonging to Brigade 2506.

The demand for freedom of expression in Cuba did not align with the systematic assassination of dissidents within the Cuban community in Miami and New Jersey. In 1985, state representative Javier Souto advocated for Hernández's pardon, claiming that the accused "was only trying to stop the agents of Soviet Imperialism from taking over this nation and the entire Western Hemisphere." Congresswoman Ileana Ros-Lehtinen and her husband, Congressman Dexter Lehtinen, wrote letters to then Florida Governor Bob Graham, appealing to his "high sense of compassion for the difficult plight of anti-communists." When critics of these campaigns in favor of terrorists, such as exiled journalists Liz Balmaseda and Francisco Aruca, mentioned the innocent victims who had been killed in these waves of terrorism, Luis Posada Carriles explained that if there were innocent deaths, it was because "they were in the wrong place at the wrong time."[317]

—Some of these perpetrators walk freely and with impunity on the streets of Miami—said Francisco Aruca—. Often, they are the same dark forces that turn around and appease both political parties, which in turn seek their support during election times.

El exilio del terror

Sponsored by the new administration in Washington, the group called *Committee 75*, made up of Cuban exiles and representatives of the Cuban government, agreed to the release of three thousand political prisoners in Cuba and permission for four thousand exiled Cubans to visit the island. Not everyone agreed. Until then, sending any package to Cuba had an additional cost of 700 dollars through Canada, and the new agreement threatened to eliminate it.

In Union City, *El Diario* and *La Prensa* suffered bomb attacks after an editorial stated that Jimmy Carter's proposal was not a bad idea and that allowing exiles to visit Cuba would help improve the family situation of many. Only the Miami magazine Réplica suffered seven bomb attacks until they managed to shut it down in 2005. According to its editor-in-chief, Max Lesnik, the weekly did not receive money from the CIA or large corporations, something entirely common in other major Miami media outlets.

—Cuba must be independent of Washington and Moscow—Lesnik had said in the 60s. At that time, he had opposed Fidel Castro's shift toward the Soviets after the Bay of Pigs fiasco, but he remained anti-Batista.

In October 1979, Eulalio José Negrín, the second member of the Committee of 75, was executed in a shooting, just before getting into his Buick in Union City, New Jersey. His twelve-year-old son had to witness the scene from the back seat. When the mercenaries in the gray Ford Granada disappeared, Richard got out of the car and saw his father bleeding, lying on the side. He was still alive. He lifted his head, but his father did not respond. Negrín died at 9:50 am, in the ambulance, in the arms of his son.

Shortly afterward, someone called an FBI office and left a message:

—We will continue these executions until all traitors are eliminated in this country.

Weeks later, bombs exploded in various Cuban diplomatic premises, the Soviet Union, and the offices of airline Aeroflot. Four more bombs exploded at the Padrón cigar factory, in retaliation for the negotiations in which its owner, José Orlando Padrón, participated, which ultimately freed three thousand prisoners that the exile community considered political prisoners of the Cuban regime. A photograph showing him sitting at a table in a courtyard in Cuba alongside banker Bernardo Benes and giving one of his cigars to Fidel Castro sentenced him to death. Padrón managed to survive.

Despite the fact that the negotiations of the Committee of 75 in 1978 achieved their goal of releasing thousands of prisoners on the island (or perhaps because of it), bombings multiplied. On other occasions, the facilities of the Padrón Factory located west of Miami were set on fire. In the 1980s, their tobacco production in Sandinista Nicaragua was blocked by the embargo imposed by President Ronald Reagan.

After more than a hundred bombs exploded in various parts of the East Coast of the United States in just two years, no one was detained or arrested. Much less brought to any court.[318] Bernardo Benes, a powerful Cuban banker from Miami, anti-Castro from day one, was also accused of being a *dialoguer*.

—I've been the number one activist of this community—Benes proudly said.

But for many in Miami, dialogue was a criminal activity, and the dialoguers were communists. There was a media campaign against Benes until his bank was bombed and surrounded for two weeks by protesters furious with his decision. Benes had to wear a bulletproof vest. His friends avoided meeting with him, and his children's friends began to avoid them.

—You see—Benes commented—no one is interested in freedom of speech in Miami. Only in Havana.

One of the characteristics of the mafia is to attack and kill other members of the same business. The Cuban mafia of the Batista supporters built one of the most prominent records in this regard, but they never called themselves the Batista Mafia—they called themselves freedom fighters.

Years later, in 1994, the coordinator of Americas Watch, Lee Tucker, wrote in a report: In Miami "there is no public defense of the right to freedom of expression or the right to dissent... No one at the local, state, or federal level has denounced the violence and threats against any moderate dissenter."[319]

—Aren't you afraid something might happen to you for publishing this too?—Hunter asked me.

—No...—I replied, still thinking—. Well, who knows. Anyway, I take precautions, like not drinking or eating anything I forgot in the office the day before.

—It's just that when something doesn't sit well with those people, instead of just passing gas like anyone else, they throw a bomb at you.

WE DON'T MIX BUSINESS WITH POLITICS

In August 1978, the Cubans Guillermo Novo Sampol, Alvin Ross Diaz, José Dionisio Suárez Esquivel, Virgilio Paz Romero, and the Chileans Juan Manuel Contreras Sepúlveda, Pedro Espinoza Bravo, and Armando Fernández Larios were indicted in the District of Columbia court and charged with perjury, conspiracy, and first-degree murder in the deaths of Osvaldo Letelier and Ronni Moffitt. In February 1979, Alvin Ross and the Novo brothers were found guilty on all charges brought against them, but the verdict was appealed.[320] Guillermo Novo and Ross were sentenced to life in prison. Ignacio Novo received a five-year sentence for each of his two perjury charges, to be served concurrently. That is, five years in total.[321]

The extradition request for the Chilean military officers from the Jimmy Carter administration was denied by Santiago in May 1979. Although Carter cut military aid to Chile, the large private corporations decided otherwise. Researchers like Alan McPhirson would find that, at that very moment, several giants rushed to support one of their allied dictators, protectors of freedom. Anaconda Copper Mining Co. signed an agreement to invest $1.5 billion, a sum twenty times greater than the aid from Washington. Chase Manhattan Bank announced the opening of its first branch in Chile. Goodyear, Exxon, St. Joe Minerals, Superior Oil, and Falconbridge increased their investments in that country. U.S. banks granted two billion dollars in credits to Chileans.[322] Between success and the miracle are always the friends.

—I don't think we lost even five minutes discussing the issue of human rights when the board approved the investment in Chile—said the Goodyear executive.

—We don't mix business with politics—said the Citibank manager, as if he had just read Orlando Letelier's latest article, "The Chicago Boys in Chile," published by The Nation two years prior:

"economic policies are always introduced to alter social structures. It's curious that the man who wrote a book titled Capitalism and Freedom *claiming that only classical economic liberalism can sustain political democracy could now so easily divorce economics from politics when the economic theories he defends coincide with an absolute restriction of all rights and all democratic freedoms. It would be expected that if those who restrict private enterprise are held responsible for the effects of their measures in the political sphere, those who impose an "unrestricted economic freedom" should also be held responsible, especially when the imposition of this policy is inevitably accompanied by mass repression, hunger, unemployment, and the perpetuation of a brutal police state... Repression for the majority and economic freedom for small privileged groups are two sides of the same coin."*[323]

—We've returned to Chile—said Ralph Cox, president of Anaconda— not only for the new possibilities in mining, but because this government has been able to create an environment of confidence for investors.

In 1980, the predictable finally happened. The military leadership and the Chilean oligarchy celebrated Carter's defeat by Ronald Reagan, who, months later, granted new credits to the government of Augusto Pinochet. At the same time, the new president's ambassador to the UN, Jeane Kirkpatrick, blocked a commission of the organization from investigating human rights violations in Chile.[324]

Kirkpatrick, an ex-socialist turned advocate for far-right values, was behind the moral, media, and financial support for the Contras in Nicaragua, despite the UN and the U.S. Congress having labeled them as terrorists. Opposed to the human rights policy pushed at the beginning of Carter's presidency, the new Kirkpatrick doctrine that prevailed in the Reagan administration stated that "the legitimacy of a policy is based on its strength." Like Henry Kissinger, Friedrich Hayek, and Milton Friedman, Kirkpatrick also visited Chile in 1981 and, upon returning, said she had seen neither disappeared people nor protests in that strange country struggling to hold onto the Andes to avoid falling into the sea. Which was equivalent to saying that, since she didn't see Santiago's sewer system, no one in Chile took a shit.

But Kirkpatrick was in search of *"a winnable war"* to lift the national spirit.[325] Chile did not provide any conflict, so his team of advisors discovered Grenada, a Caribbean island so small it didn't appear on maps.

In one of the first conversations about Cuba, the new Secretary of State Alexander Haig told the president:

—Just give me the order, and I'll turn that shithole island into an empty parking lot.[326]

Despite all the support from the U.S. government and private mega corporations, the "Chilean miracle" kept going from one economic crisis to another. In 1976, its economists, radicals of the *Free market* and *Non-intervention of the State* in the economy, attempted a disguised dollarization to stop inflation, pegging the national currency to the dollar and fixing its value at 39 pesos. By 1982, Chile had the highest per capita debt in the world, and the economy contracted by a historic 14 percent, something that had never happened during the economic blockade and social chaos instigated by Washington during Allende's three years.

Augusto Pinochet could never shake the ghost of Orlando Letelier. On March 28, 1982, Washington Post journalist Mary McGrory wrote, "A ghost haunts our policy toward Chile… From his grave, Letelier does more than any human rights envoy can do."[327]

The article was collected and archived by the CIA.[328]

THE FAILED TRADE OF GOODWILL

IN JUNE 1977, FOR THE FIRST TIME IN ITS HISTORY, the State Department sent intelligence information to Havana. Jimmy Carter had multiple fronts open and wanted to start resolving the problem of terrorist attacks in Miami. They arrested a group that was planning an attack on the island, accusing them of violating the old Neutrality Act, which was rarely enforced because it was rarely convenient.

—I don't think Washington shot down the Cubana plane—Fidel Castro told Senator Frank Church in a private conversation—but the CIA created this monster and now they can't control it.[329]

Perhaps as a gesture of reciprocity, and even though Carter was no longer president, on a Saturday in October 1984, the assistant of the Cuban Mission to the UN, Néstor García Iturbe, called the head of security for the U.S. delegation to the UN, Robert Muller, to inform him of a plan by the far-right in the United States to assassinate President Ronald Reagan in North Carolina. On Monday, Muller called García to invite him to lunch, with the news that the president's security service had detained the conspirators.

More than a decade later, in 1997, a series of bombings hit Cuba's tourist circuit, just as sugar plantations were set on fire in the

1960s or the island was infested with pathogens in the 1970s and 80s to destroy its livestock production. Several bombs exploded in hotels like the Hotel Capri, the Hotel Nacional, the Hotel Miramar, the Hotel Triton, and the Hotel Sol Palmeras. Other bombs exploded at various points in Havana. One of these destroyed the second floor of the Bodeguita del Medio, a tourist attraction associated with Ernesto Hemingway. Apart from the goal of sabotaging the island's new tourism industry, several people were seriously injured, and an Italian tourist lost his life when another bomb exploded at the Copacabana Hotel. Luis Posada Carriles showed no remorse. He simply blamed the victim for being in the wrong place at the wrong time.

Fidel Castro attributed this series of terrorist attacks to the Cuban American National Foundation of Jorge Mas Canosa in Miami. Finally, President Clinton agreed to pass intelligence information to Havana about two new attacks on other hotels. The C4 explosive attacks were aborted in time.

Shortly afterward, Fidel Castro entrusted Gabriel García Márquez with delivering information in person to President Clinton about new terrorist attacks against airlines. When the Colombian writer arrived in Washington, Clinton, an admirer of *One Hundred Years of Solitude*, was on the Pacific coast, but the information was received by intelligence services. No members of Mas Canosa's Foundation were detained. Posada Carriles gave interviews to newspapers acknowledging his participation in the recent attacks in Cuba, which he called "the fight for freedom."

The information received by Washington's intelligence services proved that, despite limited resources, Cuban intelligence was highly effective. Too effective. On September 12, 1998, the FBI launched a raid against Cuban spies, successfully detaining ten of them. The spies had infiltrated Miami groups such as Alpha 66, Brothers to the Rescue, and the Cuban American National Foundation itself.

Four managed to escape to Cuba. The five who admitted their spying activities were tried in Miami and sentenced to prison, some to life imprisonment. Neither Posada Carriles nor his collaborators, nor his financiers, nor any member of the Cuban American National Foundation was detained or brought before a court.

Everyone Wanted El Mono, Dead

ON DECEMBER 9, 1981, FOUR MEN met in Suite 1534 of the Holiday Inn in Miami to discuss in detail the attack on the *Cubana de Aviación* plane. All were familiar to local police and FBI offices: Ricardo Morales Navarrete, Francisco Chao Hermida, Osmeiro Carneiro, and Venezuelan lawyer Raymond Aguiar.

Shortly after appearing on a television program with confessions about the attacks on Orlando Letelier and the Cubana de Aviación flight, just before midnight on December 20, 1982, El Mono Morales Navarrete was murdered at the Cherries bar on Key Biscayne, an island off Miami where Richard Nixon had a vacation home. Like Orlando Bosch and many of his comrades and enemies, El Mono had spent half the day conspiring and the rest on Bacardí rum.

According to the *Washington Post* on February 6, El Mono had arrived in his red Cadillac, accompanied by Juan Fernández and Nancy Cid Lamazares, the widow of a Cuban murdered there in 1973 by Armando Elidio Ruiz, who was in turn murdered by associates of El Mono.

A .32 caliber bullet pierced his chest. He was 43 years old. Miami police labeled the case as homicide, but no one was ever convicted. Cuban Orlando Torres claimed he shot El Mono Morales in the head, not the chest, and it was in self-defense. He was acquitted.

El Mono's lawyer, John Komorowski, stated:

—I have no doubt that someone wanted Morales dead and executed him. There's no doubt about it; it was a setup. Who? Only God knows. It could have been the Cubans, the anti-Castrists, the drug traffickers, the CIA, anyone...

His acquaintances will acknowledge that El Mono Navarrete was obsessed with eliminating Rafael Villaverde, a Cuban who, like him, had participated in the Bay of Pigs invasion in Cuba. Like him, he had also been a CIA agent in Miami during the agency's destabilization campaign in the early sixties. Morales had also been a friend and probable accomplice of Edwin P. Wilson, another CIA agent who made a fortune from the illegal sale of arms to various countries in Africa, Asia, and the Caribbean. What no one could explain was the source of his hatred for Villaverde.

With the exception of General Commissioner Osmeiro Carneiro, all were murdered or died under suspicious circumstances. Among those accused of drug trafficking in Florida was Rafael Villaverde, another Cuban exile trained by the CIA. Villaverde disappeared in a yachting accident in the Bahamas, hours after his arrest, in March 1982.

Months before the execution of El Mono Morales, journalist Taylor Branch and prosecutor Eugene Propper had published *Labyrinth*, a dense and extensive book detailing El Mono's résumé as a member of Cuban paramilitary groups and as an informant for the CIA, the DEA, the Disip, the DINA, the FBI, and who knows what else.

In Miami, the Definition of Terrorism Is Flexible

In September 1986, Luis Posada Carriles disappeared from the high-security prison of San Juan de los Morros in Venezuela. He reappeared in FBI records as a CIA collaborator and security advisor to the president of El Salvador José Napoleón Duarte. In El Salvador, Posada Carriles was under the orders of Lieutenant Colonel Oliver North. This operation ended in the Iran-Contras scandal, for which, to bypass the prohibition on continuing to fund the Contras approved by the U.S. Congress, the CIA secretly sold weapons to Iran to transfer millions of dollars to the Contras through a Swiss bank account.

According to the FBI, Posada Carriles lived and operated with a fake identity card and passport issued by the government of El Salvador under the name Ramón Medina. In the same way, other CIA agents operated in that and other Central American countries, such as Guatemala, like Félix Rodríguez, the executioner of Ernesto "Che" Guevara in Bolivia, under the alias Max Gómez. Among other services, they supplied explosives from Ilopango to the Contras in Nicaragua. On February 28, 1990, he was shot near a gas station in Guatemala City. Without money to cover the multiple operations he received in Miami, his friends had to take care of the payment of $22,000—$50,000 in 2023 value. According to Posada Carriles, a friendly agent from Mossad had informed him that the attack was the work of Cuban agents, although it was also possible that it had been revenge from the Venezuelan guerrillas, whose members had been tortured under the supervision of Posada Carriles.[330]

—My enemies are many—acknowledged Posada Carriles—; they don't begin or end with Fidel Castro.

Despite the extradition treaties in force for homicide, judges in the United States will deny these requests from Cuba and Venezuela, arguing that detainees might not be tried according to international law, like the prisoners in Guantánamo, in Cuba.

In 1991, Luis Posada Carriles will admit that the attack on the Cubana DC-8 had been "the most effective sabotage against Castro."

In 2000, Guillermo Novo, Luis Posada Carriles, Gaspar Jiménez, and Pedro Remón were arrested for a new assassination attempt against Fidel Castro at the University of Panama. Before leaving the Palacio de Las Garzas, Panamanian President Mireya Moscoso granted each of them a pardon.

Like many others on the FBI's list of Cuban terrorists, Posada Carriles died free in Miami, as a hero and martyr of freedom. The rest were killed by their own comrades—none by a plot or in combat against the communists—but due to differences of opinion, mistaken statements to the press, suspicions of being double agents, debts with drug traffickers, and personal betrayals.

On April 17, 2005, the *Washington Post* published:

"In any other American city, Posada Carriles would have been met by a SWAT team; he would have been arrested and deported. But in the peculiar ecosystem of Miami, where anti-Castro politicians control both the press and the ballot box, the definition of terrorism is flexible: a terrorist to some is a freedom fighter to others."[331]

—I remember his malicious smile—wrote Cuban journalist Ann Louise Bardach after interviewing Posada Carriles— when he told me he had at least four different passports from different countries with fake names, including an American one.

—When was the last time you visited the United States?—Bardach asked him.

Posada Carriles burst into laughter.

—Officially or unofficially? I have many passports. If I want to go to Miami, I have different paths to get there. I have no problem.

—Clearly you don't— added Bardach, but Posa´da Carriles might have missed the subtlety of the comment.[332]

LET BUSH CALL HIS FATHER

BOSCH ALSO ENJOYED A PEACEFUL retirement in Westchester, Miami. An active retirement.

—They call and say that if they don't give the money they demand for The Cause—confessed former assistant prosecutor Alberto Millán— they threaten to plant a bomb.

—Alongside López Castro and Rubén Darío—said an FBI agent— Orlando Bosch is one of the godfathers of Cuban paramilitarism. We're after them, but we can never do our job.[333]

In 1987, after the intervention of the U.S. ambassador to Venezuela, the Cubans Otto Reich and Orlando Bosch were pardoned by the government of Jaime Lusinchi. In September, Bosch made the imprudent move of publishing a letter of gratitude to those who helped The Cause, including Otto Reich. Alarmed by his friend's public confession, and amid a request for a special visa for Bosch to return to the United States, Reich reported that the letter was fake, a product of Cuban propaganda.

In any case, in February 1988 Bosch flew to the United States without a visa and was arrested for violating his probation issued in Miami in 1974 in exchange for refraining from participating in violent actions of a political nature. A year later, in 1989, Cuban congresswoman Ileana Ros-Lehtinen and her secretary, the future governor of Florida and son of the president, Jeb Bush, began a campaign for the release of the patriotic hero. In support of early parole and the granting of political asylum, Jorge Mas Canosa assured the judges that his friend Orlando Bosch "would never participate in violent actions again," while the Immigration and Naturalization Service received multiple bomb threats as a way of supporting the cause in favor of Bosch.[334] The FBI agent, George Davis, wrote a report based on his investigations and reports from the local Miami police, defining Bosch as "the number one terrorist."[335] Despite all the recommendations against granting political asylum to Bosch, including from the State Department, Jeb's father, the newly minted president George H. Bush, decreed his release and political asylum in 1990 and, just two years later, granted him a green card. Almost immediately, he was hired by the Pan American Hospital in Miami. In his resume as a pediatrician, he did not include repeated malpractice in Cuba and the loss of his job at Abbey Hospital in Coral Gables thirty years earlier, due to his habit of storing bombs in the hospital's basements.

Shortly after, a police officer identified him as the organizer of a fundraiser to finance a commando that promised a new attack in Cuba. The officer reported the violation of his parole agreement, but his superior replied:

—What do you want me to do? I can call the Department of Justice and inform them that Bosch has violated his promise once again. Then Jeb will call his father, and Bosch will be back on the streets with even more authority.[336]

Bosch himself laughed at the new agreement signed with the justice system, which prohibited him from participating in any act of violence.

—It was a crude farce—he said—. They bought the collar, but they didn't buy the monkey.

In January 2001, during the last week of his presidency and following a tradition similar to the pardon of a Thanksgiving turkey, Bill Clinton granted presidential pardons, one more questionable than the other. One of the individuals who received the presidential pardon was Marc Rich, a fugitive from justice and a refugee in Switzerland for corruption and tax evasion. Rich was one of the largest donors to the campaigns of Bill Clinton and his wife Hillary when she ran for the Senate. President Clinton responded to criticisms from the Republican side:

—I swear I will answer all the questions about Marc Rich when Bush answers the questions about Orlando Bosch.

OF course, PInOCHET gave THE OrDer

IN 1987, CAPTAIN ARMANDO FERNÁNDEZ LARIOS escaped to the United States and surrendered to be tried for the crime of Orlando Letelier and Ronni Moffitt. The son of a Chilean officer, he had been born in Washington and returned two decades later to study at the School of the Americas. He participated in the assault on the Mint

House on September 11, 1973. Later, he became a supervisor of the Caravan of Death and a member of the DINA. Exactly as his father Alfredo Fernández had predicted, Armando ended up in prison, none of his superiors defended him, and the only one who could do so, his father, was already dead by then.

In January 1987, Fernández Larios secretly entered the United States and pleaded guilty to the murder of Orlando Letelier. He was imprisoned for four months. He was released and allowed to live freely in Miami, where he worked for a time in an auto repair shop, always under federal police protection. General Augusto Pinochet labeled him a deserter.

As summarized by the *Miami* News Times on November 18, 1999, Armando Fernández Larios "found refuge in the same country where he had committed a crime." He faced a trial presided over by Burlington Parker, the same judge who ten years earlier had called Guillermo Novo and Alvin Ross, implicated in the bomb that killed Letelier and Moffitt, a "black communist."

Perhaps another irony will be that the captain devoted himself to the car repair business, although, for some reason, that was the same paradox for many Cubans who were labeled terrorists by the FBI and who considered all their former associates, like Townley and Fernández Larios, traitors and war targets.

Fernández Larios was never able to free himself from his pseudonym, Romeral Jara. His accomplice, Mónica Lagos, also couldn't escape her own ghost, Liliana Walker. From then on, she attempted suicide several times and ended up sinking into drugs and alcohol, until on April 17, 1990, she was discovered in Santiago by the newspaper *La Época*.

Two years later, Lieutenant Pedro Barrientos Núñez followed the path of Captain Fernández Larios. He had lived in Miami for 34 years, until on October 5, 2023, he was detained in a routine procedure on a Florida highway and it was discovered that he was wanted by Interpol. Judge Roy Dalton stripped him of his U.S. citizenship, which had been acquired illegally. Lieutenant Barrientos and his outraged family never understood why this obsessive persecution by communist justice, filled with hatred and thirst for vengeance.

Barrientos had been one of the killers of Víctor Jara. He had been kidnapped at the State Technical University of Chile, where he worked, on September 12, 1973. He was tortured for several days. Finally, the singer was killed after his fingers were crushed. He was thrown onto an abandoned lot near the train tracks on September 16, along with others guilty of communist ideas. The autopsy report also recorded 56 bone fractures and 44 bullets in his body.

Shortly after arriving in the United States, Professor Landau interviewed Captain Fernández Larios in a motel room in Virginia. The captain gave him a list of six generals and colonels directly implicated in the murder and cover-up of Letelier.

—Of course Pinochet knew—said Fernández Larios—as did Colonels Contreras and Espinoza. It was he who gave the order to eliminate Letelier in the United States. They almost never mentioned his name, but everyone knew who they were referring to when they spoke of 'the boss.'[337]

By 1989, Michael Townley was in a Denver, Colorado prison. Perhaps too late, Mariana Callejas joined the campaign for the referendum against Pinochet in Chile. Not few recognized her as a collaborator of the dictatorship, but also acknowledged that she had repented for her crimes.

—At least this woman repented and says so—said someone who looked like a worker, someone who could have been that same worker who told Callejas's eldest son on September 11, 1973:

—Go home, son, save yourself, because none of us are getting out of here alive.

In her 1995 memoirs, Callejas would write: "I learned that the people, the working class in general, do not hold grudges and even knowing who I was, I had pleasant gatherings with residents of La Pintana, shared their communal pot…"[338]

General Pinochet continued as Supreme Chief of the Armed Forces of Chileand later as a non-elected lifelong Senator. In 1998, he was arrested in London for crimes against humanity. After five hundred days of exile in England, relieved by visits from celebrities of freedom (of capital) like Margaret Thatcher, he was released on humanitarian grounds due to his delicate health. Like Efraín Ríos Montt and dozens of other friendly dictators, he died in 2006 without ever facing trial.

In Florida, Townley became a protected informant for the FBI, pursued by militant groups in Miami. Under a secret identity, a secrecy interrupted only by a couple of interviews that only deepened the mystery, he likely resided for a long time in Fort Lauderdale, not far from his former comrades from C4 in Miami, who never stopped looking for him. General Contreras never granted him the rank of Major. Even less so when, in the 90s, the new semi-democratic regime incarcerated him, and he retreated into his own versions of history.

In 2016, the Supreme Court of Chile requested the extradition of Captain Fernández Larios, accused of at least fifteen murders. The request would sleep for many years in some office in Washington. The Court also requested the extradition of Cuban Virgilio Paz for the murder of Spanish diplomat Soria in Santiago de Chile, on July 16, 1976.

A judge in the United States convicted Paz for the terrorist attack that killed Ronni Moffitt and Orlando Letelier. As in almost all other cases, his sentence was drastically reduced to six years, with an order of deportation. Since there are no deportation treaties between the United States and Cuba, the terrorist was released and allowed to reside freely in Florida.

THE TWO SHADOWS OF THE CAR FOLLOWING US

THE DRIVER, JOSÉ DIONISIO SUAREZ, remarried a young Mexican woman in 1981. In 1990, he was living in Tampa, Florida, when the

FBI received information from some members of the Cuban exile and, after weeks of monitoring his movements, arrested him at his home on April 11. Aside from being the one who detonated the bomb that killed Ronni and Letelier, Suárez was accused of planting a bomb in New York and a murder in Puerto Rico.

—José is innocent—said his wife—. He's been working in car sales, but he's being used as a scapegoat.

Like Posada Carriles and Bosch, Suárez had dedicated himself to painting bucolic landscapes of Cuba. As in previous cases, they were appreciated as works of art in Miami. Only in Miami. As in other cases, José Dionisio Suárez, known by the nickname Charco de Sangre, participated in several executions of rebels during Batista's regime and of Batista supporters (like Lieutenant Armando Suarez Suquet) during Fidel Castro's regime.

Within a few days, several exile leaders collected thousands of dollars to pay for Suárez's defense. On May 4, once again, four Miami radio and television stations organized another media marathon to raise funds. With Guillermo Novo as spokesperson, the campaign was a resounding success, reaching the figure of $30,000, three times what they had previously achieved to help cancer patients. As moral support, three cities awarded José Suárez their honorary keys.[339]

A year later, *America's Most Wanted*, the most popular television program at the time, dedicated to the search for criminals, showed the photograph of a terrorist wanted by the FBI. Shortly after, the producers at Fox began receiving calls from South Florida.

—The guy they're looking for is Francisco Luis.

Another recorded call stated:

—That's Frank Báez.

A woman from West Palm Beach recognized him:

—That's the same guy who blasts his music. The last time I saw him was because I called the police about nuisance noise at night. Shortly after, they knocked on my door. It was him and three other men, ordering me never to call the police again.

A coworker, who worked in landscaping, recognized him.

—He has the odd habit of changing his name every so often…

On April 23, 1991, the FBI arrested Virgilio Paz. Among many other crimes in Chile, Argentina, Mexico, and Italy, Paz had participated in the 1976 terrorist attack in Washington. He was the passenger in the car that followed Letelier and the one who pressed the button on the medical beeper that detonated Townley's bomb, placed beneath the light blue Chevy.

—At least I won't have to live in hiding anymore—he said.

On September 12, 1991, the same judge Aubrey Robinson, who months earlier had sentenced José Dionisio Suárez, gave him twelve years in prison, without the right to bail, solely for the murder of Orlando Letelier and Ronni Karpen Moffitt.[340] He was released before completing the sentence.

In 2016, a judge in Chile requested his extradition (along with that of Michael Townley and Captain Fernández Larios) to stand trial for the torture and murder of the diplomat Carmelo Soria in Santiago, when Paz was a member of the DINA.

The request was archived.

Of the numerous terrorist attacks and the many directly involved in just the year 1976, only a couple of lower-ranking individuals were convicted. Their sentences did not exceed ten years or were reduced to half or nothing at all.

A New Era: Going After the Laws

IN 1997, TWENTY YEARS AFTER THE FORMER PRESIDENT of the Association of Veterans of Brigade 2506 Juan José Peruyero was executed in front of his Miami home for the crime of lukewarm anticommunism, his friend Juan Evelio Pou, a lieutenant in the United States Army, ran for president of the same Association. Pou also did not agree with continuing "terrorist acts within the United States," because they had a negative effect on public opinion in the country.[341] He preferred to carry them out outside the country, a position more in line with the jurisdiction of the CIA, his former employer.

Pou lost the election to Roberto Carballo (219 votes to 236), a more radical candidate who had opposed Carter's dialogue proponents, claiming that "a new wave of terror is inevitable, because we are at war."[342]

The file on Pou, though moderate, was also complicated. In 1979, he had been arrested by the FBI for trafficking weapons on a commercial aircraft. In 1994, along with Francisco Hernández and José Antonio Llama, he was arrested again by the Puerto Rican coast guard for trafficking rifles with a two-kilometer range and more powerful military weaponry on the private yacht La Esperanza, funded by the Cuban American National Foundation, with the purpose of assassinating Fidel Castro during the 1997 summit of leaders on Isla Margarita. The same group had rented an apartment in Venezuela to prepare for the long-sought objective.

—Owning a yacht and possessing weapons does not make anyone guilty of anything—declared defense attorney José Quinon to the *Tampa Bay Times,* on August 22, 1998—. There are political reasons behind these accusations. The U.S. government is trying to unite with Cuba… My clients are pursuing democracy in Cuba through peaceful methods.

Although the Cuban government had previously denounced several attacks organized against the island by the Cuban American National Foundation, and although the FBI confirmed having thwarted this assassination plot, the five individuals involved were cleared of charges.[343] The trial, held in the colony of Puerto Rico, will be the only attempt out of 638 to assassinate Fidel Castro that will reach a U.S. court.

On December 9, 1999, the *New York Times* reported that *"the powerful Cuban lobby,"* the Cuban American National Foundation, insisted on the same argument as the defense attorney: *"our methods of opposing the Cuban government* are peaceful... The heavy rifles confiscated were intended for personal defense."

The prosecution could not provide evidence that the defendants had any political motivation to kill a foreign leader. Without malicious intent, there is no crime.

—We want to send a message to the Cuban community—said Carlos Ávila, one of the jury members—: you are not alone.

The jury's ideological statement was crowned with a masterful maneuver by the defense attorneys, proving that the law is equal for all, but not all are equal under the law.

Awaiting the final verdict, attorney Ricardo Pesquera declared:

—The U.S. government understood that it cannot accuse any of its citizens of attempting to do what it itself had done so many times, that is, trying to kill Fidel Castro.

The defendants were found not guilty.

The Law is Equal for All; Not All are Equal Under the Law

On July 12, 1998, four years after the publication of a biography devoid of content, an enthusiastic Posada Carriles agreed to undergo two days of questioning with reporters from the *New York Times*. In a Spanish difficult to transcribe, partly due to a bullet that had pierced his jaw in 1990, Posada Carriles confessed:

—The CIA taught us everything, how to use explosives, how to kill, how to make bombs."[344]

He also acknowledged, as transcribed by the *Times*, that in 1997 he organized "*a wave of bombings in hotels, restaurants, and nightclubs in Cuba, killing an Italian tourist and alerting the Cuban government... Posada was trained in demolition and warfare by the CIA.*"

The goal was to destroy tourism in Cuba, just as sugar plantations had been destroyed with incendiary bombs in the 60s, and the family economy of farmers had been ruined with the introduction of dengue and pathogens in the 70s and 80s.

The *New York Times* also recorded that, according to Posada Carriles, *"the hotel bombings and other operations had been supported by leaders of the Cuban-American National Foundation. In turn, its founder and head, Jorge Mas Canosa, was supported by the White House, both by President Ronald Reagan and by George W. Bush and Bill Clinton."*

—Jorge Mas Canosa controlled everything—said Posada Carriles—. Whenever I needed money, I'd tell him to send me five thousand, ten thousand, fifteen thousand dollars, and he never had a problem.

According to Posada Carriles' statement to the *New York Times*, the businessman Jorge Mas Canosa sent him at least 200,000 dollars. The transfers usually came with a note: "This is for the church."[345] A significant number of transfers to cover the operational expenses of Posada Carriles and others were made through Western Union from businesses in Union City in New Jersey, some of which had paintings of Posada Carriles himself and even photographs of the artist with Jorge Mas Canosa.[346] Another of these centers was the typical Hispanic market, a supermarket, restaurant, and Western Union branch, owned by Abel Hernández. Among the small flags of various Latin American countries, one could see Posada Carriles' bucolic paintings alongside historical photographs, such as the one of the store owner posing with the millionaire and friend of presidents Jorge Mas Canosa.

José Dionisio Charco-de-Sangre Suárez also painted landscapes of rural Cuba from the Batista years. Similarly, and with no difference in style, Orlando Bosch painted bucolic landscapes of a nonexistent Cuba, especially during his time in prison in Caracas. His paintings sold like gold in Little Havana in Miami, to support The Cause. In this way, he managed to reinvest the money into a foundation he called Mortar for Masons, to fund the struggling armed resistance. For the anti-Castro community in Miami, the name didn't mean "Mortar for Masons," but "Collaboration or Bomb."

—Well—Bosch quipped in an interview— we can't say that money is going toward buying flowers and meat pies.

The businessman Mas Canosa also supported this project by sending him money, always in cash. He never wanted to know the minor details of his activities. The transfer was handled by a third party in Miami. Later, the money continued to flow, but under the names of Feliciano Foyo and Alberto Hernández.

Fearful of ending his days in an attack, like the one he suffered in Honduras in 1990, Posada Carriles tried to clarify his legacy before the journalists of the world's most famous newspaper:

—I was trained by the CIA on several occasions, such as in the camp in Guatemala, but I didn't participate in the Bay of Pigs invasion.

After escaping from the Caracas prison for the attack on the Cubana airplane, he took refuge in Central America, under the orders of Colonel Oliver North, who was then in charge of training and organizing the Contras against Nicaragua.

Over the years, Posada estimated that Mas Canosa sent him more than 200,000 dollars.

—He never said: "This is from the foundation." No. The money always arrived with a note: "This is for the church."

The generosity of millionaire Jorge Mas Canosa knew no bounds. In April 1993, he spent a fortune to rescue two of his aunts from the Cuban regime who were living in Cienfuegos.

Ingratitude knew no bounds either. After some time living in luxury and excess in Miami, the aunts returned to Cuba.[347]

—The poor will never understand what success is— said Yoani—. That's why they're poor.

IF WE DO IT, IT'S NOT TERRORISM

NELSON MANDELA AND THE AFRICAN NATIONAL CONGRESS were declared terrorists by Ronald Reagan and Margaret Thatcher for using weapons in their fight against Apartheid in South Africa. On Tuesday, March 3, 1981, the new president explained it in an interview on CBS:

—Can we— Reagan wondered— abandon a country like South Africa, which has stood by us in all the wars we have fought, a country that is essential to the Free World for its production of minerals that we all need...?

Later, in 1987, at the Commonwealth Summit in Vancouver, Margaret Thatcher confirmed the logic of Human Rights:

—A considerable number of the members of the African National Congress are communists... When the ANC says it will attack British companies, it demonstrates that it is a typical terrorist organization. I have fought against terrorism all my life... I will have nothing to do with any organization that practices violence. I have never met anyone from the ANC, the PLO, or the IRA, and I wouldn't.

In 1982, the State Department had declared that Cuba is "a state sponsor of terrorism," citing Havana's incursions in Latin America. However, as acknowledged by Presidents Cesar Gaviria and Andrés Pastrana of Colombia, Havana's contact with Colombian guerrillas focused on facilitating a peace process with the government at their own request. Something Washington attempted by contacting the FARC and failed. As a result of one of the agreements to free the brother of President Gaviria, Juan Carlos Gaviria, his kidnappers were exiled to Cuba. The second excuse was that Cuba protected Basque separatists, which was the result of another negotiation between the government of Spain and Cuba to resolve the ETA issue in Spain. The same State Department admitted it had no evidence that this group of Basques was related to any terrorist activity since their arrival on the island. Cuba was the first country designated as a sponsor of international terrorism by Washington and will remain on that list for generations. Mandela was removed from the list in 2008. Cuba was not.

Months later, in 1983, the Miami City Council created "Dr. Orlando Bosch Day" in honor of one of their greatest heroes, even though Miami police and the FBI considered him, along with Luis Posada Carriles and a long list of collaborators, a dangerous terrorist.

In August 1988, the State Department included the African National Congress among the *"organizations dedicated to terrorism."* In January 1989, Washington officially added it to the list of "terrorist groups." The publication included a preface by President George H. Bush, who equated the terrorism of the ANC with that of Al Fatah and Yasser Arafat. The ANC, the report stated, "receives support from the Soviet bloc, Cuba and several African nations" whose goal is the establishment of a "socialist and multiracial government in South Africa."[348] Something, obviously, unacceptable.

In April 2002, Noam Chomsky summed up the international principle under the hegemony of Europe and the United States:

—It's very simple. If they do it, it's terrorism. If we do it, it's counterterrorism.

From Terrorism to Lobbying

BY THE LATE 1970S, JORGE MAS CANOSA had become convinced that no bomb, sabotage, or invasion was going to overthrow Fidel Castro. If anything could be done, it was in U.S. politics, which is just as corrupt but at least legal. He did not abandon his old bomb-planting comrades, such as Bosch and Posada Carriles, but rather the opposite: he helped them with money to escape from jail in

Venezuela and with media campaigns to get them pardoned and declared heroes. He began to use his fortune and prestige to support political candidates. The first beneficiary was Paula Hawkins, the first woman elected as a U.S. senator from the state of Florida.[349]

The brothers Guillermo and Ignacio Novo were vindicated in the 1980s. Now, the Cuban American National Foundation took care of funding them. Mas Canosa hired Guillermo Novo as his bodyguard in Miami. According to his assistant Richard Allen, President Carter had shut down a clandestine radio station, privately owned by an anti-Castro group, had been excessively monitoring the Miami community, and even some had been brought to court, accused of participating in terrorist activities.

In March 1980, in the middle of the election campaign, the candidate Ronald Reagan met with Miami journalists at the Centro Vasco restaurant and repeated this version, as if he had mastered the subject. There, he said that President Jimmy Carter had been harassing the Cuban community, which only wanted freedom for Cuba…

—Can you give more details about this harassment?—a journalist asked.

—Well, I have to go—Reagan answered.[350]

The former CIA director and future vice president under Reagan, George H. Bush, supported these accusations while his son and future governor of Florida, Jeb Bush, campaigned in English and relatively fluent Spanish in favor of his father. Jeb had moved to Miami because, he said, he wanted to be immensely rich. He succeeded, with the help of some Cuban millionaires, such as Armando Codina, a few years older but still quite young. At the time, he was 32 years old. Among Jeb's many ventures was the first charter school, the Liberty City Charter School, which, along with voucher programs, was another way, like endless wars, to channel taxpayer money to large private corporations. Undoubtedly, the school had to have the word Liberty somewhere in its name.

By 1980, the future had ended; for NASA and for popular imagination. Two or three decades of rebellion by the underclass also ended. Cuban paramilitarism did not disappear, but it began to be replaced by representatives and senators in Congress. The same financial network, the same avalanche of donations from large and small businesses that in previous decades had supported terrorist groups, now redirected its capital to the new heroes: legislators. Why break the law if you can change it first? By far, a much more effective move, though never enough to kill Fidel Castro or change the communist regime for a more domestic, prosperous one surrounded by private yachts, like Miami.

This was proven almost immediately. Few months later, with 50.7 percent of the votes, Ronald Reagan became the new president. The Cuban exiles from Miami and Union City claimed the result. Not only had they gotten rid of the blond devil, not only had they placed their freedom-loving cowboy in the White House, but from then on their power in Congress would be, at the very least, disproportionate. Like the power of any lobby in the country of laws and freedom; the country proud of its democracy that never managed to shake off the tradition, the dogmas, the corporations, the banks, and even the political and electoral system from the times of slavery.

The Free World Seeks a Winnable War

FOR HENRY KISSINGER, AS WELL AS for the friendly dictatorships of the South, four years had been lost. After the defeat in Vietnam (which he negotiated in Paris and earned him a Nobel Peace Prize) and the failed invasion of Angola to restore the colonial regime that the Cubans from Cuba had helped to remove, it had not only been necessary to reinforce the unconditional support for all the friendly dictatorships around the world, but also any war that was winnable. That is, any war against a small island, that is not Cuba, like Grenada, or against a blocked and impoverished country. The

Washington Post of May 26, 1975, had already taken note of the words of the powerful Secretary of State:

—The United States—he had said, with his German accent—must take some kind of action somewhere in the world that makes clear our determination to remain the world's greatest power.[351] The law of the convert, of the super-patriotic immigrant.

A year before the election, in November 1979, the future advisor to Ronald Reagan, Jeane Kirkpatrick (a converted ex-socialist and figure of the neoconservative reaction against Carter and the hippies, she was in favor of unconditional support for friendly dictatorships, the Contras and the death squads in Latin America) was more than clear:

—If revolutionary leaders describe the United States as an imperialist, racist, colonialist, genocidal, and warlike force, then they are not authentic democrats, they are not friends; they define themselves as enemies and must be treated as enemies.

Once in the White House, Kirkpatrick, the female Kissinger, recommended to President Reagan to invade the micro-republic of Grenada and the impoverished Nicaragua:

—This is a war you can win—assured the advisor and ambassador to the UN, while the president dipped his hand into the tub of Jelly Belly candies, which never missed his desk.

A short time later, just months after moving into the White House, in an interview for CBS, the new president justified U.S. support for the apartheid in South Africa:

—Can we abandon a country that has supported us in all the wars we have fought?—answered Ronald Reagan with two questions— A country that is essential to the Free World?

Among these aids was the handover of Nelson Mandela in 1962 by the CIA, to be sentenced to life imprisonment as a terrorist rebel. There was the failed invasion of Angola in 1975, like all, supported by a powerful international disinformation campaign. The apartheid regime collaborated with the CIA to reverse the independence of Angola, partly achieved with the help of Cuba. Both Washington and Pretoria feared a new free country, governed by blacks. The same fear and the same story against the independence of Haiti in 1804 and against the independence of Cuba in 1898. Black people cannot govern themselves. This fear was confirmed years later, when in 1991 President Nelson Mandela acknowledged in a speech in Havana:

—The Cuban people hold a special place in the hearts of the peoples of Africa… There is no parallel in African history where another people have sacrificed themselves in defense of one of ours. The defeat of the apartheid army was an inspiration for the people who were then struggling in South Africa. Without the defeat of the racist army of South Africa in Angola, we would still be illegal.

Butterflies Learn To Fly

Following Ronald Reagan's victory in the 1980 elections, the wave of terrorist attacks and executions carried out by the Cuban exile in the United States began to decline. The lost confidence from the Bay of Pigs invasion and, even more, the frequent silence of the CIA in the 70s, was renewed in a new and necessary wave of trust in the government.

Just a few months after Reagan took office, businessman Jorge Mas Canosa founded the Cuban American National Foundation, a replica of the pro-Israel lobby American Israel Public Affairs Committee (AIPAC), which in turn was derived from the American Zionist Council. Automatically, the CANF gained the direct and active support of the new president, which the lobbies of the far right in the United States had struggled so hard to place in the White House after the traumatic experience of Jimmy Carter's Human Rights foreign policy and a congress positioned even further to the left, always so eager to investigate the excesses of the CIA while overlooking the excesses of Fidel Castro in Cuba.

Donations from large corporations in Latin America (at the time under rigid capitalist military dictatorships promoted by Washington) and Cuban businesses in the United States began to flow. Jorge Mas Canosa was appointed president of the new foundation and named Frank Calzón as its executive director. Among their propaganda investments, the Canf funneled several million dollars in donations to the U.S. state conglomerate Radio y Televisión Martí, which also received government funds to promote the efficiency of private enterprise through the NED. Sometimes the state and taxpayer money do serve a purpose.

As paramilitary organizations based in Miami had done before, their objective continued to not only be regime change in Cuba, but also other international interventions against any group or government that was misaligned and did not respect the sacredness of the right to free enterprise above any other right. The Canf backed allied media conglomerates, political and military interventions, such as the invasion of Grenada in 1983. It supported the reactionaries against the new government of the newly decolonized People's Republic of Angola and the apartheid regime of South Africa. All of this aligned with the policy of London and Washington to include prisoner Nelson Mandela on the list of dangerous international terrorists while his political party, the African National Congress, was classified by Washington as a "terrorist organization."[352]

The bombs did not stop. The extortions did not stop either. One night in 1989, responding to an intense media campaign by the Miami exile community, agents from the Department of the Treasury entered the home of the director of the Museum of Contemporary Art in Miami, the anti-Castro Cuban Ramón Cernuda, and seized a collection of works painted by artists residing in Cuba. Cernuda couldn't be charged with any crime, so months later a bomb exploded in front of the museum, destroying exhibited works and a considerable portion of the building. Director Cernuda was accused of displaying paintings by artists residing in Cuba and of being in favor of dialogue between Washington and Havana.[353] The critics who blew up the exhibition hall preferred the bucolic landscapes of Cuba painted by Luis Posada Carriles, Orlando Bosh, and José Dionisio Suárez.

By the early 1990s, bombs and mafia-style extortions from the Batista era amounted to just a few dozen per year, but the culture and financial structure that had developed over forty years remained intact. Thanks to new legal foundations, the flow of dollars multiplied. As is a well-known practice by the CIA, in addition to private donations, the Cuban Foundation received half a million dollars from the government through the National Endowment for Democracy, the NED, a government entity very generous to all those entrepreneurs and independent journalists who share its same business ideology and control over others.

Meanwhile, the representatives and congressmen from the exile community continued to grow in number and power. Influential Cuban Representative Ileana Ros-Lehtinen didn't need euphemisms to crystallize a social dogma that in previous decades had been a CIA secret plan and which the same national Congress of the 1970s had investigated and condemned as an illegal and criminal project under all national and international laws:

—I support any attempt to assassinate Fidel Castro.[354]

In Miami and Union City, harassment, bombings, and executions continued. For not being sufficiently anti-Castro, the weekly *Réplica* suffered seven bomb attacks, until it closed in 2005. Its owner, Cuban Max Lesnik, was rescued several times by the FBI without even knowing it. All theaters or clubs that invited artists from the island suffered bomb explosions, from New York to Miami.

In 1996, to give just one more example, El Centro Vasco (a pub and restaurant on 8th Street, frequent organizer of fundraising events for the Cuban right) invited popular Cuban actress Rosita Fornés to perform at its venue. Radio Mambí launched a campaign to discredit the restaurant. Shortly after, a bomb destroyed the facilities, forcing it to remain closed for months. Its owners, the

Saizarvitoria family, were labeled as communist traitors and had to sell the business. The buyer, Felipe Valls, a friend of Jorge Mas Canosa and owner of another restaurant, the Versailles, was one of those in charge of discrediting the Saizarvitorias for their betrayal, as they continued to receive death threats.[355]

Emilio and Gloria Estefan, Jon Secada, and Julio Iglesias maintained a deafening silence. Julio Iglesias had at least two reasons: his son Enrique Iglesias was building a successful career in Miami, and he himself knew where he stood. In 1972, at a Miami nightclub, Julio Iglesias had said he had no problem singing in Cuba. Minutes later, the police had to rescue him. Almost two decades later, when Verónica Castro visited Cuba, they destroyed her star on 8th Street and urinated on it, though the latter is just a detail, especially since urinating on 8th Street is a time-honored tradition that deserves respect.[356]

Miami remained against censorship and in favor of freedom of expression—only in Cuba. The same names, the same structure, and the same culture reconverted themselves. They did not abandon the habit of considering anyone who thought differently as an enemy combatant, nor the habit of placing bombs against their own and others, but many took the political option and imposed their own laws on them.

The political maneuver did not mean that bombs and executions had been banned from patriotic plans. In 1995, government documents were released showing that Guillermo Novo, apart from being a bodyguard and owning a furniture store in Miami, continued sending explosives to Cuba.[357] Many of these attacks were thwarted in time. Although in smaller numbers and with fewer resources, in Miami there are spies from the island just as there are CIA spies on the island. According to the government in Havana, since 1959 there have been 3,400 Cubans killed by exiles in Miami.[358] Of course, as with everything in this story, the total numbers are always debatable.

In 1989, Miami was still known as The Capital of Terrorism in the United States.[359] Its members continued to enjoy multiple privileges. Not only were they automatically treated as refugees and legalized as soon as they set foot in Florida, regardless of their criminal record, but they were protected even after committing any crime, no matter how serious. According to U.S. law, foreign criminals must be deported, but the Cuban American National Foundation pressured for an exception to be made, arguing that if they were extradited to Cuba they could suffer some form of torture by the island's government, thus violating the mandate of the UN Convention against torture. The same argument will be used to allow other terrorists like Luis Posada Carriles to be released and spend his retirement in Miami. It will not count for the innocent tortured in Guantánamo or in the hundreds of secret prisons that the CIA and Mossad maintain at their whims around the world.

—The difference here— said the Argentine writer from the *Miami Herald*, Andrés Oppenheimer— is that the dissidents are not silenced by the State, as in Cuba. Certainly, there is intolerance and repression, but it is not the government's fault.

Private censorship is censorship of freedom—protected by the government.

Freedom Lovers, Yours

THE CONGRESSWOMAN ILEANA ROS-LEHTINEN used her lobbying power and friendship with the Bush family to secure the release of Virgilio Paz and José Dionisio Charco-de-Sangre Suárez. Governor Jeb Bush also interceded with his brother, the governor of Texas and future president George W. Bush. After seven years in prison, both were pardoned in 2001 by a Florida court, the same court that would give George W. Bush the victory three months later, in the disputed elections of that year, which he won by 537 votes.[360] The history of humanity decided by a judge and 537 votes from Florida...

In some cases, the same businessmen who had donated to various terrorist organizations in Miami and Union City over the past three decades continued to donate to the new organizations—now legal, such as the Center For a Free Cuba, the Cuban Liberty Council, the Congressional Cuba Democracy Caucus, and the Cuban American National Foundation itself. The two main objectives of these groups were, first, to influence the ideological narrative of the superpower through the media to shape policies and politicians favorable to their cause. Second, to directly influence Washington and state legislatures through the practice of lobbying in the very offices of congressmen.

Other objectives and more traditional practices will not be publicly acknowledged, but their implications will continue. For instance, in 1998, Luis Posada Carriles will admit that the Cuban American National Foundation of Mas Canosa had financed the series of bombings carried out in Cuba during the previous year, although, as usual, he will later deny being the mastermind behind the attacks. Despite Posada Carriles' confessions to the press, the CANF and its president, Francisco Hernández, denied any involvement while refusing to condemn the terrorist attacks on Cuban hotels. Hernández declared to the press that "we do not consider these to be acts of terrorism." The classic "I didn't do it, but I won't condemn it" that dates back to the times of Andrew Jackson and Daniel Boone.

In the early 1990s, a series of Cuban politicians from Miami and Union City, some of them children kidnapped in Operation Peter Pan, will rise to positions in their state legislatures and the national Congress. This was the case for Republicans Mel Martínez and Marco Rubio from Miami and Democrat Bob Menéndez from Union City. In Washington, they became part of important committees, such as the Foreign Affairs Committee and the Senate Select Committee on Intelligence, which, after the scandal uncovered by the Church Commission in 1975, claimed to oversee the activities of the NSA and the CIA. Years later, one of the members of the Intelligence Committee, Norman Mineta, summarized it succinctly: "We're like mushrooms; the CIA keeps us in the dark and feeds us a load of bullshit."[361]

In all cases, the new representatives and senators not only blocked proposals to lift the embargo against Cuba but also convinced politicians from other parties to radicalize the measures that had strangled the island since the 1960s, alongside similar practices against other disobedient countries. It is no coincidence that these same politicians will advocate for pardons for Orlando Bosch and Posada Carriles, ensuring that, despite a long and well-documented history of domestic and international terrorism, they all ended their days enjoying the finest restaurants in Miami and the unanimous adoration of the local press.

Some of these influential congressmen will continue, well into the 21st century, their habit of accumulating illegal money in their homes from bribes and special favors, in addition to the tradition of legalizing other forms of corruption, such as buying and selling influence through powerful lobbies. On more than one occasion, this will be reported in the press, albeit in small and timid enough print for the public to forget it in a heartbeat.

In any case, by the second decade of the century, the ideological impact will become notable and decisive in the state of Florida as well as its influence on elections and the government in Washington. The Cuban mafia was born and consolidated during Prohibition in the United States in the 1920s and grew stronger with casinos and brothels in the 1940s and 1950s. One of its most famous centers, the Copacabana Club in Havana, never forgave the Cuban Revolution for stripping them of their special privileges. From the 1960s to the 1980s, they became known for hundreds of terrorist attacks, using bombs or direct assassinations, all in the name of a new cause, this time political or pseudo-political.

After the Triumph of Ronald Reagan in the 1980 elections, they discovered that legality was far more convenient and used the same culture and funding network to infiltrate politics, the U.S. government, the mainstream press, and a large part of American and Latin American society. All in the name of patriotism, the defense of the flag, of democracy, of freedom, and of This-Great-Country against its enemies, the undesirables. Their enemies, any dissenter—even within their own ranks.

CIA orders, sir

A FEW YEARS LATER, IN 1981, IN A CONVERSATION recorded for Miami television, the journalist from the CIA's multimedia outlet Voice of the Americas, Francisco Chao Hermida, asked El Mono Morales about his responsibility for the most notorious bombings of recent years:

—When Letelier's death occurred—El Mono said—my responsibility, as head of Venezuela's 54th Counterintelligence Division, was to inform the National Executive about what had happened. Thirty-six hours later, on his desk, President Carlos Andrés Pérez had the conspiracy, the names, everything... Orlando Letelier had been sentenced to death in May 1976. Same as the plane. He was sentenced to death and executed.

—Who sentenced Letelier to death?—asked Chao Hermida timidly.

—General Augusto Pinochet—replied El Mono, without a hint of doubt.

—And who sentenced the passengers of the Cuban plane to death?

—I sentenced them, Orlando García Vásquez sentenced them, Frank Castro sentenced them, Gustavo Castillo sentenced them,

Hernán Ricardo sentenced them, Rafael Rivas Vásquez sentenced them…

—And in the name of what, for what purpose?

—To destabilize Cubana de Aviación's operations in the Caribbean. To destabilize the Castro government's relations with the small republics of the Caribbean… The objective was to sever ties between Venezuela and Cuba.

—Was that Orlando García's objective?

—No, sir. That was the Central Intelligence Agency's objective. Orlando García is following CIA orders, sir!

—Were you in Venezuela on a CIA mission?

—Correct.

—Are you a CIA man?

—I was.

—Do you feel no shame for having been a CIA man?

—Shame would be if I had been with the KGB, or the Cuban DGI… But being with the CIA is no shame to me.

—It's no shame to you—said Chao Hermida, following his interviewee's train of thought—because you interpret the CIA as an organization defending democratic and Western countries.

—Of which I am part—confirmed El Mono.

Fifteen years later, on April 5, 2006, on Miami's Channel 41, Orlando Bosch would confirm the same impunity with the same arguments

—Did you shoot down that plane in 1976?—asked Juan Manuel Cao—Do you feel any guilt?

—If I answer that I was involved—Bosch replied—I'm accusing myself, and if I tell you I didn't participate, you'll say I'm lying to you. So, I'm not going to answer either way. I'm just going to refer you to the courts, which acquitted me five times.[362]

—In that action, 76 people died…

—In a war, kid—Bosch stated— like the one we freedom-loving Cubans have against the tyrant, you have to bring down planes, you have to sink ships, you have to be ready to attack whatever is within your reach.

—But, for those who died there, for their families, wouldn't you feel a little...

—Who could have been on that plane?—Bosch asked, in his defense— Four Communist Party members, five North Koreans, five lousy Guyanese, kid... So, kid, who was on it? Our enemies.[363]

Heroes, but not quite

BEFORE RECEIVING HIS DEATH CERTIFICATE, Carter's Human Rights Policy had moved forward like a limping man in no hurry, but soon found itself in a swamp.

—If they can do this under the nose of the CIA and the FBI and get away with it—Carter had said, lamenting the limbo into which the Letelier case had fallen— then no president can govern here.[364]

Omega 7 and Comando Zero continued killing in the United States and claiming their actions to boost donations. In any case, the champions of individual responsibility never acknowledge anything individually.

—Have you seen all the interviews produced in Miami over those twenty years?—Hunter asked.

—Almost all—I said—. Television, radio, print media, selections from the CIA, the FBI... But I'm still working on it. I'm still missing some pieces of the puzzle.

—These guys are undisputed heroes there... A terrorist is only considered a hero by other terrorists, I think someone said.

Hunter flipped through a page of the manuscript.

—When Posada Carriles was linked to a series of bombings in Cuban hotels that killed an Italian tourist—he said— he denied it with a wink and said (I quote): *"We have nothing to do with these attacks. Besides, if we did, we'd still be denying it, since that's illegal in this country.*" Almost the same words as Bosch. They drank rum together.

—Killing tourists is illegal in Cuba too. I can keep going with more statements like these, but I need to cut it short.

—I appreciate it. Leave this one just as it is.

—I don't work for you.

—Well, kid, it's an editor's suggestion.

—Other times they simply acknowledged it and then denied it. They denied it and justified it, out of professional discipline.

—But Orlando Bosch and Posada Carriles were convicted in Venezuela.

—Yes, though never for all the pending charges and they never completed their sentences, like almost everyone, with exceptions like Eduardo Arocena, who paid with thirty years in prison when the FBI proved several murders, a dozen bombings, from Miami to New York, as well as the spreading of biological pathogens in Cuba.

—An injustice, according to his wife, due to Arocena's patriotic struggle.

—Posada Carriles escaped in 1985, was readmitted to the CIA to collaborate with Contra terrorism in Central America and never entered a prison again. When he was later tried by a Texas court, he was only prosecuted for entering the country illegally. Either way, he was also pardoned for this and released. Hours later, he was drinking rum on Miami Beach.

—He died recently. He had a hero's funeral. Miami television portrayed him as a victim of Havana's propaganda.

—The hero never participated in any battle or combat. He was always behind the machinery of the CIA or the repressive police of Caracas. In short, just like all his comrades who, despite having the backing of the wealthiest men in the region and the power of the greatest superpower of the time, lost each and every one of their heroic battles.

—Bosch was also pardoned by his former boss, George H. Bush, as soon as he became president, in exchange for not continuing to commit terrorist acts, which, as in 1973, he did not comply with. More or less like giving a bottle of rum to an alcoholic in exchange for the promise of not drinking more than one glass.

—Did both retire here?

—Posada Carriles was pardoned by the president of Panama and, later, as you say, after entering the United States illegally, he was pardoned by a Texas judge. Bosch as well, like almost all of them. The ambassador to Venezuela and Undersecretary of State for Western Hemisphere Affairs, Otto Reich, organized a tribute for his return to Miami. Due to pending charges, the U.S. Department of Justice recommended Bosch's deportation, but Governor Jeb Bush launched a campaign to allow him to remain in the country.

—But the judges also ruled in their favor...

—Of course. They didn't declare them innocent. They only denied their deportation, claiming that they might not receive a fair trial in Cuba or Venezuela. They feared they would be treated as Washington treats the prisoners at Guantánamo, with the difference that almost all the prisoners tortured at that base in Cuba were declared innocent by their own accusers, despite having no friends in Washington. The friendly terrorists were protected and enjoyed all the benefits of their retirements on the beaches of Miami.

—Look, I know your opinion on all of this—said Hunter.

—I'm glad—I said, unaware that things were not going well—. You can accuse me of being wrong on any point, but never of being dishonest or complacent.

—I read somewhere that it might have been the Cubans from the island who killed Letelier and brought down the Cubana plane...

—The only problem with that theory is that there is not a single piece of evidence to support it, apart from the narrative of Calle 8. The same story as the Kennedy assassination. That it was the Cubans from the island. That Kennedy shot himself to go down in history.

Any evidence, any minimal document that would allow an investigation to begin? No. Zero. Nothing. Any evidence pointing to the CIA with the involvement of the Cuban mafia, among other mafias of the Free World? Yes, about ten thousand, and no more because the CIA itself refuses to declassify all the documents that survived the shredder and the fire.

—It's not the same.

—More similar, impossible. There's no evidence pointing to Castro, but there are a thousand pieces of evidence implicating Luis Posada Carriles and Orlando Bosch, among others, from Havana to Washington, from Caracas to Miami. Both had dedicated themselves to planting bombs wherever there were innocents, adults or children. The victims were then labeled as combatants. Both were more than informed of all those attacks in the Caribbean and the United States. Both had met with all the suspects and detainees. Both were part of clandestine organizations in Miami, in Union City and other legalized mafias, like the DISIP of Venezuela and the DINA of Chile, but they never even had the guts to acknowledge and stand by what they did, let alone go to the front, like the Che.

—Well, let's leave Che Guevara aside.

—Why?

—Because it'll turn into an endless book.

—He went to the front, whether you like it or not. The others, as CIA agent David Atlee Phillips said, had no guts. Very heroic, very brave, but landing alone on the island, in a bigger and more high-tech Granma to organize the revolution from Guantánamo or from the Bay of Pigs, not even as a joke. Heroes, *ma non troppo*.

—Let's set opinions aside—sighed Hunter, somewhat tired and perhaps frustrated— and get back to the facts. You need to finish it once and for all. You're already on (I estimate) page 550...

In 1990, the president and former CIA director, George H. Bush, nullified by presidential decree the deportation order against Orlando Bosch. As part of the agreement, Bosch promised to renounce the use of violence. As in previous times, he never kept his word, not even to those who had saved him from prison or deportation. But even this was not seen as a betrayal, but rather as a predictable formality. The same pardon would be granted to José Dionisio Suárez and Virgilio Paz through the mediation of Governor Jeb Bush and his brother, President George W. Bush.

In the year 2000, Guillermo Novo, Luis Posada Carriles and several collaborators were arrested and convicted in Panama for attempting to assassinate Fidel Castro and those around him with a fifteen-kilogram explosive device. The experienced terrorists left their fingerprints everywhere.

Immediately, Cuban congresswoman Ileana Carmen Ros y Adato contacted the White House, where Bill Clinton was still preoccupied with the dilemma of whether oral sex is sex. The four terrorists did not spend many weeks in prison, because the President of Panama Mireya Moscoso granted them, once again, a presidential pardon. All denied any involvement in the Panamanian president's free decision.

In 2004, the new president, George W. Bush, traveled to Miami during his reelection campaign, gave several speeches, and attended several meetings. Among the audience were Virgilio Paz and José Dionisio Charco-de-Sangre Suárez.

—Why don't you call the congresswoman by her name?

—Who? Carmen Ros y Adato? That's her name registered at birth in Havana. She changed it here.

—I wasn't born with the last name Hunter—said Hunter—. Everyone has the freedom to call themselves what they want.

—I'm not going to forbid it, am I?

—Well, I'd better leave—said Hunter—. It's a waste of time arguing with someone who thinks a murderer like Che Guevara is a hero.

—Do you want me to continue or should we stop here?

—Let's stop here—said Hunter—. It's another one of your dense, unpublishable books.

—Well, I'm glad.

Terrorists Yes, Poets No

IN 2005, IMMIGRATION LAWYER José Pertierra will sum it up clearly:

—If Posada Carriles were a member of the National Union of Cuban Writers and Artists instead of a terrorist, things would be different. He wouldn't be able to aspire to enter the United States. The Department of Homeland Security denies visas to Cuban poets and artists but grants free entry to the country to terrorists. Cuba is one of the seven countries that the United States considers terrorist, and with that pretext, the government of George W. Bush denies entry to Cuban musicians, poets, journalists, writers, and academics simply because, as they live and work in Cuba, they are government employees… The last Cuban terrorist to arrive in Miami, the capital of terrorism, optimistic about soon obtaining residency, is Luis Posada Carriles.

PEOPLE AND CHARACTERS

Alvin Ross Díaz. A Cuban exile in Miami, one of those in charge of the assassination operation of Orlando Letelier. Member of the Bay of Pigs invasion operation in 1961.

Antonio Veciana. Cuban CIA agent. Participated in several sabotage operations and at least one assassination in Cuba before being transferred to other Latin American countries. In his memoirs, he detailed the multiple assassination attempts on Fidel Castro and the meeting of his CIA boss with the assassin of John F. Kennedy in Dallas.

Bernardo Torres. Along with Norman Díaz, Orlando Urra, Niledo Acevedo, was accused by Rolando Otero of being CIA agents involved in the assassination of John F. Kennedy.

Blake Fleetwood. American journalist. Interviewed Orlando Bosch and Posada Carriles in a Venezuelan prison.

Carlos de la Sotta. Chilean priest, owner of the illegal channel in Concepción, supported by Channel 13 of the Catholic University. Participated in the destabilization campaign against Salvador Allende. Michael Townley murdered the night watchman who guarded the blockade equipment of the covert channel.

Carmelo Soria. Chilean-Spanish diplomat, ambassador to the United Nations. He was kidnapped, tortured, and murdered by the DINA at the Townley family's home in Lo Curro, Santiago.

Carter Cornick. FBI agent assigned to the Letelier case and one of those responsible for uncovering the perpetrators of the attack.

David Atlee Phillips. One of the most prominent CIA agents. Participated in various coups in Latin America and the failed Bay of Pigs invasion. One of his agents, the Cuban Antonio Veciana, identified him as a participant in a meeting with the assassin of John K. Kennedy, Lee Harvey Oswald in Dallas.

Eduardo Arocena. Cuban exile. Participated in several attacks and sabotage operations against Cuba, such as the introduction of pathogens that sickened 300,000 people and decimated the island's farming and agricultural production. He was one of the few Cubans convicted by a Florida court without being released through a special pardon. He was convicted for at least two murders and thirty bombings in the United States.

Eugene Propper. Lawyer in charge of the Letelier case. Along with FBI agents Robert Scherrer and Carter Cornick, he was one of those responsible for resolving the case a few years later.

Eugenio Berríos. Chilean chemical engineer, collaborator with DINA and Operation Condor. In Santiago, he worked with Michael Townley on the development of Sarin gas and other lethal agents for the Pinochet regime. He was assassinated in Uruguay in 1992.

Eulalio José Negrín. Member of the Committee of 75, he was executed by a radical Cuban commando just before getting into his car in Union City.

Felipe Rivero. Cuban exile, participant in the failed Bay of Pigs invasion. He was one of the thousand prisoners released by Fidel Castro. In 1967, he was convicted in the United States for planting bombs in Canada. The conviction sparked a protest demonstration in Miami. He was released. One of his greatest achievements was connecting Miami groups with DINA in Santiago through Michael Townley.

Félix García Rodríguez. Cuban consular attaché in New York. He was assassinated on September 11, 1980 by members of the Cuban terrorist group Omega 7.

Francisco Chao Hermida. Journalist and anti-Castro activist in Miami. Collaborator with the CIA and responsible for interviewing prominent Cuban terrorists, such as Ricardo Morales, for Miami television.

Frank Castro (Eulalio Francisco Castro Paz). Cuban CIA agent. He participated in the Bay of Pigs invasion. Leader of the paramilitary National Liberation Front of Cuba in Florida and international drug trafficker, according to the CIA.

Frank Sturgis. (Frank Angelo Fiorini). Before becoming a CIA agent, he was known in the mafia network of the Copacabana Club in Havana. Comrade of CIA agent Howard Hunt in the Watergate plot. He became a CIA agent after the Revolution. He was identified by various witnesses as the second sniper who killed Kennedy.

Freddie Lugo. One of the Venezuelan journalists hired by the Cubans in Caracas to plant the explosives that brought down Cubana Flight 455.

George H. Bush. Director of the CIA from January 1976 to January 1977. Vice President (1981-1989) and President of the United States (1989-1993). Father of Florida Governor, Jeb Bush, and of Texas Governor and two-time U.S. President George W. Bush (2001-2009).

George Junius Stinney. A fourteen-year-old Black youth, executed in the electric chair in 1944 for the crime of two white girls that he did not commit.

Guillermo and *Ignacio Novo Sampol.* Cuban exile brothers in Miami responsible, among other assignments, for the assassination operation of Orlando Letelier.

Hernán Ricardo Lozano. One of the two Venezuelan journalists hired by Cubans from Caracas to place the two bombs that brought down Cubana Flight 455 in Barbados.

Howard Hunt. One of the most powerful CIA agents in Latin America. He handled propaganda in Mexico and organized the coup d'état in Guatemala. In Uruguay, he managed to get a rural radio host elected as president. Responsible for the wiretapping scandal that led to President Nixon's resignation, his own memoirs implicate him in the assassination of John Kennedy.

Hunter. The only fictional character in this book. Editor and acquaintance of the author.

Isabel Morel. Wife of Orlando Letelier. After Letelier's death, she worked with the widower of Ronni Moffitt to clarify the assassination of her husband.

Jack Ruby. (Jacob Rubenstein), he was the killer of John F. Kennedy's assassin, Lee Oswald. He died at Parkland Hospital, the same hospital where Lee Oswald and John Kennedy had died. He was a casino owner, manager of illegal gambling operations in Texas and at the Tropicana Club in Havana. He collaborated with Cuban exiles in various attacks.

Joan Baez. Popular American protest singer, daughter of a Mexican father, a figure in Martin Luther King's civil rights movement and part of the resistance against the war in Vietnam. Alongside Orlando Letelier, she participated in the concert at Madison Square Garden against the Chilean dictatorship on September 10, 1976.

John Marciano. Professor of Ronni Karpen Moffitt at SUNY Cortland. Social activist, academic, unionist, and author of books like *The American War in Vietnam: Crime or Commemoration?*

John Roselli (Filippo Sacco). Influential mafioso in Hollywood, stripped of his casinos and brothels in Havana by the Revolution, along with Santo Trafficante Jr., he was recruited by the CIA to kill Fidel Castro. Like all others in other attempts, he failed, except in seeing President Kennedy dead. He was assassinated on April 23, 1976, shortly before testifying before the Senate Select Committee on Intelligence regarding the assassination of Kennedy.

John Rothchild. American journalist for Time and Fortune.

Jorge Mas Canosa. CIA agent and member of the failed Bay of Pigs invasion. Like the billionaire mobster José Miguel Battle, he was promoted to second lieutenant in the U.S. Army. In Miami, he became a powerful businessman and patron of terrorists like Orlando Bosch, Luis Posada Carriles, and Guillermo Novo. In the eighties, he was an advisor to Ronald Reagan, founder of the Cuban American National Foundation lobby, Radio and TV Martí (along with the CIA and government capital), and the company MasTec, founder of the Inter Miami soccer club in 2018. A bust in Miami Beach celebrates his contributions to freedom.

José Alfredo Pérez San Román. Cuban military officer under Batista's regime. He studied at military schools in Virginia and Georgia. He was one of the three commanders in chief of the Bay of Pigs invasion in 1961. He was captured by Revolution volunteers three days later and sentenced to 30 years in prison for treason. In December 1962, he was released and exiled to Miami. He repeatedly confessed to hating the United States for its failure in 1961.

José de la Torriente. Engineer and Cuban anti-Castro activist, known in Miami as a philanthropist. He was assassinated in 1974 in Miami with a shot behind his left ear by anti-Castro groups. The detail of the shot to his left ear was a code used for executions by some Cuban paramilitary groups in Miami.

José Dionisio Suárez. Nicknamed "Charco de Sangre" (Pool of Blood). Cuban exile, tasked with the assassination operation of Orlando Letelier. He was identified by witnesses in Miami as one of the executioners responsible for carrying out the killings of several individuals accused of murder and torture during the Batista regime and after the Revolution. In recent recordings made in Miami, Suárez admitted his involvement in tribunals and firing squads that executed Batista supporters accused of murder and massacres.

José Miguel Battle. Police officer under Fulgencio Batista, employee of the head of the Cuban mafia Meyer Lansky, and member of the CIA commando for the Bay of Pigs invasion. In Union City, he founded the mafia group La Corporación. He was sentenced to thirty years for his illegal gambling, drug trafficking, and murder operations in the United States, which brought him 45 million dollars annually. He pleaded guilty to murder and was pardoned two years later. In Miami, he became the wealthiest man in Florida and one of the top donors to political campaigns. In 2004, he was again accused of multiple murders and drug trafficking, a business that earned him over 1.5 trillion dollars.

Joseph Leo. FBI agent and assistant attaché at the U.S. Embassy in Caracas, and known associate of several Cubans and the Venezuelan Hernán Ricardo, whom he helped obtain visas to travel to the United States.

Juan Gabriel Valdés Soublette. Assistant to Orlando Letelier in 1976 and ambassador of Chile to the United States since 2014.

Juan Orta. Mercenary for the Cuban mafia and collaborator with the CIA, he was in charge of the assassination of Fidel Castro.

Larry Wack. FBI agent. He investigated paramilitary groups in Miami and Union City such as Omega 7 and the terrorist attacks on Cuba by CIA collaborator Eduardo Arocena.

Llano Montes. In charge of planting CIA articles in El Mundo de Caracas.

Lourdes Casal. Cuban exile poet and professor at Rutgers University, New Jersey. In the last years of her life, she supported dialogue with the Island. She was the first Cuban exile to receive a literary award from Casa de las Américas in 1981.

Manuel Contreras. First head of Chile's Secret Police (DINA). In 1995, he was sentenced in Chile to 529 years in prison for his involvement in the murder of Orlando Letelier and Ronni Moffitt, and for other charges including kidnapping, forced disappearance, and murder.

Manuel Fuentes Weddling. Head of propaganda for the far-right group Patria y Libertad of Chile and later head of publicity for the government of Augusto Pinochet.

Marcos Rodríguez and Diego Medina. Cuban exiles in charge of assassinating Fidel Castro in Chile.

Mariana Callejas (alias Anat, Ana Goldman, Ana Brooks, Ana Luisa Pizarro, and Carmen Luisa Correa Letelier). Writer, wife of Michael Vernon Townley, member of the Socialist Party of Chile and informant for the military intelligence of the dictatorship of Augusto Pinochet. Member of the far-right Chilean group Patria y Libertad. Accomplice in several terrorist attacks. In 2008, she was sentenced to twenty years in prison for the murder of General Carlos

Prats in Buenos Aires. In 2010, the Supreme Court of Chile overturned the sentence.

Marita Lorenz. German CIA agent and probable lover of Fidel Castro. In 1960, she participated in one of the Agency's 638 attempts to assassinate him. In Miami, she was the lover of the former Venezuelan dictator Marcos Pérez Jiménez, with whom she had a daughter. In the 70s and 80s, she admitted to having participated alongside Cuban exiles like Frank Sturgis and CIA agents like Howard Hunt in the plot to assassinate John F. Kennedy.

Meyer Lansky. One of the leaders of the so-called "Kosher Mafia" due to his Jewish origins, he was one of the main figures in organized crime in Cuba and the United States. Due to the Cuban Revolution, he was forced to exile in the Bahamas, where the white supremacist Bay Street Boys party was dominant at the time. He was implicated multiple times in the assassination of President John F. Kennedy.

Michael Moffitt. Research assistant to Orlando Letelier at IPS in Washington and husband of Ronni Moffitt. After the terrorist attack at Sheridan Circle and a deep depression that led him to alcoholism, he fought alongside Letelier's widow, Isabel, to uncover the truth behind the attack that killed his wife.

Michael Vernon Townley (alias Andrés Wilson, Juan Williams Rose, Hans Petersen, and Kennet Enyart). CIA agent and mercenary for DINA. He was a member of the Cuban group Chicago Junta until November 21, 1963, one day before the assassination of President Kennedy. From 1969 he was under the direction of CIA agent David Atlee Phillips, to prevent elected president Allende from taking office. He created two paramilitary groups in Chile: Orden y Libertad and Protección Comunal y Soberanía. He managed to assassinate the Chilean General Carlos Prats and his wife in 1974 using a car bomb, and the former minister Orlando Letelier and his assistant's wife in Washington, in September 1976, using the same method. In his later years, he has resided in the area of Fort Lauderdale, Florida.

Orlando García Vásquez. A Cuban CIA agent, DEA, and head of the Disip. Bodyguard of the president of Costa Rica, José Figueres and the Venezuelan presidents Rómulo Betancourt and Carlos Andrés Pérez.

Orlando Letelier. Ambassador and minister of Salvador Allende. After the coup of 9/11 in Chile, he was confined to Dawson Island. Through efforts by the government of Caracas, he was freed in 1974. In Washington, he worked for the IPS, where he became the leading figure of Chilean exiles. He was assassinated on September 21, 1976, along with his assistant Ronni Moffitt in a terrorist attack organized by Chile's DINA and Cuban paramilitary groups from Miami and Union City.

Orlando Piedra. Police chief of Fulgencio Batista, member of the smuggling and illegal gambling mafia in Havana. In Miami, he partnered with the exiled senator Rolando Masferrer. According to the FBI (doc. May 8, 1973), Piedra was responsible for the torture, murder, and disappearance of detainees in Cuba during Batista's regime.

Orlando Urra. Member of Brigade 2506 organized by the CIA, which failed in the invasion attempt of Cuba. According to the HSCA (House Committee, May 10, 1977), Urra was another of those involved in the plot to assassinate Kennedy.

Pedro Díaz Lanz. Great-grandson of José Martí, he was a CIA agent since 1960, participating in various aerial sabotage operations against the island using B-26 bombers. Member of the CIA's Operation 40 group (currently a video game) responsible for assassinations in foreign countries, in the 70s he collaborated in cocaine trafficking. Poor and abandoned in Miami, he shot himself in 2008 at the age of 81.

Perry Fellwock. Alias Winslow Peck. Secret agent of the NSA. In the 70s he leaked information about the Echelon operation, which was used to spy on American citizens. Although the U.S. Senate took note and approved limitations on these practices, in 2013 another NSA agent, Edward Snowden, would prove that the practice of mass and systematic surveillance had only increased. Always illegally.

Pete Seeger. American folk composer and singer. He was a member of the Communist Party of the United States and was blacklisted during McCarthyism.

Rafael de Jesús Gutiérrez. Intelligence officer of the Fulgencio Batista regime, recruited by the CIA after the Cuban Revolution. Involved in the terrorist attack on Cubana Flight 455.

Rafael Rivas Vásquez. Cuban anti-Castro activist, head of Venezuela's secret police, DISIP. For a brief time, he was a comrade-in-arms of Ernesto Che Guevara during the early rebellion against Batista. Later, he worked with the group of anti-Castro Cubans in DISIP, becoming a close collaborator of Orlando García Vásquez. In the 80s, he was prosecuted by Venezuelan courts for corruption and illicit enrichment. According to his daughter Ana Gloria, her father "had great faith in God."

Ramón Donestévez Domínguez. Cuban businessman, boat manufacturer, and editor of the Spanish-language nationalist newspaper Verde Olivo. Executed in Miami with a shot to the ear in 1976 as retaliation for the execution of businessman Rolando Masferrer months earlier, who had ordered a dynamite attack against Donestévez that failed. A note with his handwriting and signed by Cero, one of Miami's most feared mafia groups, was found next to Donestévez's body.

Ricardo Aníbal Morales Navarrete (alias El Mono). CIA agent, FBI informant, and DEA informant. He participated in bombings in Congo and against Angola. He was one of the Cuban chiefs of Venezuela's secret police. Member of CORU, he took part in several terrorist acts. He was one of the confessed perpetrators of the attack that brought down Cubana Flight 455, killing 73 people in 1976. He later turned to selling information and drug trafficking. He was executed in 1982 by Cuban exiles in Miami Beach.

Richard Helms. CIA Director from 1966 to 1973. In 1977, after the covert operations in Chile, Helms became the only CIA Director convicted of lying to the U.S. Congress. He retired in 1976, after serving as ambassador to Iran for three years. That same year, he swore (and committed perjury) before the Senate Foreign Relations Committee that the CIA had nothing to do with the coup in Chile. Henry Kissinger did the same on television.

Robert Scherrer. FBI investigative agent in charge of the Southern Cone, based in Buenos Aires. He investigated several assassinations under Operation Condor and interviewed Michael Townley, DINA officers in Chile and SIDE in Argentina, responsible for assassinations such as that of former Bolivian President Juan José Torres and Chilean General Carlos Prat in Buenos Aires.

Rolando Otero Hernández. Cuban CIA agent tasked with assassinating Fidel Castro and responsible for several bombings in the United States. He claimed to have been part of the CIA and its plan to eliminate President Kennedy. Failed in his attempt to assassinate Pascual Allende in Costa Rica, commissioned by the DINA in Chile. It was he who, after his trial in Jacksonville for five bombings in government buildings in Miami, identified Michel Townley in a photo under a false name.

Rolando Masferrer. One of the leaders of the Cuban exile, founder of the Miami newspaper Libertad. He was executed in 1975 with a car bomb. The Havana government was blamed, due to Masferrer's anti-Castro activities and the fact that he had been a senator under Batista and a collaborator with the Cuban mafia. According to FBI agent Robert Scherrer and scholar Saul Landau, Masferrer was assassinated by the Novo Sampol brothers, on orders from businessman Jorge Mas Canosa. Shortly before, he had ordered the execution of businessman Donestévez, but the dynamite explosion did not kill his rival, who was executed in Miami months after Masferrer's death.

Ronni Karpen Moffitt. Assistant to Orlando Letelier at IPS in Washington, alongside her husband Michael Moffitt. She died in the explosion that killed Letelier in 1976, while traveling with her husband to the IPS offices.

Sagrario Pérez-Soto. Venezuelan, Orlando's lover.

Salvatore Sam Giancana. Italian-American mobster, CIA agent. Various speculations link him to the assassination of John F. Kennedy, along with the Cuban mafia (including Johnny Roselli and Santo Trafficante), the CIA, and the Mossad. So far, Washington has not declassified all the documents that could confirm or refute these accusations. In 1975, he was killed by seven shots in his home, shortly before appearing before the Senate's Church Committee, which was investigating the role of the CIA and the Cuban-American mafia in the assassination of Kennedy.

Santo Trafficante. He operated multiple casinos in Havana until the Revolution. Alongside Johnny Roselli, Frank Ragano, and Salvatore Sam Giancana, he was one of the most powerful mafia figures in Cuba and the United States until his death in 1987. He was linked to the assassination plot of John F. Kennedy, as well as multiple attempts to assassinate Fidel Castro. For a long time, his operational base was in Miami.

Saul Landau. Journalist, documentary filmmaker, and professor at California State Polytechnic University. In 1974, he invited Orlando Letelier to join the IPS in Washington, shortly after his release. He actively participated in the investigation of Letelier's death following the 1976 attack, with his initial theory about the involvement of Chile's DINA ultimately being proven correct by the FBI.

Sheila Harris-Thompson. Barbadian nurse. An unforeseen event caused her to miss the flight of Cubana 455.

Silvia Odio del Torro. Sister of César Odio, Administrative Chief of Miami. She testified before the Warren Commission that John Kennedy's assassin, Lee Oswald and two other Cubans visited her and her sister before the president's assassination, seeking support for the Cuban Revolutionary Junta against Castro, of which Odio was a member. The psychiatrist who worked with her doubted the veracity of her testimony, which is why it was dismissed—like all the other testimonies that consistently pointed in the same direction during the 60s and 70s.

Stefano delle Chiaie. Italian fascist and conspirator. He participated in several attacks in Europe in coordination with Michael Townley. In 1974, he was recruited by DINA and settled in Chile in 1976 until moving to Bolivia, where he supported the coup d'état led by Luis García Meza Tejada in 1980.

Taylor Branch. Journalist and historian, winner of a Pulitzer Prize. Along with prosecutor Eugene M. Propper, he wrote Labyrinth, a thorough account of the investigation into the assassination of Orlando Letelier.

Vernon Walters. Number two at the CIA. He was fluent in Spanish, among other languages, which allowed him to serve as an interpreter in several diplomatic missions for U.S. presidents, in addition to being an active agent in various covert operations. He was responsible for overseeing and supporting, in different ways, the activities of Operation Condor. In 1991, President George H. Bush awarded him the Presidential Medal of Freedom.

Virgilio Paz Romero. Cuban exile in Miami in charge of the assassination operation of Orlando Letelier. Associate of Michael Townley and María Callejas, he was a collaborator with Chile's DINA of Chile and active member of several paramilitary groups in Miami, participating in terrorist attacks in Europe and other Latin American countries. From 1980, he worked in the Miami area as a gardener. In 1991, he was identified by his neighbors on the television program America's Most Wanted. He was sentenced to twelve years in prison for the assassination of Letelier and Moffitt, but was pardoned after serving half of his sentence. In 2016, the Supreme Court of Chile requested his extradition for his participation in the kidnapping, torture, and murder of Spanish diplomat Carmelo Soria. The request was denied. Like other freedom fighters, he lives freely in Miami, where he is considered a hero.

Wilfredo Pérez Pérez. Captain of flight 455 of Cubana, which was downed in the terrorist attack on October 6, 1976. He died trying to land the passenger plane, which ultimately crashed into the sea after the explosion of the second bomb placed by the team of Orlando

Bosch and Luis Posada Carriles, among other Cuban exiles from Corps.

INDEX
(excluding some of the ten most frequently mentioned names)

2506 Brigade, 172, 454
Aamco, 41, 63, 97
Abbey Hospital, 150, 474
Adlai Ewing Stevenson, 47
Adriana Corcho Calleja, 216
Agee, 179
Agustín Edwards, 218, 362
Aipac, 490
Al Capone, 17, 91, 120, 124, 126, 132, 456
Alain Mouriat, 122
Albert Anastasia, 19
Alberto del Río Aguilera, 216
Alberto Millán, 21, 128, 473
Alejandro Romeral Jara, 300, 369
Alexander Haig, 360
Alfredo Peralta Azurdia, 114
Alfredo Stroessner, 160, 293, 300
Allan Earnest, 67
Allen Dulles, 43, 105
Allen Ginsberg, 34
Allende, 22, 27, 31, 58, 60, 62, 66, 67, 70, 71, 73, 76, 78, 79, 83, 84, 96, 101, 103, 104, 145, 146, 158, 160, 176, 177, 178, 179, 183, 191, 218, 219, 220, 223, 224, 233, 235, 241, 242, 244, 245, 247, 251, 258, 277, 285, 287, 301, 311, 317, 318, 326, 327, 346, 362, 363, 403, 426, 434, 435, 444, 445, 468, 505, 511, 512, 514
Alpha 66, 40, 137, 210, 211, 256, 260, 366, 469
Alvin Ross Díaz, 86, 294, 453, 457, 505
Ana Fresno, 248
Ana Pizarro, 96, 98, 102
Andrea Project, 201
Andrés Pastrana, 485
Andrés Pérez, 74, 83, 84, 124, 125, 155, 157, 264, 265, 276, 282, 325, 326, 327, 328, 330, 331, 332, 333, 346, 347, 348, 387, 390, 392, 396, 398, 400, 405, 410, 413, 415, 425, 446, 460, 497, 512
Andrés Wilson, 67, 76, 96, 98, 307, 313, 441, 511

Andrew Jackson, 200, 361, 495
Angela Yvonne Davis, 297
Angelo Bruno, 42
Ann Louis Bardach, 396
Antonio Canaves, 113
Antonio González, 231
Antonio Veciana, 6, 36, 40, 51, 64, 66, 94, 99, 137, 211, 256, 267, 415, 462, 505, 506
Aparicio Méndez, 399
Arauco Hilton, 74, 75, 408, 410
Arbelio Ramírez, 31, 32
Argentina, 49, 66, 67, 70, 105, 158, 159, 181, 182, 183, 186, 191, 192, 193, 202, 204, 226, 227, 251, 252, 258, 262, 274, 284, 287, 290, 294, 314, 324, 328, 345, 361, 399, 459, 480, 514
Ariel Dorfman, 345
Armando Fernández, 299, 301, 357, 358, 369, 465, 475, 476
Armando López Estrada, 250, 260, 262, 264, 416
Armando Suarez, 98, 479
Arnello Romo, 181
Arturo Rodríguez Vives, 118, 206
Associated Press, 48
Augusto Lutz, 86
Avbc, 259
avenida Bergenline, 289
Bacardi, 85
Bahía de Cochinos, 216, 416
Bandera Roja, 126
Barack Obama, 240
Batallón 2506, 184
Batallón Atlácatl, 360
Batista, 15, 19, 20, 31, 32, 35, 39, 46, 59, 91, 92, 93, 95, 98, 102, 124, 132, 135, 147, 152, 205, 254, 255, 293, 320, 321, 326, 390, 416, 456, 463, 479, 483, 509, 512, 513, 514
batistero, 38, 277
Batisteros, 39
Battalion 2506, 46, 47
Bay of Pigs, 5, 31, 93, 117, 162, 172, 207, 256, 257, 260, 394

Benito Guanes, 293
Benito Nardone, 32
Bergenline Avenue, 131, 308, 341
Bermuda, 85
Bernard Cornfeld, 62
Bernardo Leighton, 104, 106, 204, 210, 226, 248, 249, 298, 334, 345, 426
Bernardo Torres, 57, 505
Bethesda, 9, 163, 164, 297, 313, 316, 334, 338, 399, 530
Beyoncé, 129
Bible, 256
Bilito Sampol, 135
Bill Clinton, 129, 130, 185, 432, 475, 483, 503
Biological Weapons, 137
Bishop, 40
Blake Fleetwood, 118, 258, 448
Blas Jesús Corbo, 230
Bob Maheu, 35
Bob Marley, 143, 144
Bolivia, 36, 37, 41, 42, 52, 64, 112, 115, 139, 159, 205, 257, 267, 449, 472, 514, 516
Bonao, 259, 260, 261, 262, 263, 265
Bosch, 32
Brasil, 177, 183
Brazil, 115, 137, 138, 246
Brigada 2506, 76, 77, 135, 142, 182, 260, 264, 364, 382, 462, 480
Brigade 2506, 46, 133, 207, 256, 363, 512
Bush, 13, 118, 120, 129, 142, 185, 364, 367, 400, 422, 423, 473, 474, 475, 483, 487, 494, 501, 503, 504, 507
C4, 38, 100, 102, 107, 124, 153, 198, 208, 266, 277, 282, 283, 288, 315, 320, 323, 324, 334, 335, 339, 342, 343, 355, 363, 377, 381, 394, 402, 409, 414, 416, 453, 456, 469, 478
Calle Ocho, 12, 15, 63, 97, 129, 152, 185, 271
Callejas, 26, 27, 28, 60, 61, 62, 63, 67, 68, 70, 71, 73, 96, 98, 99, 100, 101, 102, 103, 106, 109, 172, 174, 191, 203, 204, 214, 215, 226, 234, 284, 286, 287, 314, 317, 318, 319, 342, 354, 357, 359, 363, 426, 427, 428, 444, 446, 459, 477, 516, 530
Camilo Valenzuela, 178
Canf, 491, 495

CANF, 490
Carlo Cicuttini, 204
Carlos Altamirano, 101, 107, 249, 359, 426, 434
Carlos Bringuier, 56
Carlos de la Sotta, 190, 191, 505
Carlos Eugenio Vides Casanova, 128, 450
Carlos Godoy, 287
Carlos Marcello, 42
Carlos Menem, 328
Carlos Prats, 67, 205, 226, 250, 251, 298, 334, 346, 459, 511
Carlos Romero Barcelo, 185
Carmelo Soria, 174, 226, 248, 285, 286, 287, 480, 505, 516
Carter Cornick, 110, 278, 316, 349, 351, 373, 397, 435, 440, 460, 505, 506
Castro, 42, 53, 267
Catholic University, 342
César de Windt, 81
Cesar Gaviria, 485
Charles Horman, 87, 445
Charles Persaud, 379, 386
Chateau Renaissance motel, 314
Che, 31, 32, 93
Che Guevara, 31, 34, 37, 43, 50, 99, 112, 113, 122, 175, 253, 254, 257, 406, 407, 449, 472, 513
Chevrolet Malibu, 57, 165
Chicago Boys, 296, 342, 466
China, 186, 293, 461
Christian Herter, 30
Church Commission, 115, 138, 139, 212, 213
Ciro Orizondo, 232
Cirro Orizondo, 231
Clarence Long, 162
Cold War, 29, 31, 350, 459, 460
Colombia, 179
Columbia University, 34, 254, 335
Comisión Church, 36, 496
Condor Plan, 79
Conrado Pappalardo, 300
Contra, 449
Contras, 96, 112, 120, 175, 256, 257, 395, 450, 467, 484, 489, 500
Contreras, 26, 28, 66, 69, 81, 83, 86, 87, 96, 104, 105, 109, 146, 202, 204, 214, 220, 247, 248, 249, 250, 262, 267, 277, 293, 297, 298, 319, 356, 357,

358, 365, 366, 441, 442, 443, 444, 445, 451, 465, 477, 478, 510
Copacabana, 17, 54, 121, 123, 198, 469, 496, 507
Corps, 517
Coru, 254, 259, 260, 261, 263, 264, 266, 280, 288, 321, 391, 392, 393, 410, 416, 513
CORU, 327, 374
Costa Rica, 76, 77, 78, 79, 80, 84, 125, 145, 146, 154, 155, 158, 159, 160, 161, 223, 254, 257, 258, 265, 266, 277, 377, 388, 395, 404, 423, 449, 512, 514
Crescencio Galañega, 294
Crescencio Palenzuela Páez, 216
Cuban mafia, 31, 56, 124, 254, 509, 510, 514, 515
Cuban Nationalist Movement, 120, 131, 171, 248, 263, 313, 451, 455
Cuban Power, 120, 257
Cuban Scorpion, 120
Cubana 455, 152, 261, 333, 349, 381, 384, 396, 401, 412, 413, 414, 415, 507, 513, 515
Cubana 467, 281
Cubana 615, 281
Cubana de Aviación, 154, 265, 280, 391, 392, 422, 470
Curaçao, 146
Curtis LeMay, 153
Dallas, 21, 42, 53, 54, 55, 56, 57, 64, 79, 134, 193, 272, 505, 506
Daniel Ellsberg, 213, 239
Daniel Graham, 182
Daniel Oduber, 84, 265
Daniel Oduber Quirós, 265
David Atlee Phillips, 28, 31, 40, 42, 64, 93, 94, 177, 251, 255, 257, 402, 502, 506, 511
David Popper, 224, 243, 295
Dawson, 87, 165, 166, 167, 224, 241, 242, 336, 512
de Radio Swan, 111
DEA, 75, 94, 95, 114, 126, 152, 257, 373, 471, 512, 513
dialogueros, 116, 461, 464, 481
dialoguers, 431
Díaz Limonta, 118, 206
Díaz Radulovich, 214
Diego Arria, 241, 346, 359

Diego Medina, 52, 510
Diego Portales, 76, 338, 342, 354
Digepol, 114
Dina, 15, 16, 26, 66, 67, 69, 70, 71, 76, 78, 79, 80, 81, 83, 86, 87, 96, 98, 101, 103, 104, 105, 107, 126, 152, 202, 203, 204, 220, 223, 226, 236, 243, 249, 250, 251, 258, 267, 277, 286, 294, 297, 301, 313, 314, 315, 317, 318, 321, 335, 339, 349, 355, 357, 364, 365, 367, 368, 369, 387, 425, 439, 440, 443, 444, 453, 471, 476, 480, 502, 505, 506, 512, 515, 516
dinamita, 20, 38, 102, 216, 325, 354, 355, 456
Dinh Ba Thi, 311
Disip, 15, 16, 74, 80, 81, 124, 126, 146, 152, 264, 265, 321, 325, 326, 330, 331, 332, 333, 349, 376, 390, 393, 396, 399, 401, 402, 404, 405, 411, 412, 415, 471, 502, 513
DISIP, 111, 127, 326, 327, 405, 446
Dominican Republic, 32, 73, 82, 117, 126, 140, 146, 160, 200, 254, 258, 282, 326, 344, 417, 452
Don Bohning, 73, 81
Donald Freed, 369, 423
Donald Gregg, 449
Donald Trump, 129, 185
Douglas Fraser, 239
Drew Fetherston, 141
Duke Ellington, 33
Dupont Circle, 163
dynamite, 72, 121, 123, 124, 151, 153, 156, 157, 198, 208, 209, 229, 276, 409, 414, 513, 514
Ecuador, 179
Edgard Hoover, 107, 212
Eduardo Arocena, 135, 139, 142, 500, 506, 510
Eduardo Devreux-Bergere, 160
Eduardo Frei, 60, 61, 62, 247, 287
Edward I. Koch, 162
Edward Seaga, 144
Edward Snowden, 213, 512
Edwin Wilson, 249, 343
Efraín Ríos Montt, 478
Eisenhower, 11, 30, 34, 35, 43, 44
El Alacrán, 120
El Cajón del Maipo, 223

El Che, 37, 41, 50, 93, 122, 145, 253, 255, 407, 502, 503
El Mercurio, 174, 217, 219, 284, 358, 362, 367, 403
El Mono, 15, 16, 17, 41, 64, 74, 78, 82, 83, 86, 96, 97, 111, 116, 117, 118, 119, 126, 127, 128, 133, 135, 147, 152, 153, 154, 156, 171, 198, 211, 230, 231, 232, 261, 263, 265, 266, 277, 325, 326, 327, 331, 332, 333, 348, 349, 373, 376, 396, 401, 402, 404, 405, 406, 408, 409, 410, 411, 412, 413, 414, 423, 439, 470, 471, 497, 498, 513
el Mono Morales, 38, 75, 78, 83
El Salvador, 128, 145, 174, 175, 347, 360, 395, 433, 449, 471, 472
Elizabeth II, 279
Enrique Campos Menéndez, 284
Enrique Morel, 293
Ernest, 6, 20, 184, 295
Ernest Hemingway, 20
Ernesto Eberhard, 225
Ernesto Sábato, 227
España, 102, 189, 200, 263, 278, 334, 425, 426
Estados Unidos, 178, 267, 403
Esteban Ventura, 20
Eugene Hasenfus, 396
Eugene Propper, 212, 278, 316, 360, 367, 373, 388, 414, 434, 445, 460, 471, 506
Eugenio Berríos, 5, 87, 203, 234, 247, 248, 287, 506
Eulalio José Negrín, 136, 463, 506
Exxon, 279, 466
FACh, 223
Federico Willoughby, 219, 358
Felipe Martínez, 135
Félix Rodríguez, 112, 175, 257, 449, 472
Fernández Larios, 299, 300, 301, 307, 313, 314, 357, 369, 465, 475, 476, 477, 478, 480
Fernando Lario, 286
Fernando López Muino, 216
Fidel Castro, 15, 29, 30, 32, 33, 36, 39, 41, 43, 44, 46, 47, 48, 51, 53, 54, 56, 59, 77, 94, 96, 98, 99, 110, 112, 113, 115, 120, 122, 125, 129, 133, 146, 149, 184, 192, 209, 210, 211, 220, 254, 257, 267, 309, 313, 320, 325, 328, 330, 331, 387, 389, 390, 401, 407, 410, 415, 431, 459, 461, 463, 464, 468, 469, 472, 481, 482, 486, 488, 490, 492, 503, 505, 506, 508, 510, 511, 514, 515, 530
Filippo Sacco, 115, 508
flight 455, 152, 516
Flight 455, 85, 131, 374, 389, 401, 455, 513
Florida, 13, 16, 35, 40, 47, 54, 56, 74, 75, 81, 93, 98, 101, 106, 110, 111, 113, 117, 118, 119, 123, 127, 128, 129, 130, 151, 154, 184, 188, 197, 199, 208, 210, 229, 253, 256, 257, 259, 262, 272, 273, 274, 275, 281, 314, 325, 404, 409, 414, 417, 423, 439, 440, 450, 452, 458, 459, 471, 474, 476, 478, 479, 487, 494, 496, 506, 507, 509, 511
Fontes Pereira, 216
Ford, 62, 63, 66, 81, 192, 197, 213, 253, 318, 338, 339, 344, 355, 358, 362, 421, 441, 463
Ford Company, 63, 358
Forestier Haengsen, 358
Fort Belvoir, 46
Fort Benning, 46, 86, 112, 204, 449
Francis Bellamy, 132
Francisco Aruca, 462
Frank Bender, 30
Frank Castro, 73, 78, 79, 80, 81, 82, 85, 155, 259, 262, 264, 283, 326, 388, 392, 406, 422, 497, 507
Frank Costello, 19
FRANK SINATRA, 17, 18, 212
Frank Terpil, 249
Frank Teruggi, 445
Freddy Lugo, 281, 348, 376, 380, 386
freedom fighters, 97, 104, 177, 210, 233, 334, 394, 433, 450, 516
Freedom Fighters, 135
Friedrich von Hayek, 403
Fulgencio Batista, 19, 29, 33, 44, 92, 98, 110, 113, 120, 123, 149, 209, 254, 260, 262, 417, 449, 509, 512, 513
G-2, 16, 75, 111
Gabriel Valdés, 235, 236, 246, 337, 345, 510
Gabriela Mistral, 311
Gaeton Fonzi, 130, 366
Gamal Abdel Nasser, 34
Gary Latham, 230

gas sarín, 203, 204, 285
George H. Bush, 107, 143, 145, 175, 260, 364, 367, 368, 369, 421, 422, 423, 432, 433, 449, 450, 474, 486, 487, 501, 502, 507, 516
George Junius Stinney, 174, 507
George McGovern, 297
Georgetown, 379
Gerald Ford, 9, 73, 192, 201, 212, 247
Gerry Droller, 30
Gonzalo Facio, 160
Gottlieb, 203
Guadalajara Cartel, 257
Guantanamo, 141
Guantánamo, 199, 256, 472, 494, 501, 502
Guatemala, 29, 30, 31, 32, 42, 43, 45, 46, 47, 48, 50, 62, 111, 114, 115, 139, 177, 178, 187, 197, 198, 256, 288, 321, 325, 472, 484, 507
Guevara, 40
Guillermo Bratti, 223
Guillermo Novo, 20, 75, 85, 97, 98, 99, 106, 121, 129, 135, 136, 146, 148, 149, 180, 181, 243, 250, 251, 252, 258, 260, 261, 264, 276, 277, 289, 294, 308, 313, 314, 315, 326, 333, 369, 390, 406, 414, 443, 451, 452, 453, 454, 456, 457, 458, 465, 472, 476, 479, 487, 493, 503, 508
Guillermo Riveros, 104
Guillermo Salinas Torres, 285
Gulf Oil, 257, 279
gusanos, 133, 264
Gustavo Leigh Guzman, 219
Gutiérrez Ruiz, 227, 228
Guyana, 254, 263, 264, 266, 378, 379, 380, 381, 382, 384, 391, 392, 414
Haig, 467
Haile Selassie, 144
Haiti, 30, 121, 140, 490
Hans Petersen, 307, 441, 511
Harlem, 33, 34, 36
Haroldo Conti, 227, 228
Harry Shlaudeman, 295, 399
Hatuey, 132
Héctor Cornillot, 118
Héctor Cornillot Llano, 118
Héctor D'Avanzo Cintolessi, 158
Héctor Durán, 250, 262
Héctor Serrano, 231

Henry Kissenger, 73
Henry Kissinger, 9, 61, 71, 78, 80, 84, 137, 143, 159, 160, 183, 243, 281, 295, 302, 347, 369, 391, 392, 415, 422, 467, 488, 514
hermanos Novo, 38, 135, 198, 373, 416, 465
Hernán Ricardo, 281, 348, 376, 380, 390, 415, 498, 507, 510
Hernández-Cartaya, 260
Hialeah, 63, 416
Hilda Inclán, 405, 408, 410
Hildo Folgar, 347
Hitler, 22, 131, 138, 183, 201, 204, 219
Honduras, 111, 112, 347, 395, 433, 450, 484
Hortensia Bussi, 101
Hotel Abren Ville, 207
Hotel Algonquin, 310
Hotel Carrera, 183, 244
Hotel Emperador, 79
Hotel Theresa, 33, 34, 35, 38
Howard Callaway, 243
Howard Hunt, 32, 35, 40, 44, 49, 53, 54, 55, 57, 93, 197, 257, 263, 401, 507, 511
Hubert Humphrey, 297
Hugo Banzer, 159
Hugo Chávez, 126, 127, 395
Hugo Vigorena, 158
Humberto López, 230
Hunt, 50
Hunter, 6, 21, 24, 25, 27, 28, 29, 38, 39, 41, 43, 44, 55, 91, 93, 131, 132, 160, 185, 186, 205, 208, 224, 235, 275, 276, 309, 352, 353, 355, 398, 465, 499, 501, 502, 503, 508
IBM, 183
Ignacio Novo Sampol, 5, 54, 327, 457, 507
IMF, 328
Indonesia, 115
Institute for Policy Studies, 242, 336, 439
International Court of Justice, 175
IPS, 57, 163, 176, 179, 218, 228, 233, 235, 236, 239, 241, 242, 297, 298, 308, 313, 334, 337, 339, 340, 345, 349, 350, 351, 361, 363, 365, 399, 423, 511, 512, 514, 515
Iran, 43, 112, 115, 186, 257, 449, 471
Irán, 395, 450

Iran-Contras, 112
Irán-Contras, 450
Isabel, 11, 57, 58, 159, 161, 163, 164, 165, 182, 217, 218, 235, 240, 241, 309, 316, 334, 335, 337, 346, 347, 349, 350, 355, 359, 362, 363, 365, 451, 508, 511
Isabel Perón, 159, 161, 362
Israel, 47, 61, 67, 70, 100, 216, 286, 490
Italia, 66, 104, 106, 204
Italy, 25, 210, 226, 229, 480
ITT, 183, 362, 397
Ivanka, 129
Jack Pfeiffer, 197
Jacksonville, 12, 85, 213, 230, 232, 233, 259, 301, 408, 411, 441, 447, 514
Jacobo Árbenz, 62, 111
Jaime Roldós, 449
Jamaica, 84, 143, 200, 264, 278, 281, 283, 380, 381, 382, 384, 391, 422
James Polk, 18, 143
Javier Milei, 186
Jawaharlal Nehru, 34
Jeane Kirkpatrick, 360, 467, 489
Jeremiah O'Leary, 358, 364, 450
Jerome Sanford, 231
Jerry Sanford, 119
Jesús Galíndez, 35, 64, 254, 335
Jesús Lazo, 117, 431, 462
Jim O'Connell, 35
Jimmy Carter, 73, 116, 117, 136, 193, 280, 293, 298, 358, 365, 393, 395, 399, 432, 449, 450, 451, 461, 463, 465, 468, 487, 490
Jimmy Swaggart, 132
Joan Baez, 308, 310, 311, 508
Joao Batista Figueiredo, 293
João Goulart, 183, 287
Joaquín Balaguer, 73, 81, 258, 324
Joe Schuman, 359
John Ashbrook, 361
John Birch, 184
John Bolton, 142
John Cummings, 141
John Lennon, 213
John McCain, 185
John Roselli, 35, 115, 508
John Rothchild, 14, 405, 408, 508
John Stockwell, 171
Jorge Alessandri, 60
Jorge Domínguez, 135
Jorge Espinoza, 225
Jorge Henríquez, 189, 190
Jorge Luis Borges, 215, 226, 227, 317, 338, 342, 354
Jorge Mas Canosa, 13, 111, 112, 127, 130, 131, 157, 206, 210, 394, 395, 396, 432, 448, 449, 459, 469, 474, 483, 484, 486, 490, 491, 493, 508, 514
Jorge Romeu, 135
José Alfredo Pérez San Román, 6, 46, 509
José de la Torriente, 156, 206, 509
José Dionisio Suárez, 38, 320, 406, 465, 479, 480, 492, 503, 509
José Donoso, 284
José Elías de la Torriente, 118
José Guillermo García, 128, 450
José López Rega, 159
José Miguel Battle, 20, 91, 92, 508, 509
José Papiro González, 135
José Pertierra, 6, 504
José Pons, 399, 400
José Ramon Egues, 135
Juan Gabriel, 235, 337, 345, 510
Juan Guaidó, 126
Juan José Peruyero, 117, 462, 480
Juan Morales Salgado, 285
Juan Orta, 36, 50, 51, 510
Juan Raúl Ferreira, 227, 228, 236, 339, 340, 345
Juan Williams Rose, 300, 369, 441, 511
Julio Cortázar, 228
Julio Lobo, 40
Juscelino Kubitschek, 287, 293
Kennedy, 17, 19, 20, 30, 35, 38, 41, 42, 46, 49, 50, 53, 54, 55, 56, 64, 79, 95, 115, 116, 118, 134, 172, 200, 201, 209, 223, 239, 240, 246, 251, 257, 262, 268, 297, 322, 331, 360, 424, 458, 460, 501, 505, 506, 507, 508, 511, 512, 514, 515
Kenneth Copeland, 132
Kenneth Enyart, 68, 106, 441
Kenrick, Sharon, 379
Kissinger, 489
Klaus Barbie, 112, 139, 160, 205, 257
Kubitschek, 293
la bolita, 20
La capital del terrorismo, 38, 494
La Coubre, 121, 122
La lucha, 14, 20, 154

La Paz, 42, 52
Lalo Schifrin, 64
Landau, 22, 65, 242, 293, 294, 300, 351, 364, 457, 460, 477
Langston Hughes, 34
Larry McDonald, 360
Larry Wack, 424, 510
Las Condes, 67, 317
Lázaro Serrano, 384
Lee, 42, 53, 268
Lee Harvey Oswald, 54, 64, 506
Lee Oswald, 53, 54, 55, 56, 134, 508, 515
Legat Joe Leo, 376
LeMay, 200
Leonardo Castellani, 227
Leonor Borges, 342
Lionel Messi, 129, 130
Little Havana, 9, 11, 12, 63, 97, 131, 172, 257, 423, 483
Lo Curro, 78, 87, 109, 173, 174, 202, 226, 250, 284, 285, 297, 319, 342, 347, 356, 369, 505
Lockheed Lightning, 178
Louis Armstrong, 33
Luciano Nieves, 117, 207, 208, 431, 462
Luis Posada Carriles, 5, 15, 17, 23, 38, 40, 52, 53, 74, 83, 95, 111, 112, 116, 124, 126, 127, 128, 131, 136, 145, 156, 175, 198, 210, 253, 257, 259, 264, 265, 283, 325, 328, 329, 332, 349, 376, 384, 391, 392, 394, 396, 399, 402, 404, 406, 409, 410, 412, 416, 417, 422, 423, 431, 433, 445, 448, 450, 459, 462, 471, 472, 486, 492, 494, 495, 502, 503, 504, 508, 517
Luis Suárez, 129
Luisa Mónica Lagos, 301
Lyman Lemnitzer, 197, 201
Madison Square Garden, 308, 310, 508
mafia cubana, 36, 205, 464, 496, 502
Malcolm X, 29, 34, 35, 36, 37, 44
Manolo Revuelta, 231
Manuel Cháves, 416
Manuel Contreras, 249
Manuel de Armas, 94, 95, 96
Manuel Fuentes Weddling, 190, 510
Manuel Katz Pride, 190
Manuel Noriega, 66, 400, 432
Manuel Trucco Gaete, 344
Marcelino García, 60

Marcos Rodríguez, 52, 510
María Luisa Pizarro, 68, 96
Mariana Callejas, 5, 68, 70, 76, 96, 98, 104, 173, 190, 191, 203, 215, 234, 248, 252, 258, 284, 285, 287, 297, 334, 338, 354, 356, 426, 445, 447, 452, 477, 510
Marino Samayor Acosta, 174
Marita Lorenz, 53, 54, 55, 511
Mark Twain, 198
Martin Luther King, 37, 212, 329, 508
Mas Canosa, 111, 112, 113, 130, 147, 394, 396, 469, 483, 484, 487, 495
Matanzas, 92
Maurice Bishop, 40, 42, 64
Max Lesnik, 384, 463, 492
McCarthy, 132
Melinka, 224
Mexico, 25, 35, 117, 173, 216, 245, 257, 258, 262, 280, 314, 353, 394
México, 18, 50, 84, 94, 96, 101, 102, 106, 107, 108, 113, 114, 136, 158, 200, 211, 288, 315, 325, 333, 339, 404, 426, 480, 507
Meyer Lansky, 19, 42, 91, 92, 132, 254, 509, 511
Miami Herald, 45, 48, 73, 81, 149, 231, 262, 266, 454, 494
Miami Vice, 150
Michael Dukakis, 433
Michael Manley, 143
MICHAEL MOFFITT, 239, 240, 316, 335, 340, 354, 355, 360, 363, 365, 366, 397, 439, 440, 451, 457, 511, 514
Michael Townley, 205, 319, 323, 402
Miguel Ángel Peraza, 230
Military-Industrial Complex, 34
MIR, 76, 86, 207, 359, 361
MK-Ultra, 34, 122, 139, 204
Mohammad Gadafi, 40
Mohammed Mossadegh, 115
Monroe Doctrine, 29, 186
Morales Navarrete, 16, 38, 64, 85, 111, 116, 117, 118, 119, 152, 198, 230, 231, 260, 265, 283, 325, 387, 396, 404, 405, 414, 422, 470, 513
Mossad, 51, 472, 494, 515
motel Chateau Renaissance, 315
Movimiento Nacionalist Cubano, 288
Movimiento Nacionalista Cubano, 99, 278, 424, 456

Mulchén Brigade, 285
Nat King Cole, 33
National Security Archive, 188
NATO, 73
nazi, 181, 190, 205, 288, 357
Nazi, 131, 138, 139, 160
NED, 394, 491, 492
Negroes, 33
Neit Nivar Seijas, 324
New Zealand, 280
Nicanor Parra, 284
Nicaragua, 45, 78, 81, 96, 112, 120, 145, 158, 161, 162, 163, 175, 254, 256, 257, 265, 324, 395, 396, 433, 449, 464, 467, 472, 484, 489
Nicolás Maduro, 127
Nikita Khrushchev, 34
Niledo Acevedo, 57, 505
Nino Gavazzo, 399, 400
Noam Chomsky, 239, 486
Norman Díaz, 57, 505
Norman Manley, 281
Novo brothers, 51, 99, 323, 445, 454, 455, 457, 458, 514
NSA, 58, 133, 143, 147, 212, 213, 264, 322, 365, 366, 496, 512
OAS, 141, 181, 244, 245
OEA, 245, 302
Oliver North, 112, 175, 450, 471, 484
Omar Soto Pujol, 118
Omar Torrijos, 328, 452
Omega 7, 120, 124, 133, 135, 136, 137, 142, 256, 260, 263, 288, 289, 338, 456, 499, 506, 510
ONU, 36, 50, 99, 450, 467, 494
Operación Cóndor, 203, 236, 506
Operation Condor, 249, 262, 282, 294, 295, 399, 433, 444, 447, 514, 516
Operation Eagle, 257
Operation Mockingbird, 212
Operation Mongoose, 200
Operation Northwoods, 200
Orange Bowl, 46
Organisation de l'Armée Secrète, 104, 105
Orlando Bosch, 5, 15, 17, 20, 23, 28, 35, 38, 40, 53, 54, 55, 58, 60, 64, 75, 77, 78, 79, 82, 83, 84, 85, 91, 97, 99, 110, 113, 116, 118, 119, 121, 125, 128, 129, 135, 139, 145, 146, 149, 153, 157, 158, 159, 166, 181, 198, 209, 210, 223, 230, 231, 234, 248, 258, 259, 260, 264, 266, 276, 277, 278, 281, 283, 324, 325, 326, 332, 333, 347, 348, 365, 375, 377, 381, 384, 386, 388, 389, 391, 392, 393, 399, 401, 402, 404, 406, 408, 409, 412, 414, 416, 417, 423, 431, 445, 446, 448, 455, 456, 458, 470, 474, 475, 483, 486, 496, 498, 500, 502, 508, 517
Orlando Flores Mendoza, 159
Orlando García, 74, 77, 78, 80, 85, 116, 124, 125, 126, 263, 265, 266, 325, 332, 333, 387, 392, 399, 401, 405, 406, 413, 414, 415, 446, 497, 498, 512, 513
Orlando Letelier, 13, 24, 26, 50, 54, 57, 85, 97, 101, 110, 124, 134, 174, 176, 202, 228, 239, 240, 244, 247, 261, 262, 263, 282, 293, 296, 301, 308, 310, 326, 345, 346, 351, 358, 362, 366, 368, 369, 378, 393, 399, 400, 423, 426, 434, 439, 445, 450, 453, 455, 457, 458, 466, 468, 470, 476, 478, 480, 497, 505, 507, 508, 509, 510, 511, 512, 514, 515, 516, 530
Orlando Piedra, 20, 512
Orlando Urra, 57, 505, 512
Orson Wells, 60
Oscar Boinilla, 243
Osvaldo Bayer, 228
Osvaldo Puccio, 241
Oswald, 42, 53, 268
OTAN, 201
Otto Reich, 395, 474, 501
Pablo Escobar, 257, 433
Panama, 141, 145, 157, 185, 262, 266, 281, 283, 326, 391, 433, 442, 459
Panamá, 84, 136, 177, 200, 217, 263, 265, 392, 416, 422, 433, 452, 472, 501, 503
Pappalardo, 300
Paraguay, 159, 294, 295, 298, 299, 301, 355, 367, 368, 369, 444, 451
Pascal Allende, 76, 80, 84
Patria y Libertad, 27, 41, 67, 70, 71, 72, 172, 189, 190, 225, 317, 357, 363, 426, 460, 510
Paul, 178
Paul Wimert, 178
Pedro Espinosa, 67, 69, 71, 72, 172, 223, 285, 297, 301, 302, 444, 445

Pedro Espinoza, 251, 465
Pedro Luis Boitel, 120
Pedro Pan, 40
Pentagon, 42, 239
Pentagon Papers, 213, 239
Pentágono, 246, 395
Pepsi, 272, 362
Pequeña Habana, 133
Pérez San Román, 46
Perón, 186, 204, 226, 299, 342
Perry Fellwock, 58, 133, 147, 264, 366, 512
Peru, 318, 432, 453
Perú, 105, 179, 217, 246, 265
Pete Brewton, 260
Peter Haskell, 11, 334
Philip Habib, 399
Phillips, 40, 41, 48, 51, 52, 267
Phoenix Foundation, 452
Pinochet, 39, 57, 58, 66, 69, 75, 76, 78, 79, 86, 87, 101, 105, 124, 134, 138, 145, 146, 147, 172, 177, 179, 180, 181, 202, 204, 217, 218, 220, 223, 224, 233, 235, 236, 239, 240, 241, 242, 243, 244, 245, 246, 247, 248, 249, 250, 252, 266, 277, 278, 285, 287, 294, 295, 297, 300, 301, 310, 311, 314, 316, 325, 335, 338, 339, 345, 346, 350, 354, 356, 357, 359, 360, 362, 363, 364, 366, 368, 369, 393, 394, 395, 397, 403, 405, 410, 425, 434, 435, 442, 444, 445, 446, 447, 451, 453, 454, 459, 460, 461, 467, 468, 475, 476, 477, 497, 506, 510
Piru Seenger, 308
Plan Cóndor, 105, 277
Playa Girón, 31, 206, 255, 320
Plaza Hotel, 35
Pol Anka, 271
Pompano Beach, 62, 65
Portugal, 215, 216, 425, 427
Princeton University, 235
Pulqui, 186
Punta Arenas, 87, 166
Quetropillán, 25, 109, 202, 226, 284, 285, 286
Radio Américas, 111
Radio Mambí, 20, 492
Rafael de Arce, 113
Rafael Rivas, 126, 146, 264, 326, 498, 513

Rafael Videla, 182
Ramón Donestévez, 118, 123, 156, 205, 207, 513
Raoul Salan, 104
Raúl Alfonsín, 227
Raúl Hasbún, 189
Raúl Iturriaga, 251, 286
Raúl Martínez, 45, 47
Raymond Molina, 161, 163, 181, 182, 183, 184
Raymond Persaud, 379, 380
Red Group, 252
Renato León Zenteno, 307
René Riveros, 220
República Dominicana, 78, 81, 229, 230, 265, 335, 416
restaurant Versailles, 432
restaurante Versailles, 129
Revolución de los Claveles, 216
Ricardo Lozano, 281, 348, 386, 390, 415, 416, 507
Ricardo Morales, 5, 15, 16, 80, 83, 85, 96, 111, 116, 126, 127, 152, 171, 211, 231, 232, 260, 325, 348, 387, 404, 405, 409, 412, 439, 470, 507
Richard Helms, 61, 513
Richard Nixon, 30, 50, 61, 71, 143, 246, 263, 470
Ritoque, 224, 225, 226
Robert Maheu, 35
Robert Propper, 119
Robert Scherrer, 79, 82, 83, 110, 181, 219, 230, 365, 366, 457, 506, 514
Roberto Alejos Arzú, 114
Roberto Carballo, 259, 481
Roberto D'Aubuisson, 175
Roberto Thieme, 70, 71
Roberto Vale, 44, 45
Roberto Viaux, 178
Rodrigo Gutiérrez, 189
Rolando Masferrer, 92, 95, 118, 120, 121, 156, 206, 209, 210, 512, 513
Rolando Otero, 56, 73, 79, 82, 145, 147, 223, 229, 243, 277, 315, 408, 428, 439, 441, 447, 505, 514
Roldós, 433
Rómulo Betancourt, 125, 254, 328, 330, 413, 512
Ron DeSantis, 185
Ronald Mc-Intyre Mendoza, 315

Ronald Reagan, 112, 129, 143, 175, 213, 234, 263, 353, 395, 406, 433, 449, 450, 464, 467, 468, 483, 485, 487, 488, 489, 490, 497, 508
Ronaldo Masferrer, 20, 514
Ronni Moffitt, 13, 85, 97, 110, 134, 174, 282, 301, 394, 453, 455, 457, 465, 475, 478, 508, 510, 511, 512
Rosario del Carmen Barredo, 228
Ross Díaz, 320, 443, 454, 458
Rotonda Sheridan, 165
Rubén Blinder, 159
Ruby Hart Phillips, 31
Rusia, 91
Russia, 40, 186, 235, 452
S.W.A.T., 11
Salvador Allende, 312
Sam Giancana, 35, 115, 515
Sandinista, 162, 175
Santa Clara, 59, 150
Santo Trafficante, 19, 35, 42, 50, 91, 92, 115, 122, 123, 132, 254, 321, 508, 515
sarin gas, 109, 139, 201, 202, 214, 309, 312, 428
Saul Landau, 22, 242, 363, 457, 514, 515
School of the Americas, 86, 112, 475
Scott, 18
Sese Seco, 39
Shelburne, 32, 33, 34
Sidney Gottlieb, 34
Sierra Maestra, 59, 209, 320
Silvia Odio, 56, 134, 321, 515
Somoza, 39, 158, 161, 163, 178, 254, 265, 325
South Africa, 144, 192, 239, 280, 406, 435, 485, 489, 490
Spaggiari, 105, 253
Spain, 73, 121, 159, 285, 380, 392, 435, 485
Stanley Wilson, 359
Stefano delle Chiaie, 204, 226, 248, 516
Strom Thurmond, 182
Sud África, 216
Sun Myung Moon, 134
Susana Sienra, 236
T.D. Alleman, 120
Tariq Ali, 361
Taylor Branch, 14, 405, 408, 409, 471, 516
Ted Kennedy, 247
Televisión Martí, 491

The capital of terrorism, 115
The fight, 432
The Magnificent Seven, 65
Timothy Robinson, 363
Tom Jordache, 11, 334
Tony Baretta, 150
Tony Lapham, 368
Toribio Merino, 225
Torrijos, 433
Townley, 25, 26, 27, 28, 41, 60, 61, 63, 65, 66, 67, 68, 69, 70, 71, 72, 73, 76, 80, 84, 85, 86, 87, 96, 97, 98, 100, 101, 102, 104, 105, 106, 107, 108, 109, 134, 138, 145, 171, 172, 173, 174, 180, 189, 190, 191, 201, 202, 203, 204, 205, 209, 214, 215, 226, 234, 243, 247, 248, 250, 251, 252, 258, 262, 283, 285, 286, 287, 294, 297, 298, 299, 300, 301, 307, 308, 309, 312, 313, 314, 315, 316, 317, 318, 319, 320, 323, 324, 334, 335, 339, 341, 355, 356, 357, 358, 359, 360, 363, 369, 402, 423, 425, 426, 427, 428, 439, 441, 443, 444, 445, 446, 447, 451, 452, 453, 455, 458, 459, 460, 476, 477, 478, 480, 505, 506, 510, 511, 514, 516
Transnational Institute, 361
Trevor and Roseanne, 379
Trinidad and Tobago, 281, 390, 391, 404
Trinidad y Tobago, 380
Triple A, 158, 159
Troncoso Vivallos, 214
Trujillo, 35, 39, 64, 126, 254, 258, 259, 324, 335, 449, 452
Truman, 44
Tupamaros, 160, 361
Turkey Point, 231
UN, 33, 47, 48, 51, 144, 167, 285, 298, 347, 399, 468, 489
Union City, 22, 59, 82, 85, 92, 119, 131, 133, 136, 149, 150, 180, 184, 206, 253, 255, 259, 277, 288, 289, 307, 308, 313, 314, 315, 341, 363, 373, 405, 414, 424, 439, 454, 457, 458, 459, 463, 483, 488, 492, 495, 502, 506, 509, 510, 512
United Fruit Company, 91
United States, 42, 47, 53, 489
Universidad Católica, 190, 505

Uruguay, 31, 50, 114, 160, 227, 228, 248, 295, 327, 361, 400, 506, 507
Valentín Hernández, 117, 461
Valparaíso, 61, 224
Veciana, 42, 51, 52, 53, 267
Vernon Townley, 61, 355
Vernon Walters, 204, 249, 293, 300, 355, 367, 368, 444, 516
Versailles, 12, 129, 185, 431, 493
Versailles restaurant, 12
Víctor Jara, 311, 477
Victor Samuelson, 252
Videla, 39, 161, 182, 227, 228, 251, 274, 361
Vietnam, 18, 45, 50, 63, 70, 100, 115, 116, 140, 187, 213, 236, 239, 245, 263, 272, 274, 311, 314, 334, 337, 449, 488, 508
Violetta Parra, 310
Virgilio Paz, 28, 38, 85, 86, 100, 102, 104, 106, 134, 146, 171, 173, 174, 198, 204, 209, 248, 252, 258, 286, 294, 307, 308, 314, 315, 319, 320, 323, 335, 339, 407, 426, 443, 445, 453, 454, 455, 458, 465, 478, 480, 494, 503, 516

Virginia Prewett, 366
Vito Genovese, 19
vuelo 455, 264
Walt Disney, 212
Warren Commission, 55, 56, 134, 515
Watergate, 50, 53, 263, 343, 408
Wayne Smith, 130
Whitelaw Blanco, 228
WikiLeaks, 392
William Colby, 36
William Musto, 289
William Wieland, 30
Willoughby-MacDonald, 358
Wilson Ferreira, 227, 228, 236
Wilson Ferreira Aldunate, 228, 236
Winfield Scott, 18
Winslow Peck, 58, 133, 365, 366, 512
worms, 365
Wright Mills, 34
Wyne Phillips, 33
Yasser Arafat, 486
Yuri Gagarin, 41, 51, 99
Zbigniew Brzezinski, 451
Zelmar Michelini, 227

sources

[1] Casa de Orlando Letelier: 5818 Ogden Court, Bethesda, MD www.redfin.com/MD/Bethesda/5818-Ogden-Ct-20816/home/10638243
[2] English, T. J. "When the Mob Ruled Havana." Cigar Aficionado, Cigar Aficionado, 8 July 2019, www.cigaraficionado.com/article/when-the-mob-ruled-havana
[3] Carr, Howie. "Havana Nocturne" *New York Post*, 8 de junio de 2008, nypost.com/2008/06/08/havana-nocturne.
[4] Bardach, Ann Louise. *Cuba Confidential: Love and Vengeance in Miami and Havana*. United Kingdom, Knopf Doubleday Publishing Group, 2007, p. 116
[5] Branch, Taylor & Eugen Propper. *Labyrinth*. Penguin, 1983, p. 301.
[6] Idem, p. 311.
[7] Bardach, Ann Louise. *Cuba Confidential: Love and Vengeance in Miami and Havana*. United Kingdom, Knopf Doubleday Publishing Group, 2007, p. 113.
[8] Idem, p. 117.
[9] *Press of Atlantic City*. Lunes 18 de enero de 1965, p. 17.
[10] Bardach, Ann Louise. *Cuba Confidential: Love and Vengeance in Miami and Havana*. United Kingdom, Knopf Doubleday Publishing Group, 2007, p. 212.
[11] Branch, Taylor & Eugen Propper. *Labyrinth*. Penguin, 1983, p. 494.
[12] Callejas, Mariana. *Siembra vientos: memorias*. CESOCa., 1995. P. 42.
[13] Branch, Taylor & Eugen Propper. *Labyrinth*. Penguin, 1983, p. 496.
[14] "Cuba: Red Setback." *Time*, 8 de junio de 1959.
[15] LeoGrande, William M., and Kornbluh, Peter. Back *Channel to Cuba: The Hidden History of Negotiations Between Washington and Havana*. United States, University of North Carolina Press, 2015, p. 15.
[16] Idem, p. 18.
[17] Idem, p. 7.
[18] Idem, p. 7.
[19] Idem, p. 12.
[20] Ralph Matthews, "Going Upstairs. Malcolm X Greets Fidel," New York Citizen-Call, 24 de setiembre de 1960.
[21] Markle, Seth M. "Brother Malcolm, Comrade Babu: Black Internationalism and the Politics of Friendship." *Biography*, vol. 36, no. 3, 2013, pp. 540-67. *JStor*. www.jstor.org/stable/24570209.
[22] "The mafia: The Demise of a Don". TIME Magazine, 30 de junio de 1975. content.time.com/time/subscriber/article/0,33009,917569,00.html
[23] "Discurso pronunciado por el Comandante Fidel Castro en la Sede de las Naciones Unidas el 26 de setiembre de 1960". Cuba.cu. www.cuba.cu/gobierno/discursos/1960/esp/f260960e.html
[24] "U.S. Senate Select Committee on Intelligence".

www.intelligence.senate.gov/sites/default/files/94755_III.pdf

[25] Montes, Rafael Miguel. *Generational Traumas in Contemporary Cuban-American Literature: Making Places.* United States, Edwin Mellen Press, 2006., p. 115.

[26] Branch, Taylor & Eugen Propper. *Labyrinth.* Penguin, 1983, p. 500.

[27] Veciana, Antonio, y Carlos Harrison. *Trained to Kill: The Inside Story of CIA Plots against Castro, Kennedy, and Che.* Skyhorse, 2017.

[28] "George H. Bush' CIA Operative". CIA FOIA (2016). www.cia.gov/readingroom/document/cia-rdp99-01448r000401580069-6. Desclasificado el 23 de octubre de 2012

[29] LeoGrande, William M. y Peter Kornbluh. *Back Channel to Cuba.* University of North Carolina Press, 2014, p. 17.

[30] Majfud, Jorge. *La frontera salvaje. 200 años de fanatismo anglosajón en América latina.* Rebelde Ed. 2021. p. 329.

[31] *The Miami Herald*, Domingo 26 de marzo de 1961, p. 1.

[32] English, T. J. *The corporation.* Harper Collins Publisher, 2018. p. 45.

[33] Idem, p. 47.

[34] *The Miami Herald*, Domingo 26 de marzo de 1961, p. 9.

[35] "The President John F. Kennedy Assassination Records Collection". The National Security Archive. Geroge Washington University. Archives.gov, www.archives.gov/files/research/jfk/releases/2022/157-10011-10090.pdf

[36] Bergman, Ronen. *Rise and Kill First : The Secret History of Israel's Targeted Assassinations. First.* Random House; 2018.

[37] "The Harold Weisberg Archive." Hood.edu, 2024. jfk.hood.edu.

[38] "Cable Sought to Discredit Critics of Warren Report". *The New York Times.* Lunes 26 de Decembre de 1977, p. 32.

[39] "Sturgis: 'they' are still after him". *The Boston Globe.* Miércoles 9 de noviembre de 1977, p. 2. Wed, Nov 09, 1977, p. 2.

[40] "JFK Sparks Debate In Cuban Community". *Sarasota Herald-Tribune.* 31 de diciembre de 1991, p. 33.

[41] "The President John F. Kennedy Assassination Records Collection." Archives.gov, 2017, www.archives.gov/files/research/jfk/releases/2018/docid-32262490.pdf

[42] Branch, Taylor & Eugen Propper. *Labyrinth.* Penguin, 1983, p. 489.

[43] Idem, p. 492.

[44] Idem, p. 319.

[45] Idem, p. 495.

[46] Idem, p. 498.

[47] Alan McPherson. *Ghosts of Sheridan Circle. How a Washington Assassination Brought Pinochet's Terror State to Justice.* University of North Carolina Press, 2018, p. 54.

[48] Branch, Taylor & Eugen Propper. *Labyrinth.* Penguin, 1983, p. 173.

[49] *Miami Herald.* 21 de mayo de 1976, p. 3.

⁵⁰ Branch, Taylor & Eugen Propper. *Labyrinth*. Penguin, 1983, p. 139.
⁵¹ The National Security Archive, 2017.
nsarchive2.gwu.edu/NSAEBB/NSAEBB157/19760629.pdf
⁵² Branch, Taylor & Eugen Propper. *Labyrinth*. Penguin, 1983, p.151.
⁵³ *The Miami Herald.* 25 de enero de 1976, p. 1 y 2.
⁵⁴ Branch, Taylor & Eugen Propper. *Labyrinth*. Penguin, 1983, p. 167.
⁵⁵ Idem, p. 316.
⁵⁶ Bardach, Ann Louise. *Cuba Confidential: Love and Vengeance in Miami and Havana*. United Kingdom, Knopf Doubleday Publishing Group, 2007, p. 185.
⁵⁷ The National Security Archive. Geroge Washington University. Archives.gov, www.archives.gov/files/research/jfk/releases/2023/180-10145-10345.pdf
⁵⁸ Apoyan, Jackie. "Castro Revolution Had Major Effect on Las Vegas". The Mob Museum, Diciembre de 2016, themobmuseum.org/blog/castro-effect-las-vegas/.
⁵⁹ Idem. www.archives.gov/files/research/jfk/releases/104-10177-10239.pdf
⁶⁰ Idem. www.archives.gov/files/research/jfk/releases/104-10177-10239.pdf
⁶¹ "Cuban in Havana Cites C.I.A. Plots Against Castro". 22 de abril de 1976, p. 7. www.nytimes.com/1976/04/22/archives/cuban-in-havana-cites-cia-plots-against-castro.html
⁶² "The President John F. Kennedy Assassination Records Collection". The National Security Archive. Geroge Washington University. Archives.gov, www.archives.gov/files/research/jfk/releases/104-10177-10239.pdf
⁶³ Idem. www.archives.gov/files/research/jfk/releases/2022/104-10122-10411.pdf
⁶⁴ Branch, Taylor & Eugen Propper. *Labyrinth*. Penguin, 1983, p. 237.
⁶⁵ Latinamericanstudies.org. Audio: www.latinamericanstudies.org/audio/Suarez-Jose-Dionisio-7-18-2016.mp3.
⁶⁶ Branch, Taylor & Eugen Propper. *Labyrinth*. Penguin, 1983, p. 241.
⁶⁷ Idem, p. 243.
⁶⁸ U.S. Energy Information Administration (EIA) Independent Statistics and Analysis. (n.d.). www.eia.gov/international/content/analysis/countries_long/Algeria/algeria.pdf
⁶⁹ Branch, Taylor & Eugen Propper. *Labyrinth*. Penguin, 1983, p. 332.
⁷⁰ Idem. p. 325.
⁷¹ Fundación Rama, Bolivia. fundacion-rama.com/wp-content/uploads/2022/09/4777.-Operacion-Condor-El-vuelo-%E2%80%A6-Martorell.pdf p. 124
⁷² Branch, Taylor & Eugen Propper. *Labyrinth*. Penguin, 1983, p. 246.
⁷³ Idem, p. 177.
⁷⁴ Alan McPherson. *Ghosts of Sheridan Circle. How a Washington Assassination Brought Pinochet's Terror State to Justice*. University of North Carolina Press, 2018, p. 77.
⁷⁵ "The President John F. Kennedy Assassination Records Collection". The National Security Archive. Geroge Washington University. Archives.gov, www.archives.gov/files/research/jfk/releases/2018/180-10143-10345.pdf

[76] Bardach, Ann Louise. *Cuba Confidential: Love and Vengeance in Miami and Havana.* United Kingdom, Knopf Doubleday Publishing Group, 2007, p. 136.
[77] Idem, 138.
[78] Idem, 138.
[79] "The President John F. Kennedy Assassination Records Collection". The National Security Archive. Geroge Washington University. Archives.gov. www.archives.gov/files/research/jfk/releases/104-10178-10061.pdf
[80] The National Security Archive. Geroge Washington University. Archives.gov, nsarchive2.gwu.edu/NSAEBB/NSAEBB157/19761209.pdf
[81] The National Security Archive. Geroge Washington University. nsarchive2.gwu.edu/NSAEBB/NSAEBB157/19761209.pdf
[82] "The President John F. Kennedy Assassination Records Collection". The National Security Archive. Geroge Washington University. Archives.gov, www.archives.gov/files/research/jfk/releases/2023/180-10145-10345.pdf
[83] "4 Bombs Explode in Miami". *The New York Times*, 4 de diciembre de 1975, p. 24.
[84] "Anti-Castro Exiles Growing Tolerant of Havana Ties." *Washington Post*, 11 de junio de 1977. www.washingtonpost.com/archive/politics/1977/06/11/anti-castro-exiles-growing-tolerant-of-havana-ties/1a07fbcf-2881-42c4-9470-5132739bebb6/.
[85] Bardach, Ann Louise. *Cuba Confidential: Love and Vengeance in Miami and Havana.* United Kingdom, Knopf Doubleday Publishing Group, 2007, p. 114.
[86] "Legacy of Terror". *The New York Times*. 16 de julio de 1978, Section SM, p. 8.
[87] Bardach, Ann Louise. *Cuba Confidential: Love and Vengeance in Miami and Havana.* United Kingdom, Knopf Doubleday Publishing Group, 2007, p. 118.
[88] Idem, p. 312.
[89] "Rolando Masferrer Rojas: ¡Voló En Pedazos El Tigre" *La Jiribilla*, 16 de abril de 2005. www.latinamericanstudies.org/cuba/masferrer.htm.
[90] "Fidel Castro: 634 Plots and a True Death." *The Prisma*, 5 de diciembre de 2022, theprisma.co.uk/2022/12/05/fidel-castro-634-plots-and-a-true-death
[91] Alleged Assesination Plot Involving Foreign Leaders. *Senate Report. 1st Session.* 20 de noviembre de 1975, p. 81. www.intelligence.senate.gov/sites/default/files/94465.pdf#page=103
[92] Latin American Studies. www.latinamericanstudies.org/dialogue/donestevez-autopsy.pdf
[93] Socorro, Milagros. *ProDaVinci*, Venezuela. "Orlando García Vásquez, el hombre de los lentes junto a Pérez". historico.prodavinci.com/blogs/el-de-los-lentes-junto-a-perez-es-orlando-garcia-vasquez-por-milagros-socorro-unafotountexto/
[94] The National Security Archive. Geroge Washington University. www.archives.gov/files/research/jfk/releases/104-10177-10239.pdf
[95] Idem. www.archives.gov/files/research/jfk/releases/104-10177-10239.pdf
[96] Goodman, Joshua, and Jim Mustain. "Exclusive: Secret US Op Spied on Venezuelan Officials to Build Drug Cases." *AP News*, AP News, 1 de febrero. 2024, apnews.com

⁹⁷ Alan McPherson. *Ghosts of Sheridan Circle. How a Washington Assassination Brought Pinochet's Terror State to Justice*. University of North Carolina Press, 2018, p. 81.
⁹⁸ Bardach, Ann Louise. *Cuba Confidential: Love and Vengeance in Miami and Havana*. United Kingdom, Knopf Doubleday Publishing Group, 2007, p. 119.
⁹⁹ Idem, p. 114.
¹⁰⁰ Sesin, Carmen. "Cafecito and Presidential Sightings: A Landmark Miami Restaurant Turns 50." *NBC News*, 28 de noviembre de 2021, www.nbcnews.com/news/latino/cafecito-presidential-sightings-landmark-miami-restaurant-turns-50-rcna6509.
¹⁰¹ Bardach, Ann Louise. *Cuba Confidential: Love and Vengeance in Miami and Havana*. United Kingdom, Knopf Doubleday Publishing Group, 2007, p. 137.
¹⁰² The National Security Archive. Geroge Washington University. www.bardachreports.com/maninmiami_newrepublic
¹⁰³ "Beer Cocktails at BrewDog, Nottingham." Pub Geek, Pub Geek, 6 de agosto de 2013, lincolnpubgeek.wordpress.com/2013/08/06/beer-cocktails-at-brewdog-nottingham/
¹⁰⁴ "The President John F. Kennedy Assassination Records Collection". The National Security Archive. Geroge Washington University. Archives.gov, www.archives.gov/files/research/jfk/releases/2023/180-10143-10345.pdf
¹⁰⁵ Branch, Taylor & Eugen Propper. *Labyrinth*. Penguin, 1983, p.107.
¹⁰⁶ Alan McPherson. *Ghosts of Sheridan Circle. How a Washington Assassination Brought Pinochet's Terror State to Justice*. University of North Carolina Press, 2018, p. 83.
¹⁰⁷ Jonathan Kandell "U.S. and Brazil Sign Accord on Tie" *The New York Times*. 22 de febrero de 1976, p. 1.
¹⁰⁸ Digital Repository, University of New Mexico. digitalrepository.unm.edu/cgi/viewcontent.cgi?article=9988&context=noticen
¹⁰⁹ CIA Reading room. Desclasificado. www.cia.gov/readingroom/docs/CIA-RDP90-01208R000100220001-8.pdf
¹¹⁰ Majfud, Jorge. *La frontera salvaje*. Rebelde Editores. 2021. p. 501.
¹¹¹ CIA Reading room. Desclasificado. www.cia.gov/readingroom/docs/CIA-RDP90-01208R000100220002-7.pdf
¹¹² Ángel Cuadra. "Eduardo Arocena: el prisionero más antiguo". *Diario de la Américas*, 23 de setiembre de 2016.
¹¹³ "Terroristic Activity. Terrorism in Miami Area. Hearings before the Subcomitte to investigate the Administration of the Internal Security Act. Committe on the Judiciary United States Senate Ninety-Fourh Concress. Second Session". 6 de mayo de 1976, pg. 640.
¹¹⁴ Jorge Majfud. *La frontera salvaje*. Rebelde Ediciones, 2021, p. 389.
¹¹⁵ "Cia Henchmen Carry Out Murder Policy in Nation's Capital". CIA FOIA 2019, www.cia.gov/readingroom/document/03258180. CIA HENCHMEN CARRY OUT MU [15499938].pdf

[116] Branch, Taylor & Eugen Propper. *Labyrinth*. Penguin, 1983, p.202.
[117] Idem, p. 320.
[118] Idem, p.248.
[119] Idem, p.248 y 249.
[120] "The President John F. Kennedy Assassination Records Collection". The National Security Archive. Geroge Washington University. Archives.gov, www.archives.gov/files/research/jfk/releases/2022/124-10197-10422.pdf
[121] Idem, www.latinamericanstudies.org/belligerence/Cuban-Militant-Organizations-AB-225.pdf
[122] Idem, www.latinamericanstudies.org/belligerence/murder-exile.htm
[123] Méndez Méndez, José Luis. *Los años del terror (1974-1976)*. España, Editorial de Ciencias Sociales, 2018. p. 77.
[124] "A Heroin Smuggler Chooses U.S. Prison over the Guillotine." *The New York Times*, 2 de diciembre de 1972, pg. 1.
[125] "Former French Fascists". CIA. 13 de agosto de 1973. 25. Desclasificado el 17 de agosto de 2020.
[126] The National Security Archive. Geroge Washington University. nsarchive.gwu.edu/sites/default/files/documents/20519376/07.pdf
[127] National Security Archive. Documento desclasificado por el FBI. 15 de marzo de 1976. www.govinfo.gov/content/pkg/GPO-CRECB-1977-pt16/pdf/GPO-CRECB-1977-pt16-6-1.pdf
[128] "17 Cubans Reported Killed by Firing Squad in Angola". *The New York Times*, 12 de marzo de 1976, p. 18.
[129] The National Security Archive. Geroge Washington University. Documento desclasificado del FBI. 21 de enero de 1982. nsarchive2.gwu.edu/NSAEBB/NSAEBB8/docs/doc02.pdf
[130] Branch, Taylor & Eugen Propper. *Labyrinth*. Penguin, 1983, p. 320.
[131] "George H. Bush' CIA Operative". CIA FOIA (2016). www.cia.gov/readingroom/document/cia-rdp99-01448r000401580069-6. Desclasificado el 23 de octubre de 2012.
[132] Majfud, Jorge. *La frontera salvaje. 200 años de fanatismo anglosajón en América latina*. Rebelde Editores, 2021. p. 404.
[133] Kenneth Bredemeier, "Justice Dept. Says Group Illegally Lobbies for Chile". *The Washington Post*, 19 de diciembre de 1978.
[134] The National Security Archive. Geroge Washington University. nsarchive.gwu.edu/sites/default/files/media_mentions/2021-03-24_comisionporlamemoria.org-los_informes_sobre_la_preparacion_del_golpe_militar_que_anunciaban_una_represion_sin_precedentes.pdf
[135] Idem. nsarchive.gwu.edu/sites/default/files/documents/20519378/09.pdf
[136] Idem. nsarchive.gwu.edu/

[137] National Archives. División de Inteligencia. Doc. 15 de marzo de 1976. www.archives.gov/files/argentina/data/docid-33004374.pdf
[138] "The President John F. Kennedy Assassination Records Collection". The National Security Archive. Geroge Washington University. Archives.gov, www.archives.gov/files/research/jfk/releases/104-10074-10043.pdf
[139] "Counseling ordered for man who hit ex-PR governor", The Associated Press. 15 de enero de 2009. *San Diego Union-Tribune*; www.sandiegouniontribune.com/sdut-cb-puerto-rico-ex-governor-punched-011509-2009jan15-story.html
[140] Florida Residents Directory, www.floridaresidentsdirectory.com/person/108941627/molina-joseph
[141] Davis, E. "'A pact with the devil': US congresswoman lets rip at Argentina, CFK over China ties. *Buenos Aires Times*, 2 de marzo de 2023, www.batimes.com.ar/news/world/a-pact-with-the-devil-us-congresswoman-criticised-argentinas-military-cooperation-with-china.phtml
[142] Wallace, Danielle. "Republican warns China, Russia, Iran 'trying to invade' Western Hemisphere 200 years since Monroe Doctrine". *Fox News*, 30 de noviembre de 2023. www.foxnews.com/politics/republican-warns-china-russia-iran-trying-invade-western-hemisphere-200-years-since-monroe-doctrine
[143] "La representante republicana por Florida María Elvira Salazar elogia que Argentina tenga 'Una sola raza.'" *Telemundo*, 22 de noviembre de 2023, www.telemundo.com/noticias/noticias-telemundo/estados-unidos/la-representante-republicana-por-florida-maria-elvira-salazar-elogia-q-rcna126307.
[144] Schindler Etchegaray, Jorge. "La protección judicial para los autores de la "Operación Antena". *Interferencia*, 22 de marzo de 2023. interferencia.cl/articulos/la-proteccion-judicial-para-los-autores-de-la-operacion-antena
[145] "White House, Memorandum of Conversation between President Ford and Kissinger", March 15, 1976. National Security Archive." Gwu.edu, 15 de marzo de 1976, nsarchive.gwu.edu/document/30317-document-64-white-house-memorandum-conversation-between-president-ford-and-kissinger.
[146] Idem.
[147] Pfeiffer, Jack B. CIA: "Official History Of The Bay Of Pigs Operation Draft. Volume V CIA's Internal Investigation of the Bay of Pigs". 18 de abril de 1984. nsarchive2.gwu.edu/NSAEBB/NSAEBB564-CIA-Releases-Controversial-Bay-of-Pigs-History/cia-bay-of-pigs-v51.pdf
[148] Idem.
[149] The National Security Archive. Geroge Washington University. nsarchive2.gwu.edu/news/20010430/northwoods.pdf
[150] Mónica González. "Las armas químicas de Pinochet" CIPER Chile, 22 de Agosto de. 2013, www.ciperchile.cl/2013/08/22/las-armas-quimicas-de-pinochet/.
[151] Torrús, Alejandro. "Adiós a un criminal fascista: Delle Chiaie, una vida al servicio de la muerte. Público, 14 de setiembre de 2019, www.publico.es/politica/adios-criminal-fascista-delle-chiaie-vida-servicio-muerte-espana-italia-latinoamerica.html.

[152] Latin American Studies. www.latinamericanstudies.org/dialogue/donestevez-autopsy.pdf
[153] "Cuban Exile Found Shot to Death". *The New York Times*, 17 de abril de 1974, pg. 69.
[154] "Terroristic Activity. Terrorism in Miami Area. Hearings before the Subcomitte to investigate the Administration of the Internal Security Act. Committe on the Judiciary United States Senate Ninety-Fourh Concress. Second Session". 6 de mayo de 1976, p. 654.
[155] "Cuban Boat Inquiry Yields No Suspect". *The New York Times*, 24 de abril de 1976, pg. 4.
[156] Terroristic Activity. Terrorism in Miami Area. Hearings before the Subcomitte to investigate the Administration of the Internal Security Act. 6 de mayo de 1976, pg. 642.
[157] Branch, Taylor & Eugen Propper. *Labyrinth*. Penguin, 1983, p. 313.
[158] Bardach, Ann Louise. *Cuba Confidential: Love and Vengeance in Miami and Havana*. United Kingdom, Knopf Doubleday Publishing Group, 2007, p. 116.
[159] Branch, Taylor & Eugen Propper. *Labyrinth*. Penguin, 1983, p. 234.
[160] Idem.
[161] Steven Aftergood, "The Clapper 'Lie,' and the Senate Intelligence Committee". *Federation of American Scientists*, 20 de abril de 2023. fas.org/publication/clapper-ssci/
[162] Mónica González. *Las armas químicas de Pinochet*. CIPER Chile. 22 de agosto de 2013. www.ciperchile.cl/2013/08/22/las-armas-quimicas-de-pinochet/
[163] "Two Cubans Die in Bombing of Embassy in Portugal". *The New York Times*, 23 de abril de 1976, pg. 3.
[164] O'Keefe, Thomas Andrew. "Most Chileans Know Military Invented Plot". 29 de julio de 1990, Sección 4, p. 18.
[165] Fundación Rama, Bolivia. fundacion-rama.com/wp-content/uploads/2022/09/4777. Operacion-Condor-El-vuelo-%E2%80%A6-Martorell.pdf
[166] Testimonio por correo privado de Juan Raúl Ferreira con el autor.
[167] Latin American Studies. www.latinamericanstudies.org/belligerence/Otero-1976.pdf
[168] Idem.
[169] Idem.
[170] Douthat, Bill. "Court Crucified Me, Otero Says" The Miami News. Viernes 28 de enero de 1977, p. 54.
[171] *The Miami News*. 18 de octubre de 1976, p. 4.
[172] Branch, Taylor & Eugen Propper. *Labyrinth*. Penguin, 1983, p.163.
[173] "Cuban Exile Terrorism". Metro Dade County, Florida. Organized Crime Bureau, Metro Dade County Police. Cuban Information Archive. Doc. 0073. *CubanExile.com*, 2014, cuban-exile.com/doc_051-075/doc0073.html.

[174] Amalia Bertoli, Roger Burbach, David Hathaway, Robert High, Eugene Kelly. *Human Rights..."In the Soul of Our Foreign Policy*. NACLA, 25 de setiemrbe de 2007. nacla.org/article/human-rightsin-soul-our-foreign-policy
[175] Conversación con el autor. 2023.
[176] Branch, Taylor & Eugen Propper. *Labyrinth*. Penguin, 1983, p. 321.
[177] Hersh, Seymour M. "Kissinger Said to Rebuke U.S. Ambassador to Chile". *The New York Times:* Viernes 27 de setiembre de 1974, p. 18.
[178] Ortega Frei, Eugenio. "La verdadera razón de los atentados de 1976 contra Orlando Letelier y Eduardo Frei Montalva". *El Mostrador*, 7 de setiembre de 2023. www.elmostrador.cl/noticias/opinion/columnas/2023/09/07/la-verdadera-razon-de-los-atentados-de-1976-contra-orlando-letelier-y-eduardo-frei-montalva/
[179] Adriana Arce, María Paula Pontoriero, Laura Pereiras, María Rosa Roble, Cecilia Vanin y Baltazar Gastón Real. *Operación Cóndor: 40 años después*. Editado por la Dirección Nacional del Sistema Argentino de Información Jurídica, Editorial Ministerio de Justicia y Derechos Humanos de la Nación, Buenos Aires, 2015. www.cipdh.gob.ar/pdf/Operacion_Condor.pdf p. 73.
[180] CIA. Documento desclasificado. www.cia.gov/readingroom/docs/CIA-RDP91-00901R000700060054-9.pdf
[181] Branch, Taylor & Eugen Propper. *Labyrinth*. Penguin, 1983, p. 323.
[182] Simkin, J. (2023). *Michael V. Townley*. Spartacus Educational. spartacus-educational.com/JFKtownleyM.htm
[183] Serrano, María. *The Assassination of Orlando Letelier: An Example of Chilean and American Teamwork*. The Mirror. Undergraduate History Journal, vol. 31, no. 1 de Marzo de 2011, p. 25-40.
[184] Majfud, Jorge. *La frontera salvaje*. Rebelde Ed. 2021. p. 274.
[185] Pfeiffer, Jack B. CIA: "Official History Of The Bay Of Pigs Operation Draft. Volume V CIA's Internal Investigation of the Bay of Pigs". 18 de abril de 1984. nsarchive2.gwu.edu/NSAEBB/NSAEBB564-CIA-Releases-Controversial-Bay-of-Pigs-History/cia-bay-of-pigs-v51.pdf
[186] Majfud, Jorge. *La frontera salvaje*. Rebelde Ed. 2021. p. 389.
[187] The National Security Archive. Geroge Washington University. nsarchive2.gwu.edu/NSAEBB/NSAEBB202/19761018.pdf
[188] Simkin, John. "Eulalio Francisco Castro Paz (Frank Castro)." *Spartacus Educational*, 2024, spartacus-educational.com/JFKcastroFr.htm.
[189] Simkin, John. *Michael V. Townley*. Spartacus Educational. spartacus-educational.com/JFKtownleyM.htm
[190] Johnson, Haynes. "The CIA's Secret War on Cuba': Laying Bare Our Painful Legacy". *Washington Post*, 9 de junio de 1977.
[191] Rafael, Antonio. "Ricardo 'El Mono' Morales Navarrete." YouTube, 15 Oct. 2016, www.youtube.com/watch?v=NiSBUn8csTw.
[192] CIA: Documento desclasificado. www.cia.gov/readingroom/docs/CIA%20HENCHMEN%20CARRY%20OUT%20MU%5B15499938%5D.pdf

[193] Branch, Taylor & Eugen Propper. *Labyrinth*. Penguin, 1983, p.204.
[194] *The Miami Herald*, 3 de julio de 1974, p. 129.
[195] Fundación Rama. fundacion-rama.com/wp-content/uploads/2022/09/4777.-Operacion-Condor-El-vuelo-%E2%80%A6-Martorell.pdf
[196] "Terroristas de Miami sirvieron al fascismo en Chile". Cubadebate. 29 de setiembre de 2011. www.cubadebate.cu/opinion/2011/09/29/terroristas-de-miami-sirvieron-al-fascismo-en-chile
[197] Branch, Taylor & Eugen Propper. *Labyrinth*. Penguin, 1983, p.120.
[198] Anderson, Peter. "Concord folks ready to land, 'sea' and air", *The Boston Globe*, Martes 11 de marzo de 1975, p. 18.
[199] Hornblower, Margot. "Unusual Bicentennial Exhibits Plot Your Revolution Aptitude". *Anderson Independent-Mail*. 18 de diciembre de 1975, p. 27.
[200] Beard, Lanford. "Princess Anne Was Exempted from 'Gender Testing' When She Went to the Olympics". *People*. 15 de Agosto de 2021.
[201] "A family affair: The royal visit that wound up at the 1976 Olympics". *CBC*, Canadá. 12 de julio de 2019. www.cbc.ca/archives/royal-visit-1976-queen-princess-anne-olympics-1.5204216
[202] "Possible plans of Cuban exile extremist to blow up a Cuban airline". CIA. 21 de junio de 1976. Desclasificado en 1997. https://nsarchive2.gwu.edu/NSAEBB/NSAEBB153/19760622.pdf
[203] Callejas, Mariana. *Siembra vientos: memorias*. CESOC, Santiago, 1995.
[204] Latin American Studies, www.latinamericanstudies.org/omega/MH-7-25-1976-30.pdf
[205] "Cubans at rally urges to back bomb suspects"/ "Cuba sobre todo". *The Jersey Journal*. Lunes 16 de agosto de 1976, p. 1.
[206] Small, Richard. "Cubans Arks Byrne Intercede on Behalf of Anti-Castro Plotter". *The Jersey Journal*. Martes 8 de enero de 1974, p. 1.
[207] "To rally for bombs suspects". *The Jersey Journal*. Viernes 30 de julio de 1976, p. 5.
[208] Fundación Rama, Bolivia. fundacion-rama.com/wp-content/uploads/2022/09/4777.
[209] "The 'Chicago Boys' in Chile: Economic Freedom's Awful Toll." *The Nation*, 21 de setiembre de 2016. www.thenation.com/article/archive/the-chicago-boys-in-chile-economic-freedoms-awful-toll
[210] Townley Papers, "Relato de Sucesos en la Muerte de Orlando Letelier. 21 de setiembre de 1976". National Security Archive". *Gwu.edu*, 14 de marzo de 1978. nsarchive.gwu.edu/document/30799-document-3-townley-papers-relato-de-sucesos-en-la-muerte-de-orlando-letelier-el-21.
[211] CIA, Doc. desclasificado. www.cia.gov/readingroom/docs/CIA-RDP91-00901R000700060054-9.pdf
[212] González, Mónica. "Las armas químicas de Pinochet", *CIPER* Chile. 22 de Agosto de 2013. www.ciperchile.cl/2013/08/22/las-armas-quimicas-de-pinochet/

[213] "Privación de nacionalidad chilena. Orlando Letelier". Doc. desclasificado, Santiago, 2 de setiemrbe de 1976. media-front.elmostrador.cl/2016/09/Decreto-privacion-nacionalidad-Orlando-Lettelier-ilovepdf-compressed.pdf
[214] *Transcript of Orlando Letelier's Speech at the Felt Forum. Transnational Institute.* 13 de julio de 2023. Transnational Institute. www.tni.org/en/article/transcript-of-orlando-leteliers-speech-at-the-felt-forum
[215] Callejas, Mariana. *Siembra vientos: memorias.* CESOC., 1995.
[216] Branch, Taylor & Eugen Propper. *Labyrinth.* Penguin, 1983, p.182.
[217] Callejas, Mariana. *Siembra vientos: memorias.* CESOCa., 1995. p. 38.
[218] Idem, p. 39.
[219] Idem, p. 39.
[220] Idem, p. 40.
[221] Idem, p. 41.
[222] Idem, p. 42.
[223] "The President John F. Kennedy Assassination Records Collection". The National Security Archive. Geroge Washington University. Archives.gov, www.archives.gov/files/research/jfk/releases/docid-32262517.pdf
[224] Church, Frank. "Select Committee To Study Governmental Operations With Respect To Intelligence Activities United States Senate". 14 de abril de 1976. www.intelligence.senate.gov/sites/default/files/94755_III.pdf. Pg. 160.
[225] Idem.
[226] The National Security Archive. Geroge Washington University. Doc. desclasificado. nsarchive2.gwu.edu/news/20071115/01-CIA_on_Posada_Bosch.pdf
[227] Metropolitan Briefs. "Jury Selection Starts on Bronfman Kidnapping Gimbel's Strike Settled Soviet Ship Damaged Strike Halts Tramway 2 Admit Faking Accidents Retail Sales Increase". *The New York Times.* 17 de setiemrbe de 1976, p. 26.
[228] Conversación del autor con Juan Raúl Ferreira. Con su autorización.
[229] Bob Woodward y Ben Weiser. "Ex-CIA Aide, 3 Cuban Exiles Focus of Letelier Inquiry." *Washington Post,* 12 de abril de 1977. www.washingtonpost.com/archive/politics/1977/04/12/ex-cia-aide-3-cuban-exiles-focus-of-letelier-inquiry/e92eb95a-71f5-4ab1-a650-ed3fccd399f9/.
[230] "Ex agent nabbed in arm case". *The Akron Beacon Journal.* 16 de junio de 1982, p. 2.
[231] National Security Archive. GMU. CIA, 26 de noviembre de 1976. nsarchive2.gwu.edu/NSAEBB/NSAEBB157/19761209.pdf
[232] "Transcript of Orlando Letelier's Speech at the Felt Forum". *Transnational Institute.* 13 de julio de 2023. www.tni.org/en/article/transcript-of-orlando-leteliers-speech-at-the-felt-forum
[233] CIA. Documento desclasificado. www.cia.gov/readingroom/docs/CIA-RDP91-00901R000700060054-9.pdf
[234] Alan McPherson. *Ghosts of Sheridan Circle. How a Washington Assassination Brought Pinochet's Terror State to Justice.* University of North Carolina Press, 2018, p. 121.

[235] Callejas, Mariana. *Siembra vientos: memorias*. CESOC, 1995.
[236] Burniiani, David. "Cubans in Letelier Case Linked to a 2d Murder Plot". *The New York Times*, 16 de enero de 1979, Sección A, p. 2.
[237] Haberman, Clyde. "Laying out a Case for Deporting Human Rights Abusers." *The New York Times*, 9 de noviembre de 2014.
[238] Branch, Taylor & Eugen Propper. *Labyrinth*. Penguin, 1983, p. 55.
[239] Congressional Record Senate. 24 de setiembre de 1976. p. 32292 en delante.
[240] Alan McPherson. *Ghosts of Sheridan Circle. How a Washington Assassination Brought Pinochet's Terror State to Justice* y University of North Carolina Press, 2018, p. 13. Augusto Pinochet, quoted in U.S. embassy in Santiago to secretary of state, 10 de marzo de 1978, Letelier (FOIA) document generado por el Department of State, 6 de febrero de 1980, vol. 1, box 8, LC, NSA.
[241] Robinson, Timothy S. y Stephen J. Lynton. "Evidence Links Letelier Death to Anti-Castro Unit". *Washington Post*. Primero de febrero 1977.
[242] Katrina Vanden Heuvel. "This Week in 'Nation' History: Saul Landau's Investigations of US Ties to the Pinochet Regime." *The Nation*, 13 de setiembre de 2013.
[243] CIA. Documento desclasificado. *CounterSpy*. Peck, Wislow. "CIA Covers Up Murder Web of Chilean Gestapo with False Stories And Terrorist Operations".
[244] Branch, Taylor & Eugen Propper. *Labyrinth*. Penguin, 1983, p. 75.
[245] Branch, Taylor. "The Letelier Investigation". *The New York Times*. 16 de julio de 1978, Sección SM, p. 7.
[246] "Pinochet's Role in the Letelier Assassination and Subsequent Coverup". National Security Archive, George Washington University. Directorate of Intelligence. Primero de mayo de 1987.
[247] "The President John F. Kennedy Assassination Records Collection". The National Security Archive. Geroge Washington University. FBI, Memorandum a Mr. Galangher, 26 de octubre de 1976.
[248] "Possible plans of Cuban exile extremist to blow up a Cuban airline". CIA. 21 de junio de 1976. Desclasificado en 1997.
[249] Branch, Taylor & Eugen Propper. *Labyrinth*. Penguin, 1983, p. 273.
[250] Salim Lamrani, "Conversations with Max Lesnik ", *Études caribéennes*, 7 de julio de 2021.
[251] Bardach, Ann Louise. *Cuba Confidential: Love and Vengeance in Miami and Havana*. United Kingdom, Knopf Doubleday Publishing Group, 2007, p. 111.
[252] Alan McPherson. *Ghosts of Sheridan Circle. How a Washington Assassination Brought Pinochet's Terror State to Justice*. University of North Carolina Press, 2018, p. 110. (Omang, "Terrorist Plot," A17.)
[253] 'By All Means at Our Disposal' Orlando Bosch." *YouTube*, 28 de abril de 2011, www.youtube.com/watch?v=E-om6WubPhk.
[254] Alan McPherson. *Ghosts of Sheridan Circle. How a Washington Assassination Brought Pinochet's Terror State to Justice*. University of North Carolina Press, 2018, p. 110.

²⁵⁵ Branch, Taylor & Eugen Propper. *Labyrinth*. Penguin, 1983, p. 217.
²⁵⁶ Bardach, Ann Louise. *Cuba Confidential: Love and Vengeance in Miami and Havana*. United Kingdom, Knopf Doubleday Publishing Group, 2007, p. 189.
²⁵⁷ National Security Archive. George Washington University. FBI. "Suspected Bombing of Cubana Airline DC-8 Near Barbados". Doc. clasificado el 7 de octubre de 1976.
²⁵⁸ WikiLeaks. "Us Position On Investigation Of Cubana Airlines Crash". 9 de octubre de 1976.
²⁵⁹ Bardach, Ann Louise y Larry Rohter "A Bomber's Tale: Decades of Intrigue; Life in the Shadows, Trying to Bring Down Castro". *The New York Times*. 13 de julio de 1998, Sección A, p. 1
²⁶⁰ Servicio de Información de Defensa (SID). Archivos del Terror de Uruguay. Archivo SID (Berrutti). Rollo 1100. p. 270.
²⁶¹ Bardach, Ann Louise. *Cuba Confidential: Love and Vengeance in Miami and Havana*. United Kingdom, Knopf Doubleday Publishing Group, 2007, p. 190.
²⁶² Idem, 190.
²⁶³ Rafael, Antonio. "Ricardo 'El Mono' Morales Navarrete" (1981) YouTube, 15 de octubre de 2016, www.youtube.com/watch?v=NiSBUn8csTw.
²⁶⁴ FBI Cornick to Propper, October 8, 1976, Letelier (FOIA) documents produced by the FBI, vol. 11, box 2, LC, NSA.
²⁶⁵ Majfud, Jorge. "Uruguay, los dictadores tienen quién les escriba". *Rebelion*. 29 de abril de 2007.
²⁶⁶ Rafael, Antonio. "Ricardo 'El Mono' Morales Navarrete." YouTube, 15 Oct. 2016. www.youtube.com/watch?v=NiSBUn8csTw.
²⁶⁷ Idem.
²⁶⁸ Majfud, Jorge. *La frontera salvaje. 200 años de fanatismo anglosajón en América latina*. Rebelde Ed, 2021. p. 413.
²⁶⁹ Idem, p. 416.
²⁷⁰ CIA. Document declassification. "Henchmen Carry out murder policy in nations's capital". *CounterSpy*.
²⁷¹ "Excerpts from an Interview with Walter Cronkite of CBS News. The American Presidency Project." University of California, Santa Bárbara. 3 de marzo de 1981.
²⁷² "The President John F. Kennedy Assassination Records Collection". The National Security Archive. Geroge Washington University. Document declassification. June 2, 1977.
²⁷³ Pfeiffer, Jack B. CIA: "Official History Of The Bay Of Pigs Operation Draft. Volume V CIA's Internal Investigation of the Bay of Pigs". 18 de abril de 1984.
²⁷⁴ William Tucker e Hilda Inclan. "US Reporters ousted in Venezuela intrigue"; Taylor Branch. "Caracas secret police chief: A Cuban exile with CIA past"; Associate Press. "Bosch Denies Bombing". *The Miami News*. 23 de octubre de 1976, ps. 1 y 4.
²⁷⁵ Inclan, Ilda. "Brigade's baby talk campaign". *The Miami News,* Miércoles 16 de marzo de 1977, p. 51.

[276] Branch, Taylor & Eugen Propper. *Labyrinth*. Penguin, 1983, p.116.
[277] Idem, p.108.
[278] CIA. Doc. desclasificado. Harold H. Sounders. "Castro's Alegations". 18 de octibre de 1976.
[279] Latin American Studies. www.latinamericanstudies.org/espinosa/bank-espionage.htm
[280] Messersmith, Al, y Jay Ducassi "Commando Camp Leader Arrested". *The Miami Herald*. Sábado 27 de febrero de 1982, p. 30.
[281] "The President John F. Kennedy Assassination Records Collection". The National Security Archive. Geroge Washington University. CIA doc. "Luis Clemente Posada Carriles, Anti-Fidel Castro Activities/Commandos L". 8 de enero de 1966.
[282] The National Security Archive. Geroge Washington University. "FBI, Letter to Kissinger, [Regarding Ricardo Morales Navarette]". 5 de noviembre de 1976.
[283] Tarpley, Webster G. y Anton Chaitkin. *George Bush: The Unauthorized Biography*. Chapter XV: "CIA Director". Progressive Press, 2004.
[284] Alan McPherson. *Ghosts of Sheridan Circle. How a Washington Assassination Brought Pinochet's Terror State to Justice*. University of North Carolina Press, 2018, p. 114.
[285] Branch, Taylor & Eugen Propper. *Labyrinth*. Penguin, 1983, p. 323.
[286] Idem, p. 324.
[287] "Four Sought in Florida in '75 Slaying of Exile". *The New York Times*. 5 de diciembre de 1976, p. 32.
[288] "The President John F. Kennedy Assassination Records Collection". The National Security Archive. Geroge Washington University. Archives.gov, 4 de julio de 1977.
[289] "Reagan Terms Nicaraguan Rebels 'moral Equal of Founding Fathers'". *The New York Times*, 2 de marzo de 1985, Sección 1, p. 1.
[290] Anderson, Jack. "A Mysterious Turn to Letelier Murder". *The Miami Herald*. 20 de diciembre de 1976, p. 192.
[291] Branch, Taylor & Eugen Propper. *Labyrinth*. Penguin, 1983, p. 329.
[292] Idem, p. 301.
[293] Idem, p. 334.
[294] Idem, p. 336.
[295] González, Mónica. "Las armas químicas de Pinochet". CIPER Chile. 22 de agosto de 2013.
[296] Branch, Taylor & Eugen Propper. *Labyrinth*. Penguin, 1983, p. 224.
[297] Idem, p.504.
[298] Fleetwood, Blacke. "I am going to declare war". *New Times*, 13 de mayo de 1977.
[299] Bardach, Ann Louise. *Cuba Confidential: Love and Vengeance in Miami and Havana*. United Kingdom, Knopf Doubleday Publishing Group, 2007, p. 191.
[300] Idem, 192.
[301] Idem, 192.

[302] Idem, 206.
[303] Alan McPherson. *Ghosts of Sheridan Circle. How a Washington Assassination Brought Pinochet's Terror State to Justice*. University of North Carolina Press, 2018, p. 173.
[304] Idem, 179.
[305] *"The Miami Herald.* 6 de mayo de 1978, p. 16.
[306] Idem.
[307] Alan McPherson. *Ghosts of Sheridan Circle. How a Washington Assassination Brought Pinochet's Terror State to Justice*. University of North Carolina Press, 2018, p. 183.
[308] Idem, 180.
[309] Hasson, Judi. "Michael Moffitt, who survived a car bomb that killed" UPI Archives. 13 de mayo de 1981.
[310] Alan McPherson. *Ghosts of Sheridan Circle. How a Washington Assassination Brought Pinochet's Terror State to Justice*. University of North Carolina Press, 2018, p. 195.
[311] UPI. "2 Cuban Exiles Acquitted At Retrial Of Letelier Murder". The *New York Times.* Domingo 31 de mayo de 1981, p. 10.
[312] Latin American Studies. www.latinamericanstudies.org/MNC/Letelier-bail.pdf
[313] Idem. www.latinamericanstudies.org/exile/miami-nov-1-30-1980.pdf
[314] Alan McPherson. *Ghosts of Sheridan Circle. How a Washington Assassination Brought Pinochet's Terror State to Justice*. University of North Carolina Press, 2018, p. 180.
[315] Idem p. 168.
[316] Idem, p. 204.
[317] Landau, Anya K. y Wayne S. Smith. "Keeping things in perspective: Cuba and the question of international terrorism". 20 de noviembre de 2001.
[318] Alan McPherson. *Ghosts of Sheridan Circle. How a Washington Assassination Brought Pinochet's Terror State to Justice*. University of North Carolina Press, 2018, p. 181
[319] Bardach, Ann Louise. *Cuba Confidential: Love and Vengeance in Miami and Havana.* United Kingdom, Knopf Doubleday Publishing Group, 2007, p. 116.
[320] "United States of America v. Guillermo Novo Sampol, Appellant.united States of America v. Alvin Ross Diaz, Appellant.united States of America v. Ignacio Novo Sampol". U.S. Court of Appeals for the District of Columbia Circuit, 636 F.2d 621, D.C. Cir. 1980.
[321] "United States of America v. Guillermo Novo Sampol". D.C. Circuit, 14 de setiembre de 1980.
[322] Alan McPherson. *Ghosts of Sheridan Circle. How a Washington Assassination Brought Pinochet's Terror State to Justice*. University of North Carolina Press, 2018, p. 217
[323] Letelier, Orlando. "The 'Chicago Boys' in Chile: Economic Freedom's Awful Toll". *The Nation*, agosto de 1976. Republicado el 21 de setiembre de 2016.

[324] Alan McPherson. *Ghosts of Sheridan Circle. How a Washington Assassination Brought Pinochet's Terror State to Justice*. University of North Carolina Press, 2018, p. 219.
[325] Majfud, Jorge. *La frontera salvaje. 200 años de fanatismo anglosajón en América Latina*. Rebelde editores, 2021, p. 459.
[326] Idem, p. 449.
[327] McGrory, Mary. "The Ghost Who Haunts Our Chile Policy." *Washington Post*, 28 de marzo de 1982. También citado en McPherson, Alan. *Ghosts of Sheridan Circle: How a Washington Assassination Brought Pinochet's Terror State to Justice*. United States, University of North Carolina Press, 2022, p. 221.
[328] CIA. Doc. desclasificado. www.cia.gov/readingroom/docs/CIA-RDP90-00552R000403680019-2.pdf
[329] LeoGrande, William M., and Kornbluh, Peter. Back *Channel to Cuba: The Hidden History of Negotiations Between Washington and Havana*. United States, University of North Carolina Press, 2015, p. 332, 334.
[330] Bardach, Ann Louise. *Cuba Confidential: Love and Vengeance in Miami and Havana*. United Kingdom, Knopf Doubleday Publishing Group, 2007, p. 206.
[331] Bardach, Ann Louise. "Our Man's in Miami. Patriot or Terrorist?". The Washington Post. 17 de abril de 2005.
[332] Idem.
[333] Bardach, Ann Louise. *Cuba Confidential: Love and Vengeance in Miami and Havana*. United Kingdom, Knopf Doubleday Publishing Group, 2007, p. 117.
[334] Idem, 202.
[335] Idem, 203.
[336] Idem, 203.
[337] Heuvel, Katrina Vanden. "This Week in 'Nation' History: Saul Landau's Investigations of US Ties to the Pinochet Regime." *The Nation*, 13 de setiembre de 2013.
[338] Callejas, Mariana. *Siembra vientos: memorias*. CESOC., 1995.
[339] Alan McPherson. *Ghosts of Sheridan Circle. How a Washington Assassination Brought Pinochet's Terror State to Justice*. University of North Carolina Press, 2018, p. 237.
[340] Reuters. "12-Year Term for Assassin of Chilean Envoy". 13 de setiembre de 1991, Sección A, p. 16.
[341] Inclan, Hilda. "Pro-Fidel magazine goes by the Bible". *The Miami News*. 22 de abril de 1977, p. 8.
[342] "Anti-Castro Exiles Growing Tolerant of Havana Ties." *Washington Post*, 11 de junio de 1977.
[343] "Cuban-American Group's Chief Linked to Seized Rifle Gun Is 1 of 2 Suspected in Plot to Kill Castro VTC." *Baltimore Sun*, Baltimore Sun, 22 de diciembre de 1997.
[344] Bardach, Ann Louise y Larry Rohter "A Bomber's Tale: Decades of Intrigue; Life in the Shadows, Trying to Bring Down Castro". *The New York Times*. 13 de julio de 1998, Sección A, p. 1

[345] Bardach, Ann Louise y Larry Rohter. "A Bombers Tale: Taking Aim at Castro; Key Cuba Foe Claims Exiles' Backing. *New York Times*, 12 de julio de 1998, sección 1, p. 1.
[346] Bardach, Ann Louise. *Cuba Confidential: Love and Vengeance in Miami and Havana*. United Kingdom, Knopf Doubleday Publishing Group, 2007, p, 210.
[347] Idem, 139.
[348] Windrem, Robert. "US government considered Nelson Mandela a terrorist until 2008". *NBC News*. 7 de diciembre de 2013.
[349] Bardach, Ann Louise. *Cuba Confidential: Love and Vengeance in Miami and Havana*. United Kingdom, Knopf Doubleday Publishing Group, 2007, p. 139.
[350] Cannon, Lou, and Martin Schram. "Reagan: Administration Harasses Cuban Exiles." The Washington Post, 10 de marzo de 1980.
[351] Lamb, Chris. "Belief Systems and Decision Making in the Mayaguez Crisis." Political Science Quarterly, vol. 99, no. 4, 1984, pp. 681-702. JASTOR.
[352] Windrem, R. "US government considered Nelson Mandela a terrorist until 2008". NBC News, 7 de diciembre de 2013.
[353] Torres, María de los Angeles. *In the Land of Mirrors: Cuban Exile Politics in the United States*
"Cuban Exile Politics at the End of the Cold War". University of Michigan Press, 1999, p. 140.
[354] Alan McPherson. *Ghosts of Sheridan Circle. How a Washington Assassination Brought Pinochet's Terror State to Justice*. University of North Carolina Press, 2018, p. 286
[355] Bardach, Ann Louise. *Cuba Confidential: Love and Vengeance in Miami and Havana*. United Kingdom, Knopf Doubleday Publishing Group, 2007, p. 111.
[356] Idem, 112.
[357] Alan McPherson. *Ghosts of Sheridan Circle. How a Washington Assassination Brought Pinochet's Terror State to Justice*. University of North Carolina Press, 2018, p. 286
[358] Bardach, Ann Louise. *Cuba Confidential: Love and Vengeance in Miami and Havana*. United Kingdom, Knopf Doubleday Publishing Group, 2007, p. 109.
[359] Idem, 113.
[360] Alan McPherson. *Ghosts of Sheridan Circle. How a Washington Assassination Brought Pinochet's Terror State to Justice*. University of North Carolina Press, 2018, p. 287.
[361] "America's Secret War". CIA FOIA, Doc. desclasificado. 10 de octubre de 1983.
[362] *News, Darias*. "Orlando Bosch: Escambray, Cuba". 10 de julio de 2006. *YouTube*, 22 de julio de 2017, www.youtube.com/watch?v=opXB3MCZh1Q.
[363] Pertierra, José. "La Historia Que Reclama Ser Contada al Pueblo Estadounidense". *Cubadebate*. 14 de abril de 2006.
[364] Cummings, John. "Foreign terrorists hit the US". *The Fresno Bee*, domingo 9 de noviembre de 1980, p. 27.

www.ingramcontent.com/pod-product-compliance
Lightning Source LLC
Chambersburg PA
CBHW071641160426
43195CB00012B/1321